Buddhist Education
Theory and Practice

Buddhist Education
Theory and Practice

Dr. Ch. Venkata Siva Sai

PRASHANT PUBLISHING HOUSE
DELHI-110094

Published by :
Prashant Publishing House
C-34, 28 Foota Road, Gali-3,
West Karwal Nagar, Delhi-110094
Phone : 011-22963970, Mob. : 9810396373
e-mail.: prashantpublishinghouse@gmail.com

Buddhist Education: Theory and Practice
Reserved
First Published 2014

ISBN 978-93-80565-46-0

PRINTED IN INDIA
Published by Mr. R.K. Jha M/s Prashant Publishing House and Published at H.S. Offset House Press, Delhi.

Preface

The motivating factor for Buddha's inquiry was to find means, which would annihilate the suffering of man. The cause for man's suffering in the world arises from the ignorance (*avidya*) coupled with desires (*tanha*) that bonds man to the wheel of repeated existence (*Bhava chakra*). Buddhist education is the practical dimension, whereby the Buddhist percepts – Dhamma can be translated from word to deed (*carita*). Buddha rightly stated that 'mind' is the locus, wherein the formulation of wrong knowledge (ignorance) takes place .This ignorance is twofold namely imputed ignorance (*parikalpita-avidya*) and innate ignorance (*sahaja-avijja*).

Realizing the need for cleansing the mind, the Buddha rightly propounds that knowing *the mind, shaping the mind and freeing the mind* constitutes the threefold means to annihilate suffering. He states that with the removal of theoretical ignorance the prime cause for suffering can be overcome and freedom achieved. Buddhist education shows the path (marga), but it insist on man following the process of personal inquiry which is based on direct experience of the mind. It is only through concentration-mindfulness (*Satipattana*) that an individual can perceive 'things' as they are'. Man, herein gains wisdom which enables one to draw a distinction between things as they are subjectively characterized by the subject mind and things devoid of subject characterization i.e., the real nature (*svabhava-satta*).

Education, in the modern context, is a means not only for getting knowledge but should lead to meaningful employment, which can be achieved only when the individual apart from possessing knowledge should be equipped with skills to transmit the knowledge acquired into are useful application that can generate wealth. In this context, Buddhist Education has utmost relevance in the contemporary education scenario as there is paradigm shift in the processes and method of teaching-learning -pedagogy. It is no longer a means for gaining of information and knowledge, but the effective means for transmission from the domain of knowledge to understanding, wisdom and development of skills as enunciated in the Vissudhimagga. Buddha speaks of three levels of wisdom. First, "General and All Knowledge Wisdom", it refers to the correct understanding of the nominal, or essence, of the universe. It is the wisdom of knowing the general aspect of all existences. The next higher level of wisdom "Differentiation Wisdom" refers to the wisdom that will enable one to correctly comprehend all the infinite phenomena of the universe, the wisdom of knowing the discriminative aspect of all existences. The highest level of wisdom "Overall and Perfect Knowledge Wisdom" refers to the exhaustive and perfect perception whereby one can comprehend truth of life and the universe without the slightest doubt or error. Only when one possesses all three of these kinds of wisdom, one can completely understand the true reality of life and the universe. The present day education system at the most provides the first level of wisdom, the education planners have to introduce changes both in the subject content and pedagogy, which is the methods of teaching, if they desire to equip the students to attain the higher levels of wisdom. It is also necessary for it will enable the individual to understand the meaning and purpose of life.

Buddha was a teacher par excellence, who stressed that do not accepts anything on blind faith; think for yourself, test it out and see if it actually does make sense. He laid emphasis on principle of verification of the facts by examining it by oneself, and only then accept it as a fact. Buddhist thought and its educational philosophy is open to scientific investigation and invites people to examine it in that way.

Buddha adapted the method of *upaaya-kosalla,* wherein the traditional ideas and practices formulated his sermons to suit the aptitude of people. It is a skilful process and effective means of transmitting knowledge to people. Teacher educators should develop the intellectual ability to comprehend the dispositions of his students (*naanaadhimuttikataa*). He apart from using the dialogue and debate method, he invariable adopted the 'illustrative approach', which refers to the use of analogy, simile, parable (*upamaa)*, the use of fable and story drawn from ordinary life for the effective transmission of knowledge.

Buddha opines that the teacher should not only transit knowledge, but should have a critical outlook, so that the stated facts could be verified and realized by the intelligent .Further, he should be 'an analyst' (*vibhajjavaada),* which refers to the teacher's capacity to analyze the meaning (*attha),* the reasons, the conditions (*dhamma)*, the educational medium (*nirutti)*, and the intellectual mastership (*patibhaana):. There by the Teacher educator* should be capable of grasping the 'analysis of meaning', specifically and according to the letter, to explain the lesson in various ways, to teach it, expound it, lay it down, open it up, classify it and make it comprehendible to the learner.

Dr Ch. Venkatasivasai, in his Book Buddhist Education: Theory and Practice has dealt in detail all the aspects pertaining to Education in general and Buddhist education in particular. His book provides the reader with rare insights into the philosophical foundations, the curriculum, the role of the teacher and the methodology adopted in Buddhist education. It has great relevance for the present day educational thinkers and planners especially in India in there strive to make India regain its place as a nation of creative thinkers rather than men of mere knowledge.

—Dr M. V. Ram Kumar Ratnam
Professor, Centre for Mahayana Buddhist Studies
Acharya Nagarjuna University, Guntur

Contents

Introduction

The ultimate goal of Buddhist education is to destroy ignorance, the root cause of suffering. Specifically, education in a Buddhist sense should seek to eliminate from the students' mind a variety of wrong views, which form the theoretical basis of ignorance. These purely conceptual contents of the mind comprise the so-called "imputed ignorance" (parikalpita-avidyā), as opposed to the "innate ignorance" (sahaja-avidyā). It is "conceptual" or "acquired" ignorance. Innate ignorance cannot be accessed until there is conceptual ignorance (or misconceptions), so first one has to eliminate the "imputed" ignorance, i.e. wrong views.

Wrong views in the Buddhist sense contradict the three marks of conditioned existence, i.e. impermanence, suffering and selflessness. To think that there are any permanent phenomena in conditioned existence is certainly a wrong view, just as much as to think that there is any lasting happiness to be gained. However, the root of all wrong views is the belief in a concrete and permanent self, seeking to gain happiness. Samsāra revolves around a notion of self – the most difficult and impenetrable of all our misconceptions. This notion of the self is particularly important in modern Western society, and both socially and economically institutionalized, such that all our dominant institutions are dedicated to the personal and economic development of the self. Education does not escape this stranglehold.

The materialist view in the West that began with Descartes has evolved into the scientific view that the universe is an object out there, to be dominated and mastered. Following this, most education processes imply that there is some kind of result to be gained from the process of learning. A student, for instance, studies a certain subject in order to master it and put it to use in his/her life, thus becoming more knowledgeable, wealthier, gaining higher status in society etc. This is what we may call the social value of education. This highly abstract value is concretized in the diploma or certificate issued on completion of one's studies. It is usually assumed that by getting a diploma, one somehow becomes a more valuable person and he/she can turn this extra value to his/her advantage. Many young people entering higher education today are conditioned by such expectations. The value system of modern education obviously implies belief in a concrete and permanent self, which can become "better" (more knowledgeable, educated etc.) and happier through education.

In First Chapter I discuss about An Introduction to Buddhist Education. It includes Education and learning, Goal of Education, Education in Buddhist period in India, Merits of Buddhist Education, Demerits of Buddhist Education, Cultural Dimensions of Buddhist Education, Buddhist way of Education, Need for Modern Buddhist Education etc in detailed way.

The ultimate goal of Buddhist education, i.e. to attain liberation from the misconception of a permanent self, and the purpose of modern Western education, which is to strengthen and secure one's mistaken sense of identity? How can we resolve this contradiction in the context of modern Buddhist education? I would like to offer four interlinking approaches to solve the dilemma:

(1) Transforming students' motivation

(2) Presenting formal education as skilful means

(3) Emphasizing the role of meditation

(4) Opening up new vistas of learning.

Transforming Students' Motivation

Modern society may put great stress on students to obtain some definite goal in life, such as a good job, social status, carrier etc. These social expectations will inevitably affect students, even if they are well-motivated and genuinely interested in Dharma. Many of them will wonder how to integrate their Buddhist learning with survival in modern society. Though there are different means to address this question, one important aspect of the solution is to transform students' motivation. Relying on the basic Buddhist truths of impermanence, 'suffering' and selflessness – students' minds should be turned towards higher values: contentment, spiritual liberation and kindness to others – so that, rather than trying to conform with the expectations of modern society in order to gain something in return, they might begin to think about how they can contribute to well-being in their society. Their self-concern may thus be transformed into concern for others.

Formal Education as Skilful Means

One of the ways to counterbalance the modern view of education as life investment is to emphasize its traditional Buddhist use as skillful means. Buddhist institutions and forms of education may appear in conformity with the world, but their main function is to provide the opportunity for studying the Dharma, which is beyond this world. Any formal qualification (such as a diploma in Buddhist studies) is merely a by-product of one's study rather than an end in itself. Competence in matters relating to the Dharma does not depend on any formal recognition, nor does a diploma obtained in 3-5 years of formal study guarantee such competence. Advancement in the higher trainings of morality, concentration and wisdom cannot be objectively measured or evaluated by the quantitative standards of modern education. While maintaining humility to the Buddhist tradition, Dharma studies should be pursued in the spirit of free inquiry and free from the competitiveness that often characterizes mainstream education. Through emphasizing the role of Buddhist education as skillful means, we can safeguard students against over-expectation and encourage them to use their precious study opportunity to the best of their abilities.

The importance of meditation: In contrast with modern education, Buddhism values first-hand experience higher than theory. Buddhist education should be concerned with more than just handing over factual knowledge. The Buddha taught a path of personal inquiry to put an end to suffering, and that path depends on direct experience. Therefore, the traditional methods of Buddhist mind-training – contemplation, meditation – could be taught at schools. The Buddhist view on the integral nature of human experience, where the intellectual and emotional sides of mind are equally appreciated, is highly relevant in the modern world, which is overly fragmented. Buddhism presents a path of mind-training, and education is nothing but that path. Since the full meaning of the Buddhist texts and teachings is not fully understood before one has direct experience in meditation, meditation is an indispensable part of Buddhist education. In fact, Buddhist educational institutions, if they have not been tainted by the values of the West, could well define themselves as schools of mental training. The usefulness of mindfulness methods in developing the "seven factors of enlightenment" (such as peace, joy, concentration etc.) has been demonstrated even outside the context of Buddhist education. It has been found indispensable for realizing true education in general. (Brady, Kassabian)

Finally, to encourage active Buddhist engagement in everyday affairs, we must open up new vistas of learning. Hearkening back to spirit of the great Indian Buddhist universities such as Nalanda, we should try to apply the Buddhist principles in all walks of life, testing their truth in different disciplines. Just as Buddhist philosophy in India developed in constant dialogue with other schools of philosophy, we should also try to be at constant dialogue with science and the other religions.

In second Chapter I would like to discuss about the Buddhist Education and Modern Education. It includes significance of Buddhist Ethics, System of Buddhist Education particularly system of Pabbaja, upasampada, Dr. B.R.Ambedkar contribution to Buddhist Education in India, Buddhism as Education, How to spread to South and South East countries Srilanka, Indonesia, Malaysia, Thailand, Mynamar, Bangladesh, Cambodia, Vietnam, Japan, China, Tibet etc their Theravada Buddhist education systems. The Theory of dependent origination can bring new perspectives to many social, economical and ethical issues that humanity faces today. Moreover, it has been shown that scientific notions of cause and effect in the natural world agree with the Buddhist understanding, which can potentially enrich the natural sciences with an ethical dimension. (Waldron) Buddhist education therefore should not be concerned with simply transmitting the knowledge and methods of the past, but should also be creative in the application of Buddhist principles. It is mainly the task of Buddhist institutions of higher education to keep the spirit of Buddhist wisdom alive and turn it to the benefit of humankind. Viewed from this perspective, Buddhist education has a practical role to play in the modern world.

Buddhism has a great deal to offer in terms of its insights into the mind, and hence into its development through education. With its emphasis on 'things as they are', it provides a path, an individual and collective means of inquiring into our minds, and the arising conditions that are invaluable in these days of global chaos. In this way, it can enable young people to work towards wisdom rather than knowledge, and find a way of working together harmoniously, co-creating institutions based on compassion rather than greed. With new motivation, meditation, and an emphasis on skillful means, Buddhism needs to find new forms for helping break through ignorance and open up new vistas of learning.

In Chapter Three I discuss about Three Domains of Learning in Buddhist Education, Buddhist Education and Pedagogy its challenges and opportunities etc. It is a matter of great significance, especially in the context of learning psychology, which the Buddha had over 2600 years ago, identified three distinct levels or domains of learning namely, pariyatti, patipatti and pativedha. According to Buddhist Education, pariyatti constitutes the theoretical foundation that is required in learning and understanding the Buddha Dhamma. However, we have to be mindful that a theoretical foundation would only enable a person to experience the Dhamma at a superficial level. On the other hand, a person could still experience the deeper meaning and relevance of the Dhamma without having to be erudite in the scriptures and to eloquently recite suttas. Buddhist scriptures are replete with examples of how disciple monks and lay followers of the Buddha, possessing relatively low intelligence, could attain great spiritual uplift. A classic example was Cula Pantaka who could not even commit a simple verse to memory. Yet, he was able to attain Arahanthood simply by practicing concentration and removing defilements from his mind. Simply put, in Buddhist Education possession of a high level of intelligence is not a qualifying pre-requisite or pre-condition for spiritual advancement.

A theoretical study of the sacred texts must not therefore be looked upon as the be-all-and end-all of Buddhist Education for this will limit one to only a superficial involvement with the profound Teachings of the Buddha. From possessing a theoretical foundation of the Dhamma, one should advance to patipattior the practice of the Dhamma through inquiry, investigation and self- experience. Skilful practice of the Dhamma in daily life is absolutely necessary for one to progress to the third domain of learning and self-training namely, pativedha — the realization of Insight Wisdom. The Buddha had always stressed that in order for one to come to grips with the realities of life one has to come to terms with one's own spiritual development. To really understand and benefit fully from the Dhamma, one has to progress beyond the theoretical plane and immerse oneself in the method and technique of practicing and applying the Buddha's Teachings in daily life.

The Buddha had always stressed that in order to benefit from the Dhamma one has to practice his Noble Teachings with understanding and depth. This is because the Dhamma is a complete education and training programme which we are to infuse into our day-to-day living. The Buddha persistently admonished His disciples and lay followers that he was only a Teacher, Guide and Role Model of one who had understood, lived and experienced the Dhamma. Throughout His forty-five years in teaching the Dhamma, He laid stress on the Eternal

Doctrine as a way of wholesome living rather than an esoteric philosophy for scholarship or for theorising. On many occasions he refused to be drawn into useless speculation and debate when he knew that the discussion would not lead the opponent to understand the nature of his existence and the realities of life.

The development of the mind is central in Buddhist Education. In the context of daily living, this helps one to discriminate, for example, between wholesome and unwholesome thoughts and actions. In terms of practicing and internalizing the Dhamma, the affective domain of learning and training is without question an essential ingredient and is linked to harnessing the pool of information and facts in the Dhamma that is to be relied upon for one to arrive at sound conclusions, decisions and actions in our daily life.

The psychomotor domain of learning advances an individual a step further in learning. As the term itself suggests, this level of learning deals with the total person, that is, the body and mind concurrently. In this domain, both the psychological (meaning the thinking, attitude, mental make-up, emotions, sentiments and feelings) and the behavioral (in reference to personal skills, talents, conduct and volition or actions) aspects of learning are involved in unison. It is in this domain that the practical application and practice of the Dhamma impacts forcefully on the development of the individual. Viewed from the perspective of Buddhist Education, the psychomotor and the affective domains of learning, relates to the living or 'being' aspects of Buddhism. Here the individual becomes mindful of living the Dhamma. The focus of the learning and training is on developing. Human values and virtuous qualities such as metta, karuna, muditha, upekkha.

The Future of Women in Buddhism: The future of humanity relies on the procreative power of women, since the future of the human species literally depends on women's special power to give birth to children. Yet women's procreative potential is not the only reason to believe that women hold the key to the future. In addition to our biological gifts, we women have many other skills and talents to offer humanity. And Buddhist women have unique strengths and potential to succor our crisis-ridden planet.

In recent decades, attention to the topic of women in Buddhism has expanded dramatically. Since the 1960s, interest in Buddhism has grown exponentially throughout the world, facilitated by great Buddhist teachers, new research and publications on Buddhism in modern languages, the Internet, the growth of outstanding Buddhist educational centers, and an abundance of vibrant Buddhist social service activities. Especially in Western countries, the Buddha's teachings on peace, compassion, ethics, and human psychology have had a significant impact.

Buddhist thought and culture have permeated Western culture to a remarkable degree, from religion to politics, the arts, and the marketplace. This new wave of interest in Buddhism has coincided with new educational and professional opportunities for women and an increasing awareness of women's capabilities and potential. Yet, unfortunately, women do not always have access to Buddhist education, nor are they equally represented in Buddhist institutions. Although the Buddha taught a path to liberation for the benefit of all beings, full recognition and equal opportunity do not extend to women in many Buddhist traditions. If the Buddha's teachings are liberating, shouldn't they be equally liberating for both women and men?

The place of Women in Buddhism: The position of women has been a subject of considerable interest in recent decades. In all societies, particularly in the West, there has been a rethinking of the position accorded to women in all spheres of activity. This has resulted in a significant change in the role played by women in social, economic and even political life. This reappraisal has also touched on the question of the position accorded to women in the main religious traditions of the world. In Christian countries the issue of the ordination of women has become a highly controversial topic, and some Churches are facing the prospect of dissension, and even schism, on this question. It is therefore opportune to consider the place accorded to women in Buddhism.

The role of women in Buddhism could be considered in several ways. We can, for instance, compare the position accorded to women in both the religious and the secular life in India before the Buddha's time with that after the establishment of Buddhism, and consider whether the Buddha's teaching resulted in a change radical or otherwise. We can see whether the Buddha's teaching accords to women a position different to that accorded to men, as is the case in many other religious. We may consider whether the accident of the sex of one's birth helps or retards progress on the Buddha's path, and indeed whether gender is itself a chance event or caused by pre-existing factors. The part played by women in the early history of Buddhism, notably during the Buddha's own time, could be considered as providing a clue to the place accorded to women in Buddhism. In this connection the events surrounding the establishment of the Bhikkhuni Order need to be re-examined, as there is a measure of misunderstanding on this question. The influence of Buddhism on the position of women in the countries where Buddhism became a living presence could be highlighted. In this connection the significant facts pertaining to the mission of Sanghamittā to Sri Lanka deserves notice. Finally the position of women in Buddhism could be contrasted with that accorded to women in the other great religious traditions of the modern world.

While the attitude of the Buddha to the role of women was an enlightened one, even when judged by the standards of the modern age, it must not be thought that everything that is said on this subject in Buddhist writing, even in the Pali Canon itself, measures up to the high standard expected of a Buddha. There are many explanations for this, not least of which is the fact that most of these works were written down several centuries after the Parinibbāna of the Buddha, and that during this time the teachings were sustained by monks, some of whom might not have been entirely free from the prejudices of the age. It is interesting to note that such "backsliding" occurs most commonly in the later works, e.g. in the prose sections of the Jataka (which incidentally are non-Canonical). And popular Buddhism took liberties of its own with this aspect of Buddhist teaching as it did with several others.

It is not possible to consider all these issues in a talk of this length. Only a few comments can be made on each of these questions. In particular it is not possible to comb the Buddhist texts to collect all the relevant issues relating to the position of women ill Buddhism. Fortunately this is not necessary as a small literature on this subject has accumulated since the late Ms I. B. Horner wrote her book *Women under Primitive Buddhism* well over 50 years ago. This book presents a comprehensive account of this question, and is still in many ways the best source on this question. But no apology is needed to revive this question at a time when the position of women in religious life is undergoing a critical re-examination in many places.

Women and the Buddha's Path: There is very little, if any at all, in Buddhism that identifies it with a particular sex. The Buddha himself was historically a man, but the essence of Buddhism does not involve any extolling of the personality of the Buddha (unlike say the Christian extolling of the person of Jesus in his capacity as the Son of God). What the Buddha discovered was a universal law which existed independently of all the Buddha's, and which others, male or female, can discover by following the directions of the Buddha. The cult of the Buddha's person, the worship of relics, the conduct of the "Buddha pûjās" and the like, were all later developments, both in the Theravada and the Mahayana, and have scant justification in the discourses of the Buddha.

Later academic speculation has raised the question whether a female could become a Buddha or a Bodhisattva. Mahayanists have taken an affirmative position (e.g. the cult of Kwan Yin as a Bodlihisattva who heeds the pleas of those in distress), but the Theravadan position is less clear. Some have claimed that the Buddha's have to be males; others have taken a more ambiguous position. The correct way to approach this question is to regard it as another of those profitless questions which the Buddha left unresolved (avyākata), as it is irrelevant to the question of release from samsāra. There can be only one Buddha in a given Buddha-era (despite what some of the Jātakas may imply), and the present era happened to have been inaugurated whether by necessity or coincidence, by a male, Siddhartha Gautama.

In essence, Buddha means wisdom. In application or function, it means enlightenment. There are three levels of wisdom. First, "General and All Knowledge Wisdom" is the correct understanding of the nominal, or essence, of the universe. It is the wisdom of knowing the general aspect of all existences, the wisdom of Theravada sages. Second, "Differentiation Wisdom" is the wisdom that can correctly comprehend all the infinite phenomena of the universe, the wisdom of knowing the discriminative aspect of all existences, the wisdom of Bodhisattvas. How did these phenomena arise? From where? In what way? What were their results? Third, "Overall and Perfect Knowledge Wisdom" is the exhaustive and perfect perception and comprehension of the truth of life and the universe without the slightest doubt or error, the wisdom of Buddha's. Buddha Shakyamuni, possessing all three of these kinds of wisdom, completely understood the true reality of life and the universe.

The function of wisdom is enlightenment. There are three classifications of enlightenment. First is "self-enlightenment", a state in which one possesses no erroneous thoughts, views, speech or behavior. Arhats and Pratyekabuddhas in Theravada Buddhism have attained this level of self-enlightenment, but have not yet generated the Bodhi mind to help others achieve enlightenment. Second, is "enlightenment of self and others", a state in which one helps others to reach enlightenment after achieving his or her own. Bodhisattvas in Mahayana Buddhism have attained this level. Third is "Perfect Complete Enlightenment", a state in which one reaches perfection in both enlightenment for self as well as helping others to reach enlightenment. This is the state of Buddha's.

In Chapter five I discuss about The Fundamentals of Buddhist Education in Practice. The path of Buddhist Education, Ultimate goal of Buddhist Education, How to get perfect, and Complete Enlightenment etc.What is the ultimate goal of the Buddha's teachings? It is to attain the Perfect, Complete Enlightenment. Transliterated from Sanskrit, it is called Anuttara-samyak-sambodhi. Out of respect, this phrase was maintained in its original form rather than translated. There are three stages within this enlightenment: "Proper Enlightenment", "Equal and Proper Enlightenment", and "Perfect, Complete Enlightenment".

The Buddha told us, that although scientists, philosophers and religious scholars may have reached a good understanding about life and the universe, this realization is neither complete nor proper. Why? Although they have obtained some understanding, they are far from having freedom from worries, from ending their afflictions. They still indulge themselves in the Five Poisons of greed, anger, ignorance, arrogance and doubt. They remain mired in all the troubles of human relationships and are swayed by personal feelings. In other words, they are human.

If a person has severed greed, anger, ignorance, arrogance, doubt and afflictions, it will be acknowledged that this person has attained the first level, that of Proper Enlightenment. He or she will be called an Arhat, similar to the initial academic degree in Buddhism. Arhats differ from Buddha's in the way that they use their mind. They use it in the same manner we do. The difference is that we still have afflictions while Arhats do not.

So, a Buddha is one who has fully comprehended the truth of life and the universe and acquired the ultimate and perfect wisdom. This is also the goal of Buddhist education; to enable beings to attain this same level of wisdom. Therefore, Buddhism is an education of wisdom.

The Objectives of the Buddha's Teachings: The principle of Buddhism is to break through all superstitions and delusions.

It is to resolve delusion to attain happiness and enlightenment, to eliminate suffering to gain serenity and purity of mind. What is delusion? When we do not thoroughly and properly understand the phenomenon around us, we tend to be deluded, to have wrong ideas, which lead us to make mistakes. Then we suffer ill consequences as a result. However, if we have correct understanding about life and the universe, we will be free from mistakes in thought, judgment and behavior. Then our result, or effect, will be favorable. Thus, resolving delusion to attain enlightenment is the cause and eliminating suffering to attain happiness and purity is the effect.

Only through resolving superstition and delusion, can enlightenment be attained. This is the objective of the Buddha's teaching. This wisdom will enable all beings to differentiate true from false, proper from improper, right from wrong and good from bad. It can help us to establish a dynamic and caring attitude toward life and our surroundings. So, we can clearly see that Buddhism is neither passive nor obsolete, nor is it retreating from society. As said in the "Buddha Speaks of the Infinite Life Sutra of Adornment, Purity, Equality" and "Enlightenment of the Mahayana School" or the "Infinite Life Sutra," Buddhism can perfectly solve all afflictions and problems. It enables us to obtain true and ultimate benefits by creating fulfilling lives, happy families, harmonious societies, prosperous nations and a peaceful world. These are the objectives of the Buddha's teachings for our world now. The ultimate objectives of abandoning all worries thus transcending the six realms are even more incredibly wonderful. Therefore, we can see that it is an education that will enable us to attain truth, virtue, beauty, wisdom and genuine eternal happiness.

1

An Introduction to Buddhist Education

Ideally, education is the principal tool of human growth, essential for transforming the unlettered child into a mature and responsible adult. Yet everywhere today, both in the developed world and the developing world, we can see that formal education is in serious trouble. Classroom instruction has become so routinized and pat that children often consider school an exercise in patience rather than an adventure in learning. Even the brightest and most conscientious students easily become restless, and for many the only attractive escape routes lie along the dangerous roads of drugs, sexual experimentation, and outbursts of senseless violence. Teachers too find themselves in a dilemma, dissatisfied with the system which they serve but unable to see a meaningful alternative to it.

One major reason for this sad state of affairs is a loss of vision regarding the proper aims of education. The word "education" literally means "to bring forth," which indicates that the true task of this process is to draw forth from the mind its innate potential for understanding. The urge to learn, to know and comprehend is a basic human trait, as intrinsic to our minds as hunger and thirst are to our bodies. In today's turbulent world, however, this hunger to learn is often deformed by the same moral twists that afflict the wider society. Indeed, just as our appetite for wholesome food is exploited by the fast-food industry with tasty snacks devoid of nutritional value, so in our schools the minds of the young are deprived of the nutriment they need for healthy growth. In the name of education the students are passed through courses of standardized instruction intended to make them efficient servants of a demeaning social system. While such education may be necessary to guarantee societal stability, it does little to fulfill the higher end of learning, the illumination of the mind with the light of truth and goodness.

A major cause of our educational problems lies in the "commercialization" of education. The industrial growth model of society, which today extends its tentacles even into the largely agrarian societies of South and Southeast Asia, demands that the educational system prepare students to become productive citizens in an economic order governed by the drive to maximize profits. Such a conception of the aim of education is quite different from that consistent with Buddhist principles. Practical efficiency certainly has its place in Buddhist education, for Buddhism propounds a middle path which recognizes that our loftiest spiritual aspirations depend on a healthy body and a materially secure society. But for Buddhism the practical side of education must be integrated; with other requirements designed to bring the potentialities of human nature to maturity in the way envisioned by the Buddha. Above all, an educational policy guided by Buddhist principles must aim to instill values as much as to impart information. It must be directed, not merely toward developing social and commercial skills, but toward nurturing in the students the seeds of spiritual nobility.

Since today's secular society dictates that institutional education is to focus on preparing students for their careers, in a Buddhist country like Sri Lanka the prime responsibility for imparting the principles of the Dhamma to the students naturally falls upon the Dhamma schools. Buddhist education in the Dhamma schools should be concerned above all with the transformation of character. Since a person's character is molded by values, and values are conveyed by inspiring ideals, the first task to be faced by Buddhist educators is to determine the ideals of their educational system. If we turn to the Buddha's discourses in search of the ideals proper to a Buddhist life, we find five qualities that the Buddha often held up as the hallmarks of the model disciple, whether monk or layperson. These five qualities are faith, virtue, generosity, learning, and wisdom. Of the five, two — faith and generosity — relates primarily to the heart: they are concerned with taming the emotional side of human nature. Two relate to the intellect: learning and wisdom. The second, virtue or morality, partakes of both sides of the personality: the first three precepts-abstinence from killing, stealing, and sexual abuse- govern the emotions; the precepts of abstinence from falsehood and intoxicants help to develop the clarity and honesty necessary for realization of truth. Thus Buddhist education aims at a parallel transformation of human character and intelligence, holding both in balance and ensuring that both are brought to fulfillment.

The entire system of Buddhist education must be rooted in faith (*saddha*) — faith in the Triple Gem, and above all in the Buddha as the Fully Enlightened One, the peerless teacher and supreme guide to right living and right understanding. Based on this faith, the students must be inspired to become accomplished in virtue *(sila)* by following the moral guidelines spelled out by the Five Precepts. They must come to know the precepts well, to understand the reasons for observing them, and to know how to apply them in the difficult circumstances of human life today. Most importantly, they should come to appreciate the positive virtues these precepts represent: kindness, honesty, purity, truthfulness, and mental sobriety. They must also acquire the spirit of generosity and self-sacrifice *(caga),* so essential for overcoming selfishness, greed, and the narrow focus on self-advancement that dominates in present-day society. To strive to fulfill the ideal of generosity is to develop compassion and renunciation, qualities which sustained the Buddha throughout his entire career. It is to learn that cooperation is greater than competition, that self-sacrifice is more fulfilling than self-aggrandizement, and that our true welfare is to be achieved through harmony and good will rather than by exploiting and dominating others.

The fourth and fifth virtues work closely together. By learning *(suta)* is meant a wide knowledge of the Buddhist texts which is to be acquired by extensive reading and persistent study. But mere learning is not sufficient. Knowledge only fulfills its proper purpose when it serves as a springboard for wisdom *(pañña),* direct personal insight into the truth of the Dhamma. Of course, the higher wisdom that consummates the Noble Eightfold Path does not lie within the domain of the Dhamma school. This wisdom must be generated by methodical mental training in calm and insight, the two wings of Buddhist meditation. But Buddhist education can go far in laying the foundation for this wisdom by clarifying the principles that are to be penetrated by insight. In this task learning and wisdom are closely interwoven, the former providing a basis for the latter. Wisdom arises by systematically working the ideas and principles learned through study into the fabric of the mind, which requires deep reflection, intelligent discussion, and keen investigation.

It is wisdom that the Buddha held up as the direct instrument of final liberation, as the key for opening the doors to the Deathless, and also as the infallible guide to success in meeting life's mundane challenges. Thus wisdom is the crown and pinnacle of the entire system of Buddhist education, and all the preliminary steps in a Buddhist educational system should be geared toward the flowering of this supreme virtue. It is with this step that education reaches completion, that it becomes illumination in the truest and deepest sense, as exclaimed by the Buddha on the night of his Awakening: "There arose in me vision, knowledge, wisdom, understanding, and light."

EDUCATION AND LEARNING: A BUDDHIST PERSPECTIVE

I am pleased that I was asked to write about education and learning from a Buddhist perspective rather than 'A Buddhist Philosophy of Education'. How could one person encapsulate the entire Buddhist canon and history and its many different paths into one definitive statement on education? This author could not, so a more modest and less presumptuous title is appropriate.

One could structure this article in a host of different ways and part of the challenge in taking on a task such as this is to find a way in which thoughts can be marshalled into some semblance of order which makes sense to Buddhists and non-Buddhists alike. I have chosen to identify two key concepts: citta which translates as 'heart or mind'; and the four 'divine abidings' or mental states - the Brahma Viharas – which many Buddhists try to develop and which are a very important part of my own practice. These two concepts present one way, a 'skilful means', by which this large and difficult question can be addressed. There are, no doubt, many others.

Citta

I think it was on Desert Island Discs that I heard George Steiner draw attention to the fact that in English we talk about 'learning by heart'. We don't talk about 'learning by mind' or 'learning by brain', but 'by heart'. It points to a very significant fact about learning and therefore about education as a whole. Real learning is transformative and it changes us as people, deep inside our hearts and minds, and this is why the Pali word citta is so important in considering a Buddhist approach to education. It lies somewhere between 'mind' and 'heart' and thus combines what we have sometimes called in educational jargon the 'cognitive' and the 'affective'. No such dichotomy exists within Buddhist thinking: there is rather something which is whole and complete and which does not give primacy to one rather than the other. The primacy of mind and reason has dominated western thinking since the (European) Enlightenment, resulting in the relegation of the heart and emotions to a lower order. It is not so and we know it! The Buddha was perhaps the original post-modernist who provides a model for education in which the heart and mind are rightly inextricably joined. It is the basis for a truly holistic philosophy of education.

If we put this into practice in our schools the acquisition of knowledge and skills would not be more important that the development of attitudes and values, they would have equal status. Then areas of scientific learning would not be separated from the ethical questions they raise; historical facts would not be acquired without full consideration of their impact and their continuing significance on our lives and our culture; there would be time for reflection right across the curriculum and ultimate questions would no longer be the preserve of the RE (and perhaps the English) department. There would be a deep understanding of the 'wholeness' of the child and emotional and spiritual intelligence would be rated as highly as good SATs results. The joy of teaching in such an environment!

The Buddhist path is about the cultivation of the mind – bhavana - and, as the Dhammapada says in its opening verses: 'Your life is the creation of your mind'. The development of wisdom (one of the three parts of the Noble Eightfold Path) is the intended outcome of Buddhist practice and it is nurtured through mindfulness, that paying of bare, non-judgemental attention to what the mind is doing. Concentration (the second of the three parts) and mindfulness are the basis of meditation practice, the purpose of which is the development of wisdom – thus the Noble Eightfold path perpetually nurtures and reinforces itself, combined as it is with the third part, morality (of which more later).

It is, I hope, self-evident that all of this – mind and wisdom - is the philosophical basis from which a Buddhist view of education can be. articulated. Mindfulness and wisdom enable insight and understanding of the true nature of reality which means that gradually delusion begins to fade. From a Buddhist perspective the nature of reality is summed up in the three essential elements of all contingent existence: unsatisfactoriness (dukkha), impermanence (anicca) and insubstantiality or non-self (anatta). Children and young people – and their teachers – know plenty about unsatisfactoriness and impermanence; what is harder is understanding insubstantiality but, again, from a Buddhsit perspective, this is not merely cognitive; it is, rather, a deepening understanding of one's own mental formations that comes through the practice of meditation.

This brings us back to the key concept of 'mental cultivation' - bhavana. Buddhism is quite clear that for all human beings there is the possibility of self-transformation through mental development and that resonates clearly and profoundly with what educationists believe about the power and significance of the learning process.

The Brahma Viharas - Mental States

There are four mental states which Buddhists try to develop through their practice. They are known as the brahma viharas and they are: metta or loving kindness; karuna or compassion; mudita or sympathetic joy; and upekkha or equanimity. Each of these, it seems to me, has something important to say about the purpose and meaning of education and the principles that should underpin that process, wherever it is practised.

METTA – LOVING KINDNESS

Loving kindness is the fundamental attitude that underpins all behaviour, speech and thought in Buddhist teaching and stands diametrically opposite to anger. This is not just loving kindness towards one's fellow human beings but, importantly, towards oneself – how that would raise our pupils' self-esteem!– and towards all living beings. It implications and applications are endless: it is about our relationships, our responsibilities towards others and since, in Buddhist teaching, everything is interconnected, our relationship with the whole of the natural world. Practising loving kindness towards others entails behaving morally and the five precepts of Buddhism give simple guidance on what how this can be done:

Avoidance of destroying living creatures

Not taking that which is not given

Avoidance of sexual misconduct

Not using incorrect speech

Abstaining from drugs and alcohol.

These are not commandments but 'rules of training' to develop one's practice further. Morality (sila) is at the heart of Buddhist practice and it is, therefore, also at the heart of any philosophy of education that stems from it. The combination of morality and loving kindness is immensely powerful and is potentially transformative in the ways in which we structure our schools and the relationships and ethos that exist within them.

KARUNA – COMPASSION

It is well known that the recognition of unsatisfactoriness or suffering was the catalyst that inspired Siddhattha Gotama to begin the search that led ultimately to his enlightenment and thus to the formation of the religion we now know as Buddhism. In Buddhism the appropriate response to suffering is compassion, which is without limit or condition. The causes of suffering are greed or desire, hatred or anger and delusion – none of us is free from these (unless we have already achieved enlightenment) and thus we are all on the same continuum. This is not a fixed state - we all move along that continuum perpetually as we make appropriate or inappropriate responses to our circumstances. A simplistic dualism of good and evil is entirely absent from Buddhism; there is rather a recognition that all beings are engaged in a difficult struggle, and easy judgements of others' behaviour are inappropriate. It might seem that the outcome of this would be to adopt an indiscriminating, relativistic toleration of anything and everything but this is not the case in Buddhist thinking, for, as I have already said, morality is the heart of the practice. Here there is another immensely powerful combination of morality with compassion; its opposite is hardness of heart.

This can form the foundation of exploration of issues that arise across the curriculum: in Citizenship, in political education, in global education, in RE and PSHE and in the questions that are raised through studying history and literature. At an individual level it is also the basis for counselling and listening to pupils.

MUDITA – SYMPATHETIC JOY

Mudita is about our ability to enjoy the achievements of others, their talents, theirskills and their qualities; its opposite is jealousy. It is about everyone within a school participating in and celebrating the well-being of each other and it applies to all areas of school life. A school that practises mudita would be a school where collaboration, rather than competition, is central to activities and where praise for some does not alienate others. At the heart of mudita is love and that should be at the heart of education. It isn't always easy to love one's pupils (or one's colleagues) but that is the ideal and a school where pupils are genuinely loved and affirmed is always successful. It is also happy - and what is more important than that?

Upekkha – Equanimity

It is with this mental state that Buddhism is perhaps more recognisably on home territory. The development of equanimity is a long and complex process for most people and develops from an understanding of the true nature of reality, including its impermanence and its insubstantiality. It requires silence and space for its growth and is often linked in schools to spiritual development and stilling exercises. However, we do not need equanimity when we are comfortable and calm and still. We already have it. We need equanimity in the face of criticism and pain and loss and grief – the dark side of spiritual experience that is all too often forgotten in a quietist and pietistic view of 'the spiritual'. Equanimity is not uncaring or escapist; it is rather the ability not to be swept hither and thither by the forces of life. The still, calm mind has depth and strength and, crucially, awareness of the true nature of what is taking place around itself; its opposite is agitation. Enabling pupils (and ourselves) to develop such equanimity would, I believe, have huge impact on the nature of schools – their rush and bustle and frenetic activity being replaced by a more reflective and quieter way of being. That is not to say that there wouldn't be fun and laughter and friendship and all those other vital elements of daily life but there would be a recognition that they too are as they are – just in that moment, impermanent and insubstantial.

Conclusion

Now, you might feel that all this is pie-in-the-sky philosophy that has no place in the 'real' world. Bur defining the real world is Buddhist practice and living with equanimity and joy in the real world is what this is all about. I am convinced that the key concepts outlined above can provide a sound base from which a more humane, spiritual and effective education can be developed and sustained. But, I hear you ask, what about my SATs or GCSE results? What about league tables? Well, what about them? Of course every responsible professional working in education is going to enable their pupils to learn and achieve but what is more important is to recognise a deeper and higher purpose in learning that goes beyond the utilitarian and the measurable to something that is life-long and life-enhancing in the fullest sense of the word. Buddhism helpfully recognises conventional truth, that there are ways of doing things that have to be done while recognising simultaneously that there is a higher truth that is there to be perceived.

Look back on your own education and what do you remember and treasure? The tables you learned in arithmetic? The spelling tests on Friday mornings? Or the nature table and the Beethoven symphony and the poetry of the First World War? I know which I remember and I know which have utilitarian value and which improve the quality of my life, then and now.

An education that genuinely embraces a whole concept of the child and that has at its heart loving kindness, compassion, sympathetic joy and equanimity is an education that can transform the lives of the children and young people in its care and ultimately increase the sum of human happiness. It might just help the professionals as well.

THE GOAL OF BUDDHIST EDUCATION

What is the ultimate goal of the Buddha's teachings? It is to attain the Perfect, Complete Enlightenment. Transliterated from Sanskrit, it is called Anuttara-samyak-sambodhi. Out of respect, this phrase was maintained in its original form rather than translated. There are three stages within this enlightenment: “Proper Enlightenment”, “Equal and Proper Enlightenment”, and “Perfect, Complete Enlightenment”.

The Buddha told us, that although scientists, philosophers and religious scholars may have reached a good understanding about life and the universe, this realization is neither complete nor proper. Why? Although they have obtained some understanding, they are far from having freedom from worries, from ending their afflictions. They still indulge themselves in the Five Poisons of greed, anger, ignorance, arrogance and doubt. They remain mired in all the troubles of human relationships and are swayed by personal feelings. In other words, they are human.

If a person has severed greed, anger, ignorance, arrogance, doubt and afflictions, it will be acknowledged that this person has attained the first level, that of Proper Enlightenment. He or she will be called an Arhat, similar to the initial academic degree in Buddhism. Arhats differ from Buddhas in the way that they use their mind. They use it in the same manner we do. The difference is that we still have afflictions while Arhats do not.

The next higher level of enlightenment is that of Equal and Proper Enlightenment, represented by Bodhisattvas. They resemble Buddhas in motivation but have not yet reached the same level of enlightenment. The minds of Bodhisattvas are genuine; they remain forever unchanged and are similar to those of Buddhas. Buddhas use the full and perfect true heart. Buddhas represent the highest level of enlightenment, which is the Perfect Complete Enlightenment.

In Buddhist classic literature, the perfect, true mind of a Buddha was symbolized by a full moon. The mind of a Bodhisattva was symbolized by a crescent moon, which was neither full nor perfect. And the mind of an arhat was symbolized by moonlight reflected from the surface of water, it is not real.

These three levels of enlightenment can be compared to our college educational system. The level or degree of Arhat is similar to earning an undergraduate degree. The level of Bodhisattva is similar to earning a Master's degree and the level of Buddha is similar to earning a Doctorate's degree. The word Buddha is not exclusive to Buddha Shakyamuni, but is a common title for any being who has attained the perfect complete enlightenment. Thus, Buddha, Bodhisattva and Arhat are only names or titles to represent the levels of enlightenment or a degree we receive in Buddhism. And they are most certainly not deities to be worshiped.

So, a Buddha is one who has fully comprehended the truth of life and the universe and acquired the ultimate and perfect wisdom. This is also the goal of Buddhist education; to enable beings to attain this same level of wisdom. Therefore, Buddhism is an education of wisdom.

The Objectives of the Buddha's Teachings

The principle of Buddhism is to break through all superstitions and delusions. It is to resolve delusion to attain happiness and enlightenment, to eliminate suffering to gain serenity and purity of mind. What is delusion? When we do not thoroughly and properly understand the phenomenon around us, we tend to be deluded, to have wrong ideas, which lead us to make mistakes. Then we suffer ill consequences as a result. However, if we have correct understanding about life and the universe, we will be free from mistakes in thought, judgement and behavior. Then our result, or effect, will be favorable. Thus, resolving delusion to attain enlightenment is the cause and eliminating suffering to attain happiness and purity is the effect.

Only through resolving superstition and delusion, can enlightenment be attained. This is the objective of the Buddha's teaching. This wisdom will enable all beings to differentiate true from false, proper from improper, right from wrong and good from bad. It can help us to establish a dynamic and caring attitude toward life and our surroundings. So, we can clearly see that Buddhism is neither passive nor obsolete, nor is it retreating from society. As said in the Buddha Speaks of the Infinite Life Sutra of Adornment, Purity, Equality and Enlightenment of the Mahayana School or the Infinite Life Sutra, Buddhism can perfectly solve all afflictions and problems. It enables us to obtain true and ultimate benefits by creating fulfilling lives, happy families, harmonious societies, prosperous nations and a peaceful world. These are the objectives of the Buddha's teachings for our world now. The ultimate objectives of abandoning all worries thus transcending the six realms are even more incredibly wonderful. Therefore, we can see that it is an education that will enable us to attain truth, virtue, beauty, wisdom and genuine eternal happiness

A Buddhist Philosophy of Education

A Buddhist philosophy of education is based on a Buddhist social philosophy. No society will manage education without associating it with beliefs in regard to justice, freedom and equality. The system of education will be one of the systems relying on the social systems.

Buddhism and Education: Buddhist education should teach people to be good people and abandon any animal instincts and bad behaviors. Moreover, it teaches people the path to attain mental freedom. One of the way to carry out Buddhist education is to establish the Buddha as the primary philosophy and to derive an educational philosophy from that. The other way is to teach Buddhism in schools and institutions so as to enrich the youth with Buddhist teachings. This is a good way to train the youth to be good person and purify their mind with moral merits. But it doesn't mean that we will make Buddhism as the basis of the system of education, but to reinforce the existing education system.

The Goal of Buddhist Education: The critical goal of Buddhist education is to attain wisdom. Buddhism believes that the ultimate of wisdom is inherent in each person's nature, stating that everyone has the potential to achieve wisdom. However, the majorities are distracted by misunderstanding and misconceptions, therefore, are incapable of being aware of this kind of potential. In this sense, Buddhism aims to teach us recognize the intrinsic part of human nature.

Buddhist wisdom varies from individual to individual. It is related to the degree to which one's delusion is and there is no inherent difference among all human beings. Buddhism helps us remove delusion and regain the wisdom to remove confusions of individual potential and achieve happiness.Buddhism considers deep meditation and concentration as the crucial factors in order to attain wisdom. Buddhism teaches the way of meditation and the mindfulness of concentration.

BEGINNING AND DEVELOPMENT OF BUDDHIST EDUCATION IN VIETNAM

No systematic examination of how Buddhist education began and developed in Vietnam has been hitherto attempted, to the best of my knowledge. The importance of tracing the history of Buddhism in general and Buddhist education in particular is enhanced by the fact that Vietnam is geographically the meeting point of the eastern expansion of Indian culture and the southern expansion of Chinese culture. These two significant cultures met and flourished in Vietnam. Its study is an extremely urgent academic task because the few currently available sources could disappear due to the prevailing political and cultural developments, on the one hand, and the dispersal of scholars due to the Vietnamese Diaspora, on the other. In the ensuing chapters, the history of Buddhism and Buddhist education in Vietnam is reconstructed to the extent possible under the present conditions. Some of the conclusions are, therefore, tentative. The basic hypothesis on which the research has been established: (1) Adequate data are gleanable from available resources, textual and oral, to reconstruct this history; (2) Such data and the recording of the experience of educated monastics could serve to understand the main features and challenges of Vietnamese Buddhist education; and (3) A history of Buddhist education thus reconstructed could be the basis for further examination of issues on which disagreements exist among scholars. The research adopted a combination of four approaches: (a) A desk research on primary sources in Chinese and Vietnamese; (b) A critical examination of secondary sources in Chinese, Vietnamese, English and French; (c) A phenomenological analysis of my personal experience as a Buddhist and student of Buddhism and the experiences of my immediate colleagues, friends and teachers; and (d) Validation of data through a field survey conducted with a questionnaire. The result of this research is presented in eight substantive chapters. Following the opening Chapter outlining the methodology and the plan of the study, Chapter Two on the contextual background to Buddhist education examines (A) the culture and education of Vietnam before the advent of Buddhism, and (B) how Buddhism came to be introduced to Vietnam. An investigation into the earliest form of Buddhist education in Vietnam is taken up in Chapter Three and continued into Chapter Four with a detailed analysis of the development of Buddhist education up to 1975. Chapter Five surveys the information available on educational institutions and records the contribution made by pagodas in various parts of the country. Special attention is given in Chapter Six to the content of Buddhist education, which is presented historically under the three domains of educational objectives, namely cognitive, affective and skill-based. This analysis brings out most eloquently the richness of the substantive content which Vietnamese Buddhist education has inherited from its primary sources of inspiration and further developed through its own ingenuity. An equally significant observation results from Chapter Seven in which traditional methods of instruction are examined with reference to the experience of Vietnamese educators. Chapter Eight takes note of the large number of nationally famous educators and teachers, of both Thiê n (Zen) and Pure Land traditions, whose literary and instructional contributions could be outlined. In doing so, special notice has been taken of the role which poetry played as a vehicle of spiritual and philosophical communication among them. Chapter Nine summarizes the substantial findings of the research and ends with a brief note on the present and future of Buddhist education in Vietnam.

The Need for Modern Buddhist Educcation

In Asian Buddhist communities, both in Asia and abroad, an increasing number of people who have been raised in nominally Buddhist homes have come to regard Buddhism as mere superstition and turn to other religions. Upon talking with these people, their misconceptions about Buddhism are evident. Again, this is due to a lack of modern Buddhist education.

Buddhism has never been an evangelical religion, nor should it become one. However, clear explanation of the Buddha's teachings should be made available to people who are interested. The Buddha showed the path to happiness, and it is desirable for this to be made accessible to others, so that they can benefit from it. This is the duty and responsibility of Buddhists who have compassion for others.

In what ways can Buddhist education be made relevant to people today? First, if oral teachings were given in the language with which people are most familiar, the language in which they are educated, then they could understand the meaning better. Colloquial language communicates much better to lay people than does classical language. For scholars and serious practitioners, knowledge of Pali, Sanskrit, and ancient Chinese is necessary, but for the general public and young people who are used to television colloquial language and everyday examples are more suitable. One university student told me that he was reluctant to come to talk with me because he feared that I would use many Pali words and he would not understand! I wonder how many others there are who avoid going to teachings or reading books because they cannot understand the language well.

Secondly, it is essential that Buddhist principles be clearly and logically explained. Today's youth is well-educated. They have knowledge of science, philosophy, psychology, and so forth. Not satisfied with hearing only the story of Buddha's life and the Jataka tales and thereby generating faith, they now want to know how the doctrine of selflessness relates to quantum physics and how Buddha's teachings on patience can be integrated into modern psychology. Young people who have a modern secular education will not believe in rebirth just because Buddha said so. They want to understand the logical proof for it and to know current examples of people who have memories of their previous lives.

EDUCATION IN BUDDHIST PERIOD IN INDIA

In India during the time of Buddha, there was a racial discrimination in the society. This discrimination was according to profession of man, and according to birth. In the society there were four division of man of whom Brahman was superior. Brahmanism dominated the society and established their supremacy in the country. They enjoyed rights for religious training and education. But other category of people deprived of their religious and educational rights. At that time there were 62 heretical doctrines in existence and priesthood got upper hand. In this background a religious revolution started in ancient India in 600 B.C. and a new doctrine or system developed which is called Buddhist doctrine or Buddhist philosophy. It is to be said that on the foundation of Buddhism a new and special Education System originated in ancient India. Buddhism made a tremendous movement which played a valuable role in the development of Education System in ancient India or ancient Buddhist world. It is well-known that with the rise of Buddhism in India there dawned the golden age of Indias culture and civilisation. There was progress in all aspects of Indian civilisation under the impact of Buddhism There arose many centres of learning which did not exist before

Aims of Education

The goal of Buddha's teaching-the goal of Buddhist education is to attain wisdom. In Sanskrit, the language of ancient India, the Buddhist wisdom was called ¯Anuttara-Samyak-Sambhodi meaning the perfect ultimate wisdom. The Buddha taught us that the main objective of our practice or cultivation was to achieve this ultimate wisdom. The Buddha further taught us that everyone has the potential to realize this state of ultimate wisdom, as it is an intrinsic part of our nature, not something one obtains externally.

The chief aim of Buddhist education was all round development of child's personality. This included his physical, mental, moral and intellectual development.The aim of Buddhist Education is to make a free man, a wise, intelligent, moral, non-violent & secular man. Students became judicious, humanist, logical and free from superstitious. Students became free from greed, lust and ignorance. Buddhist Education was wide open and available to the people of all walks of life. The principal goal of the Buddhist Education is to change an unwise to wise, beast to priest.

The Buddhist education system aimed at regaining our intrinsic nature. it also teaches absolute equality which stemmed from Buddha's recognition that all sentient beings possess this innate wisdom and nature. Buddha's teaching helps us to realize that innate, perfect, ultimate wisdom .With wisdom, we can then solve all our problems and turn suffering into happiness.

In the Buddhist era, religion was given top priority and education was imparted through it. The chief aim of education was propagation of religion and inculcation of religious feelings and education served as a mean to achieve salvation or nirvana. Preparation for life, there was a provision for imparting wordily and practical knowledge along with religious education so that when the students entered normal life they may be able to earn their livelihood.

The Nature of Mass Education

In the early period Buddhist Education was limited within the monasteries and only for the members of the monastery. But later on it was open to all, even lay people got scope to have education in those institutions. In modern days Buddhist Education became wide open and embraced people of all walks of life. The aim of Buddhist Education is to change an unwise to wise, beast hood to Buddha hood.

Buddhist Education made revolutionary change in the society. The Buddhists in the world first made Education open to all. Students irrespective of caste, creed, and religion got opportunity to have education which was denied by the superior class in the society. In India also, in Vedic Educational schools students from lower classes were refused to get admission.

The monasteries or Buddha Vihars were the chief centres of learning and only the Budhist monks could be admitted to them for education. Thus there was no planned arrangement for mass education as such during the period. It forms this position it would be wrong to construce that the Buddhist monks were unmindful of the education of the people in general. So at the time of begging alms the monks used to remove the religious doubts of the people through their interesting conversation or short and alp lectures. Thus the people in general received moral and religious education from the monks.

Women Education

Women education during Buddhist period was at its lowest ebb, as the women folk were despised in the sense that Lord Buddha had regarded them as the source of all evils. So he had advised during his life time not to admit women in monasteries .but after some time due to the insistence of his dear pupil Anand, Buddha had permitted about 500 women along with his step mother for admission in the Vihars with many restriction and reservations.

When Buddhist monasteries had developed into colleges of international reputation, women did not receive any education because of their early marriages. In the early history of Buddhism, however the permission was given to women to enter the order and gave a fairly good impetus to female education, especially in aristocratic and commercial sections of society. Large number of ladies from these circles joined the order and became life-long students of religion and philosophy. Their example must have given an indirect encouragement to the spread of education among lay women as well. Besides this, the rules of admission of women in Sangh were hard enough.

Two years of probation was fixed for women-monks for their permanent membership .Strict rules were enforced for women monks. . The women monks were not allowed to meet any male monk in loneliness and their residence was arranged separately at a distant place. They were not given any permanent post in the sangh. Some monk could give her religious instruction twice a month in the presence of another monk. The assent of the whole Sangh was also considered essential. Moreover, they had to live separately, and they were instructed by a special monk twice in a month. They could not live lonely with the teacher too. Buddhist Sangh had given attention to the cultural development and social uplift of the women. Mostly women entered the Sangh out of keen interest and deep religious feelings. Some had also joined it to get rid of the troubles of the wordly affairs. As the Bhikshunis did not like to maintain inferior position, so they naturally were more interested in the studies leading pious life. Though, Buddhist literature does not speak much of the system of the education of Bhikshunis, yet there are some references of new comer Bhikshunis and taking charge of their education. It makes clear that there must have been some arrangement for their education.

There were Bhikshunis whose spiritual knowledge was very high and they could influence a good number of people.Many Bhikshunis took the duties of social services also. They serve the sick, orphans, etc., and considered it to be their prime duty. Some of them had studied the philosophy deeply and had become poetess and writers. . Some of them had studied even politics and took active part in politics of the day. Some of them had even gone to foreign countries to preach Buddhism. Sheelbhattarika, Prabhudevi and Viyanka were famous in those days as poets and writers. The sister of the Emperor Asoka Sanghamitra was very famous Bhikshunis, who had done remarkable services of Buddhism

Qualities and Responsibilities of the Teacher

The teacher himself must spend at least ten years as a monk and necessarily must have the purity of character, purity of thoughts and generosity. Both the teacher and student were responsible to the monastery. But regarding education, clothes, food and residence of the student monk, the teacher was fully responsible. The teacher was also responsible for any treatment of the student whenever he fell ill.

The duties of the teachers were imparting education to the students, writing Book, propagation of religion, discussion, and arrangement of debate for the clarification of serious subjects. The teachers were responsible for physical, mental, spiritual and moral development of the students. Teachers loved the students and helped them in every affair. They also took care of them during their diseases and agony. The teachers were responsible for their food, accommodation and other necessaries of livelihood. They kept eyes on the all round development of the students. Especially they were serious about the obeyance of the Sangha rules, meditation and concentration to their learning.

Both the teacher and the student were responsible to the monastery or the Buddhist order. But regarding education, clothes, food and residence of the student monk, the teacher was wholly responsible. The teacher was also responsible for any treatment of the student whenever he fell ill. The teacher used to bestow all the affection to his student and used to educate his through lecture and question answer method.

Buddhist philosophy admits the possible of attaining peace here and now, though, it starts with a pessimistic note. Teacher, therefore, need not have any cry of despair. Bhikshus were the teacher. Buddhist vihar as or monasteries have their methods of Imitation and training for the apprentices. The preceptor must give his disciple, all possible intellectual and spiritual help and guidance. There was mutual esteem between the teacher and the pupil. There relations were like father and son. The teacher was regarded as spiritual father or intellectual father of the student.

During Budhist period the place of teacher in the scheme of education was very important. There were the categories of teachers – Acharyas and Upadhayas. According to Sutras

Literature Acharya may admit according to his unfettered discretion, a number of pupils, who would have to live with him at this house, for a minimum period of twelve years. He would not accept any fees from the pupils under this instruction. The progress shown by pupil was the only factor that determined the continence of his apprenticeship.

Concept of Student

The teachers were highly qualified. The aim of Buddhist Education is to make a free man, a wise, intelligent, moral, non-violent & secular man. Students became judicious, humanist, logical and free from superstitious. Students became free from greed, lust and ignorance. Buddhist Education was wide open and available to the people of all walks of life. The principal goal of the Buddhist Education is to change an unwise to wise, beast to priest.

The teachers were the guardian of the students. They were responsible for physical, mental, spiritual and moral development of the students. Since Educational Institution (Monasteries) was residential therefore the relationship between the teachers and the students were very very cordial.

The student was expected to serve his teacher with all devotion. On rising in the morning the student will arrange everything for the daily routine of the teacher. He will cook his food and clean his clothes and utensils. Whatever he acquired through begging alms, he would place before teacher. The student had to prepare himself to receive education at any time whenever the teacher required him.

The Budhist system, enjoins upon the pupil the duty of serving this preceptor as a part of education. The pupils is to rise early in morning from the bed and give his teacher teeth-cleanser and water to rinse his mouth with; then, preparing a seat for him, serve him rice- milk in rinse his mouth with; then, preparing as seat for him, serve him rice milk in rinsed jug, and after his drinking it, wash the vessel and sweep the place. Afterwards he is to equip him for his begging round by giving him fresh undergarments, girdle, his two upper garments, and his alms- bowl rinsed and filled with water and then is to dress and equip himself similarly if he wants to accompany his teacher but must not walk too far from or near wants to accompany his teacher but must not walk too far from or near wants to accompany his teacher but must not walk too far from or near him. He is not to interrupt his teacher in speaking, even if he makes a mistake. There were also rules for the expulsion of a pupil by his teacher. In five cases a Saddhiviharika ought to be turned away; when he does not feel great affection for his Upajjhaya, nor great inclination towards him, nor much shame, nor great reverence, nor great devotion. Sangha (Monastic) life was residential; therefore a cordial relationship between the teachers and the students grew up. Their relationship can be compared with the relationship of a father and a son. The teachers were the guardians and sincere for their mutual relationship, happiness, development and responsibilities.

Admission

Admission in monastery-monasteries was the centre for imparting education during the Buddhist period. For admission the student had to present himself before the teacher and request him for giving education. The teacher was fully responsible for education of his pupil. In turn, the pupil had also to be responsive to the instructions received from the teacher. The student was not at all accountable to any other Bhikshuk in the monastery.

The novices first entered into the Sangha (Bhikkhu Sangha), then had to follow the monastic rules and Sangha rules. Even today these rules are followed. There are many rules regarding food, dress, bed room, meditation, dedication and other rules as laid down by the Sangha. They had to undergo with physical exercise for maintenance of their health. They had to clean the campus, rooms, halls, serve the teachers (Achariya) and assist them in various field. This was the primary duties of the students After admission the students had to follow monastic rules along with their syllabus and they were classified according to merit. The period of Education was 12 years. They had to follow the advice of the teachers and obey them. In this way they had to pass twelve years in learning. Students put questions to the teachers; teachers answered the question and discussed matters related to their Education. Students had to perform daily routine works beyond learning.

The teacher of a budhist monastery were empowered to expel any student on charge of misconduct or any type of serious disobedience. However, the student was expelled only when it was definitely ascertained that he lacked faith and respect for the teacher and the other things related to the sanctity of the monastery. After the death of the teacher or when the teacher changed his religion or left the monastery for elsewhere, the students also deserted the monastery. The education of the concerned students ended then and there.

Pabbaja Ceremony

Pabbaja was an accepted ceremony of the Buddhist monasteries. Pabbaja means going out. According to this ceremony the students after being admitted to a monastery had to renounce all his worldly and family relationship. An individual belonging to any caste could be admitted to a monastery and after being admitted he did not belong to any caste. '.After admission he had to change his old clothes and all old ways and the manners of living. For the Pabbajja ceremony the minimum age was eight years.

For pabbaja ceremony the individual had to get his head fully shaved and put on yellow clothes. In this shape he was presented before the presiding Bhikshu. On presentation this individual would pray for admission to the monastery. On his prayer the head Bikshu would administer three basic advices:

(1) I take refuse with Budha.

(2) I take refuge with religion.

(3) I take refuge with the order.

The aspirant for admission used to pronounce these advices very distinctly. Then his admission was permitted. On being admitted the individual was called a Sharman.

Rules for shramner—

1. Not to kill any living being
2. Not to accept anything given to him.
3. Live free from the impurity of character.
5. Not to tell lie
6. Not to take food at improper time
7. Not to use luxurious things.

Upasampada Ceremony

After pabbaja the Buddhist monk had to undergo the Upasampada ceremony. This ceremony was different from pabbaja ceremony. After the Pabbajja ceremony education continued for twelve years. When the student received twelve years education he had to undergo the Upasampada ceremony, that it is at the age of twenty years,Upasampada ceremony was performed. This ceremony was democratic in nature. The Sharman has to present himself in front before all other monks of the monastery. One could be admitted for this ceremony only when the majority of the monks voted in favour of the same. After this ceremony the Sharman was regarded as full- fledge member of the monastery. On this occasion all his worldly and family relationships ended.

Discipline

The Core of Buddha's teaching-the Buddha teaching contains three major points discipline, meditation and wisdom. Wisdom is the goal and deep meditation or concentration in the crucial process toward achieving wisdom. Discipline through observing the precepts, is the method that helps one to achieve deep meditation; wisdom will then be realized naturally. Buddha's entire teaching as conveyed in the sutras never really depart from these three points.

After getting education in the Buddhist schools, colleges and universities one can not do any injustice, tell a lie, commit theft, can not kill, can not be addicted in wine and make himself free from moral turpitude. In this way students become free from greed, lust, enmity and ignorance. Buddhism encompasses the entire collection of works by Buddha Shakyamuni and is called the Tripitaka.This can be classified into three categories sutra, Vinaya (precepts or rules) Sastra (Commentaries) which emphasize meditation, discipline and wisdom respectively.

The monk and the students in Buddhist period were following the simple living and high thinking principle.their lives were full of purity, nobelness, dutifulness and humanity and are suppose to follow the Astang Marg- the word Samma means 'proper', 'whole', 'thorough', 'integral', 'complete', and 'perfect' -

1. Samma-Ditthi — Complete or Perfect Vision
2. Samma-Sankappa — Perfected Emotion or Aspiration,
3. Samma-Vaca — Perfected or whole Speech
4. Samma-Kammanta — Integral Action.
5. Samma-Ajiva — Proper Livelihood.
6. Samma-Vayama — Complete or Full Effort, Energy or Vitality
7. Samma-Sati — Complete or Thorough Awareness.
8. Samma-Samadhi — Full, Integral or Holistic Samadhi.

Syllabus

Buddhist Education system developed on the basis of some basic principles. This education gave emphasis on the moral, mental and physical development and also to divert the students towards the Sangha rules and guide them to follow it. The main stress was given to have a clear idea of Tripitaka which consists of Sutta Pitaka, Vinaya Pitaka and Abhidhamma Pitaka. The entire Tripitaka consists of Buddha's teachings, message, philosophy and rules for the Bhikkhus and Bhikkhunies.

The curriculum was chiefly spiritual in nature. It was because the chief aim of education was to attain salvation. So the study of the religious books was most important. This type of curriculum was meant only for the monks. Besides these spinning, weaving, printing of the clothes, tailoring, sketching, accountancy, medicines, surgery and coinage were the other subjects of Budhist education.

At the initial stage medium of education was mother tongue, later it included Pali and Prakrit and in the following days Sanskrit also included as a medium of instruction. Specially the Mahayana Teachers achieved distinction in practicing Buddhism in Sanskrit. A special Sanskrit Buddhist literature developed. Mention may be made here that at the hands of Nagarjun, Asanga, Basubandhu, Santideva, Aryadeva and Candrakisti Buddhist philosophy and literature made tremendous progress through Sanskrit. In later period according to the demand of the society and professional education, art, sculpture, architecture, medicine also included in the syllabus. Buddhist Education came out from the religious arena and went out for the benefit of the mankind.

There were two types of education primary and higher education. In primary education reading, writing and arithmetic were taught and in higher education religion philosophy Ayurveda, military training was included. Everyone was free to choose his subject without any restriction.

Vocation education was not ignored during the budhist system of education. The monks of Vihar were taught spinning, weaving and sewing in order that they meet their clothing requirement. They were taught architecture as well. Education in architecture enabled them to build up new Vihars or repair the old ones. Similarly the householders following Buddhism but living outside Vihar were given training in different type of and also earn their livelihood.

It is to be mentioned that Buddhist Educational Syllabus included Vedic subjects also. In this way difference of Buddhist & Vedic Education wiped out and united. This was a historic development in the history of Education in India.

TEACHING METHOD

At first there was a private and group teaching. Later it developed into class room. In due course Sangharamas developed into residential college and universities. In the history of Education those universities played major role in the propagation of Buddhism, Buddhist history, Art & Culture. In those universities world famous scholars like Atisa Dipankar, Silabrada, Santarakshit were the teachers. Many valuable books were written. We still remember the glory of the universities like Nalanda, Vikramsila, Sompuri, Salban, Jagaddal, Pandit Vihar, Taxila. The supremacy of those universities were unparallel. Students from China, Myanmar, Thailand, Gandhara and all parts of ancient India came to have their education in those universities. Buddhist Education is a combination between individual and classroom educatio

The main of the Budhist monks was to propagate Buddhism .Hence some Acharyas like Sariputta, Mahayaggalva, Aniruddha, Rahula, etc gave the importance to tours for educating peopleAfter completion of the education the student were encouraged to undertake long tours to gain the real and practical knowledge.Conferences were arranged on every full moon and 1st day of month in the Budhist sanghs. The monks of different sanghs assembled and put forward their doubts freely. The attendance of every monk was compulsory in such conference.On the beginning and close of every month learned people used to assemble together. This type of assembly together was a very important part of Budhist education. The purpose of this assembly was to maintain the moral standards of all the monks, because the total education was based on morality. It was compulsory for all the monks to be present in this assemble so much so that even ill monks used to try to attend it anyhow. If due to illness it was not possible for monk to come, then assembly was held near his residence. This assembly was quite democratic and it has immense moral impact on all concerned. In order to win discussion or Shastrartha and impress the general public, it was necessary to improve the power of discussion. This was also needed to satisfy the critics and opposing groups and establish ones own cult. Thus, rules were framed for discussion. : The importance of discussion encouraged the logic in the Budhist period. The controversial matters could not be decided without logical argument. Logic was also useful in the development of the mental power and knowledge to established the disputes point the following evidences of eight kinds were required theory, cause, example,parallelism, contradiction, evidence, argument and induction. the important of discussion encouraged the logic in the Buddhist period. The controversial matters could not be decided without logical arguments.

The curriculum was spiritual in nature. The aim of education was to attain salvation. So the study of religious books was most important. Sutta, Vinaya and Dhamma Pitak were the main subjects prescribed for study. Budhist education aimed at purity of character. Like Vedic education it was training for moral character rather than psychological development of the students. One has to attain the stage of Bodhisattva. Mental and moral development was emphasized:

The method of teaching was mostly oral in nature. Though the art of writing had been well developed up to Budhist period yet, due to shortage and no availability of writing materials, verbal education was prevalent as it was in Vedic age. The teacher used to give lessons to the novices who learnt them by heart. The teacher used to put questions on the learning the lesson by heart. Teacher gives lecture on good behaviour and required topics and students were listen with attention In early days teaching was a hearing system. The teachers gave lectures; students heard it and kept it in their memory. In due course it developed into dialogue and comparison method. The teachers used to teach the students on the basis of telling stories, arranging dialogue. Sometimes debate and discussions were arranged to give idea of the subject matter as well as determination of truth, subsequently writing system introduced.Afterwords students were expected to memories the same. The teacher educates the students through lectures and question answer method. Attendance of every monk was compulsory. The medium of Buddhist education was the common language of the people.

Some Buddhist monks are more interested in isolated spiritual meditation in lonely forests and caves. Only those monks were considered fit for lonely meditation who had fully renowned the worldly attraction and had spent enough time in the Sanghs has gained the efficiency for solitary meditation.

Merits of Buddhist Education

1. Well organized centers- Buddhist education was imparted in well organized centers, monasteries and Vihara which were fit places for the purpose.
2. Cosmopolitan-Buddhist education was free from communal narrowness.
3. Simple and austere-Bhikshus led a life of austerity and simplicity.
4. Total development- Buddhist education laid much emphasis on the physical mental and spiritual development of the students.
5. Disciplined Life- both the teachers and students led disciplined life.
6. Ideal student teacher relationship.
7. International importance- Buddhist education helped to gain international importance it also developed cultural exchange between India and other countries of the world.

Demerits of Buddhist Education

1. Buddhist education could not give the proper attention to the occupational, industrial and technical education.
2. It gave severe blow to the social development because it derided family ties. Leaving their family life Buddha Bhikshus devoted their whole lives to sangh and Buddhism.

In the ancient period Buddhist Monasteries and in the later period Buddhist Universities played major role in developing Buddhist Education. In the institutions teachers were highly qualified and sincere to their duties. The main aim of Buddhist Education is to make a free man, an intelligent man, a wise, moral, talented, non-violent and secular man. Buddhist Education makes man judicious, humanist, logical and free from superstitions

It is a matter of great pride that Buddhist Education crossed Indian Sub-continent and expanded upto China, Korea, Japan, Tibet, Mongolia, Srilanka, Myanmar, Thailand, Cambodian, Laos, Vietnam, Malaysia, Singapore, with the rise and development of Buddhism in those countries. In those countries Buddhist Education has made tremendous progress with the inclusion of modern subjects in the syllabus. Today in order to make more popular more useful and modern subjects have to be included such as English, Science, Medicine, Engineering, Commerce, Computer and Information Technology. We are happy that the name of the countries which I mentioned has made tremendous development of Buddhist Education with the inclusion of modern subjects. They have made more facilities for the lay students. I Buddhist Education syllabus shall have to be incorporated with modern subject.

THE CULTURAL DIMENSIONS OF BUDDHIST EDUCATION

Here I am discussing Buddhism and Education with Thai Experience (with students). Since the advent of Buddhism in Thailand nearly 1,000 years ago, monks have had crucial roles especially in the moral education of the public. The Thai mind, in general, is thus inculcated with compassion, friendliness, and love of peace.Nevertheless, having lacked knowledge of the Buddhist scriptures and modern academic knowledge, the Thais were superstitious and unable to improve their way of life. King Rama V (1868-1910) was aware of his people's inadequate knowledge susceptible to Western imperialism. He began the process of educational reform in the country. The two Buddhist colleges, Mahamakuta and Mahachula, were built in order to properly train monks to be efficient Buddhist teachers and good followers of the *dhamma*. After their graduation, monks went to work in temple schools in villages throughout the country. They taught Buddhist ethics, Thai language, mathematics, history, and so on, and tried to improve folk ways of life. In the reign of King Rama V, Thai people were more educated and contented with their prosperity.

Problems of Education in Thailand Today

Though Thai education has been improved since the reign of King Rama V, the government is still unable to push all children through the process of compulsory formal education. The failure of educational management and administration as well as a rapid increase of population call for non-formal education, e.g., a Temple Pre-school Centre, a Buddhist Sunday School, etc.

It is obvious that only a well-to-do family is able to send children to a good school. Many poor children in Bangkok and those in villages far away are condemned to stay with their parents to work for the rest of their lives. The sight of youngsters selling newspapers and garlands in the street is just an ordinary experience for everyone in Bangkok. Similarly, outside Bangkok, far away in the countryside, small boys and girls watch cattle in the fields without any chance to enter school.

The Roles of the Government and Monks

In order to prepare children for school and provide the socially disadvantaged with the chance to be literate, the Ministry of Education initiated Temple Pre-school Centres in 1963. The project gained good support from the Buddhist Sangha, which allowed any temple to establish a temple school. Monks became teachers of pre-school children. The outcome of the project was successfully accepted by the public.

The Temple Pre-school Centre is a kind of social welfare promoted by the government. It invites people of all ages to come to the temple, be morally cultivated, and fulfil their human qualities. It widely interests the public with its following features:

1. It works on a basis of charity and gives free service.
2. It can be established in any temple.

3. Children eligible are five to eight years old.
4. Any illiterate adult is welcome to enrol.
5. Monks and novices are teachers. Lay people can be teaching assistants.
6. Children are prepared to enter compulsory school and their morals and manners are cultivated.

Since 1988, the Temple Pre-school Centre has changed to 'the Centre of Pre-school Children in the Temple'. It is open to children three-to-six years old.

Apart from the project of the Ministry of Education, there are some other projects for poor children launched by developer monks. One worth mentioning is Phra Khamkhian Suvanno of Sukhato Forest hermitage in north-eastern Thailand.

Phra Khamkhian Suvanno founded the Centre for Child Development in 1978 in order to take care of small children whose parents had to work in the fields all day. Most north-eastern villagers were poor farmers. They had to bring their children to the fields because there was nobody at home to look after them. Waiting for their parents to finish work, children played in the rain or were exposed to the sun the whole day. Some were severely ill and died. Phra Khamkhian thus decided to set up the Centre so that children would be taken care of and would learn to read and write elementary Thai language. At first, there were 20 children in the Centre. Phra Khamkhian brought up these children himself. They were fed with the food given to monks everyday. They had soy milk to drink and sweetmeats to eat regularly. The Centre gave a free service to the community for 8 months of the year from March to November. It was closed on the Buddhist Sabbath days. Some years later, a few volunteer assistants came to teach the children. Parents could leave their children in the centre and go to work happily in the fields.

Apart from 2,554 pre-school centres around the country, the government and the Buddhist order also carry on the project of the Buddhist Sunday School. The Buddhist Sunday School originated in Sri Lanka in 1886. It teaches various fields of Buddhist knowledge and languages. From 1953 to 1957, Phra Bimaladharma of Mahachulalongkorn Buddhist College, Bangkok, had visited Sri Lanka and witnessed moral and cultural teaching in the Sunday School. He deeply appreciated the success of its work. After his return to Thailand, he established the first Buddhist Sunday School in Mahachulalongkorn Buddhist College in 1958.

The Buddhist Sunday School was founded and has been carried on until today in order to inculcate moral discipline and general knowledge in children. Many social problems, e.g., juvenile delinquency, drug addiction, etc., arise from a lack of moral training and moral cultivation. If children are acquainted with the Buddhist teachings and properly follow the Buddhist precepts, they will be able to attain peaceful happiness and live successful lives.

In order to save young people from ignorance and worthless life, Mahachulalongkorn Buddhist College thus began the Buddhist Sunday School with the following objectives:

1. To make young people and children familiar with Buddhism.
2. To inculcate moral discipline and cultural appreciation in young people and children.
3. To teach young people and children to lead their lives according to Buddhist principles.
4. To train young people and children to work for public welfare.

Now-a-days there are 995 branches of the Buddhist Sunday School around the country. Class levels are arranged according to students' grades as follows:

1. There are 4 elementary classes for primary school pupils of grades 1, 2, 3 and 4.
2. There are 3 intermediate classes for secondary school students of grades 1, 2 and 3.
3. There are 3 advanced classes for high school students of grades 4, 5 and 6.

4. There are 2 final classes for college students.

It takes 12 years to complete the entire course. Monks and some lay teachers, due to their compassion and loving kindness towards students, work in the programme on a voluntary basis. Their work is much appreciated by all Buddhists and considerably helps improve public morality.

Apart from Mahachulalongkorn Buddhist College's public service of education, there are some other Buddhist leaders, both monks and lay people, who actively work for the sake of disadvantaged children. Worth mentioning here are Phra Vidya Cittadhammo of Mount Sarb Temple School and Mr Pai Soisaklang, the head of Sa Koon village.

According to Thai Buddhist tradition, only a male has the privilege of becoming a novice or a monk and is able to stay in a monastery for further education. A female can be merely a lay attendant and cannot closely associate with monks. Thus, male children have a good chance to fulfil their education through ordination. The case of Mount Sarb Temple School may well illustrate the point.

Phra Vidya Cittadhammo, the developer monk who runs the school, explains that all other secondary schools in the country emphasise only academic knowledge. They pay less attention to the moral cultivation of students' minds. Mount Sarb Temple School, on the contrary, accepts all underprivileged boys whose parents are too poor to send them to a formal school. These children are ordained in the temple and have studied in its secondary school, free of charge, for 3 years. The subjects are Thai, English, mathematics, and social studies. Children and young people who are novices hold to the ten Buddhist precepts during their 3 years of education, which covers both secular knowledge and *dhammic* knowledge.

It is very important nowadays to pay attention to juvenile development. Samanera Vidya, a young novice, points out that due to his poverty, he cannot enter any other school and that most youngsters are wayward and delinquent. He stresses that the Mount Sarb Temple School tremendously helps young people cultivate their minds, fulfil their human qualities, and be able to survive happily in this suffering world.

Another example of service for young students is the Sa Koon Village School, founded by the headman Pai Soisaklang and all villagers. Pai Soisaklang uses Buddhist teachings as a guide for village life. He and the villagers built the school, without any support from the government, in order to prevent youngsters from wrongdoing. By means of education, children learn to differentiate right from wrong and be sufficiently knowledgeable to depend on themselves. He also encourages the villagers to live according to the Buddhist precepts, for their own peaceful happiness, through the following village rules:

1. Do not kill animals, since it is forbidden by the first Buddhist precept.
2. Do not fire a gun within the village since it will frighten others.
3. Do not drink alcoholic beverages in the village since the drunkenness may cause trouble to others.

During the Buddhist Lent, young people are persuaded to listen to a sermon and join a religious ceremony in the temple. They learn to stay close to their parents and follow the traditional way of life. During weekends, children stay home to help their parents work in the fields and dig fish-ponds. They are happy to make themselves useful to their community.

A Look to the Future

The changing role of Thai monks from ascetics to social developers is indispensable for Thai society nowadays. This phenomenon does not diminish monks' sacred status at all since they still preserve their monastic discipline.

Once when I spent a week at the Sukhato Forest Hermitage in north-eastern Thailand, I had the opportunity to examine Phra Khamkhian Suvanno's community development. I found that his work was much beneficial to the villagers and indispensable for community life. The three villages around the hermitage are located quite far away from the helping hand of the government and cannot survive without monks' assistance.

Phra Khamkhian's method of work is a combination of *dhammic* practice and social development. He follows the Buddhist teaching that a good mind yields a good practice. If one has learned to purify oneself and is able to lessen one's own defilements, one can live for the sake of others and thus can yield benefits to one's community and to the rest of the world. Phra Khamkhian teaches the villagers to abstain from all evil deeds and to practise meditation in order to learn more about themselves and to understand the nature of the world.

Under the sponsorship of the Thai Khadi Research Institute, Thammasat University, Bangkok, I spent nearly 2 months interviewing many villagers, monks, and government officials who were responsible for the well-being of these villages. The outcome of Phra Khamkhian's work, however, is unsatisfactory. Most projects are initiated and run only by Phra Khamkhian. Villagers are merely participants and thus have no motivation to carry on and fulfil their work. For example, even though the Centre for Child Development still operates today, Phra Khamkhian is the only one who manages it and takes responsibility for all the work. Due to poverty and the lack of self-dependent orientation, the villagers would rather leave all problems to Phra Khamkhian than participate in the Centre or donate some money to support it.

Phra Khamkhian is well conscious of his role as a Thai monk venerated by lay people. His community development has been done within the context of Buddhist discipline. Thus, his monastic status is always held as sacred by the villagers.

Furthermore, it can be noted that most private agencies working for community development do not like to communicate or seek assistance from governmental officials. They prefer working by themselves. The case of Phra Khamkhian is an example of a leading developer monk who devotedly works for the sake of the poor community but lacks internal cooperation and external support.

In Thailand the traditional system of primary education is as important as the modern system since ethical training is no less crucial than academic proficiency. The Thai traditional system of primary education began in a temple or a monastery where monks were teachers and preachers. Its aim was to moralise the public as well as to improve the folk ways of life. According to Buddhist beliefs, the cultivation and purification of the mind is the source of all good deeds. Thus, if we properly bring up children at the earliest, they will become good citizens and good human beings in the future. Their knowledge will be applied to save the world. Right now, the Ministry of Education in Thailand is well conscious of this fact and mandates that all primary school pupils should study Buddhist ethics and should be trained to be morally good in their own traditions. It seems that the traditional system of education emphasises the role of religion for the good of students while the modern system honours academic knowledge and Westernization as signs of educational achievement.

I believe that both moral cultivation and academic training are equally important for students. We would rather have a morally knowledgeable person than an evil brilliant guy or a virtuous idiot. In order to train children both morally and academically, the government and all private agencies need to cooperate in supporting educational projects in all schools and in providing all illiterates throughout the country with compulsory education and elementary knowledge suitable for their folk lives and local environment.

An ideal primary school or centre of education should be well equipped with pictorial lessons and audio-visual materials in order to draw pupils' attention and make the entire process of teaching attractive. The size of the centre depends on the number of pupils in a community. Nevertheless, it is better to have 15-20 pupils in each class so that the teacher is able to train and look after everyone. Children who are ready to enter a primary school and be able to fulfil their course are ideally 5 years old. The curriculum should emphasise knowledge useful for children, encouraging optimistic viewpoints and leading to the fulfilment of their potential. The characteristics of a teacher and parents' education are no less important. Teachers should love children and be cheerful enough to make the lessons interesting. They should be trained particularly for their profession. Needless to say, if the government really wants to support public education and fight against illiteracy, it needs to provide the public with free and compulsory primary education. Since the children of today are the adults of tomorrow, as a Thai proverb says, the attempt by all means to make the best of children is thus worth the investment.

THE BUDDHIST WAY OF EDUCATION

The Lord Buddha is the Greatest Teacher of Gods and Men alike. During the Buddha's journeys into India and many other parts of the world, he has systematically designed his teachings to the intellectual aspirations and spirtual understandings of individuals whom he had come into contack with and to adapt it to their varied cultural backgrounds. This article, which is originally written by a Japanese scholar of Buddhism, Prof Sui Ye Hong Yuan, examines how the Buddha was able to educate and lead thousands of his students from varied family backgrounds with vast intellectual differences to achieve from mundane happiness to successive spiritual progress culminating towards the ultimate goal of supramundane experience, and his emphasis on cultivating mindfulness meditation.

The Blessed One's approach to education can be broadly classified into 2 ways, the ekayano magga and the anupubbi katha. From the scriptures, the suttas and the vinaya pitakas, the Buddha often talks about the beginner and the advanced level of spiritual attainment. He introduced different levels of teachings and approaches to suit individuals of different intellect and wisdom and to lead them towards the ultimate summit of knowledge and liberation.

The ekayano magga path refers to the direct meditative practice, which consists of the meditational teachings of the Buddha and of taking practical steps to practice and adopt them through experiences to achieve spiritual levels of attainments. The anupubbi magga refers to the gradual path approach, as the individual progress gradually from his perspective of religious understanding, background and belief. Depending on the individual intellectual level and at different level of spiritual attainment, different concepts are introduced to meet that level of understandings and spiritual developments.

The education system of present society is similar to that of the anupubbi katha path. For example, the teaching of mathematical concepts. At the primary school level, students are taught simple arithmetic. Students at the upper and post-secondary school level are introduced to more advanced concepts sucg as modern mathematics or further mathematics concept depending on their intellectual level and aspirations and their ability to grasp these concepts. As one advances the academic ladder right up to university, mire sophisticated and abstract ideologies are being introduced. Again, depending on their inclination, students are channelled to different streams or to one that they are best suited to excel.

The ekayano magga path, however, is little known or emphasized in today's educational context. In the olden days, much of the learning was based on memory, little children of three to four years old were able to memorise and regurgitate volumes after volumes of great philosophical ideas which they knew very little of but yet had to subscribe to. With experiences and the passing of time did they come to realise the significance of what they had learned in those younger days.

Let us now examine from the sutta's perspective, how the Buddha teaches the ekayano magga path. Ekayano magga means the one sole way, which refers to contemplation on the four foundations of mindfulness. In the long discourses, the Mahasatipatthana Sutta states : " There is the one sole way, monks, for the purification of beings, for overcoming sorrow, lamentation, grief and despair, for reaching the right path, for attaining enlightenment, namely the four foundations of mindfulness."

These are common verses found in various Buddhist scriptures. Besides emphasizing on the four foundations of mindfulness as the one sole way to enlightenment, the Buddha also gave teachings on developing the four right efforts, the six recollections and the noble eightfold path, as objects of practice and contemplation. He taught his students to practice morality, develop their minds by concentration and insight meditation, right up to the summit of the spiritual path.

In the scriptures, however, the ekayano magga way of expressing the truth is not used. One can only assume that the goal and method of practice are similar to that of the anupubbi katha.

One begins on the path of an ordinary undeveloped spiritual practitioner to that of an advanced meditator. He progresses to become one with the lineage of enlightened beings, the stream winner, the once-returner, the non returner and the perfected one. These realisations are the fruits of their practice and are also similar, and so is their experience of insight. The silent Buddhas and the Fully Enlightened Buddhas also seek enlightenment through similar method.

Then, how do the enlightened ones realise the truth from the same practice? One can assume that they had all realised the truth by comtemplating on subjectssuch as the four noble truths, the nature of the five aggregates and so sorth and the development of the five faculties (confidence, energy, mindfulness, concentration, wisdom) etc. He contemplates on subjects like the establishment of the four foundations of mindfulness up to the development of the seven factors of enlightenment (mindfulness, investigation of states, energyjoy, bliss, concentration, equanimity), the noble eightfold path, mindfulness of breathing etc. The scriptures mentioned other subjects of contemplation too but primarily practise is to realise the four noble truths and the nature of the five aggregates, that every nature is subjected to the same phenomena - rise and fall. The scriptures mentions a way in which the Buddha teach Yasa, a lay follower the gradual path (anupubbi katha),by first explaining to him the benefits of performing acts of charity, of keeping morality and the fruits of being born in heaven.

Subsequently, the Buddha expounds to him the faults underlying in being attached to sensual pleasure and the benefits of early detachments. When the layman Yasawas ready for higher spiritual understandings, the Buddha would then teach him the fundamentals of Buddhism.In essence then, we see that there are no differences in practice. Whether one chooses to contemplate on the four noble truths, the four foundations of mindfulness, the five aggregates, the philosophy and experience are similar and thus constitute the right path of Buddhism. The difference, however, lies in the practitioner's own character and intellectual capacity. From this point onwards, the Buddha would introduce the teachings to the layman Yasa in successive stages.

The teaching was initially meant for people who did not have knowledge of the laws of cause and effect. The Buddha would emphasize to them the need to be generous towards the poor and the religious monks. He also taught people to be discipline and to observe the five precepts: namely to avoid acts of killing living beings, stealing and lying and adultery. With the accumilation of past merits and the observance of the moral precepts, one would be reborn in the heavens after death.

When the Buddha knows that Yasa had a purified mind, freed from mental hindrances, joyful, happy and full of faith, he imparts to him the knowledge of all Buddhas most sublime teachings, the four noble truths. Like a piece of white cloth being thoroughly cleased of impurities and dirts, it is able to absorb varied colours. Similarly, when asa's mind is pure, he is able to receive the various teachings from the Buddha. When he realises that whatever all phenomena has a nature of rise and fall, his mind is freed from defilements, attaing the purified eys of wisdom.

On the other hand, if one does not practise generousity and break the moral precepts, he will be reborn in the lower realms of existence. Thus the laws of cause and effect dictates that doing good deeds result in good returns and evil actions read evil rewards. The first stage is to eliminate wrong views of not believing in the laws of cause and effect, and the second stage is when the mind becomes receptive to the essence of the teachings, the higher philosophy will be taught.

Besides, human lifestyle evolves around many enjoyments which results in the danger of being attached to such sensual pleasures. The essense of freedom is to be devoid of such attachment. Thus, if one still clings to and is unable to detach one's mind of sensual pleasures, one is not ready or receptive to the advanced level of Buddhism. Rather than teaching that person detachment, it is better for him to realise that for himself and come to term with it.

For those who are able to accept the teachings and understand the philosophy of dependent origination, they will certainly realise the wisdom of Buddhas and their eyes of wisdom will be eliminated. Regarding Buddha's global philosophy and life's philosophy, this is the initial stage of realisation. At the later and more advanced stages, it means seeing the deeper aspects of the path.

People who has just realised the eyes of wisdom and attained to realisation would naturally teach the truth from his own experience, transforming theory into direct experience. Initially, when the Buddha attained enlightenment, he taught the four noble truths to his first disciples, the five monks, thus enlightening them on the right path and practice. Subsequently, he taught them to realise the true nature of the five aggregates, the impermanent, unsatisfactory and empty nature of the bodily and mental phenomenon.

The supramundance path requires the meditator to contemplate with a clear comprehening mind and to reflect on the nature of the aggregates. From this point onwards, he realises insight. Emptiness is realised through comtemplation and listening to the discourse on the four noble truths. This way of developing faith and wisdom can be found in the scriptures. From contemplating on the four foundations of mindfulness, reflecting on the repulsiveness of the body, recollection on death, the four immerasurable thoughts, the four formless absorptions and mindfulness of breathing, one progressively develops the seven factors of enlightenment. From contemplating on the breath, one enters into developing the four foundations of mindfuless, then to developing the factors of enlightenment. In that order, he successively realises the highest knowledge and liberation. From this process he purifies himself through virtue.

Pali Buddhism, the Theravada Buddhist tradition has seven stages of emancipathion of practise. THe Mahayana tradition advocates the three causes of noblehood, cultivating the three good roots, seeing, practising and leading to stages of noblehood. Such complicated spiritual practises emphasizes on the fifty-two stages of cultivating the bodhisatta path. This can be a said to be a more complicated and comprehension approach of the anupubbi katha or gradual path.

Why is it so important to bring forth all three aspects: intellectual, moral, and social?

Today, academic educational institutions focus on intellectual instruction, on bringing forth what lies within the mind. Looking around it's not hard to see where this has all too often gotten us: some very smart people making very poor moral choices, which have egregiously harmed society. What has gone wrong?

These institutions focus on economic progress instead of ethical progress, on commercializing the mind not illuminating it. Self-interest has been placed as number one, with the benefit for the many being relegated far down the list. Short-term profits, regardless of the long-term costs reign. The balance of the three aspects has shifted to a concentration on just one—intellectual. The moral and social aspects have been seriously neglected.

Is the Intellectual Aspect Unimportant?

Not at all. The intellectual is important. After all we need to learn the appropriate information and skills in all areas of our lives. We need to learn how to support ourselves, meet our own various societal responsibilities, and be able to function in the world in a manner that helps, not harms, others. We need to learn about others, how they live, their values, the many things we have in common, and the wonderful differences that make humanity so fascinating.

Apart from academic learning, Buddhism looks more at helping us to grow spiritually. For this, we need to learn from wise teachers and teachings in areas like morality, virtues, and causality. These will help enable us to live in the world, but not become ensnared by it. Becoming ensnared will lead to wanting more and more, and, invariably, harming more and more.

With good instruction, we will bring forth the good values that already lie within our very essence, what we call our prajna, our innate, wisdom. Every being has this innate wisdom deep within them. Every being has the ability to function with spontaneous, unconditional care and compassion. Our learning and practice have the goal of illuminating this innate wisdom and goodness so it will arise and shine forth in everything we do. Practice is why we learn. Practice is fulfilling the teachings.

What of Moral Instruction?

Good moral values instruction will enable us to get along better with others and will thus bring in social instruction as well. To accomplish this, we need teachers who understand the teachings as the original teachers intended. One way to see if the teacher understands the moral teaching is to observe whether he or she puts them into practice in daily life, in everything they do.

This role modeling is a teaching in itself because it shows that the principles are indeed applicable and appropriate for us. They're not out-dated or out-of-touch. The role modeling also gives real-life examples of how to apply the principles in daily situations like those we ourselves encounter.

And vitally important, seeing the teacher putting the teachings into action, deepens our confidence in the teachings, and the teacher. This is not just some noble principle I learned last week, this is a genuine teaching that works and can help me. Not only that, it can be seen to help others as well. Someone not taking something without permission or saying what is untrue gives those who observe this a feeling of safety, of not needing to worry in this person's presence.

What of the person who chose not to commit a wrongdoing? They too are less anxious! There is no need to try to remember what they told one person as opposed to what they told another. No need to worry about being found with something they have no right to possess. No need to fear that something they said or did is wrong and will come back to haunt them. No need to feel ashamed of having hurt a person they hold dear.

By worrying, fearing, and stressing less, both mind and heart will gradually become more calm. The calmer they are the better they learn and function. And the better that innate, true nature and wisdom will shine forth.

Education—giving the three aspects of intellectual, moral, and social instruction—ennobles us all. It ennobles the one who teaches, for this person has given completely of their knowledge, without holding back, without putting self- interest above the interests of others. Education ennobles the one who is taught, for this person has learned better how to not merely survive but to grow in the world, how to be a caring, moral person who seeks to help not harm others.

Education ennobles all those who are touched by the teachings for they too are touched by the spirit of the teachings through simply being in the presence of good people and learning how to emulate them.

Education benefits us all for it allows us to become wiser, to be more caring of those who need our help, more respectful of others' viewpoints, more patient with those we interact with, and happier with ourselves.

THE GOAL OF BUDDHIST EDUCATION

What is the ultimate goal of the Buddha's teachings? It is to attain the Perfect, Complete Enlightenment. Transliterated from Sanskrit, it is called Anuttara-samyak-sambodhi. Out of respect, this phrase was maintained in its original form rather than translated. There are three stages within this enlightenment: "Proper Enlightenment", "Equal and Proper Enlightenment", and "Perfect, Complete Enlightenment".

The Buddha told us, that although scientists, philosophers and religious scholars may have reached a good understanding about life and the universe, this realization is neither complete nor proper. Why? Although they have obtained some understanding, they are far from having freedom from worries, from ending their afflictions. They still indulge themselves in the Five Poisons of greed, anger, ignorance, arrogance and doubt. They remain mired in all the troubles of human relationships and are swayed by personal feelings. In other words, they are human.

If a person has severed greed, anger, ignorance, arrogance, doubt and afflictions, it will be acknowledged that this person has attained the first level, that of Proper Enlightenment. He or she will be called an Arhat, similar to the initial academic degree in Buddhism. Arhats differ from Buddhas in the way that they use their mind. They use it in the same manner we do. The difference is that we still have afflictions while Arhats do not.

The next higher level of enlightenment is that of Equal and Proper Enlightenment, represented by Bodhisattvas. They resemble Buddhas in motivation but have not yet reached the same level of enlightenment. The minds of Bodhisattvas are genuine; they remain forever unchanged and are similar to those of Buddhas. Buddhas use the full and perfect true heart. Buddhas represent the highest level of enlightenment, which is the Perfect Complete Enlightenment.

In Buddhist classic literature, the perfect, true mind of a Buddha was symbolized by a full moon. The mind of a Bodhisattva was symbolized by a crescent moon, which was neither full nor perfect. And the mind of an arhat was symbolized by moonlight reflected from the surface of water, it is not real.

These three levels of enlightenment can be compared to our college educational system. The level or degree of Arhat is similar to earning an undergraduate degree. The level of Bodhisattva is similar to earning a Master's degree and the level of Buddha is similar to earning a Doctorate's degree. The word Buddha is not exclusive to Buddha Shakyamuni, but is a common title for any being who has attained the perfect complete enlightenment. Thus, Buddha, Bodhisattva and Arhat are only names or titles to represent the levels of enlightenment or a degree we receive in Buddhism. And they are most certainly not deities to be worshiped.

So, a Buddha is one who has fully comprehended the truth of life and the universe and acquired the ultimate and perfect wisdom. This is also the goal of Buddhist education; to enable beings to attain this same level of wisdom. Therefore, Buddhism is an education of wisdom.

THE OBJECTIVES OF THE BUDDHA'S TEACHINGS

The principle of Buddhism is to break through all superstitions and delusions. It is to resolve delusion to attain happiness and enlightenment, to eliminate suffering to gain serenity and purity of mind. What is delusion? When we do not thoroughly and properly understand the phenomenon around us, we tend to be deluded, to have wrong ideas, which lead us to make mistakes. Then we suffer ill consequences as a result. However, if we have correct understanding about life and the universe, we will be free from mistakes in thought, judgement and behavior. Then our result, or effect, will be favorable. Thus, resolving delusion to attain enlightenment is the cause and eliminating suffering to attain happiness and purity is the effect.

Only through resolving superstition and delusion, can enlightenment be attained. This is the objective of the Buddha's teaching. This wisdom will enable all beings to differentiate true from false, proper from improper, right from wrong and good from bad. It can help us to establish a dynamic and caring attitude toward life and our surroundings. So, we can clearly see that Buddhism is neither passive nor obsolete, nor is it retreating from society. As said in the Buddha Speaks of the Infinite Life Sutra of Adornment, Purity, Equality and Enlightenment of the Mahayana School or the Infinite Life Sutra, Buddhism can perfectly solve all afflictions and problems. It enables us to obtain true and ultimate benefits by creating fulfilling lives, happy families, harmonious societies, prosperous nations and a peaceful world. These are the objectives of the Buddha's teachings for our world now. The ultimate objectives of abandoning all worries thus transcending the six realms are even more incredibly wonderful. Therefore, we can see that it is an education that will enable us to attain truth, virtue, beauty, wisdom and genuine eternal happiness.

According to Oxford Advantaged Genie Dictionary, education means a process of teaching, training and learning, especially in schools, or colleges, to improve knowledge and develop skills. Here we will examine in brief how much Buddhism has taught, and done as regards to this.

Buddhism gives the highest regard for wisdom (paññā) and purity (visuddhi) of the mind from mental defilements, and the worst condemn for ignorance. In Buddhism wisdom is the sharpest means to cut off all impurities. But what we are talking here is knowledge (ñāna), of course, knowledge and wisdom are not equivalent terms. For one can collect knowledge by learning, but not wisdom. Wisdom is not something that is accumulated, but it comes from a deep reflection. Therefore, of the three roads, to wit: Suta- learning, Cinta- thinking, Bhāvana- meditation, only the third one gives rise to wisdom. But Buddhism does not overlook the fist two steps. It always emphasizes on learning and teaching as the way to dispel ignorance. And some times the two terms knowledge and wisdom are interchangeable.

First, the Buddha is an extraordinary Teacher (sattha). He is endowed with the five qualities:

1. Attaññû: He knows what is good/ beneficial;
2. Dhammaññû: He knows what is true/righteous;

3. Mattaññû: He knows the measure;
4. Kālaññû: He knows the right time;
5. Parisaññû: He knows the assemblage or the person.

Among his nine precious attributes one is "Anuttaro purisadammasarathi" which means an excellent tamer of who should be tamed; and another epithet is "Satthā devamanussānam" which means the teacher of gods and men.

The Buddha said he had enlightened by himself without a teacher but it does not means that he had never learnt. Actually he had trained to be mastered of all the skills of statecrafts and sciences of the day. He also had a proficient religious knowledge of Brahmanic and Samana traditions. What he said is that he had realized the unrealizable of *the Samanas' experiences, and he proclaimed the unheard Dhamma that were lacking in the Vedic scriptures, and he gave a new interpretation for the ancient knowledge.*

He is a skilful teacher and strongly believed in the power of transferring knowledge to convince people to change their way of life. Once, the Buddha and his large company of monks were in the city of Nalanda, a lay follower named Kevamma came to pay respect to him and requested the Buddha commending his great disciples to exhibit miracles so that the entire inhabitants of prosperous Nalanda city would become his followers. The Buddha rejected his request and said that *of the miracles, the miracle of instruction is the best* -anusāsanî-pāmihāriya And only this miracle he himself used and encouraged his disciples to use. After he has trained the first group of disciples, the Buddha sent them to different directions to teach the Dhamma "for the good of the many, for the benefit of the many, for the happiness and welfare of the world." He himself went to Uruvella and converted one thousand fire-worship ascetics by famous "Aditta sutta"- the discourse on fire.

The Buddha expounded Dharma in many ways to fit the different types of individuals. He used many different methods and devices to transfer his knowledge to people: similes, parables, analogies, analyses, synthetic, etc. By his ability of reading other's minds and their past experiences, he gave a suitable discourse so that his listeners would easily understand and put into practice. Now we see some discourses are lengthy, some are medium size and some are very short; some are rich of lofty philosophy, some are with deep and nuanced psychology, some are simple and common day to day life for the peasants.

He requested his listeners to pay close attention at what is being taught (Tena hi bhikkhave sunātha, sādhukam manasi kārotha...), willingly to learn, and remember it well, then folder and examine it's meaning. (sutvā dhāreti dhātānam dhammānam attham upaparikkhati attham upparikkhato dhammā nijjhanakkhamanti; or: Dhammam sotukāmo sutānam dhammānam dhārakajātiko. Dhātānam dhammānam atthûpaparikkhāyi..).

In Sammosa sutta of the SN it is stated: Idha bhikkhave bhikkhû na dhammam pariyāpunanti suttam geyyam veyyākaranam gatham udānam itivuttam jātakam abbhutadhammam vedallam ayam pathamo dhammo saddhammassa sammorāya antarādhānaya pavattati.- Herein, bhikkhus , if the bhikkhus do not master the dhamma: the discourses, mixed prose, expositions, verses, inspired utterances, brief saying, birth stories, marvelous accounts, miscellanies, this is the first cause of the disappearance of the true teaching." Thus *the Buddha emphasized on the learning and mastering the Dhamma, made it a crucial factor which constitutes the longevity of the Dhamma.*

Another interesting event recorded in Mahaparinibbana sutta (DN) is that the Mara-evil one requested the Buddha terminated his life right after he attained enlightenment, the Buddha refused this unreasonable request with the consideration that until the Tathagata's fourfold disciples (Bhikkhus-monks, bhikkhunis-nuns, Upasaka-laymen followers, Upasika-lay women followers) have mastered the Dhamma taught by him, he will not enter into eternal peace of Nibbana. *This incident reveals that the Buddha had dedicated his time for teaching, instructing and enlightening people. During forty-*

five years of his Buddha's career he was the noblest example of a Teacher.

In Buddhist terms, the knowledge acquired by learning is called 'sutamaya ñ āna'. The other two are 'cintamaya ñ āna'- the knowledge acquired by thinking, and 'bhavanāmaya ñ āna'- the knowledge acquired through practicing meditation.

One of the factors that give rise to right view is named 'paratoghosa' which literally means hearing the sound of other. This is not a kind of revelation secretly revealed by the God or gods. It simply means one listens to the wise and gains some knowledge or suddenly realizes some essential there in.

Another word to describe the person of much knowledge is 'buhussuta'. A person who is endowed with 'heard much' is regarded as a blessing. (Mangala sutta). 'Sutadhanam' is the treasure of having 'heard much', sutadharo is remembering a lot, and 'sutasanniccaya is collection of hearing. 'Suta'is one of the five treasures-(dhana). To wit: confidence-saddha, virtue-sîla, learned-suta, benevolence-cāga, and wisdom-pa ñ ñ ā for lay persons, and it is among the seven treasures of bhikkhus-monks and bhikkhuni- nuns.

But the Buddha also reminded his audiences to be careful about accepting what were being taught. "Nay, Kālāma, do not be led by revelation, or by tradition, or by hearsay, not by authority of the secret scriptures, or by mere reasoning, not by seeming logical, not by mere believing in the person who spoke it,..".

In another occasion, the Buddha pointed out five things that should not be taken for granted. They are saddha- faith, ruci- liking (emotional inclination), anussava- oral tradition, akāraparivitakka-reasoned cogitation, and dimmhi nijjhānakkhanti-reflective acceptance of view. "These five things can turn into different ways here and now. Now some thing may be fully accepted out of faith, yet, it may be empty, hollow, and false, but some thing else may be not accepted but it may be factual, true and unmistaken..."

There are three stages in the course of Buddhist Education: *Pariyatti*-learning, *Pamipatti*- practicing, and *Pamivedha*-realization. Thus learning is the first step on the way to Nibbāna.

The four aspects of knowledge:

(1) Dimmha- what is seen.

(2) Suta- what is heard.

(3) Muta- what is thought of.

(4) Viñ ñ āta- what is understood.

Suta-learning is the first step to acquire knowledge. Another term for learning is 'ugganhatam'.

Sikkhā is the higher training. Three kinds of trainings are essential in Buddhism. They are: Sila sikkhā-the higher training of morality; Samādhi sikkhā-the higher training of concentration; and Pañ ñ ā sikkhā- the higher training of wisdom. In Singāla sutta (DN), the Buddha taught the young Sigāla about five duties of students toward teacher as follows:

(1) Ummhānena- Rising up to show respect (when the teacher comes).

(2) Uppatthānena- supporting the teacher.

(3) Sussūsāya- listening to him carefully or showing obeisance.

(4) Pāricariyāya- attending on the teacher.

(5) Sakkaccam sippapamiggahanena- duly comprehending the accepted teaching.

The word sippa means skill/knowledge in crafts or arts, this surely denotes the worldly knowledge. Thus the fifth duty of a pupil is to be carefully/attentively learning whatever he is taught. In Mangala sutta it is stated: 'bāhu-saccañ-ca sippañca, vinayo ca susikkhito-learned and perfect in skills, disciplined and well trained.'

On the part of teachers, they have to:

(1) Suvinitam vinenti-trains him in whatever discipline well trained.

(2) Suggahitam gāhāpenti- makes him hold fast that which must be well held.

(3) Sabba sippassutam samakkhāyino bhavanti- thoroughly instructs him in every skill of the art.

(4) Mitta maccesu patiyādenti-speak well of him among his friends and companions. Disāsu parittānam karoti- do protect him in every direction.

Thus the duties of teachers as instructed by the Buddha are heavier than nowadays. This is because the conditions of education in the Buddha's time were much difference than in the modern time. In the ancient time the pupils lived dependent on the teachers. They often learn with one teacher at a time. And there were no government schools. The Jataka stories reveal that Takkasita was the well- known center of learning and teaching in India. The youngsters were sent there and they found a teacher who possesses the knowledge that they want to learn, there they remain with the teacher for long time, under his care and protection. The term for teachers are: sattha, Acariya, upajjhāya- preceptor, mentor; and antevāsiko is a pupil. The teacher should show compassion for the pupil. Cûna vagga Pali, vattakhanddhaka describes in details the duties of teachers (ācariya, upajjhāyā,...) to the pupils, and the duties of a pupil toward his mentor/ preceptor/ teacher.

A Sutta in Anguttara Nikaya vividly describes the method of monastic training as follows:

(1) Approach a teacher with due respect and conscientious;

(2) Interrogation to clear out the meaning;

(3) Having learnt sufficient knowledge, he lives in comfort (citta viveka & kayaviveka);

(4) He is virtuous, live by the training of the Patimokkha, restraining his sense organs, seeing danger in the slightest fault.

(5) Having learnt much, memorized, recited verbally, investigated with the mind, and penetrated well by right view.

(6) He is energetic;

(7) Does not engage in pointless talk, he talks only on the Dhamma, or keeping noble silence.

(8) He dwells contemplating on the rise and fall of the five aggregates.

Sangha, the community of monks and the community of nuns are not only the congregation of contemplatives, but also the religious training schools. In a traditional way the new comer has to remain with a teacher (upajjhaya) for as least five years in order to learn the way of monastic as well as scriptures, meditation subject, etc. The methods of learning are: listening, memorizing, reciting (verbally), investigating the meaning by himself or interrogating with dhamma friends or teacher to clear the meaning.

Many monasteries become the great centre of learning, even there were some large Buddhist university such as Nalanda in eastern India and Valabhi in Western India that lasted for centuries, dated back over one thousand five hundreds ago. It was reported that there were times Nalanda University hosted around twenty thousand students from many different countries.[6] In Sri Lanka, in ancient time there were Mahavihara, Abhayagiri (Anuradhapura period); in modern time there were Vidyalankara pirivena, Kaleniya Pirivena, Vajira Pirivena,... to name a few. In Myanmar in the past Pyu, Thaton, Bagan, Amarapura were the great centre of Buddhism where children were sent to monasteries to acquire knowledge. Before the colonial period, Buddhist monasteries were the main schools for children of countries of the Theravada Buddhist tradition (Sri Lanka, Thailand, Myanmar, Lao, Cambodia and some southern provinces of Vietnam).

In modern time, Buddhist monks and nuns still actively give their services in educational field. Building school, write and distributing books, giving lectures, supporting poor students, and giving Dhamma talks are the most popular way to educate people. Follow the Teacher's footsteps Buddhist monks and nuns wander place to place to awaken people to the reality of life. A typical progressive talk start from charity (dana), to morality (sila), to heavenly states (sagga), to renunciation (nekkhamma), and finally to the Four Noble Truths that embody the liberation from all form of suffering. Thus Buddhist education is the way leading upward, though it does not stress much on the skills and knowledge for material gains, but it always encourages people "to be able" in supporting oneself and one family, to benefit society, and above all, to be detached, liberated from greed, hatred, and delusion.

BUDDHIST MONTESSORI MODEL

Although there is no definitive statement on the subject of Buddhist education, from our point of view, it is based on the opening verses of the ancient *Dhammapada*, in which the Buddha says, "We are what we think. All that we are arises with our thoughts. With our thoughts we make the world." Our mind is forerunner to inner happiness and well as to material success. Likewise, if we neglect the mind, we are vulnerable to our blind passions, making wrong decisions, and unwholesome living. By developing mindfulness, ethical development and understanding, students can unfold an attitude of inner awareness and compassion, and live wholesome, productive and happy lives. Through the cultivation of the mind, students can realize the interdependent nature of things and may be inspired to become positive agents of the dharma for the benefit of society and the world.

Our educational approach is encouraged by the *Kalama Sutta*. The Buddha gave this famous discourse to the Kalama people on how to handle the seemingly contradictory religious teachings of the times. Here, the Buddha sets the parameters on free inquiry with the goal of discovering meaningful spiritual truth. However, this approach can be used in any educational endeavor. It is the attitude of a scientist who objectively seeks the truth with a mind open to all possibilities but balanced with reason and experience. The Buddhist attitude would add the realization that we should never forget our interdependence with other beings.

To the Kalama people, the Buddha said, "Do not believe anything based on mere hearsay or rumor. Do not believe in traditions because they are ancient and handed down through the generations. Do not believe anything because it is written down in scripture. Do not believe anything just because you like the idea. Do not believe anything based on mere belief and because you carried this assumption for many years or because you feel it is inspired by a deity. Do not believe because your teachers or priests told you so. However, only after a thorough investigation and reflection, based on reason and experience, as conducive to the benefit of the many, should you accept it as real. Only then, should you embrace it and live by its truth."

Our school creates a new and powerful educational model by uniting the Buddhist teachings and its educational perspective with the Montessori educational approach that focuses on the child's innate curiosity and the natural learning process. Its student centered learning approach is a proven way to create autonomy, self-discipline, self-esteem and the love of learning. Wikipedia.com explains that a "Montessori education is an educational approach developed by Italian physician and educator Maria Montessori and characterized by an emphasis on independence, freedom within limits, and respect for a child's natural psychological, physical, and social development. Montessori education is practiced in an estimated 7,000 schools worldwide, serving children from birth to eighteen years old."

Similar to Buddhism, a Montessori education focuses on the student's mind and character, and encourages concentration and a sense of order. Like Shin Buddhism, teachers are guides along the path, respecting the dignity of the child, and promoting an environment of peace and collaboration. The Montessori approach develops the inner confidence and skills of children to become resourceful problem solvers, life-long learners, and community leaders. We believe it is a complimentary educational approach to the Shin Buddhist Way.

Below are some basic characteristics of the Montessori educational approach as prescribed by the Association

Montessori Internationale (AMI) and the American Montessori Society (AMS).

- Mixed age classrooms based on cycles or approximate age ranges.
- Student choice of activities based from a number of prearranged alternatives.
- A "discovery" model, where students learn from working with materials, rather than by direct instruction.
- Freedom of movement within the classroom.

BUDDHIST EDUCATION AND PEDAGOGY: CHALLENGES AND OPPORTUNITIES

The emerging profit-driven global economy is guided by unbridled development and gigantism. Such an economy is also coming under ever increasing domination of science and technology. Such a development is not only cutting us off from nature and one another but also undermining natural and cultural diversity. One major consequence of this is that our very survival is threatened. Moreover, the global economy is overwhelmingly controlled and run by consumerism and salespersons in which things are bought not because people need them but because they want them. The modern economic notion that more production of goods would make people happy is misplaced.

As pointed out by Schumacher, "An attitude to life which seeks fulfillment in the single-minded pursuit of wealth- in short, materialism- does not fit into this world, because it contains within itself no limiting principle, while the environment in which it is placed is strictly limited... The modern economy is propelled by a frenzy of greed and indulges in an orgy of envy, and these are not accidental features but the very causes of its expansionist success... such causes... carry within themselves the seeds of destruction" (1973: 17-18). Thus, we need to seriously examine not only our attitudes and lifestyles but also our policies that govern the use of renewable and non-renewable resources, science and technology, and the scale and direction of industrialization. As compared to this, Buddhist economy is based on the motto of happiness and welfare of maximum number of people (bahujanahitāya bahujanasukhāya: Vinaya Pitaka.I.21). Buddhist Economics does not necessarily see unbridled modernism and westernization as a positive phenomenon as it is responsible for many of the major problems that we face today. A modern Buddhist scholar, for instance, has pointed out that "Modernity is rejected because it is seen as a form of life that has in a short period of time despoiled the landscape and done irreparable damage to the environment (Lancaster 2002: 1-2).

Not only the inherent value of life itself but also the interdependence and reciprocity of human and other forms of life are a fundamental Buddhist belief. Thus, nature and humanity on the one hand and humans amongst themselves on the other are seen as mutually obligated to each other. A living entity can neither isolate itself from this causal nexus nor have an essence of its own. In other words, as part of the Dependent Arising (paticcasamuppāda), humans are seen as affecting their environment not only through the purely physical aspects of their actions, but also through the moral and immoral qualities of such actions.

That is, karmic effects sometimes catch up with people via their environment. It is thus said that, if a king and his people act unrighteously, this has a bad effect on the environment and its gods, leading to little rain, poor crops and weak, short-lived people (Anguttara Nikāya.II.74-76). This message is also strongly implied by the Aggañña Suttanta of the Dîgha Nikāya (III.80-98), which shows how in the beginning nature was bountiful, but it became less so when humans began to take greedily from it. When they began to harvest more rice than they needed, it was not naturally able to grow quickly enough.

This necessitated cultivation which in turn caused division of land into private fields, so that property was invented. Origin of private property became the root cause of different social and economic ills. Here, then, is a vision of how sentient beings are affected by what they take from their environment.

Our current socioeconomic system promotes competition rather than cooperation. This is bound to generate conflict and resentment-.

A society founded upon the Buddhist Dharma recognizes that one should aim at promoting the good of the greater unit to which one belongs, and as a minimum one must not look for one's own satisfaction in ways that may cause harm to others. Thus, in Buddhist approach to social and economic develop-ment, the primary criterion governing policy formu-lation must be the well-being of members of the society as a whole. Production must serve the real needs of the people, not the demands of the economic system. In such a system, economic de-velopment would be guided not by maximum consumption but sane and rational consumption furthering human well-being.

Buddhism promotes a wide distribution of basic necessities so that no one has to suffer deprivation as deprivation is the root cause of social conflict. Thus, talking about the cause of social conflict, the Buddha pointed out that, "goods not being bestowed on the destitute poverty grew rife; from poverty growing rife stealing increased, from the spread of stealing violence grew apace, from the growth of violence, the destruction of life became common" (Dīgha Nikāya.III.67).

Hoarding wealth in any form is looked down upon in Buddhism (A.III.222) and if a wealthy person were to enjoy his wealth all by himself only, it would be a source of failure for him (Sn.v.102). In fact, pride of wealth or economic snobbery is given in Buddhism as a cause of one's downfall (Sn.v.104). As pointed out by From, the present system generates greed and selfishness in which personal success is valued more highly than social responsibility. "It is no longer shocking when political leaders and business executives make decisions that seem to be to their personal advantage, but at the same time are harmful and dangerous to the community... At the same time, the general public is also so selfishly concerned with their private affairs that they pay little attention to all that transcends the personal realm" (Fromm 1976: 10-11). Our modern dinosaur society has become a greedy society and we do not know when enough is enough. A society driven by greed loses the power of seeing things in their wholesomeness.

"The hope... that by the single-minded pursuit of wealth, without bothering our heads about spiritual and moral questions, we could establish peace on earth, is an unrealistic, unscientific, and irrational hope... the foundations of peace cannot be laid by universal prosperity, in the modern sense, because such prosperity, if attainable at all, is attainable only by cultivating such drives of human nature as greed and envy... making inordinately large demands on limited world resources and... (putting rich people) on an unavoidable collision course- not primarily with the poor (who are weak and defenceless) but with other rich people" (Schumacher 1973: 18-19). Thus, "given unlimited desires, even the greatest production cannot keep pace with everybody's fantasy of having more than their neighbors. Necessarily, those who are stronger, more clever, or more favored by other circumstances will try to establish a favored position for themselves and try to take advantage of those who are less powerful, either by force and violence or by suggestion... (Conflict in the society) cannot disappear as long as greed dominates the human heart" (Fromm 1976: 114).

Buddhism, even though speaking in atheistic and secular terms, aims at the liberation of human beings from egoism and greed as they are the main cause of misery and harm. There is no doubt that environmental disaster is to a great extent due to the insatiable greed of humans. Buddhism on the whole, though does not mind wealth and prosperity, but they have to be acquired and used in full accord with the ethical norms. Human tendency to have- to possess- which the Buddha called craving (tanhā), is the basis of present profit-driven global economy fostering greed. As compared to this, Buddhist economy would base itself on what Fromm called 'to be'- to share, to give, to sacrifice (Fromm 1976: 105-106).

In the present profit-driven global economic system anything that is 'uneconomic' is sought to be obliterated out of existence. "Call a thing immoral or ugly, soul-destroying or a degradation of man, a peril to the peace of the world or to the well-being of future generations; as long as you have not shown it to be "uneconomic" you have not really questioned its right to exist, grow, and prosper" (Schumacher 1973: 27).

However, in Buddhist view of things, profitability alone cannot be an adequate measure of whether something is "economic" or not. Buddhist economics would take into account not only the profitability of a given activity, but also its effect upon people and environment, including the resource base. The higher animals have an economic value because of their utility, but they are not a meta-economic value in themselves. "If I have a car, a man-made thing, I might quite legitimately argue that the best way to use it is never to bother about maintenance and simply run it to ruin. I may indeed have calculated that this is the most economical method of use. If the calculation is correct, nobody can criticise me for acting accordingly, for there is nothing sacred about a man-made thing like a car. But if I have an animal-be it only a calf-or a hen-a living, sensitive creature, am I allowed to treat it as nothing but a utility? Am I allowed to run it to ruin? It is no use trying to answer such questions scientifically. They are metaphysical, not scientific, questions. It is metaphysical error, likely to produce the gravest practical consequences, to equate "car" and "animal" on account of their utility, while failing to recognize the most fundamental difference between them, that of "level of being"(Schumacher 1973: 84-85).

By pointing out that the vulgar chase of luxury and abundance is the root-cause of suf-fering, Buddhism encourages restraint, voluntary simplicity, and con-tentment. "The cultivation and expansion of needs is the antithesis of wisdom. It is also the antithesis of freedom and peace. Every increase of needs tends to increase one's dependence on outside forces over which one cannot have control, and therefore increases existential fear. Only by a reduction of needs can one promote a genuine reduction in those tensions which are the ultimate causes of strife and war" (Schumacher 1973: 20). Thus, Buddhist economics based on ideals such as being content with little, avoiding wastefulness, voluntary simplicity i.e., fewness of desires (appicchatā), and contentment (santutthi) aspires to pave the road to peace and happiness. Contentment is the mental condition of a person who is satisfied with what he has or the position in which he finds himself (santussamāno itarîtarena: Sutta-Nipāta.v.42).

The question arises as to how a person can remain content in the midst of so many economic difficulties. From the Buddhist point of view, economic and moral issues cannot be separated from each other. From the Buddhist point of view mere satisfaction of economic needs without spiritual development can never lead to contentedness among people. Just as poverty is the cause of much crime, wealth too is responsible for various human ills. In the consumer society wealth is merely seen from a materialistic point of view. The result of such an attitude is that its possessor is never satisfied and does not have the correct attitude towards it. However correct attitude towards wealth from the Buddhist point of view is very important because it views material wealth as only required to meet bare necessities. Moreover, wealth must be earned only through righteous and moral mean.

Generosity (dāna) and liberality (cāga) are always linked in Buddhism with virtue. Moreover, by doing so one gets rid of selfishness and becomes more unacceptable to others because "one who gives makes many friends" (Sutta-Nipāta.187). It is not necessary to have much to practice generosity because giving from one's meager resources is also considered very valuable (Samyutta Nikāya.I.18; Dhammapada.224). Generosity is one of the important qualities that make one a gentleman (Anguttara Nikāya.IV.218). The Buddha compares the man who righteously earns his wealth and shares it with the needy to a man who has both eyes, whereas the one who only earns wealth but does no merit is like a one-eyed man (Anguttara Nikāya .I.129-130). To build up a healthy society, therefore, liberality and generosity have greatly to be encouraged.

As pointed out by Schumacher, "(f)rom the point of view of Buddhist economics... production from local resources for local needs is the most rational way of economic life... the modern economist... tends to take statistics showing an increase in the number of ton/miles per head of the population carried by a country's transport system as proof of economic progress, while to the latter- the Buddhist economist- the same statistics would indicate a highly undesirable deterioration in the pattern of consumption" (1973: 42).

The fig-tree glutton (udumbarakhādika) method blamed by the Buddha (Samyutta Nikāya.IV.283), the method of shaking down an indiscriminate amount of fruit from a fig-tree in order to eat a few, is precisely the same as the one employed in drift-net fishing, where many more animals are killed than utilized. Today we understand natural capital as the sum total of renewable and non-renewable resources, including the ecological systems and services that support life. It is different from conventionally defined capital in that natural capital cannot be produced by human activity. What was unimaginable 50 years ago was the speed with which the loss of natural capital would affect humankind. Humanity cannot continue to consume the planet's limited resources at the rate to which it has become accustomed. Such an attitude is bound to have catastrophic consequences. The human economy does not operate in an infinite expanse capable of providing an inexhaustible supply of re-sources. When the economy expands, it does so by absorbing into itself more and more of the re-source base of the extremely fragile and finite ecosystem and by burdening the ecosystem in turn with its waste. But long before the human economy reaches that limit, it will cross a threshold point beyond which the delicate fabric of the ecosystem will be damaged so badly that it shall no longer be capable of sustaining higher forms of life.

We may already be very close to that threshold and as human population grows further, the stress on the environment is bound to rise to even more perilous level-s.

Since human beings are social creatures who naturally come together for common ends, this means that a social order guided by Buddhist principles would consist primarily of small-scale communities in which each member can make an effective contribution. Only small-scale social arrangements can rescue people from the portending future disaster. Considered from a Buddhist point of view, the huge polluted mega-cities and uncaring bureaucrats and politicians typical of our age are unsuitable for a proper welfare of sentient beings.

The most suitable and compatible economy would be small-scale and localized. Such an .economy would use simple technology which would not drain natural resources and in it production would be aimed principally at local consumption, so that there would be direct face-to-face con-tact between producers and consumers. Large-scale technologies are dehumanizing and morally wrong. Schumacher called for human-scale, decentralized, and appropriate technologies. People can only feel at home in human-scale environments. If economic structures become too large they become impersonal and unresponsive to human needs and aspirations. Under these conditions individuals feel functionally futile, dispossessed, voiceless, powerless, excluded, and alienated. "Wisdom demands a new orientation of science and technology towards the organic, the gentle, the nonviolent, the elegant and beautiful" (Schumacher 1973: 20).

Thus, in the Buddhist concept of economic development, we should avoid gigantism, especially of machines, which tend to control rather than serve human beings. If bigness and greed can be avoided, the Middle Path of Buddhist development can be achieved, i.e., both the world of industry and agriculture can be converted into a meaningful habitat. "Some in the industrial countries have learned at first that material prosperity without spiritual development is ultimately unsatisfying" (Anonymous 1983: 18). "Strange to say, technology, although of course the product of man, tends to develop by its own laws and principles, and these are very different from those of human nature or of living nature in general. Nature always, so to speak, knows where and when to stop. Greater even than the mystery of natural growth is the mystery of the natural cessation of growth. There is measure in all natural things- in their size, speed, or violence. As a result, the system of nature, of which man is a part, tends to be self-balancing, self-adjusting, self-cleansing. Not so with technology... (which) recognises no self-limiting principle- in terms, for instance, of size, speed, or violence. It therefore does not possess the virtues of being self-balancing, self-adjusting, and self-cleansing" (Schumacher 1973: 120).

Our economy is already big enough and our technologies too smart and too powerful. What we need most of all is streamlining and downsizing: cutting down on weapons production, on industries dedicated to wasteful luxuries, on conspicuous con-sumption as the engine that drives the economy. Instead we need qualitative improvements to make our technologies more humble and humane, more benign towards the total bio-sphere.

Economic justice and social equity are essential so that no one is deprived of a fair standard of living. As Schumacher said the problem children of the world are the rich societies and not the poor (1973: 126). "To live peacefully, we must live with a reasonable degree of equity, or fairness, for it is unrealistic to think that, in a communications-rich world, a billion or more persons will accept living in absolute poverty while another billion live in conspicuous excess. Only with greater fairness in the consumption of the world's resources can we live peacefully, and thereby live sustainably, as a human family" (Elgin 1993: 42).

Well-documented scientific studies have now clearly established that each living creature has its place in the biosphere, whereby it plays its unique role is part of the collective balance. The egalitarianism of rights to life is therefore based on scientific realities such as the unity of the living world, its vast diversity (a key factor in evolution) and the complementary nature of its different components. The right to have humanizing work that is dignified and meaningful- right livelihood (Sammā-ājîva) as it is known in Buddhism. "The study of Buddhist economics·could be recommended even for those who believe that economic growth is more important than any spiritual or religious values... It is a question of finding the right path of development, the Middle Way between materialist heedlessness and traditionalist immobility, in short, of finding "Right Livelihood" (Schumacher 1973: 45). The righteous householder aims at harmonious living (dhammacariya, samacariya) (Majjhima Nikāya.I.289; Samyutta Nikāya.I.101) and compassion (karunā) which is "the desire to remove what is detrimental to others and their unhappiness" (Sutta-Nipāta.v.73). This is the concept of the well-adjusted and balanced person, who while he seeks pleasure, exercises a degree of restraint and limits his needs and avoids greed (visamalobha) (Dîgha Nikāya.III.70).

The Buddhist values mean that environment should not be over exploited. As the Tibetans say very wisely that not too much of anything that is precious should be taken from the earth, as then its quality fades and the earth is destroyed (Morgan & Lawton 1996: 93). The Buddhist ideal, in fact, is co-operation with nature, not domination. As pointed out by E.F. Schumacher, the world is ruled from towns where the feeling of belonging to an ecosystem is not realised. This results in a harsh and improvident treatment of things upon which we ultimately depend, such as water and trees. Moreover, modern economics does not distinguish between renewable and non-renewable materials, as its very method is to equalise and quantify everything by means of a money price. The cheapest is automatically the one to be preferred, as to do otherwise would be irrational and 'uneconomic.' From a Buddhist point of view "non-renewable goods must be used only if they are indispensable, and then only with the greatest care and the most meticulous concern for conservation. To use them heedlessly or extravagantly is an act of violence... The Buddhist economist would insist that a population basing its economic life on non-renewable fuels is living parasitically" (Schumacher 1973: 43-44).

Thus, a new relation must be established between people and nature, one of cooperation not of exploitation. Buddhism enjoins a respectful and non-violent attitude towards ecology. "Every follower of the Buddha ought to plant a tree every few years and look after it until it is safely established, and the

Buddhist economist can demonstrate without difficulty that the universal observation of this rule would result in a high rate of genuine economic development independent of any foreign aid" (Schumacher 1973: 43).

Pollution and accumulation of large amounts of highly toxic substances is an important feature of the emerging global economy. However, as pointed out by Schumacher, this is an ethical, spiritual, and metaphysical monstrosity which "means conducting the economic affairs of man as if people really did not matter at all" (1973: 119). "An entirely new system of thought is needed, a system based on attention to people, and not primarily attention to goods- (the goods will look after themselves!). It could be summed up in the phrase, "production by the masses, rather than mass production." What was impossible, however, in the nineteenth century, is possible now. And what was in fact- if not necessarily at least understandably- neglected in the nineteenth century is unbelievably urgent now. That is, the conscious utilisation of enormous technological and scientific potential for the fight against misery and human degradation- a fight in intimate contact with actual people, with individuals, families, small groups, rather than states and other anonymous abstractions" (Schumacher 1973: 56).

The driving force of such an economy would be the pro-motion of well-being both material and social, not commercial profit and unrestrained expansion. As pointed out by Fromm, the development of profit-oriented "economic system was no longer determined by the question: What is good for Man? But by the question: What is good for the growth of the system? One tried to hide the sharpness of this conflict by making the assumption that what was good for the growth of the system (or even for a single big corporation) was also good for the people. This construction was bolstered by an auxiliary construction: that the very qualities that the system required of human beings- egotism, selfishness, and greed- were innate in human nature; hence, not only the system but human nature itself fostered them. Societies in which egotism, selfishness, and greed did not exist were supposed to be "primitive," their inhabitants "childlike." People refused to recognize that these traits were not natural drives that caused industrial society to exist, but that they were the products of social circumstances" (Fromm 1976: 7-8). "The technology of mass production is inherently violent, ecologically damaging, self-defeating in terms of non-renewable resources, and stultifying for the human person. The technology of production by the masses, making use of the best of modern knowledge and experience, is conducive to decentralisation, compatible with the laws of ecology, gentle in its use of scarce resources, and designed to serve the human person instead of making him the servant of machines" (Schumacher 1973: 126).

We are trying to satisfy nonmaterial needs with material goods. For Buddhism material satisfaction merely pro-vides a starting point for the pursuit of higher goals. The Buddha called upon people to wake up and liberate themselves from the illusion that craving for things leads to happiness. It is not cleverness but wisdom which can "enable us to see the hollowness and fundamental unsatisfactoriness of a life devoted primarily to the pursuit of material ends, to the neglect of the spiritual. Such a life necessarily sets man against man and nation against nation, because man's needs are infinite and infinitude can be achieved only in the spiritual realm, never in the material. Man assuredly needs to rise above this humdrum "world"; wisdom shows him the way to do it; without wisdom, he is driven to build up a monster economy, which destroys the world, and to seek fantastic satisfactions, like landing a man on the moon. Instead of overcoming the "world" by moving towards saintliness, he tries to overcome it by gaining preeminence in wealth, power, science, or indeed any imaginable "sport"" (Schumacher 1973: 24). Spiritual health and material well-being are not enemies: they are natural allies. A Buddhist approach to economics would distinguish between misery, sufficiency, and glut. Economic growth would be good only to the point of sufficiency. Limitless growth and consumption would be disastrous.

Further, whereas Buddhist economics would be based squarely on renewable resources, modern economics is based on the ruthless exploitation of nonrenewable resources and recognizes no limits to production and consumption- a non-sustainable system. "Economics without Buddhism, i.e., without spiritual, human, and ecological values, is like sex without love... While the materialist is mainly interested in goods, the Buddhist is mainly interested in liberation. But Buddhism is "the Middle Way" and therefore in no way antagonistic to physical well-being. It is not wealth that stands in the way of liberation but the attachment to wealth; not the enjoyment of pleasurable things but the craving for them... From an economist's point of view, the marvel of the Buddhist way of life is the utter rationality of its pattern- amazingly small means leading to extraordinarily satisfactory results... For the modern economist this is very difficult to understand. He is used to measuring the "standard of living" by the amount of annual consumption, assuming all the time that a man who consumes more is "better off" than a man who consumes less. A Buddhist economist would consider this approach excessively irrational: since consumption is merely a means to human well-being, the aim should be to obtain the maximum of well-being with the minimum of consumption... The ownership and the consumption of goods is a means to an end, and a Buddhist economics is the systematic study of how to attain given ends with the minimum means" (Schumacher 1973: 38-41).

Buddhist economics is very different from the economics of modern materialism, "since the Buddhist sees the essence of civilisation not in a multiplication of wants but in the purification of human character. Character, at the same time, is formed primarily by a man's work... properly conducted in conditions of human dignity and freedom" (Schumacher 1973: 39). It is unBuddhistic to consider goods as more important than people and consumption as more important than creative activity. Such an aim was made explicit in the Green Buddhist Declaration, prepared by members of the international Buddhist community for discussion at the World Fellowship of Buddhism in Colombo (1980): "We believe that since world resources and the ecosystem cannot support all peoples at the level of the consumption of the advantaged nations, efforts towards global equity must be coupled with efforts towards voluntary simplicity, in one's individual life-style and through democratically-determined policies. The economic structures which encourage consumeristic greed and alienation must be transformed." Unfortunately, in present-day globalizing world, moral sentiments are viewed as irrelevant to business and economics. Business principles are taken to be essentially restricted to profit maximization. Moreover, as pointed out by Amartya Sen, "a departure from profit maximization need not necessarily be benign, nor need moral sentiments be invariably noble. Some of the worst barbarities in the contemporary world have been committed by self-sacrificing racists- ready to do harm to some people even at great cost or risk to themselves. Indeed, this process continues today with relentless persistence... The rejection of a self-centered life can go with the attempted advancement- sometimes violent promotion- of the perceived interests only of a particular group or community (excluding others), and even with wilfully inflicting damages on another group or community" (Sen 1997: 6). This is where Buddhism and the value-system proposed by it become important.

Briefly, Buddhist Education is a practical, clear-cut, tried and tested holistic training programme to be followed in one's daily life. It encompasses a method and technique of living to help one to meet the problems and challenges in life as well as to make the best of the limitless opportunities that life has to offer. In this sense, Buddhist Education is a holistic education programme, based on the practice and practical application of the Dhamma. It is far from being an academic study to satisfy one's intellectual gratification. On the contrary, Buddhist Education calls for resolute self-effort and a firm self-commitment to not only learn but to also skilfully train oneself in the Teachings of the Buddha. As such, Buddhist Education engages all of one's faculties – the emotions as much as one's intellect and will.

The Buddha did not want anyone to blindly follow the Noble Path He unravelled for the benefit of all humankind without regard to a person's own life-experience. He wanted disciple monks and lay-adherents whose own experimentation provided them shraddha or confidence obtained through a right understanding of the Dhamma. It was for this reason that the Buddha consistently underlined this cardinal requirement of self-inquiry and self-development in one embracing the Dhamma. We must therefore not overlook this basic requirement of Buddhism which we are to first fulfil. So before everything else, one has to undergo oneself, the spiritual experimentation or orientation.

THREE DOMAINS OF LEARNING IN BUDDHIST EDUCATION

It is a matter of great significance, especially in the context of learning psychology, which the Buddha had over 2600 years ago, identified three distinct levels or domains of learning namely, pariyatti, patipatti and pativedha. According to Buddhist Education, pariyatti constitutes the theoretical foundation that is required in learning and understanding the Buddha Dhamma.

However, we have to be mindful that a theoretical foundation would only enable a person to experience the Dhamma at a superficial level. On the other hand, a person could still experience the deeper meaning and relevance of the Dhamma without having to be erudite in the scriptures and to eloquently recite suttas.

Buddhist scriptures are replete with examples of how disciple monks and lay followers of the Buddha, possessing relatively low intelligence, could attain great spiritual uplift. A classic example was Cula Pantaka who could not even commit a simple verse to memory. Yet, he was able to attain Arahanthood simply by practicing concentration and removing defilements from his mind. Simply put, in Buddhist Education possession of a high level of intelligence is not a qualifying pre-requisite or pre-condition for spiritual advancement.

A theoretical study of the sacred texts must not therefore be looked upon as the be-all-and end-all of Buddhist Education for this will limit one to only a superficial involvement with the profound Teachings of the Buddha.

From possessing a theoretical foundation of the Dhamma, one should advance to patipattior the practice of the Dhamma through inquiry, investigation and self- experience. Skilful practice of the Dhamma in daily life is absolutely necessary for one to progress to the third domain of learning and self-training namely, pativedha — the realisation of Insight Wisdom.

The Buddha had always stressed that in order for one to come to grips with the realities of life one has to come to terms with one's own spiritual development. To really understand and benefit fully from the Dhamma, one has to progress beyond the theoretical plane and immerse oneself in the method and technique of practicing and applying the Buddha's Teachings in daily life.

The Buddha had always stressed that in order to benefit from the Dhamma one has to practise his Noble Teachings with understanding and depth. This is because the Dhamma is a complete education and training programme which we are to infuse into our day-to-day living.

The Buddha persistently admonished His disciples and lay followers that he was only a Teacher, Guide and Role Model of one who had understood, lived and experienced the Dhamma. Throughout His forty-five years in teaching the Dhamma, He laid stress on the Eternal Doctrine as a way of wholesome living rather than an esoteric philosophy for scholarship or for theorising. On many occasions he refused to be drawn into useless speculation and debate when he knew that the discussion would not lead the opponent to understand the nature of his existence and the realities of life.

It is significant to note that in modern teaching psychology too, three distinct levels of learning are recognised namely, the cognitive, affective and psychomotor domains. The cognitive domain of learning deals with bare knowledge such as facts, figures, data and theories. This essentially knowledge-based learning focuses on the acquisition and retention of facts or information such as Siddhartha was a Sakya prince; his father was King Suddhodana; he attained Supreme Enlightenment and so on. As these learning deals essentially with acquiring and regurgitating knowledge, the inner being, in terms of one's emotional feelings, thinking process and mind-set remains largely uninvolved or affected. It is because of this fact that the cognitive level or domain of learning is referred to as a 'passive' process.

On the other hand, the affective and psychomotor domains of learning involve, among other things, critical observation, self-reflection, self-analysis and the synthesis of different facts, ideas and viewpoints.

The thrust of the affective domain of learning is for one to develop a deep, probing, inquiring mind. This is similar to the penetrating, analytical and objective, mental make-up and thinking that is typical of the Buddha's life since his childhood.

Here the individual has to establish for him or herself what is significant in a subject, analyze and synthesize the facts, ideas and viewpoints that are involved and to independently form objective judgments and conclusions. In this way, the individual progresses from the domain of possessing knowledge or facts on a specific subject to developing his or her observational skills, ability to reflect, sieve, conceptualise and evaluate the different facts and details. In the process objectivity is sharpened objectivity which enables a person to think clearly and with a critical mind.

The development of the mind is central in Buddhist Education. In the context of daily living, this helps one to discriminate, for example, between wholesome and unwholesome thoughts and actions.

In terms of practising and internalising the Dhamma, the affective domain of learning and training is without question an essential ingredient and is linked to harnessing the pool of information and facts in the Dhamma that is to be relied upon for one to arrive at sound conclusions, decisions and actions in our daily life.

The psychomotor domain of learning advances an individual a step further in learning. As the term itself suggests, this level of learning deals with the total person, that is, the body and mind concurrently.

In this domain, both the psychological (meaning the thinking, attitude, mental make-up, emotions, sentiments and feelings) and the behavioral (in reference to personal skills, talents, conduct and volition or actions) aspects of learning are involved in unison. It is in this domain that the practical application and practice of the Dhamma impacts forcefully on the development of the individual.

Viewed from the perspective of Buddhist Education, the psychomotor and the affective domains of learning, relates to the living or 'being' aspects of Buddhism. Here the individual becomes mindful of living the Dhamma. The focus of the learning and training is on developing. human values and virtuous qualities such as metta, karuna, muditha, upekkha. Thus it is in the psychomotor domain that the practical application of Buddhism in terms of actual day- to -day practice of the Dhamma is ingrained.

Buddhist Education in Modern World

"Equally, to strive for leisure as an alternative to work would be considered a complete misunderstanding of one of the basic truths of human existence, namely that work and leisure are complementary parts of the same living process and cannot be separated without destroying the joy of work and the bliss of leisure."

The tragedy of the developing countries is that they have been encouraged by the West during the colonial era, and by their own Western-educated elites in the post-colonial era, to copy the Western social institutions into the smallest detail. In most cases they have failed miserably, whether they were copying the British parliamentarian system or the Western educational system.

The educational system has usually failed in the developing countries, often simply because too little money is invested in it, governments are too poor or disinterested in investing more; textbooks are propagandistic and outdated; educational authorities ignorant and corrupted, teachers underpaid and undertrained.

The Western-type of approach alienates the children from their own environment. Traditional education was destroyed by the colonial authorities, or, in the modernisation process, by the Westernised elite.

Traditional education has, however, experienced a revival in many parts of the world, where Western education has turned out to be a failure. In the Theravada Buddhist world, traditional education was given by the monks to the boys in the temples.

Nowadays, many Thai children study in schools located in the temple compounds, but they follow the Western-inspired curriculum. In the Asoke schools, the children do study English, natural sciences and computer skills, but they also learn to appreciate the traditional skills of the rural Thais.

Samma Sikkha - The Right Study

"It is clear therefore, that Buddhist economics must be very different from the economics of modern materialism, since the Buddhist sees the essence of civilisation not in multiplication of wants but in the purification of human character, at the same time, is formed primarily by a man's work. And work, properly conducted in conditions of human dignity and freedom, blesses those who do it and equally their products." (Schumacher, 1999, 39)

The Asoke schools are called Samma Sikkha schools, with reference to the Noble Eightfold Path and its steps of Right Understanding, Right Thought etc. The secondary schools were established some 10 years ago and, at the moment, there are more than 500 students in the Samma Sikkha secondary schools. Recently, also primary schools and vocational schools have been opened. All teachers work as volunteers. Some of the teachers originate from the outside schools and try sometimes push the Asoke schools more to the line of state schools. Many monks and nuns work as teachers in the Asoke schools, teaching everything from Buddhism to English and Mathematics.

The Samma Sikkha schools are in constant process of change as new teachers join the schools wanting to reform them along the lines of their private visions. The children learn to become quite tough and are well-prepared to defend their rights and interests. The school children have regular meetings where they learn to discuss their problems, negotiate solutions to conflicts and take certain responsibility for their own behaviour and for the behaviour of their fellow students. This process is supported by the teachers.

Many students leave Asoke schools for various reasons. The ones who stay, often stay on in the Asoke communities even after graduating. Some join the vocational schools at the Asoke centres, some study at the Asoke "university" (Sammasikkhalaya Wang Jiwit) or at the open universities like Ramkhamhaeng University. Very few leave the community permanently, it is more common to stay in the geographic and spiritual vicinity.

Asoke schools take a holistic approach to education where theoretical knowledge goes together with practical skills such as gardening, cooking, cleaning, producing and selling goods, repairing cars and engines, sewing, and nursing. The Asoke centres are presently also training their own "barefoot doctors" in cooperation with a hospital in the Northeast.

Asoke school is a place for the lay practitioners to show devotion, which is regarded as an important part of Asoke Buddhism. To donate money to the Asoke temples or foundations is not enforced. Visitors who come for the first time are not at all allowed to donate money before they have visited the temple seven times and understand the teachings of the temple. Working for the temple is valued higher than any material contribution, as work is regarded as spiritual practice.

NIRVANA: Simplicity and non-violence are obviously closely related. The optimal pattern of consumption, producing a high degree of human satisfaction by means of relatively low rate of consumption, allows people to live without great pressure and strain and to fulfill the primary injunction of Buddhist teaching: Cease to do evil; try to do good." (Schumacher 1999, 42)

To donate one's devotion and labour to the temple originates from the Asoke teaching about Enlightenment or Nirvana. (Thai: Niphaan).

Enlightenment is the highest goal of all Buddhists, but, in many Buddhist countries, it is usually regarded as unattainable for an ordinary lay person. An American researcher specialised in Burmese Buddhism, Melford Spiro has therefore divided Buddhist practice into two different categories: Karmic Buddhism and Nibbanic Buddhism. Karmic Buddhism strives to improve one's karma for this life and for the next life, whereas Nibbanic Buddhism is reserved only for the monks.

Asoke interpretation has demystified the concept by dividing nirvana into "small" and "big" nirvana (parinirvana). The small nirvana is here and now and can be reached by getting rid of defilements (kilet). In the present life, nirvana is signified as a state of mind. The development into the state of nirvana goes through certain stages, which Buddhists can reach through their own struggle.

In mainstream Buddhism these stages are seen as steps on the long path of several rebirths (samsara). The first stage is a sotapanna (Thai: Sodaban), a stream enterer who will become a saint (araha) within seven rebirths.

The next stage is a sakadagami (Thai: Sakitakhami) a once-returner, who has destroyed the intermediate forms of sensual delight and ill-will. The next stage will be an anagami (Thai: Anakhami), a non-returner, and the highest stage is finally an araha, who will enter nirvana at the time of his death.

The Asoke members are all encouraged to strive to become enlightened. According to the Asoke interpretation, these stages can be reached within this present life: the lowest stage sotapanna requires that the person is free from the following six vices: addiction, roaming at unseemly hours, frequenting shows, gambling, association of bad companions, and idleness. In addition, the person should be able to follow the five precepts - abstain from killing, stealing, practising illicit sex, lying and becoming addicted.

The person should also pay respect to the "Triple Gem" (Ratana Trai), i.e. to be a good practising Buddhist respecting the Buddha, the dhamma and the sangha. According to the Asoke interpretation even a married person can practise to become a sotapanna. To practise by working in the temple gives the person a chance to reach the nirvana of a sotapanna.

The next stage, sakadagami, can be reached by becoming free of passion and anger. The person should be able to follow the eight precepts. This requires that the person can, first of all, follow the five precepts, and furthermore this requires him or her to reduce the number of daily meals, refrain from singing, dancing and decorating him/herself, and to refrain from sleeping on elevated beds and sofas. The third precept in this case requires celibacy.

The next step is anagami, when the person has become free from all worldly affairs, the person feels no temptation to worldly pleasures and worldly events do not have any effect on him or her. The person at this level still has some defilements within his or her mind, but they are not shown outside. The final stage is araha, when the person is completely free from the idea of "self", and can work for the benefit of others because he or she is not selfish any longer. This stage is nirvana, which is a state of mind, in which the person has no selfishness, anger, greediness or delusion.

The concept of nirvana differs in the Asoke ideology from the general ideas of the Thai Buddhists. Nirvana is traditionally described as being something very distant, unimaginable and unreachable. Only monks might have a realistic chance of reaching nirvana. Ordinary lay people do not even orientate themselves towards nirvana, instead they concentrate on earning enough merit (bun) to be born in more favourable socio-economic conditions in the next life. Asoke group teaches that nirvana can be reached in this life since it is a state of mind. Nirvana is not something supernatural or otherworldly. To be enlightened means to be peaceful and calm due to having no more selfishness.

Opportunities and Challenges for Buddhist Education in Europe

In contrast with most Asian countries represented in this symposium, Europe does not have a tradition of Buddhist education. This is not surprising. The Dhamma actually arrived to Europe fairly recently, just about one century ago, which is not a very long time for the Dhamma to take root. Every beginning is difficult – and one-hundred years can only be considered as a beginning.

Even the very concept of Buddhism is quite problematic in the Western setting. It is generally characterized as a religion, but as the Venerable Dr. Yifa also said: many western Buddhists are uncomfortable or are getting uncomfortable with that classification and they prefer to treat Buddhism as a science, psychology or philosophy. These western concepts, whether we talk about religion or science, do not do justice to Buddhism, because it seems to cut across all of these conceptual categories.

Individual people who practice the Dhamma may overcome these conceptual distinctions and realize that the Buddha's teaching is a method to see through dukkha [pain/suffering]. Nevertheless, Buddhism cannot be considered a scientific method – in the western use, or western sense of the word, because it comes from a completely different cultural background – with quite different suppositions.

But when we consider Buddhism as a religion, it can be basically studied in two ways: from within, or from without.

Non-historical religions, in the European sense, those not rooted in the European culture are traditionally studied from without – that is, scientifically, objectively – without any emotional or personal involvement.

As Europeans started to become fascinated with the [East] about two or three centuries ago, the eastern cultures became objects of scientific investigation. Consequently, European universities developed the tradition of oriental scholarship, focusing mainly on the study of texts. Insofar as these texts are Buddhist, we may speak of the study of Buddhism in those institutions.

However, these studies come under the rubric of linguistics or philology, or history of religion, and thus cannot be considered as examples of Buddhist education in the traditional sense – with textual studies as only part of the training. More recently, based on the study of various Buddhist sources and combining methods of philology and cultural anthropology, the science of Buddhology developed, which aims to study Buddhism in its historical context.

Though these studies may greatly enhance our understanding of Buddhism, they do not go beyond the academic style of objective inquiry and, hence again, cannot rightly be characterized as Buddhist education. Individual development in a mental or spiritual sense, which is the ultimate goal of traditional Buddhist training, is clearly outside the scope of Western academia, which, thus cannot be expected to host Buddhist educational programs.

Now, Buddhism can also be studied from within in Europe, in different Dhamma centers, but their training programs do not have any academic accreditation; and, thus, do not qualify as higher education, however high their academic standards may otherwise be. So we come to the conclusion here that Buddhist education, Buddhist higher education is virtually non-existent in Europe.

Now, about why it should exist. First, a fully qualified Buddhist education in Europe must meet two quite different sets of criteria: one set by the Buddhist tradition and another by western scholarship. These two are not easy to bring into line. Generally speaking, Western standards are based on the objective measurability of one's knowledge and skills in a certain area, without much concern for the rest of the person's demeanor. In the Buddhist sense, however, the development of skills and understanding goes hand in hand with personal advancement with morality, concentration – and these mental skills are not easy to measure.

But more significantly, academic commitment demands impartiality towards one's object of study which is in striking contrast with what is expected in a traditional Buddhist school. So the basic difference between these two sets of expectations seems to lay in their respective understanding of the use of knowledge, that is: what knowledge is good for – that is, why we study.

In Europe, it is shown by some post-modernist thinkers that knowledge is power, in the first place; so, it is a means to control and manipulate the world around us, ourselves, and the environment, and by objectifying one's field of study – rendering it manageable. Also, we define ourselves in relation to that object. Learning in the Buddhist sense is something quite different. It cannot be used to control or manipulate. (Quite on the contrary, it reveals the futility of these human concerns.)

All of this goes to show that Buddhism does not conform to our western categories and expectations of what a religious or scientific discipline should look like. This distinction between science and religion is a European cultural heritage, which can be traced to a split in between reason and faith – as Christian dogma failed to accommodate the findings of scientific observation. As the scientific method proved more and more successful in predicting the behavior of objects in the natural world, religious modes of understanding came to be discredited or relegated to a transcendent world. These two seem to have no relation to each other. This characteristically western duality is reflected in the epistemic compatibility between objective scientific study and subjective religious experience. When Buddhism is considered as a religion, it is reduced to a belief system; when it is treated as a science, it tends to be divested of its devotional aspect.

So, institutionally speaking, the challenge for Buddhist education in Europe, in the 21st Century, seems to be to develop an institutional framework, which is free from the academic/religious distinction, and we should also devise programs which avoid one-sided emphasis on either intellectual or spiritual training, thus helping to restore the integrity of human experience.

This is one of the main messages which I would like to put across, here: let us try to get rid of this duality! Spiritually speaking, our main challenge seems to be to heal that very split, in the western mind, or psyche, which makes the categorization of Buddhism so difficult. It is the dominance of reason, resulting from that split that lies at the heart of the so called 'evils' of modern society and what we associate with globalization.

But from its internal dimension, the divided western mind sought to control its surroundings and set out to conquer the outside world – intellectually by developing science, economically by applied technology, and physically through imperialism. The technical revolution, which changed the face of the Earth so drastically, also derives from the dominance of the rational ego. Starting out from Europe, the white-man colonized the people of other races, exploited their natural and human resources, and still continue to do so, albeit in a different guise. So thinking along those lines, we can see that Buddhism can give us key insights into the re-evaluation of our culture.

THE NEED FOR MODERN BUDDHIST EDUCATION

In Asian Buddhist communities, both in Asia and abroad, an increasing number of people who have been raised in nominally Buddhist homes have come to regard Buddhism as mere superstition and turn to other religions. Upon talking with these people, their misconceptions about Buddhism are evident. Again, this is due to a lack of modern Buddhist education.

Buddhism has never been an evangelical religion, nor should it become one. However, clear explanation of the Buddha's teachings should be made available to people who are interested. The Buddha showed the path to happiness, and it is desirable for this to be made accessible to others, so that they can benefit from it. This is the duty and responsibility of Buddhists who have compassion for others.

In what ways can Buddhist education be made relevant to people today? First, if oral teachings were given in the language with which people are most familiar, the language in which they are educated, then they could understand the meaning better. Colloquial language communicates much better to lay people than does classical language. For scholars and serious practitioners, knowledge of Pali, Sanskrit, and ancient Chinese is necessary, but for the general public and young people who are used to television colloquial language and everyday examples are more suitable. One university student told me that he was reluctant to come to talk with me because he feared that I would use many Pali words and he would not understand! I wonder how many others there are who avoid going to teachings or reading books because they cannot understand the language well.

Secondly, it is essential that Buddhist principles be clearly and logically explained. Today's youth is well-educated. They have knowledge of science, philosophy, psychology, and so forth. Not satisfied with hearing only the story of Buddha's life and the Jataka tales and thereby generating faith, they now want to know how the doctrine of selflessness relates to quantum physics and how Buddha's teachings on patience can be integrated into modern psychology. Young people who have a modern secular education will not believe in rebirth just because Buddha said so. They want to understand the logical proof for it and to know current examples of people who have memories of their previous lives.

Young people are often queried by their classmates and colleagues about Buddhist theory and practice. Why is paper money burned for the deceased? What is the use of praying to a statue? If Buddha was just a man, how can he save us? In which galaxy of our universe is the Western Pure Land located? If the youth do not received a good Buddhist education so that they know what is Buddhist practice and what is not, if they do not understand the purpose and meaning of chanting and rituals, if they do not understand well exactly what the Triple Gem is and how taking refuge benefits oneself, then they become full of doubts and may eventually abandon Buddhism for another religion.

Or, they may become tempted to criticize and denigrate other religions in an effort to defend their own. Both of these unfortunate reactions could be avoided by directly dealing with these issues through education. If Buddhism is explained clearly and logically, people will naturally see its validity and worthiness, and they will be able to answer questions posed to them.

In the past, Buddhist philosophical education was reserved for the monks and nuns, with the role of the laity being to have faith and make offerings to the monastic community. However, with the rise in the literacy rate and standard of education, the laity wants to and is more capable of taking responsibility for the practice and spread of Buddhism. People have more time and ability to study the Dharma in a weekly series of teachings, to engage in a daily meditation and chanting practice at their homes, and to attend week-end retreats. They can teach Sunday school classes for children and prepare educational materials about Buddhism. It would be suitable for modern Buddhist education to reflect this increasing capability and changing role of the lay devotees.

Thirdly, Buddha's doctrine becomes extremely clear in the minds of the youth when it is explained explicitly in relationship to modern, twentieth century lifestyle and problems. In this way the profound meaning of the Buddha's teachings is directly made relevant to current situations, and the people easily see the value of practicing the Dharma. Teachers can explain how to live according to ethical values in corporate business, how to practice patience in international politics, and how to develop detachment in discotheques. They can answer questions such as: how can one be compassionate towards people who try to take advantage of us?

How can Dharma practice improve relationships with our family and colleagues? What is the value of becoming a monk or nun in the twentieth century? Should Buddhists become more involved in projects to benefit society, such as operating schools, hospitals, drug counseling centers and old age homes? How can meditation prevent stress?

One way to make the teachings relevant to contemporary society is by using stories and examples of current situations during teaching sessions. Another is by having discussion groups where people share their experiences and consider how to solve daily life difficulties by employing Dharma methods.

Fourth, Buddhism can be explained by using a variety of media. Traditionally, education was done by the disciple listening to the teacher in a strict teaching situation, or by children mimicking their parents actions. But now videos, television, radio, comic books, weekly articles in the city newspaper, theater, and modern music are viable media for people to learn about the Dharma and to express what they have learned. If these media are used more, then young people will feel that Buddhism fits into their modern culture. I was very impressed when one teenage Buddhist society sang Buddhist songs that their members had written in modern lyrics to the accompaniment of guitar music. The songs created a wonderful atmosphere of faith in the Buddha and spiritual friendship among the devotees. Theater provides a way to use humor in teaching Buddhism, and comic books (for the youngsters) and videos easily catch people's attention.

Fifth, it is beneficial for explanations of Buddhist theory and practice to be made available to the public in general. The purpose is not to be evangelical, but to avoid misconceptions arising in non-Buddhists' minds about Buddhism and to give interested people an opportunity to learn about the Dharma without getting involved in rituals and devotional practices. Here Buddhism is explained in a more academic way, without people feeling obliged to call themselves Buddhists or adopt Buddhist practices. To this effect, public talks could be given in libraries and auditoriums, as well as courses on comparative religion or philosophy could be taught in universities and adult education courses.

Lastly, inter-religious dialogue is extremely valuable, especially in multi-religious societies. In our rapidly-shrinking world, people need to respect, and not antagonistically criticize, other religions. This can be achieved only by knowing about other belief systems and emphasizing the common, uniting points. It is important not only that religions be harmonious among themselves, but also that leaders of all religions present a united front in encouraging world peace and better living conditions. This would truly be an inspiring example of openness and tolerance for all peoples of the world.

In short, conventional Buddhism is at a critical juncture. The path to liberation and enlightenment that the Buddha described from his own experience is a timeless one. Compassion and wisdom, the essence of the doctrine, are always needed to make our lives meaningful and beneficial to others. However, if we neglect to express these principles in a form that is easily understood by the people of today, then we are denying them access to the beauty of the teachings. Having huge temples and elaborate statues will not guarantee the continuation of the doctrine in the minds and actions of people. Performing rituals which few understand while neglecting to give advice suitable to people's mentality and problems is not sufficient to ensure that people actually benefit from the Dharma. For people to touch the real meaning of the Dharma and to enrich their lives through Buddhism, education that is relative to their modern culture, lifestyle and language is necessary. To provide this is the responsibility and the joy of those of us who ourselves cherish having met the precious doctrine of the Buddha.

REFERENCES:

[1] Kevatta sutta, DN; AN iii, 60. Three kinds of supernormal powers or miracles: Iddhipada- dive into the earth, fly on the sky, etc; paracitta ñ na- thought reading, and anusssani- the miracle of instruction "you should think in this way and not in that way! You should attend to this and not to that! You should give up this and should dwell in the attainment of that."

[2] Mahavagga pali, p14

[3] Kesamutti sutta, AN

[4] Canki sutta, MN

[5] A viii, 2.

[6] Huien Tsang record.

2

Buddhist Education and Modern Education

In previous Chapter, I explored some aspects of the ethical tension between modern education, based on Western academic standards, and traditional Buddhist education. As I stated, "Western standards are based on the objective measurability of one's knowledge and skills in a certain area, without much concern for the rest of the person's demeanour. In the Buddhist sense, however, the development of skills and understanding goes hand in hand with personal advancement in morality and concentration." (Agocs 2007) Now, I would like to further investigate this rift between the two different value systems and offer some practical guidelines as to how to harmonize the two, seemingly incompatible, systems of education. The question is not how to assimilate, but how to integrate Buddhist Education into the modern educational system, while retaining its basic values and identity.

The ultimate goal of Buddhist education is to destroy ignorance, the root cause of suffering. Specifically, education in a Buddhist sense should seek to eliminate from the students' mind a variety of wrong views, which form the theoretical basis of ignorance. These purely conceptual contents of the mind comprise the so-called "imputed ignorance" (parikalpita-avidyâ), as opposed to the "innate ignorance" (sahaja-avidyâ). It is "conceptual" or "acquired" ignorance. Innate ignorance cannot be accessed until there is conceptual ignorance (or misconceptions), so first one has to eliminate the "imputed" ignorance, i.e. wrong views.

Wrong views in the Buddhist sense contradict the three marks of conditioned existence, i.e. impermanence, suffering and selflessness. To think that there are any permanent phenomena in conditioned existence is certainly a wrong view, just as much as to think that there is any lasting happiness to be gained. However, the root of all wrong views is the belief in a concrete and permanent self, seeking to gain happiness. Samsâra revolves around a notion of self – the most difficult and impenetrable of all our misconceptions. This notion of the self is particularly important in modern Western society, and both socially and economically institutionalized, such that all our dominant institutions are dedicated to the personal and economic development of the self. Education does not escape this stranglehold.

The materialist view in the West that began with Descartes has evolved into the scientific view that the universe is an object out there, to be dominated and mastered. Following this, most education processes imply that there is some kind of result to be gained from the process of learning. A student, for instance, studies a certain subject in order to master it and put it to use in his/her life, thus becoming more knowledgeable, wealthier, gaining higher status in society etc. This is what we may call the social value of education. This highly abstract value is concretized in the diploma or certificate issued on completion of one's studies. It is usually assumed that by getting a diploma, one somehow becomes a more valuable person and he/she can turn this extra value to his/her advantage. Many young people entering higher education today are conditioned by such expectations. The value system of modern education obviously implies belief in a concrete and permanent self, which can become "better" (more knowledgeable, educated etc.) and happier through education.

Increasingly, and perhaps alarmingly, in Western educational institutions, success is now measured in terms of how much money that institution earns – how many students attend courses, how much money has been brought in for research grants. The quality of the curriculum or dedication to learning about ourselves, in the world, is not a consideration. The education system becomes increasingly dominated by 'market considerations'; the work of academics is measured in terms 'customer satisfaction' offered. For example, large multinational companies can sponsor courses, which raise significant questions about the objectivity and value of the final diploma. Students are less concerned about the skills they obtain, but more with the diploma they receive. Pioneering and critical thinking, the traditional driving force in educational establishments is costly, time-consuming and dangerous since it challenges the status quo.

Is there not then, a contradiction between the ultimate goal of Buddhist education, i.e. to attain liberation from the misconception of a permanent self, and the purpose of modern Western education, which is to strengthen and secure one's mistaken sense of identity? How can we resolve this contradiction in the context of modern Buddhist education? I would like to offer four interlinking approaches to solve the dilemma:

(1) Transforming students' motivation

(2) Presenting formal education as skilful means

(3) Emphasizing the role of meditation

(4) Opening up new vistas of learning

Transforming Students' Motivation

Modern society may put great stress on students to obtain some definite goal in life, such as a good job, social status, carrier etc. These social expectations will inevitably affect students, even if they are well-motivated and genuinely interested in Dharma. Many of them will wonder how to integrate their Buddhist learning with survival in modern society. Though there are different means to address this question, one important aspect of the solution is to transform students' motivation. Relying on the basic Buddhist truths of impermanence, 'suffering' and selflessness – students' minds should be turned towards higher values: contentment, spiritual liberation and kindness to others – so that, rather than trying to conform with the expectations of modern society in order to gain something in return, they might begin to think about how they can contribute to well-being in their society. Their self-concern may thus be transformed into concern for others.

Formal Education as Skilful Means

One of the ways to counterbalance the modern view of education as life investment is to emphasize its traditional Buddhist use as skillful means. Buddhist institutions and forms of education may appear in conformity with the world, but their main function is to provide the opportunity for studying the Dharma, which is beyond this world. Any formal qualification (such as a diploma in Buddhist studies) is merely a by-product of one's study rather than an end in itself. Competence in matters relating to the Dharma does not depend on any formal recognition, nor does a diploma obtained in 3-5 years of formal study guarantee such competence. Advancement in the higher trainings of morality, concentration and wisdom cannot be objectively measured or evaluated by the quantitative standards of modern education. While maintaining humility to the Buddhist tradition, Dharma studies should be pursued in the spirit of free inquiry and free from the competitiveness that often characterizes mainstream education. Through emphasizing the role of Buddhist education as skillful means, we can safeguard students against over-expectation and encourage them to use their precious study opportunity to the best of their abilities.

The Importance of Meditation

In contrast with modern education, Buddhism values first-hand experience higher than theory. Buddhist education should be concerned with more than just handing over factual knowledge. The Buddha taught a path of personal inquiry to put an end to suffering, and that path depends on direct experience. Therefore, the traditional methods of Buddhist mind-training – contemplation, meditation – could be taught at schools. The Buddhist view on the integral nature of human experience, where the intellectual and emotional sides of mind are equally appreciated, is highly relevant in the modern world, which is overly frágmented. Buddhism presents a path of mind-training, and education is nothing but that path. Since the full meaning of the Buddhist texts and teachings is not fully understood before one has direct experience in meditation, meditation is an indispensable part of Buddhist education. In fact, Buddhist educational institutions, if they have not been tainted by the values of the West, could well define themselves as schools of mental training. The usefulness of mindfulness methods in developing the "seven factors of enlightenment" (such as peace, joy, concentration etc.) has been demonstrated even outside the context of Buddhist education. It has been found indispensable for realizing true education in general. (Brady, Kassabian)

Opening up New Vistas of Learning

Finally, to encourage active Buddhist engagement in everyday affairs, we must open up new vistas of learning. Hearkening back to spirit of the great Indian Buddhist universities such as Nalanda, we should try to apply the Buddhist principles in all walks of life, testing their truth in different disciplines. Just as Buddhist philosophy in India developed in constant dialogue with other schools of philosophy, we should also try to be at constant dialogue with science and the other religions.

BUDDHIST EDUCATION AND MODERN EDUCATION

The Theory of dependent origination can bring new perspectives to many social, economical and ethical issues that humanity faces today. Moreover, it has been shown that scientific notions of cause and effect in the natural world agree with the Buddhist understanding, which can potentially enrich the natural sciences with an ethical dimension. (Waldron) Buddhist education therefore should not be concerned with simply transmitting the knowledge and methods of the past, but should also be creative in the application of Buddhist principles. It is mainly the task of Buddhist institutions of higher education to keep the spirit of Buddhist wisdom alive and turn it to the benefit of humankind. Viewed from this perspective, Buddhist education has a practical role to play in the modern world.

Summary: Buddhism has a great deal to offer in terms of its insights into the mind, and hence into its development through education. With its emphasis on 'things as they are', it provides a path, an individual and collective means of inquiring into our minds, and the arising conditions that are invaluable in these days of global chaos. In this way, it can enable young people to work towards wisdom rather than knowledge, and find a way of working together harmoniously, co-creating institutions based on compassion rather than greed. With new motivation, meditation, and an emphasis on skillful means, Buddhism needs to find new forms for helping break through ignorance and open up new vistas of learning.

PUTTING THE HEART INTO PRACTICE BUDDHIST ETHICS AND EDUCATION

Buddhism is a religious ideological system rooted in seeking detachment against perplexity, improper thoughts, and distresses of birth and death; and it is a life-education system aimed at guiding human beings towards a more civilized and perfect life.

Buddhist ethical thoughts are built on the basis of the particular conceptions of life-view, values-view, and liberation-view of Buddhism. The implications of Buddhist Ethics consist of three relationships. The first is the relationship between the individual and Buddhas/Bodhisattvas – emphasizing the belief in *tri-ratna* [homage to the Buddha, Dharma and Bodhisattvas/ Sangha].

The second is the relationship between individuals – stressing the abidance of five precepts, the practice of ten good acts, and the coordination and consummation of harmonious relationships between them. The third is the relationship between humans and other sentient beings; between individuals and the cosmos, which advocates the respect for life and protection of the natural environment – the healthy development between humans and the nature. In this respect, ethics is a very important part of Buddhist doctrine, and also the fundamental belief and approach for Buddhists to realize liberation and completion of life.

Over its long history, Buddhism has been like a bright light shining on India, China, Southeast Asia, and the rest of the world; and it plays an important role in enlightening one away from ignorance, developing social-progress *[development]*, guiding life, purifying society, and so on. Buddhist ethics and Buddhist moral theories, moral concepts, moral standards, and moral practices – these all play an important role in the history of global civilization and in real life. This paper portrays the implications of Buddhist Ethics and its instructive significance to people in modern society.

The Implication of Buddhist Ethics

1. On "Abstention from the Evil and Cultivation of the Good"

The ultimate purpose of Buddhist ethics can be generalized as "abstention from the evil and cultivation of the good", an indispensable approach for realizing the purpose of *moksa* and to be in the pursued: tranquil state. Thus, the distinction between good and evil becomes a principle of Buddhist Ethics and the standard of moral judgment.

This intensively shows that Buddhist ethical concepts and moral thought for Buddhist views of good and evil is an orientation-value for Buddhist morality, and value-standards based on Buddhist doctrine.

In Buddhism, the very nature of worldly life, including the circumstances in which one lives and the world one confronts, is "suffering". To transcend these pains in the world and realize an ultimate and complete life – one deals with the ignorance and greed found within ourselves; abstains from evil and cultivates good. Getting rid of existing evil, working not to produce additional evil; to work at nurturing goodness, to destroy any pre-existent evil – when doing this, one achieves liberation and bliss for oneself and others. The good dharma of Buddhism is a dharma of purity with a nature of tranquility benefiting both oneself and others in this present life and future lives. For example, from the *Abhidharmakosa-sastra* (Treasury of Metaphysics): "Calm karma is called the good.[1]

The *Vijnaptimatratasiddhi-sastra* (Discourse on the Theory of Consciousness-only) states : "Dharmas which are beneficial to present life and the other life is called the good."[2] In simple words, Good Dharma is that which can give oneself and others good effects in present life and the future life. The "Good" and the "Evil" in Buddhist ethics cannot be differentiated at the point of "ego", nor are they founded on the judgment between the good and the evil in "the present life"; compared to the corresponding good and evil in the mundane ethics, they transcend Buddhist ethics, and the principle of "transmigrating the effects between the triple world". Buddhism claims good or evil karma of present will determine the good or evil effects in the future life; the effects suffered in the present are determined by the good or evil practice in the past life. These thoughts transcend spatio-temporal localization of being one's personal benefit and temporal gain and loss, and are particularly valuable as far as ultimate concern is concerned.

In realistic ethical-education, one realizes that the cause and effect principle: "good will be rewarded with good, and evil with evil"; and the theory of "abstention from evil and cultivation of good" derived from Buddhist ethics – this shows particular Buddhist viewpoints enrichening and exalting implications of mundane ethics. At the same time, this plays a positive driving-role in ethical education – persuading others to abstain from evil and following good examples.

2. *Equality and Compassionate Views*

Equality and compassion view are essential principles for the relationship between individuals and between humans and other life in Buddhism. Equality refers to the same respect towards other people or life; compassion refers to the care towards them. Equality is the ideological foundation of compassion; compassion is the ethical expression of equality.

Equality means indiscrimination. Early in original Buddhism, Sakyamuni Buddha was against the four castes – held by Brahmins. He proclaimed that the four castes: Brahmin, Ksatriya, Vaisya, Sudra – are equal. The equality here means: four castes are equal in the achievement of practice in renunciation and in Buddhist groups; and the four castes are equal as far as karma and its effects are concerned, whether someone is of high-caste or low-caste: they all gain or lose corresponding to the effects of their own karma. According to the idea that all beings have the Buddha nature, Buddhism claims “all beings are equal”, which is one of distinctive characters from other religions.

Buddhism & Ethics In Chinese: compassion *(ci bei)* always refers to the combination of its two characters' meanings of “kindness” *(ci)* which means loving all sentient beings and giving them happiness; and “pity” *(bei)* which means feeling pitiful to all sentient beings and driving away those pains. The nature of compassion is the expression of sympathy and love – the refinement of love.

The compassion principle of Buddhist ethics is based on the thoughts of dependent origination and no self. In terms of the theory of dependent origination, nothing can exist singularly without causes and conditions. Everyone has close relationship with other sentient beings; in the cause and effect relationship of three worlds, other sentient beings may be one's parents or relatives. This close relationship between individuals is the supreme sympathetic heart of Buddhism – the start of “great compassion without conditions”. In terms of the theory of no-self, an ‘individual’ does not have substantial existence, hence arose the idea of the ‘oneness’ of oneself and others, and the heart of “great compassion of oneness”. The equality and compassion of Buddhism is not confined to humans, it includes all living creatures, even those things without sensation, which is called “both sentient beings and non-sentient beings achieves the perfect Buddha-wisdom simultaneously”. This is the greatness of containing everything with sublime love. This broad-thought is significant: to alleviate the narrow and selfish mind, and correct the belief that 'humans are at the core of everything' – as prominently held in current society; and furthermore, to coordinate better relationships between human and nature.

3. *Self-benefit and Altruistic Views*

Self-benefit refers to benefits gained from the good effect of one's vigorously practice for one's own *moksa*. Altruism refers to dedication of doing well for saving all sentient beings. Self-benefit saves one; altruism saves and benefits all sentient beings. Self-benefit and altruism is the way of Bodhisattva – the pursuing the way of Buddha is also the saving all sentient beings. As far as the enlightenment of truth and saving all sentient beings are concerned, it is also called: "enlightenment of self and enlightenment of others". Mahāyāna Buddhism request the combination of self-benefit and altruism, and the realization of the state of perfect nirvana.

The ethical principle of self-benefit and altruism in Mahāyāna Buddhism has close relations with the 'oneness' view of "non-duality between self and others". Mahāyāna Buddhism believes that one and others are not opposite, but interdependent. In the long transmigration, the liberation of oneself and others are not separate. Thus, to treasure oneself, one must treasure others; to liberate oneself, one has to liberate others. Only through helping sentient being and liberating sentient beings can one become liberated. It can be said that at the core of the ethical principles of self-benefit and altruism in Mahāyāna Buddhism is altruism which is a greater development from compassion thought. The ethical thought of self-benefit and altruism in Mahāyāna Buddhism is helpful to promote Buddhist believers to care more about the mundane life, and impel Buddhist ethics to become more social and more open.

From all of the implications mentioned above – abstention from evil and cultivation of the good, equality and compassion, self-benefit and altruism – can be called the essential principle of Buddhist ethics; but the detailed ethical content can be seen in the three practices, five precepts, ten good acts, six perfections, four dharmas of attraction, etc. of Buddhism.

Of the numerous, so-called: eighty-four thousand bundles of dharma – many of them teach to remove one's own ignorance and affliction, to abstain from evil and cultivate good, to cherish the heart of equality and compassion, and to practice the deeds of self-benefit and altruism.

For example, by observing five precepts and pursuing ten good acts (i.e. not killing, not stealing, not committing adultery, not lying, not speaking harshly, not speaking divisively, not speaking idly, not being greedy, not being angry, not having wrong views) – the individual can increase one's compassionate heart, correct bad habits, improve accomplishments. As far as social functions are concerned, precepts promote: the moral accomplishment of its members; bring steadiness and harmony into the social-order; preserve the survival and development of human society – because the five precepts and ten good acts are ethical standards of universal significance. It can be said that the five precepts and ten good acts are experience, as summarized in the process of survival for the sustainable development of humanity, of the living wisdom of human beings, and holding these are important for society and the universe.

Actually the four dharmas of attraction: giving the gift of Dharma or something that people like; using kind words; acting for the purpose of benefit to them; physically working together with them – in the way of Bodhisattva, are four principles for living together harmoniously. These are ways for one to get along with others: the first and third show a great humanitarianism spirit – playing a positive role to restrain polarization between the rich and the poor, harmony in human relationships -these relax conflicts between people, resolve societal disorder and crisis in this global human society which is undergoing a sharp gap between the rich and the poor, and a difficult living state for the vulnerable groups.

In terms of the law of causation and the theory of dependent origination, Buddhism stresses interdependent relationships between people, and hence approves of coexistence and mutual prosperity, mutual coordination between individual and another's interest, and individual survival and social development. These serve, perfectly, as the solid ideological foundation of social morals.

CONTEMPORARY EDUCATIONAL SIGNIFICANCE OF BUDDHIST ETHICS

There are spiritual resources available for modern ethics in all of the main religious-theoretical systems of the world. Buddhist ethical thought is an important part of the whole theoretical system of Buddhism, an indispensable ethical thought-resource, and the ethical system plays an important role in the ethical-thoughts for the world. Currently, with the increasing abundance of material-life, just the opposite is occurring, with the 'spirit and heart' facing grim crises day by day: lack of beliefs, selfishness, lonely hearts, people becoming deficient in their responsibilities, collapse of value systems, and so on. Ethical ideas such as self-discipline, transcendence, equality, compassion, etc., derived from Buddhist ethical-thoughts could alleviate crises, and to warn and awaken oneself in the present human society. It is also important for contemporary people to build up their ethical-living principles peacefully and to enhance their sense of responsibilities. We should make full use of the advantages of Buddhist ethics, and exert its educational and social strengths in and for modern society.

Constrain Egoism and Hedonism in Modern Society through Buddhist Ethics

Owing to the advancements in the development of social and material civilization – extreme individualism, materialism, and hedonism have become very popular in modern society. More and more people place emphasis on the realization of one's personal 'value' by paying particular attention to one's personal interests, safeguarding personal dignity, and pursuing personal happiness. In these processes, they move through one extreme to another extreme – sticking to nothing, using various means, and finally leading to intensification of conflict-of-interests between people -causing social turbulence and unrest. If these problems can be instructed by the principle of causality of good and evil, transmigrate between the three-worlds of Buddhism – the extremes of pursuing personal happiness or hedonism would be moderated into mutual respect and mutual safeguards – to ensure each other's legal interest for the improvement of harmony and stabilization of global-humanity.

Encourage Helping People in Distress, Relieve Those in Need, and Propel the Development of Social/Charitable Causes through Buddhist Ethics

There are abundant theoretical resources of 'mercy' and 'saving the world' in Mahāyāna Buddhism, such as: "all sentient beings are equal", "mercy and benefiting the world", "the causality of good and evil", etc., as the source of spiritual power -when many Buddhist groups and social organizations are doing charitable causes. Therefore, by using Buddhist ethical thoughts to encourage people to take active parts in charitable activities would be beneficial for all sentient beings, with the mercy-spirit of Buddhas and Bodhisattvas – to improve reality, perform efforts beneficial to every sentient-being, cultivate good fortune, and benefit society with Buddhist ideals. This would be a powerful force to close the increasingly-deeper gap between the rich and poor in current society, ease serious social conflicts, and promote harmony and prosperity in society, and further human-happiness and benefit.

Mediate Conflicts between Humans and Nature, Promoting the Sustainable Development of Global Society, Economy, and Environment – through Buddhist Ethics

Development is one of the basic issues in contemporary society. Over the past two centuries, with the accelerating steps of global modernization, economies have become greatly developed, and with this, unexpected problems arose, such as:

over-population, resource shortages, environmental pollution, ecological destruction, etc. Additionally there are things like: famines, and floods not brought on by humans; terrorism, the threat of war or chaos, and mental unrest – leading to the danger of an unbalanced planetary life-system; and even restrictions placed upon principles for global sustainable development, economic systems, and society. For the sustainable development of human society – one would need to change one's ideological concepts -Buddhism has abundant ideological-resources available that could be used for reference. For instance: "not killing" is definitely against war according to Buddhist ethics – which refers to not only to killing humans, but also towards not killing bird ts, insects, and fishes, etc. – including not chopping trees arbitrarily. In addition to the precept of "not killing" – Buddhism advocates the birds,small animals,seeing of captive animals, which is directly beneficial to maintain the natural ecological balance. Other ideological resources include: "not stealing" or "not being greedy" – as beneficial for the improvement of public social-order conditions, and the stabilization of such a social order. The theory of dependent origination also serves as the theoretical foundation of Buddhism, stressing that humanity and the natural environment are interdependent. Buddhism's principle of the maturation of karma suggests that in the environment, all sentient beings live – interpretations also state that this includes mountains, rivers, land, and even all the global environment – all subjected to the effects of prior karmas of sentient being's own behaviors. The idea that subject and environment are un-separated, that subjective activities affect changes in the objective environment, is of great enlightening and instructive significance – that humans need to respect nature, treat nature well, and protect nature.

Human-oriented thoughts, and good-wishes towards the pursuance of harmony, stabilization, and development can be found everywhere when implying Buddhist ethics. It can be said that Buddhist ethics are expressions of humanity's living wisdom and summary of experience towards the process of survival and human-development. If we can pursue these principles from the Buddha, instruct more people in the principles, and to develop the Buddhist ethical principles, of: the abstention from evil and cultivation of good, equality and compassion, self-benefit and altruism, and related moral standards. If the principles are popularized into the common people, and penetrate into all kinds of human endeavors – indifference would lessen, conflicts would ease, enmity between people would disappear – and a friendly, harmonious, and sincere society would build solid relationships. Individuals would have a purified mind, perfected 'spirit', and an enlightened life; to wider extent, it would be beneficial to the State and the people – to improve the social morale, promote peace, safety, and a sustainable and healthy developed world.

BUDDHIST EDUCATION OF WOMEN: A FEMINIST PERSPECTIVE

Here I am discussing the someo of case study and discussion (*Maithree Wickramasinghe is a senior lecturer at the Department of English of the University of Kelaniya and wife of Opposition and United National Party leader Ranil Wickremaesinghe)* among the womens in Srilanka. Here then is a woman, who in the late 19th century, decides, simply on the strength of a modest advertisement, to embark on a journey to the other hemisphere, alone, to a land known to her only through her reading. Of course, we need to contextualise her journey in the context of her times.

No doubt she may have been grieving for her husband; no doubt that she may have been already familiar with Colonel Olcott through the Theosophist movement, but she was also part of an intellectual dynamic of the times and (like other educated fellow liberals and radicals), she was questioning the rise of a social order created by industrialism, the ethics of the colonial enterprise and the contradiction between social needs and orthodox religion in Europe and the US. Like a number of other white women who came to South Asia, (Feminist researcher Kumari Jayawardena records their journeys) Helena

Blavatsky, Annie Besant, Madeline Slade, Margret Noble, Mira Richard, Agnes Smedley and Katherine Mayo, Ms. Higgins too was willing to give up the familiarity and security of her life in Washington DC to pursue educational and social activism in Sri Lanka under the British.

In other words, she was a woman actively engaging with the intellectual currents and politics of Sri Lanka; agitating for social change. Remember, she later co-founded the Ceylon Reform Society along with Anne Besant.

In its indomitable strand of social activism was what led her, along with Peter de Abrew (with the help of William de Abrew's generous donation of land), to establish the wattle and daub hut with a cadjan roof that was to serve as a school for a group of 18 students in 1891 .

This was what led her to continue her work of educating generations of young women — despite a climate somewhat hostile to her constitution, despite the primitive conditions of those early years and despite the relentless attacks of white ants on the mud walls of the original school.

This was what led her to continue to fundraise with her friends and acquainted philanthropists to upgrade the school; moving to a two-storied building within a couple of years, adding a shrine room, and then a nursery as well as a cottage at different times, and ultimately, launching a women's teacher training college to further the cause of women's Buddhist education in English in Sri Lanka.

Imagine how gratified Marie Musaeus and Peter de Abrew would have been to see the school today — with its multistoried buildings, its indoor swimming pool and its hi-tech auditorium — a school which provides an education to 6,700 girls and which, I am told is the largest private girls' school in South Asia. In fact, even I am amazed when I think back to the homely quadrangle bordered by flowers that served as the heart of the school during my days.

Nineteenth century Musaeus College was not confined to Buddhists. An article in the Island in 2009 maintains that its gates were open to students from all communities; and of course, it had members of various nationalities and communities in its teaching staff. I think it is important for us to make a distinction here — despite the title of the institution as a 'Buddhist Girls' Schools', Musaeus was founded to provide an education based on Buddhist ethics, not as an institution to provide an education for Sinhala Buddhist girls only.

Similarly, Ananda College, started in 1886 to provide a Buddhist education in English for boys, did not impose limitations on its students at its inception.In the occasion of this memorial lecture then, I would like to express my gratitude to both Marie Musaeus Higgins and Peter de Abrew for their vision and their action, which led to tremendous transformations in the lives of generations of young women.

Consequently, the topic that I would like to focus on today is that of The Buddhist Education of Women – from a Feminist Perspective. As such, I would like to explore the historical trajectory of women's education and contemplate what is meant by an education and especially what is meant by a Buddhist education over time.

As a feminist scholar, I will be subscribing to feminist and gender perspectives in so doing. You may wonder why I have chosen a somewhat tedious and perhaps even 'tired' topic such as women's education.

Let me tell you. Is not only because of the current woes and vagaries that the education system in Sri Lanka is experiencing; but it is also because of the distinct role that our school, Musaeus College, historically played in Sri Lankan women's education; and because, as an academic and an educationist, my life is interlaced with the field of education.

Women's Education in Antiquity

To contemplate women's education we need to return to the sepia tones of the distant past, to the threadbare ola leaf chronicles of the Sinhalese; to the religious zeal of the Christian missionaries disembarking on the island's shores; to the colonial impulse of the British and the distinct religious politics pertaining to education in this country; as well as the revolution brought on by the welfare reforms of the 20th century. As a feminist, I find it extremely tempting to conceptualise an island cloaked in the mists of antiquity, inhabited entirely by women (yakkinis), and to trace the education of Sri Lankan women to the proud Queen Kuveni.

Kuveni's educational prowess, as we know, was in the occult rather than in traditional education or the competence of all rulers — military warfare. Kuveni practised her knowledge of witchcraft to protect her dominion from invaders like Vijaya. While we must be cautious about the validity of speculating on legendary material, we must also remember that we will always be dependent, by and large, on the imagination, when it comes to narratives claiming the origin of a nation.

So, if the choice were concerning Suppadevi of the Vanga kingdom (and her keeper -- the Lion), or the incestuous, patricide Sinhabahu or the marauding coloniser Vijaya, personally, I would prefer to go with Kuveni. With the advent of Theravadha Buddhism in the 2nd century BC, the bhikkhuni order established by Sangamittha Theri provided a rich source of spiritual education as well as a religious sanctum for women from the higher tiers of Buddhist society to the lesser.

However, as we are well aware, the bhikkuni order was socio-culturally a lower order than the bhikku order, and today, in complete decline. Further, women's historian Sirima Kiribamuna contends that there were fewer bhikkunis than bhikkus throughout the centuries -- going by the inscriptions and chronicles of the dhanas given by the monarchy and records of vihara ceremonies. Moreover, the remains and ruins of nunneries are scarcer than monasteries. Perhaps this can be related to the multiple roles and responsibilities within the domains of the family and home to which women were consigned, which prevented them from 'renouncing the secular world' to pursue knowledge and enlightenment within the Buddhist scope of life. For, when they did take to the saffron robes they did so not only to attain nirvana and be freed from the gyration of birth, death and rebirth but also for a range of reasons as poetised in the Theri Gathas and noted in the Chulavamsa.

These include an impassioned desire to be free — free from domestic violence and kitchen drudgery, free from being captured by enemy armies, free from compulsory submission and service to her family, and free from sexual obligation to her husband. While the bhikkunis who attained renown in the Dipawansa were essentially vinaya teachers, it is plausible that these bhikkunis were equally conversant with other aspects of the dharma; and that they took part in the critical debates and controversies relating to the different intellectual strands of Buddhism -- given their affiliation to the three historical nikayas of the Mahavihara, the Abhayagiri and the Jethavana. In fact, Sirima Kiribamuna contemplates the bhikkuni order of having possibly impressed the Chinese pilgrim Fahsien to such an extent that Sinhala bhikkunis were invited to Nanaking, China to establish a bhikkuni order there in the 5th century AD. Note that the practice of proselytisation or spreading the religious word is common to all religions not only to the Christian churches.

THE FOUNDATIONS OF MODERN EDUCATION

The systematic education of girls and women does not seem to have had a place in this country until colonial times — barring a few exceptions where women from the upper strata were perhaps privately versed in Sanskrit, Sinhala or Tamil. The Buddhist pirivena education carried out in the temples and monasteries was open principally to men. In the 16th century, the Portuguese explorers who stumbled onto the island began a string of parish schools — although these too did not necessarily provide the opportunity for the education of girls.

However, in the 18th century, there was a flowering of literature — including women's literature as a result of a folk revival of Sinhala literature in Southern Sri Lanka as well as some women being able to access the Dutch parish schools in the Maritime Provinces. For instance, Dona Isabella Cornelia Perumal, better known as Gajaman Nona of the Matara School of poets; her sister Dona Arnolia Perumal as well as her daughter Dona Katherina, Attaragama Kumarihamay, Dissanayake Lamathani, Ranchagoda Lamaya and Runa Hamine.

Some of Gajaman Nona's impromptu poetry focused on the blend of indigenous cultural concerns and the growing influence of westernisation during her time — issues that still preoccupy some individuals even in the 21st century. But she is equally famed for having defied convention -- dressing up as a boy to obtain a pirivana education (whether historically accurate or not), and later dressing up in the attire of a Dutch gentlewoman, writing letters and verses for money, 'daring to' correspond with erudite men, going about unaccompanied and of course, her erotic and highly risky poetic exchanges with the Elapatha Dissawa.

Runa Hamine too is noteworthy for having transformed much of the Bible into popular Sinhala verse — even though she was neither officially recognised for having done so nor adequately compensated. Interestingly, she thus complains in verse (I am referring here to Kumari Jayawrdena's citation of Denham): 'If this work had been done by a man, he undoubtedly would have received both money and fame, but since it was done by a woman she received no such reward'.

Yet by the mid-19th century, Christian missionary education schemes in English began to focus on girls and women — not only to propagate religion but also to provide suitable wives for the native men in the middle rungs of the British administration as well as the emergent capitalist class, and later on, the bourgeoisie — all who were increasingly adopting the values of the English colonizers.

Consequently, the curricular in girls' schools, imported wholesale from England comprised English, British history, English literature, arithmetic, geometry, Latin, French, German, Pali, Sanskrit, trigonometry, botany, physics, animal physiology, book-keeping, shorthand, (notice, it did not include any knowledge of Sinhala/Tamil or local history). It did, however, contain domestic economy, needlework, drawing, dressmaking, and music. These were value additions for girls in making them into presentable housewives and mothers — you can detect how the gender ideology relating to women's education during the period was transformed into educational practice.

The backlash against the Christian schools consolidating their influence over the island came in the form of the Hindu revivalist movement in Jaffna headed by Arumuga Navalar in the mid-1860s, which was swiftly followed by the Buddhist revival initiated by Hikkaduwe Siri Sumangala and Nigatuwatte Gunanada Theros. This was coupled with the campaign against the colonial government's liquor policies — the Temperance movement, and the local members of the Legislative Council of Ceylon insisting on controlling finance in government.

Clearly anti-colonial feeling was building. The demand for a 'Buddhist education in the English medium' for girls (as well as boys) arose in this context — assisted by the liberal impulses of the Theosophical movement, which stood for 'the universal brotherhood of humanity without race, creed, sex, caste or colour'. In this context, Olga Weerakoon was the first Sri Lankan woman to mount a public stage to speak out on women's education at the opening of Sangamitta School in Maradhana — the first girls' high school to give a Buddhist education in English.

As we all know Marie Musaeus Higgins, Helena Blavatsky, and Anne Besant were the key women Theosophist social activists and educationists who worked alongside local activists — particularly members of the Women's Education Society of Ceylon (founded in 1889) such as Mallika Hewavitarne, Madelina Perera Dharma Gunawardana, A. de Livera, Dona Madelena, E. Wijeysinghe, Margaret E. de Silva, and Isabella Dharma Gunawardana, as well as local funders such as William and Peter de Abrew, Ms. Wijeratne from Galle, and Cecilia Illangakoon from Matara. Yet despite this resurgence for what was called 'protestant Buddhism' by Richard Gombrich and the introduction of a Buddhist education in the English medium modelled on the protestant educational system, we must remember that there were patriarchal strands of Buddhism then, as well as there are now, which strove to control women's education and confine their lives.

Unfortunately, some of these narrow thinking emanated from some of the women themselves. Hilda Peiris -- the wife of a prominent civil servant of the time, Paul E. Peiris, felt that educating girls simply to become 'good Buddhist wives and mothers and homemakers' was adequate — similar to the Christian missionary objectives. She, in fact, states (as narrated by Kumari Jayawardena). '...A good deal more might be done by devoting the time which is wasted on obtaining a valueless smattering of Latin, French, theory of music and trigonometry ... to studying music drawing, dressmaking, and fine needlework, subjects which will not only add to the charm of a girl's home life but will also lead to a considerable saving in household expenditure'.

You will note that women's education is considered an asset in home making; education is not seen as an individual right — probably because women were not considered as individuals. However, Musaeus graduates seem to have far exceeded these patriarchal expectations by emancipating themselves through secondary, professional and tertiary education.

Ms. N. K. Pilapitiya records the progress of some of the Musaeus students in those early days. Elsie de Silva passed the junior Cambridge Examination in 1897, and Lucy de Abrew became the first Sinhala girl to enter the Medical College in 1902 (and the first woman to win the Jeejeebhouy scholarship). Jane de Zoysa, another pupil, became the first principal of the Teacher Training College for women teachers.

Some Statistics on Contemporary Education & Employment

In complete contrast to the situation at the turn of the 19th century, today, the landscape of education shows a surge of girls and women in both secondary and higher education (I am moving away from the topic of women's Buddhist education for a moment).

Statistics from the Ministry of Education show that in 2011, of the country's total student population of 3,973,847 at school level, 50.5% were girls and 49.5% were boys.

Each year, there are more boys enrolling into primary schools than girls; but there are more girls in Advanced Level classes. This indicates that boys drop out mid-stream during their education. There were 62,607 men teachers and 157,279 women teachers confirming that teaching is indeed a female-dominated service.

In sharp contrast, the university statistics for 2011 (given by the University Grants Commission) discloses that there were virtually 60% women undergraduates enrolling into the universities as opposed to 40% men undergraduates — indicating a clear feminisation of higher education — at least in terms of undergraduate numbers.

Moreover if we were to break that down to look at the gender proliferation within disciplines — women undergraduates are a majority in all streams; except engineering, architecture, quantity surveying, computer and the sciences — the most significant gender gap being in engineering.

On the other hand, when it comes to university teaching staff there are more men than women in all levels of academia with the sharpest gender differences between women and men being at the professorial level. For examples, of 512 professors in the island only 129 are women.

These statistics communicate significant increases in the numbers of girls' participation in secondary and tertiary education; in fact, there have been more girls in education than boys for a number of years. There are no available gender disaggregated statistics of teachers in relation to their educational qualifications and positions.

Within universities, not only are women lecturers lesser in number than men lecturers; but many women lecturers have yet to reach the topmost rungs on equal terms with men.

When correlating education with employment in a wider sense, although women have been in the workforce for decades (both formally and informally), there are distinctive gender inequalities in the labour market. Given the relative invisibility of women in the informal sector, the labour force participation rate of women is significantly lower than that of men. For instance, in the fourth quarter of 2012, the labour force participation rate of men was 67.9% while the rate of women's participation was 31.3%.

Male participation in the labour force has been approximately twice as that of females for the last four decades (the gender disparity being particularly broad among youth and those with secondary education).

No doubt it has been reiterated over and over that in Sri Lanka's three leading foreign exchange earning sectors (garments, foreign remittances and tea), women constitute the bulk of the work force, thereby making a valuable contribution to the GDP, balance of payments and overall economic development.

What we should note in addition is that they are employed only at the lower end of the employment ladder -- as assembly line operators, in overseas domestic service, and as plantation workers.

Thus while women may have access to education, their participation in the labour force, in comparison to men, is half that of men's.

Furthermore, they do not occupy the higher echelons of work institutions. Except for a minority of much publicized exceptions in high places, our often-cited woman prime minister and president in politics, a handful in public administration (including a woman Chief Justice and Attorney General) and a few CEOs in the private sector, women as a sex/gender have not breached the glass ceilings at workplaces.

As such the link between education and the employment of women remains highly problematic. Suffice to state then that despite over a century of women's education the dividends expected for women as a sex/gender have not materialized. While there is no harm in education being an end in itself – as opposed to the means to an end – can young women afford to be self-indulgent? Or do they remain officially uncounted because they are in the informal sector or in domestic work? How do their educational levels compare with their income levels? The lack of a means of income generally signifies economic dependency, which as we know, can act as a barrier to women's independence and empowerment.

Extracurricular Activities: In this scenario, let us now consider the quality of education today. What concerns me, in particular, is not necessarily the curricular of formal education (which is, in today's context, governed by both local market needs as well as the commercialisation of education worldwide amongst other factors), but extracurricular education and value--? based education. When it comes to extra curricular activities, I believe that Musaeus is in the lead.While I was researching for this speech, I happened to surf the website of Musaeus College – I was vastly impressed by the scope and spectrum of academic disciplines, fields, programs, services, sports, hobbies and activities that current students can access – aside from the regular curricular.For those of you, who are, perhaps like me, unfamiliar with current school activities, I have listed some of them. They include an Astronomy Society, a Commerce and Bank Society, a Creative Writers' Club, a Diabetic Task Force, a Drug Preventing Society, an Environment Society, a Young Inventors' Club, an English Debating Circle, an ICT Society, a Music & Drama Society, a Media Unit, a Mathematics Society, a Photography Club, an Orchestra, a Scrabble Club, a Social Worker's Club, a St. John's Ambulance Brigade, a United Nations Club, a Welfare Society, a Young Entrepreneurs' Club as well as Squash, Chess, Rowing, Table Tennis and Wushu.

This is in stark contrast to what was available to us thirty years ago. Value--?based Education While it is apparent that these girls do benefit from a highly versatile all-rounded education — beyond the textbook, my question remains -do they also gain a value-based education based on ethical principles? What about core understandings of sincerity and faithfulness; care and compassion; honesty and integrity; gratitude and generosity? Do today's young women try to understand, respect and include those who are different from them – whether it is a case of sex/gender, language, ethnicity, religion, sexual orientation, age, disability or whatever? What about the capacity to be free from egoism or the strength to admit responsibility for one's actions? Are our young women able to display equanimity in joy and suffering, in honor and dishonor, and in success and failure? Are they taught to be open to all forms of knowledge; are they able to achieve a degree of balance and independence of thought? And most importantly, are they able to express these values through thought, feeling and action? Or are these young women (and perhaps their parents) hopelessly entangled in an educational system- where the parents themselves seem to be going to school; avidly pursuing the 'best' — the 'best of schools' the 'best of teachers', the best of classes; aiming to win at all costs, constantly looking to score marks; trudging to innumerable tuition classes, collecting dozens of certificates and perhaps even using their children's achievements for social prestige?

Recently I watched a Japanese documentary, which showed how teachers and pre-teen students after having watched a movie (about a man who had done a great disservice to another man) were deliberating on the need to articulate the word 'sorry'. These children were discussing when and why and actually how to say sorry: the effect of saying sorry with emotion and without, as well as the politics of saying sorry.

They were discussing what we usually understand to be an expression of politeness from the perspective of ethics, religion, etiquette, public relations, politics, and psychology and so on as part of their formal education.

In contrast, I have been told that one of the first principles that you learn in a particular media class in Sri Lanka is not to ever say that one is sorry (though I must confess that I am not too sure about the veracity of this statement). In universities, we are concerned with the wider social implications of primary / secondary education that is based on the current objectives of single-minded achievement, the ethic of winning, and consumerism.

How do such values impact on law and order? On ethnic and religious relations? On those who are weak and poor? On gender equity / equality? One of the initiatives that I am involved with is the Centre for Gender Studies at the University of Kelaniya. Our goal is to promote gender equity and equality in Sri Lankan universities and society. This involves, integrating gender issues and women's specific concerns into university curricular as well as gender--?perspectives into academic courses. Yet, our work does not stop at education. It encompasses changes to policy and practice as well. We are also advocating that equal numbers of competent women be appointed to University Councils and the management of universities; the institution of mechanisms within higher educational institutions to support and offer redress to those affected by ragging, sexual harassment, and sexual and gender-based violence; the recognition of the importance of a healthy work/life balance given that women's multiple roles as well as rigid employment conditions are seen as possible reasons for the stagnation of women in lower employment ranks; and the development of gender-sensitive infrastructure and facilities such as crèches, areas for breast-feeding, and dry toilets in accessible places.

I am not raising the issue of toilets for humorous effect — but if women's toilets do not match the increase in numbers; or if they are located in close proximity to male dominated areas such as security offices or monks' rest areas then it poses problems for the women who use these toilets – given inequitable gender ideologies and cultural values.

In this sense we are attempting to operationalize value-based education relating to gender equity / equality into university practice. Challenge to Buddhism and Social Responsibility During the past forty minutes I traced women's education in this country, discussed the promise made by educationists like Marie Musaeus Higgins, Peter de Abrew, and others, pointed out the significant achievements over the following decades and appraised the disappointing failures in realizing women's emancipation on a larger scale.

I would now like to turn my attention to the imperative issues of education that we, as Musaeites, or for that matter, educated Buddhist women all over the country have the responsibility to engage with today. I believe that one of the biggest threats to a Buddhist education comes from within – from the fundamentalist corps of Sinhala Buddhists, who not only distort the very goals of education and enlightenment propounded by the Buddha — but who also misinterpret the very doctrine of the dharma for personal and political gain. I am talking about parochial worldviews of Sinhala Buddhism that, for instance, may padlock the spirit of peace, compassion, respect, tolerance and inclusion of others when it comes to different gender, ethnic or religious groups.

For instance, views which yoke together Buddhism with cockeyed notions of culture that may curtail or deny women their human rights (including the right to live a life free from sexual and gender-based violence).

I am talking about a siege-mentality adopted by certain Sinhala Buddhist groups – who bind together Sinhala Buddhism with misguided concepts of patriotism, who refuse to practice insight or self-knowledge, and thereby, abuse Buddhism for political advantage.

I am talking about discriminative worldviews of Sinhala Buddhism – based on pungent notions of racial purity, supremacy and exclusivity that stridently deny the flexibility of a religion that allows for inter-religious practices and beliefs.Consider how many of you have not sought solace at a church or kovil- aside from the temple in times of crisis I am talking of militant worldviews of Sinhala Buddhism that currently promote the persecution of Muslims, Tamils and Christians, through scorching populist rhetoric and criminal acts of arson - burning down churches, mosques and kovils, forcing the closure of selective business enterprises-chiefly because they are sanctioned by various powers to do so. In this context, it is possible for us to turn to the historical strands of Buddhism in Sri Lanka for guidance. From the arrival of Sangamitta onwards there has been a tradition of openness, respect and inclusion in Buddhism in Sri Lanka, which promoted the integration of what was worthy and valuable from a variety of cultures and countries throughout the eras.

Archives and archeology tell us that we are all the descendants of waves of migrants over the centuries — not only from the crotch of Bengal but also from the eastern rims of the Bay of Benagal (popularly called Javakas), the shores of Malabar, the Coramandal coast, and the Persian Gulf; furthermore, the invading Portuguese along with kaffirs (slaves from the East of Africa), the Dutch and British with indentured labour from Maduari have all mingled their genes amongst us. The island has also been hospitable to silk and spice traders sailing the cusp of the Indian subcontinent from Rome, Greece, Central Asia to the lands of India, the islands of Java, ancient Sinae (or China) and perhaps even beyond.Within institutionalized Theravadha Buddhism, we know that monks had to be brought down from Thailand and Myanmar in the 18th and 19th centuries to give upasampadha so as to re-establish the Buddhist order through the dominant Siyam, Amarapura, and Ramanna nikayas.

In the 19th century, in setting up the Ceylonese chapters of the Theosophical society, Colonel Olcott was amply supported by Migettuwatte Gunananda Thera, Hikkaduwe Sri Sumangala Thero, Walane Sri Siddhartha Thero and Ratmalane Dhammaloka Thero, along with Walisinghe Harischandra, and D.B. Jayatilaka. If some of today's Sinhala Buddhist attitudes were in place at that time Musaeus College would never have materialized because we all know how closely Peter de Abrew worked with Marie Musaeus to establish our school.

The cross-fertilisation of ideas and collaboration of people as well as the peaceful coexistence with all faiths and communities of this land (for the most part) has been the greatest strength of Buddhism historically. But in the face of the dangerous strands of so called 'Sinhala Buddhism' in today's context, the challenge for women who want to identify themselves as Sinhala Buddhists, is firstly, to stop being silent. For, I believe that it is exceedingly important to speak out against what you do not believeing even if you are in the minority. Often we tend to ignore extremism if we ourselves do not subscribe to it.Yet this only serves to crystallize fanaticism as the dominant opinion. At this juncture, speaking out is the least one can do. It will not be easy. After all — if doing the right thing were easy, I doubt that all religions would have to keep urging us to do it. We can all take heart from the young Pakistani girl, 15-year-old Malala Yousafzai, who was shot in the head by the Taliban for her educational activism. Luckily, she survived, and went on to win education for all girls in Pakistan, and is today addressing the UN asking global leaders to ensure that every child goes to school – what is considered to be a shockingly achievable goal. If you found a guiding principle or abiding value in my speech, take note; If you found passing inspiration, take it to heart; If you found something of usable worth take it away and use it; The rest – you may throw out. In fact, you may throw out the whole thing if so inclined! The writer is a professor and the director of the Centre for Gender Studies at the University of Kelaniya.

EARLY BUDDHIST EDUCATION AND ITS MODERN BUDDHIST MONASTERIES BECOME THE CENTRE OF EDUCATION

Buddhist Education gave emphasis on the moral, mental and physical development. The main stress was given to have a clear idea of Tripitaka. In the later period according to the demand of the society and professional Education art, sculpture, architecture, medicine also included in the syllabus. At the initial stage medium of Education was mother tongue, later it included Pali & Prakrit and in the following days Sanskrit also introduced. It is to be mentioned that Vedic subjects also included in the syllabus. This was a historic development .Sangharamas the centre of Buddhist Education later developed into colleges

& universities. Nalanda, Vikramsila, Sompori, Salban, Pandit Vihar, Taxila were the unparallel universities. Students from China,Myanmar, Thailand, Gandhara came to have their studies there.

The teachers were highly qualified. The aim of Buddhist Education is to make a free man, a wise, intelligent, moral, non-violent & secular man. Students became judicious, humanist, logical and free from superstitious. Students became free from greed, lust and ignorance. Buddhist Education was wide open and available to the people of all walks of life. The principal goal of the Buddhist Education is to change an unwise to wise, beast to priest.

At present Buddhist Education in China, Korea, Japan, Thailand, Myanmar, Srilanka made tremendous progress with the introduction of modern subjects. They have made more facilities for the lay people. Education has been incorporated with modern facilities. Buddhist Education in Bangladesh is still in a traditional position and could not succeed due to financial assistance. So, it needs help and guidance from the Buddhist World. Buddha, the founder of Buddhism was born in Lumbini present Nepal. In ancientdays, Nepal,Srilanka, Bangladesh Pakistan, Myanmar was one country and known as Indian Sub-Continent. In Buddhist text it is known as Jhambudipa. Buddha attained enlightenment in Bodhgaya, Bihar presently situated in India. He spent 45 years after Buddha hood in different parts of India and propagated his religion. In India during the time of Buddha what was the condition of society. How education had come into assistance. There was a racial discrimination in the society. This discrimination was according to profession of man, and according to birth. In the society there were four division of man of whom Brahman was superior. Brahmanism dominated the society and established their supremacy in the country. They enjoyed rights for religious training and education. But other category of people deprived of their religious and educational rights. At that time there were 62 heretical doctrines in existence and priesthood got upper hand. In this background a religious revolution started in ancient India in 600 B.C. and a new doctrine or system developed which is called Buddhist doctrine or Buddhist philosophy. It is to be said that on the foundation of Buddhism a new and special Education System originated in ancientIndia. Buddhism made a tremendous movement which played a valuable role in the development of Education System in ancient India or ancient Buddhist world.

Centre of Education

The main centre of Buddhist Education was sangharama (Monastery / Vihara, Temple) where monks and samanaras reside sangharamas were open to all. Here students from different caste, creed, colour and religion got free admission. Buddhism was a strong protest against orthodox Vedic (Hindu) religion and also Education System. Buddhism established democracy, universalism and monastic life. There was no racial discrimination and nobody was deprived of his rights. Buddhist Monasteries became the Centre of Education.

Admission : The novices first entered into the Sangha (Bhikkhu Sangha), then had to follow the monastic rules and Sangha rules. Even today these rules are followed. There are many rules regarding food, dress, bed room, meditation, dedication and other rules as laid down by the Sangha. They had to undergo with physical exercise for maintenance of their health. They had to clean the campus, rooms, halls, serve the teachers (Achariya) and assist them in various field. This was the primary duties of the students. After admission students were classified according to their merit and put under the guidance of different teachers. They had to follow the advice of the teachers and obey them. In this way they had to pass twelve years in learning. Students put questions to the teachers; teachers answered the question and discussed matters related to their Education. Students had to perform daily routine works beyond learning.

Duties of the Teachers

The duties of the teachers were imparting education to the students, writing Book, propagation of religion, discussion, and arrangement of debate for the clarification of serious subjects. The teachers were responsible for physical, mental, spiritual and moral development of the students. Teachers loved the students and helped them in every affair. They also took care of them during their diseases and agony. The teachers were responsible for their food, accommodation and other necessaries of livelihood. They kept eyes on the all round development of the students. Especially they were serious about the obeyance of the Sangha rules, meditation and concentration to their learning.

Relation between the Teachers and the Students

Sangha (Monastic) life was residential; therefore a cordial relationship between the teachers and the students grew up. Their relationship can be compared with the relationship of a father and a son. The teachers were the guardians and sincere for their mutual relationship, happiness, development and responsibilities.

Syllabus

Buddhist Education system developed on the basis of some basic principles. This education gave emphasis on the moral, mental and physical development and also to divert the students towards the Sangha rules and guide them to follow it. The main stress was given to have a clear idea of Tripitaka which consists of Sutta Pitaka, Binoy Pitaka and Abhidhamma Pitaka. The entire Tripitaka consists of Buddhas teachings, message, philosophy and rules for the Bhikkhus and Bhikkhunies.

In later period according to the demand of the society and professional education, art, sculpture, architecture, medicine also included in the syllabus. Buddhist Education came out from the religious arena and went out for the benefit of the mankind. At the initial stage medium of education was mother tongue, later it included Pali and Prakrit and in the following days Sanskrit also included as a medium of instruction. Specially the Mahayana Teachers achieved distinction in practicing Buddhism in Sanskrit. A special Sanskrit Buddhist literature developed. Mention may be made here that at the hands of

Nagarjun, Asanga, Basubandhu, Santideva, Aryadeva and Candrakisti Buddhist philosophy and literature made tremendous progress through Sanskrit. It is to be mentioned that Buddhist Educational Syllabus included Vedic subjects also. In this way difference of Buddhist & Vedic Education wiped out and united. This was a historic development in the history of Education in India.

Teaching Method : In early days teaching was a hearing system. The teachers gave lectures; students heard it and kept it in their memory. In due course it developed into dialogue and comparison method. The teachers used to teach the students on the basis of telling stories, arranging dialogue. Sometimes debate and discussions were arranged to give idea of the subject matter as well as determination of truth, subsequently writing system introduced.At first there was private and group teachings. Later it developed into class room. In due course Sangharamas developed into residential college and universities. In the history of Education those universities played major role in the propagation of Buddhism, Buddhist history, Art & Culture. In those universities world famous scholars like Atisa Dipankar, Silabrada, Santarakshit were the teachers. Many valuable books were written. We still remember the glory of the universities like Nalanda, Vikramsila, Sompuri, Salban, Jagaddal, Pandit Vihar, Taxila. The supremacy of those universities were unparallel. Students from China, Myanmar, Thailand, Gandhara and all parts of ancient India came to have their education in those universities. Buddhist Education is a combination between individual and classroom education.

Contribution of Buddhist Education

In the ancient period Buddhist Monasteries and in the later period Buddhist Universities played major role in developing Buddhist Education. In the institutions teachers were highly qualified and sincere to their duties. The main aim of Buddhist Education is to make a free man, an intelligent man, a wise, moral, talented, non-violent and secular man. Buddhist Education make man judicious, humanist, logical and free from superstitions. After getting education in the

Buddhist schools, colleges and universities one can not do any injustice, tell a lie, commit theft, can not kill, can not be addicted in wine and make himself free from moral turpitude. In this way students become free from greed, lust, enmity and ignorance.

Buddhist Education made revolutionary change in the society. The Buddhists in the world first made Education open to all. Students irrespective of caste, creed, religion got opportunity to have education which was denied by the superior class in the society. In India also, in Vedic Educational schools students from lower classes were refused to get admission.

In the early period Buddhist Education was limited within the monasteries and only for the members of the monastery. But later on it was open to all, even lay people got scope to have education in those institutions. In modern days Buddhist Education became wide open and embraced people of all walks of life. The aim of Buddhist Education is to change an unwise to wise, beast hood to Buddha hood.

BUDDHIST EDUCATION & MODERNIZATION

It is a matter of great pride that Buddhist Education crossed Indian Sub-continent and expanded uptoChina, Korea, Japan, Tibet, Mongolia, Srilanka, Myanmar, Thailand, Cambodian, Laos, Vietnam,Malaysia, Singapore, with the rise and development of Buddhism in those countries. In those countries Buddhist Education has made tremendous progress with the inclusion of modern subjects in the syllabus. Today in order to make more popular more useful and modern subjects have to be included such as English, Science, Medicine, Engineering, Commerce, Computer and Information Technology. We are happy that the name of the countries which I mentioned have made tremendous development of Buddhist Education with the inclusion of modern subjects. They have made more facilities for the lay students. it is my suggestion that Buddhist Education syllabus shall have to be incorporated with modern subject. In Bangladesh, Buddhist Education is still concentrated in the monasteries. Because of financial assistance it could not precede upto expectation. Buddhist Education in Bangladesh needs help, assistance and guidance from the Buddhist World.

Buddhism and Education

Once, when the Buddha was passing through an area known as Kalama, some people came to ask his guidance. Since the area was well situated, different teachers regularly passed through. Invariably, they would claim that they were right and the other teachers, and their teachings, were wrong.

The Kalamas, who were not the Buddha's students, requested he tell them how to proceed in discerning and choosing a teacher who did indeed speak the truth.

Knowing the Kalamas to be intelligent, moral people, the Buddha gave them several guidelines, including: "Do not go upon what has been acquired by repeated hearing; . . . nor upon rumor; . . . nor upon surmise; . . . nor upon specious reasoning; nor upon a bias towards a notion that has been pondered over; nor upon another's seeming ability; nor upon the consideration, 'The monk is our teacher.'"

The Buddha continued explaining to the Kalamas, but for our purposes today, we can stop here. The Buddha was not advising that one should throw out the baby with the bathwater by ignoring all existing doctrine and faith, but rather to proceed wisely—not blindly—when choosing a teacher and his or her teaching, and to test the teaching through experience.

True teachings will withstand examination through experience, through experimentation. If I am told that I will be happy by giving to others, I may be skeptical. But when I give, and see how much my actions mean to another, then I truly know happiness.

If we are not to believe blindly, how do we proceed? With education: the act of being educated.

From a very broad, all-encompassing perspective, the New Oxford American Dictionary defines educate as "give intellectual, moral, and social instruction . . . ." Educate comes from the Latin word meaning to lead out, to bring forth. In the process of leading out, of bringing forth, there is a starting point and that which is brought into view. Something that is already intact, which is uncovered in order to function.

Why is it so important to bring forth all three aspects: intellectual, moral, and social?

Today, academic educational institutions focus on intellectual instruction, on bringing forth what lies within the mind. Looking around it's not hard to see where this has all too often gotten us: some very smart people making very poor moral choices, which have egregiously harmed society. What has gone wrong?

These institutions focus on economic progress instead of ethical progress, on commercializing the mind not illuminating it. Self-interest has been placed as number one, with the benefit for the many being relegated far down the list. Short-term profits, regardless of the long-term costs reigns. The balance of the three aspects has shifted to a concentration on just one—intellectual. The moral and social aspects have been seriously neglected.

Is the Intellectual Aspect Unimportant?

No at all. The intellectual is important. After all we need to learn the appropriate information and skills in all areas of our lives. We need to learn how to support ourselves, meet our own various societal responsibilities, and be able to function in the world in a manner that helps, not harms, others. We need to learn about others, how they live, their values, the many things we have in common, and the wonderful differences that make humanity so fascinating.

Apart from academic learning, Buddhism looks more at helping us to grow spiritually. For this, we need to learn from wise teachers and teachings in areas like morality, virtues, and causality. These will help enable us to live in the world, but not become ensnared by it. Becoming ensnared will lead to wanting more and more, and, invariably, harming more and more.

With good instruction, we will bring forth the good values that already lie within our very essence, what we call our prajna, our innate, wisdom. Every being has this innate wisdom deep within them. Every being has the ability to function with spontaneous, unconditional care and compassion. Our learning and practice have the goal of illuminating this innate wisdom and goodness so it will arise and shine forth in everything we do.

Practice is why we learn. Practice is fulfilling the teachings.

What of Moral Instruction?

Good moral values instruction will enable us to get along better with others and will thus bring in social instruction as well. To accomplish this, we need teachers who understand the teachings as the original teachers intended. One way to see if the teacher understands the moral teaching is to observe whether he or she puts them into practice in daily life, in everything they do.

This role modeling is a teaching in itself because it shows that the principles are indeed applicable and appropriate for us. They're not out-dated or out-of-touch. The role modeling also gives real-life examples of how to apply the principles in daily situations like those we ourselves encounter.

And vitally important, seeing the teacher putting the teachings into action, deepens our confidence in the teachings, and the teacher. This is not just some noble principle I learned last week, this is a genuine teaching that works and can help me. Not only that, it can be seen to help others as well. Someone not taking something without permission or saying what is untrue gives those who observe this a feeling of safety, of not needing to worry in this person's presence.

What of the person who chose not to commit a wrongdoing? They too are less anxious! There is no need to try to remember what they told one person as opposed to what they told another. No need to worry about being found with something they have no right to possess. No need to fear that something they said or did is wrong and will come back to haunt them. No need to feel ashamed of having hurt a person they hold dear.

By worrying, fearing, and stressing less, both mind and heart will gradually become more calm. The calmer they are, the better they learn and function. And the better that innate, true nature and wisdom will shine forth.

Education—giving the three aspects of intellectual, moral, and social instruction—ennobles us all. It ennobles the one who teaches, for this person has given completely of their knowledge, without holding back, without putting self- interest above the interests of others. Education ennobles the one who is taught, for this person has learned better how to not merely survive but to grow in the world, how to be a caring, moral person who seeks to help not harm others.

Education ennobles all those who are touched by the teachings for they too are touched by the spirit of the teachings through simply being in the presence of good people and learning how to emulate them.

Education benefits us all for it allows us to become wiser, to be more caring of those who need our help, more respectful of others' viewpoints, more patient with those we interact with, and happier with ourselves.

DR. B.R.AMBEDKAR'S CONTRIBUTION TO BUDDHIST EDUCATION IN INDIA

"Noble is your aim and sublime and glorious is your mission. Blessed are those who are awakened to their duty to those among whom they are born. Glory to those who devote their time, talents and their all to the amelioration of slavery. Glory to those who would reap their struggle for the liberation of the enslaved in spite of heavy odds, carpine humiliation, storms and dangers till the downtrodden secure their Human Rights."- Bharat Ratna Babasaheb Dr.B.R.Ambedkar.

Today's Ambedkarites may have reduced their mentor to a symbol to center their electoral campaign on, but history will view Babasaheb Bhim Rao Ambedkar differently—as a man whose genius extended over a diverse arrange of human affairs. Born to Mahar parents, Babasaheb would have been one of the many Untouchable of his times condemned to a life of suffering and misery, had he not doggedly overcome the oppressive circumstances of his birth to rise to pre-eminence in India's public life. Ambedkar was, of course, a towering leader of the Untouchables, but he was also much more- patriot, scholar, thinker and Founding Father of the Indian Constitution.

Ambedkar started the Bahishkrit Hitkarini Sabha and the Samaj Samanta Sangh for the uplift of untouchables. He led processions and dharnas for his community, demanded separate electorates for them, parted ways with Gandhi, violently differing with Gandhi's approach toward the Untouchables, and finally, left the Hindu fold, embracing with thousands of his followers the more egalitarian faith of Buddhism.

India got Independence 55 years ago, till today Dalit has to suffer for basic needs for their day to day living i.e. Drinking water, food, shelter and Right to live as human being in society. The Untouchables "Dalit" were denied even Human Rights, which are essential for a bare existence of human life. They were not allowed to drink water from public well; and even their shadow was supposed to pollute the so- called upper Castes. The Hindu social order made the life of the Dalit miserable in every sense of the term. The Hindu Dharmashastra gave sanction to this evil Caste system and the practice of Untochability. This continued for the Centuries.

Then arose on the horizon Dr. BabaSaheb Ambedkar, the liberator of the Millions of downtrodden in India. He made abolition of the Caste system and Untouchability a mission of His life. Perhaps it would take a rebirth by the Mahatma Gandhi to end the abominable evil of Caste. As he he had said: "If I do not want to attain moksha, I do not want to be reborn. But if I were to be reborn, I should be born an Untouchable... not as a Brahmin, Kshatriya, Vaishya or Shudra But as an Atishudra, a Bhangi."

Babasaheb Ambedkar raised the banner of Buddhism and brought back to his motherland the Buddha who suffered an exile for over twelve hundred years. Ambedkar, a man of provocative learning, challenged opponents of Buddhism to hold discussions with him, and was confident that he would defeat all Pandits. He propagated Buddhism in India. He made the provision for the study of Pali in the Indian constitution. The Government of India had declared Buddha Jayanti a holiday mainly through his efforts. Dr. Ambedkar was the greatest Pioneer of Buddhist revival in India.

India, no doubt, continues to be proud of its Buddhist heritage. Since regaining independence, Buddhist symbols like the Wheel of Dhamma and the Asoka Capital, have become national symbols and the Mathura Buddha adorns the house of Parliament and inspires Indian lawmakers.

The Buddha established a classless society by opening the gates of the Sangha to all deserving individuals, making no distinction between caste and class. The fundamental principle of Buddhism is equality... Buddhism was called the religion of the Shudra's... " There was only one man who raised his voice against separatism and Untouchability and that was Lord Buddha... Buddhism is the only religion, which does not recognize caste and affords full scope for progress.

Dr. Ambedkar's speech on the Eve of the great conversion at Nagpur on October14, 1956, Dr. Ambedkar said Buddhism can serve not only this country, India, but the whole World at this juncture in the world affairs; Buddhism is indispensable for world peace you must pledge today that you, the followers of Buddha, will not only work to liberate yourself, but will try to elevate your country and the world in general.

Dr. Ambedkar declared: "By discarding my ancient religion which stood for inequality and oppression today I am reborn. I have no faith in the philosophy of incarnation; and it is wrong and mischievous to say that Buddha was an incarnation of Vishnu. I am no more a devotee of any Hindu god or goddess. I will not perform shradha. I will strictly follow the eightfold path of Buddha. Buddhism is a true religion and I will lead a life guided by the tree principles of knowledge, right path and compassion. Dr. Ambedkar denounced Hinduism, its customs and traditions and declared that from that moment onwards he would strive for the spread of equality among human beings.

Emancipation and empowerment of Dalits is possible only through education. The present Dalit leadership, unlike Spartacus or Ambedkar, is suffering from intellectual bankruptcy. It fails to criticize the ruling classes or follow Ambedkar's philosophical and ideological roots. Nearly 60 to 70 per cent of India's wealth belongs to Dalits. It is their blood and sweat. But they are the principle victims of the system.

Dr. Ambedkar explained to his people that "a great responsibility had fallen on their shoulders in connection with the upholding of Buddhism; and if they would not follow rigidly and nobly the principles of Buddhism, it would mean that the Mahars reduced it to a miserable state, no other person under that the sum was burdened with such unparalleled responsibility as he was, he concluded.

Dr. Ambedkar set the wheel of Dhamma in motion once again, spreading the message of his Master to all the corners of the world. The Buddhists said the "the Dhamma Chakra was set revolution by Dr.Ambedkar and it was the greatest religious revolution which India had witnessed in modern times."

Dr. Ambedkar dedicated himself to the propagation of the Buddhist faith in India. He wrote a book on Buddhism titled "Buddha and His Dhamma" explaining its tenets in simple language to the common man. His two other books "Revolution and Counter Revolution in India' and "Buddha and Karl Marx"

The malafide intentions of including the Buddha in the Avatara pantheon are also clear from the fact that the Brahmins never worshiped the Buddha and no temples were built in his honour. Logically, the theory that Buddha is an incarnation of Vishnu is dubious one. Therefore, Dr. Ambedkar exhorted Buddhists not to believe that the Buddha was an incarnation of Vishnu. Now even a Brahmin Priest agrees that the Buddha was not an incarnation of Vishnu. Principal Vipassana Teacher, Shri S.N.Goenka and Sankaracharya of Kanchikam Kote Peetham Sri Jayendra Saraswati made a joint declaration on 11.11.1999 at Sarnath that Gotama the Buddha was not an incarnation of Vishnu.

"I am reported to be against peace. This is not correct. I am for peace. But, the peace, which is, based on justice not the peace of a graveyard. So long as justice is not respected in the world there cannot be any peace. Buddhism and Buddhism alone can save the World."

Dr. B.R.Ambedkar a great scholar, Lawyer and freedom fighter along with hundreds of thousands of Mahar's an untouchable caste, converted to Buddhism and changed the face of Buddhism in India. Dr. Ambedkar's conversion was a symbolic protest to the oppressions of caste inequality. His conversion was an intellectual decision that would meet with the least opposition from the Hindu majority.

India, have no leader of the kind Dr. Babasaheb Ambedkar, Indian Crusader for Social Justice and Champion of Human Rights. One of the greatest contributions of Dr. Ambedkar was in respect of Fundamental Rights and Directive Principles of State Policy enshrined in the Indian Constitution. The fundamental Rights provide for freedom, equality, abolition of Untouchability and remedies to ensure the enforcement of rights.

Fifty-five years after independence, Caste prejudices in India have not erased very much. And now there is a deliberate attempt to revive these prejudices to their former position.

Grundtvig's conception about Nordic mythology and Christian "Anskuelese" may be compared with Ambedkar's views on the original tradition of Buddhism as a source of inspiration. In describing the work of on Buddhism he said" we have started this movement to develop and educate our minds" Explaining the need for religion among the poor as a need arising for hope, Ambedkar referred to a German professor of his, Professor Wintermitz.

"The Watergang Rabelan Depth was the book which he recommended and by which I was much inspired. It is only the poor, he said who need religion." Hope is the spring of action in life. Religion affords hope. Therefore, mankind finds solace in the religion, and that is why the poor cling to religion."

Those who are turned to Buddhism, but remained within Hinduism but wanted Hinduism to change, Ambedkar made the following suggestion:

"You must give a new doctrinal basis to your religion-a-basis that will be in consonance with Liberty, Equality and Fraternity, in short, with Democracy."

Dr. BabaSaheb Ambedkar once commented, "Dalit representatives elected from reserved seats open their mouth in the Indian parliament only when they have to yawn."

It was the Buddha who, for the first time in the known history of mankind, attempted to abolish slavery and "invented the higher morality and the idea of the brotherhood of the entire human race, and in striking terms condemned" the degrading caste-system which in Indian society at that time was firmly rooted. The Buddha declared: "By birth is not one an outcast, By birth is not one a Brahmin, By deeds is one an outcast, By deeds is one a Brahmin."

Dr. Ambedkar in His book "Annihilation of Caste" reproduces his major difference with the Mahatma Gandhi. While he was for abolition of the caste system, prescribed by Hindu sage Manu, Gandhi was for giving up caste prejudice, and for reform of the system, so that the stigma of Untouchability may be removed, but function of various castes remains.

As Dr. Ambedkar could not abolish the caste system, when Mahatma Gandhi asked for dedication on the shared cause of struggle for freedom, he asked for separate electorates for the so-called "outcastes" whom the Mahatma called "Harijan"- sons of the 'God'

Dr. Ambedkar turned on Gandhi too: The Dalits leaders converted to Buddhism perhaps the least dogmatic or hierarchic of world religions. Dr. Ambedkar's response to Gandhi was that he wanted to treat the symptom, not the cause of the disease- you can't abolish Untouchability without addressing the Caste and the Dharma system, which is at the root of it.

" Gandhiji, felt that the high castes should change their hearts: Dr. Ambedkar said that we' ve been suffering for over 2000 years, many Hindu saints have come and gone; but nothing has changed, so he legally empowered to challenge it." Article 17, of the Constitution that abolished "Untouchability" The problem is if you implement it half of India would be in Jail."

There have been many Mahatmas in India whose sole object was to remove Untouchability and to elevate and absorb the depressed Classes, but every one of them has failed in his mission. Mahatmas have come, Mahatmas have gone. But the Untouchables have remained as Untouchables.

Buddhists of India need the friendship, understanding and cooperation for uplifting themselves and for strengthening the hands of those who are striving for peace, equality and justice. Let the scent of the Dhamma spread in all directions and illumine the minds of those who put much faith in steel and fire but ignore the value of peace, loving kindness and compassion.

Venerable Anagarika Dharampal, great son of Sri Lanka, came to India and was distressed to find even the great Bodhi Gaya Temple in a dilapidated condition under the control of Brahmin Mahant. He struggled to take possession of Boudh - Viharas of the Buddhist but failed owing to the hostile attitude of the British Government and the Upper Caste Hindus. He founded Maha-Boudhi Society to propagate the Dhamma and to continue the struggle for reviving Buddhism.

Dr. S. Radhakrishna, Late -President of India and Philosopher said; Buddhism brought about a profound change in the lives of the Indian people. "For us in this country the Buddha is an outstanding representative of our religious tradition."

Dr. G.P.Malalasekera said: Let us not forget that some of the leaders of religion have themselves been revolutionaries. The Buddha, for instance, was one of the greatest rebels in human history. He denied the assumptions on which religion in His day was based and gave the religious quest an entirely new orientation. He refused to accept the sincerity of the Vedas or the power of the Priesthood. He refuted the illusion that human problems could be solved with sacred rituals and incarnations. He was a sworn enemy of the Caste –System on which the World structure of Indian Society rested. He was ridiculed and persecuted and several attempts were made on his life.

Dr. Ambedkar said, my final words of advice to you is "Educate, Agitate, Organize" have faith in yourself. With justice on our side, I do not see how we can lose our battle. The battle to me is a matter of joy. The battle is in the fullest sense spiritual. There is nothing material or social in it. For ours is a battle not for wealth or for power. It is a battle for freedom. It is a battle for reclamations of the human personality.

Amedkar was Bharat Ratna in the refuge of Tri- Ratna Buddha, Dhamma and Sangha. Therefore all Ambedkarites must call themselves as Buddhist and nothing else. Thus Ambedkar's whole life and mission was a practical contribution to humanistic Buddhist education in India and not just intellectual and philosophical which is common these days. Though he was not a Buddhist by birth but by practice and at heart he was a Buddhist.

BabaSaheb Ambedkar had said Tuesday July 31, 1956, at his official residence 26 Alipur Road, New Dehli at 17-50 to his Honorary Personal secretary Mr. Nanak Chand Rattu… Tell my people Nanak Chand: "Whatever I have done, I have been able to do after passing through crushing miseries and endless troubles all my life fighting with my opponents. With great difficulty, I have brought this caravan where it is seen today. Let the caravan march on and further on despite the hurdles, pitfalls and difficulties that may come in its way. If my people, my lieutenants are not able to take the caravan ahead, they should leave it where it is seen today, but in no circumstances should they allow the caravan to go back?"

The most significant development in the resurgence of Buddhism in modern India was the movement inaugurated by BabaSaheb Ambedkar, as a result of which mass conversions of Buddhism have been taking place in many parts of the country. The Neo-Buddhist is progressively gaining self-sufficiency as regards temples and shrines, monastic leadership and guidance, educational institutions and religious literature. In India, too, Buddhism is numerically the fastest growing religion.

I, for one, truly believe that individuals can make a difference in society. Since periods of great change such as the present one come so rarely in human history, it is up to the each one of us to make the best use of our time to help create a happier world for new generation to live with peace, freedom and love for mankind on planet earth. This century is the most important century of humankind said: His Holiness the Dalai Lama.

BabaSaheb Ambedkar said: The first point, which makes off Buddha from the rest, is his self-abnegation. JESUS insists that he is the Son of God. MOHAMMED went a step further. He claimed that he was the messenger of God on earth and insisted that he was the last messenger. Lord KRISHNA went a step beyond both Jesus and Mohammed. He claimed that he was "Parameshwar" – the God of Gods. BUDDHA never arrogated to himself a status. He was born a son of man and was content to remain common man and Krishna claimed for them selves a role of MOKSHADATA, Buddha was satisfied with playing the role of MARGADATA.

Buddha's Teachings are based on wisdom, morals and concentration, which are applicable not only for Buddhist nations but are of Universal application. He is the giver of path of sublime promotions and reliever from painful demotions. Hence let us all practice His teachings without hesitations walking on the path of noble truth realization and making "Nibbana" as our final destination.

The socio-cultural movement, which gradually transformed the original teaching of Buddha to popular Buddhism as practiced by millions of people, needs to be given due consideration in a study of Buddhism as religion.

"The Hindus wanted the Vedas and they sent for Vyasa, who was not a caste Hindu. The Hindus wanted an Epic and they sent for Valmiki, who was an Untouchable. The Hindus wanted a Constitution, and they sent for me."-Dr. B.R.Ambedkare.

"Law is secular, which any body may break while fraternity or religion is sacred which everybody must respect. My philosophy has a mission. I have to do the work of conversion: for I have to make the followers of Triguna theory to give it up and accept mine. Indians today governed by two different ideologies. Their political ideal set out in the preamble to the Indian Constitution affirms a life of liberty, equality and fraternity. Their social ideal embodied in their religion, denies them." Dr. B.R.Ambedkar (All-India Radio broadcast of speech on October 03, 1954)

Buddhism makes enlightenment the sole aim of life. This was the philosophy that Ambedkar accepted and tried to revive. Besides this there was another reason. Buddha, whose life and movement Ambedkar had studied, was a believer of the educatability and the creativity of the people. Under the influence of those teachings, the most rejected peoples of India has once risen and uplifted their life as well as that of the whole society. If that was once possible in India, it must be possible again. He had a solid historical basis to trust India's ordinary folk as India's future democrats.

This is what Jawaharlal Nehru wrote of the commitment of Ambedkar to the untouchables: "Dr.B.R.Ambedkar would be remembered mostly as the symbol of revolt against all the oppressing features of Hindu society. In a way he symbolized the hopes and aspiration of the oppressed and the Untouchables." Buddha was the first religious leader of the world, who expounded peace and equality in the history of man.

Five precepts (Panchsheeel) of Buddha's life are principles of building world peace the precepts Panchsheel based on Buddha's life would help to build world peace and harmony among the Nations.

Our Humanity is cultivated through our emotions. Each day we should look not only to be moved by others, But also to move them through kindness, patience and caring. Said Venerable Master Hsing Yun.

It is my hope and prayer that we will always live a happy, joyful, peaceful life based on non-violence, truth, equality, love and compassion, this great message of Buddha is relevant today.

Nishikant Waghmare, Peace Representative, The World Peace Prayer Society, USA. Director- Asia & Pacific, Airline Ambassadors International UN NGO USA.

RULES OF ADMISSION OF BUDDHIST SYSTEM

Admissions into Buddhist monasteries were based more or less on the rules and regulations observed by Gurukulas as in Vedic period. Like the students of 'Vedic' period, here also the students had to present themselves before the teacher to ask for the admission.

Like the 'Upanayan', 'Pabbaja or pravrajya' is to go out. The boys went out of their families and joined the monasteries. Everyone had the opportunity to undergo 'Pabbaja' and become a 'Buddhist' monk. After admission into 'Sangh' they could remain a monk.

They had to change the former caste, dress, character, etc. Though theoretically, all the castes were allowed to get admitted into the monastery but practically and mostly the people of higher classes were admitted there.

However, it is also true that some of the monks were derived from the lower castes. At the time of entering into the 'Sangh' the disciple must have attained the age of 8 years and during this period the new monk made his preparation for the sangh-life. Afterwards at the age of 20 years, he accepted 'Upsampada' and became full-fledged member of the 'Sangh'.

THE SYSTEM OF PABBAJA

At 8 years of age, one could go to any 'Vihar' or 'Sangh' according to his own will. With head shaved and a yellow cloth in hand he went to the principal monk and requested him for admission in 'Sangh'. He thus surrendered himself fully. The monk caused him to put the yellow clothes on and surrendered to the three words of shelter in a loud voice-

I go into the shelter of Buddha.

I seek the shelter of Dharma.

I enter the shelter of Sangh.

After taking the above three vows, one became entitled admission. No one could get admission into the 'Sangh' without consent of his parents Patients of infectious diseases like Leprosy. T B., Eczema, etc. and Government servants, slaves and soldiers were not allowed to be admitted into 'Sanghs'. However, there was no discrimination of any kind on the basis of caste or creed.

Rules for the Students

Now the admitted student was called "Samner". He had to follow the following rules:

1. Not to kill any living being.
2. Not to accept anything given to him.
3. Live free from the impurity of character.
4. Not to tell a lie.
5. Not to use any intoxicating thing.
6. Not to take any interest in music, dance, play show, etc.
7. Not to take food at improper time.
8. Not to speak ill of any body.
9. Not to use luxurious and scented things.
10. Not to accept the gifts of gold or silver, etc.

The ten rules were essentially observed by the new monk. The 'Upajsata' i.e., the teacher took all responsibilities up to the age of 20 years when he became mature and capable for accepting 'Upsampada'.

For the teacher, he was 'Sadvi Biharak'. Lord Buddha himself taught that teacher should recognise his taught (Sadvi Biharak) as his son and the taught (Sadvi Biharak) should recognise the teacher (Upajsaya) as his own father.

Upasampada

After completing the education for twelve years, the 'Monk' had to undergo the 'Upasampada' ritual at the age of 20 years and then he became the permanent member of the 'Sangh'.

Limited period, 'Upsampada' was permanent. It was for the whole life. Celibacy or chastity was considered essential for Brahmanic education. While among Hindus those observing celibacy for the whole life were; in 'Buddhistic' education it was a common feature. In this respect, Buddhistic education was more austere than Brahmanic education.

At the time of 'Pabbaja' the new monk of 8 years would go to the teacher and say with folded hands, "You are my teacher (Guru)". Thus, their relationship was established. The 'Upsampada' was performed before the entire 'Sangh'. Therefore, 'Upsampada' was given unanimously or on the decision of the majority.

Restrictions on Admission

In 'Buddhist' education also, like 'Vedic' education, the eligibility and the competence of the entrant was taken into account. A candidate could not be admitted into 'Sangh' in the following conditions:

1. Without the permission of his parents.
2. Patient of any infections or serious disease.
3. Convict of any serious moral sin.
4. Under any legal responsibility and who was not free from legal bondage.

5. Not found generous and laborious during the probation period, which sometimes were four or five days

Thus Buddhist sanghs did not intend to destroy the family system. No one was admitted into 'Sangh' without the due permission of his parents. Similarly those who wanted to get rid of their social, moral and economic obligations were not admitted.

Moreover, only those were allowed admittance who was healthy both mentally and bodily. Hence Buddhism spread rapidly and in an organised manner, in so many countries of the world.

HISTORY OF BUDDHIST EDUCATION

The history of education in Buddha period is interrelated with Story of monasteries and 'Vihars' because there were no independent educational institutions or centres, other than those religious centres. Only monks and shramanas were authorised to impart education to the people.

Thus, the monasteries and 'Vihars' took the place of sacrificial altars and as a result, these places became the centres of cultural life. Thus, the methods of these monasteries and 'Vihars' were the educational methods of that time.

Rules and regulations of Buddhist monasteries and 'Vihars' were not framed by Lord Buddha. They had been taken from Hinduism and the various sects of Sadhus and nuns so they resembled 'vedic' systems.

The teaching method introduced by the Buddha to the field of education is still highly utilized in the system of modern education. The Buddha first started his teaching career wandering from house to house, village to village and street to street. Then he founded his centers of educations in the monasteries such as Veluvanarama in Rajagaha, Jetavanarama, and Pubbarama in Savatthi. It was the starting point of monastic education in the history of education. While the Buddha was the master in all these monastic institutions, his great disciples such as Sariputta, Moggallana, Anuruddha, Maha Kaccana and so on immensely contributed to bring forth his teaching in many different ways with their unsurpassed knowledge of the Dhamma. It is evident from the canonical references that most of the analytical discourses of the canon such as Samm–üditthi, Saccavibhanga and Dhatuvibhanga were delivered by the great disciples of the Buddha. Sometimes, when the Buddha left half through his lessons, for some reason, one of his disciples came forward to complete the remaining part of the lesson. The Madhupindika sutta of Majjhima nikaya is a collaborated lesson of the Buddha and the Venerable Maha Kaccana.

There were many disciples of the Buddha who developed different skills in the fields of Dhamma due to the monastic education during the time of the Buddha. We can find canonical references to such competent monks, such as Dhamma-dharas, Vinaya-dharas, Matikadharas, Dhamma-kathikas, Vicita-bhanakas, and so on. These monks, who were competent in the different fields of the Dhamma, continued to preserve and propagate the teaching of the Buddha by way of monastic education, even after the passing away of the Buddha.

Teaching of the Dhamma became a traditional heritage of the monks. Teacher-pupil lineage of the monks has contributed much for the development of Buddhist literature in different directions. Thanks to their efforts, today we are fortunate enough to possess a wide range of Buddhist literature comprising the canon, pre-commentarial literature, commentaries, sub-commentaries, manuals etc. The history of Buddhism records a wide variety of Buddhist schools, which presented different interpretations of the teachings of the Buddha during the time in between the passing away of the Buddha and the third Buddhist Council. These Buddhist schools of the interpretation of Buddhist thought no doubt emerged from the different Buddhist educational institutes headed by the Buddhist scholars who held different views on Buddhism.

When Buddhism was introduced to Sri Lanka in the third century BC., the system of Buddhist education began to flourish on a solid ground. The Mahavihara in Anuradhapura was a center for Theravada Buddhist education after the establishment of Buddhism in Sri Lanka. It is a well-known fact that the Pali commentaries brought to Sri Lanka by Venerable Mahinda were elaborated and translated into Sinhalese language in the Mahavihara, the education center of Buddhism.

The great commentator Venerable Buddhaghosa, who went to Sri Lanka in the 5th Century AD, was reported to have studied Theriya tradition in Mah%üvih%üra. Beside Mahavihara, Abhayagiri and Jetavana were other centers of Buddhist education in ancient Sri Lanka, which conducted their own ways of Buddhist learning. Sri Lanka is still maintaining its unbroken tradition of Buddhist education. The system of pirivena education, which confined itself to Buddhist education in Srilanka, has immensely contributed not only to the development of Buddhism, Buddhist culture and Buddhist values of the people, but also to gain much fame and honour to the country.

While Buddhist education was gaining its culmination in Sri Lanka on the one hand, Buddhist scholarship of India was able to build up a golden era of Buddhist education in India on the other. History of Buddhist education records its utmost development in India during the 4th to the 12th centuries AD. When the western world was unaware of the concept of university, Indian Buddhist scholarship gave rise to six monastic universities during that period. They were known as Nalanda, Wikramasila, Odantapuri, Somapura, Jagaddala, and Wallabhi. Among these six universities, Nalanda received much more popularity among both local and foreign students. It was a light house of wisdom and learning, the first of its kind in the world. According to Hieun Tsang, a Chinese brilliant scholar monk, who studied at Nalanda, when he entered the university, there were 10,000 resident students who came from all parts of India and different foreign countries such as Tibet, China, Japan, Korea, Java, Sumatra and Sri Lanka. There were 1510 teachers and about 1500 workers. 100 lectures were delivered daily. Before it was set to fire by Muslim invaders, it was a leading university for several centuries in India.

All the six universities maintained high standards in education, administration and discipline. The course of studies of these universities included Buddhist studies pertaining to all three Buddhist traditions, comparative religion, the six systems of Hindu Philosophy and various other secular subjects such as politics, economics, law, agriculture, astrology, science, logic, medicine, fine-arts and literature.

Buddhist education aims at a personality transformation into a highest form of humanity through ethical, intellectual and spiritual perfection. These three faculties of perfection of human life undoubtedly lead a man through mundane happiness to supra mundane happiness, which is the highest achievement we all are equally looking for. Therefore, the Buddhist education is grounded on the primary psychological need of all living beings, that is to say as the Buddha pointed out "sukhakama hi satta dukkha patikkala". All living beings like happiness and they dislike unhappiness. I think Buddhism is growing so well in the West. I will use the acronym PURE to summarize four key strategies that have helped extend the spread of Buddhism:

1. Presentation – in ordinary language
2. User friendly — inviting and accessible,
3. Relevant — concerned with everyday Problems
4. Examples — monks leading by example

Presentation

If we want the wonderful Teachings of Buddhism to reach our modern generation, then it needs to be presented in a modern way. It is not the essence of the Dhamma that needs to be changed; it is the presentation that needs continual adjustment. The generations of tomorrow are not going to listen to boring monks droning on giving irrelevant sermons.

We all know that the Lord Buddha said to teach the Dhamma in ordinary language (e.g. Aranavibhanga Sutra). Let me give an example of what I think this means. Last century, Western priests and scholars dismissed Buddhism as pessimistic, saying that it only focuses on suffering. This was even repeated by

Pope John Paul II in his controversial book on world religions. To avoid this misunderstanding one may rearrange the central Dhamma Teaching of the Four Noble Truths as Happiness (Dukkhanirodho); the Cause of Happiness (the Eight-Fold Path); the Absence of Happiness (Dukkha); and the Cause for the Absence of Happiness (Craving). This shifts the focus onto happiness.

This is a simple re-packaging of the Dhamma that retains the essence while being more attractive to modern audiences. It is justified by the Lord Buddha's statement that "Nirvana is the highest happiness" (Dhammapada 203, 204). When I present the Four Noble Truths in such a way, I find all generations listen and come back for more.

User Friendly

Presenting the Dharma in ordinary language is the first step to making Buddhism user friendly. However, I have found many cases of people, in the West and in the East, who want to learn about Buddhism but are too afraid to come into the temple or monastery because they are not familiar with the traditional customs, or even because they are scared of scowling monks! When Buddhist temples are more welcoming to their visitors, and more accommodating to newcomers, when the monks are more approachable, then the temple is user friendly.

In these modern times, though, people are so busy that they rarely have time to visit the temple. So the temple should go to the people with books, audiocassettes, CDs and, of course, the Internet. Our Buddhist Society of Western Australia has a large web-site that loads weekly spoken Dharma talks in English so that anyone, anywhere in the world can listen to Dhamma in the comfort of their own homes convenient to them. This has been highly successful with a large audience of regular disciples all over the world, with no need for expensive and extravagant buildings.

Relevant

Religions like Christianity are declining in the West because they are seen as irrelevant to most people's lives. Few are concerned about abstract philosophy, rituals with no apparent meaning, or with speculations that go against reason. However, they are very concerned about how to find more happiness amid the common problems of life.

I have found it easy to explain that keeping moral precepts raises one's average level of happiness, just as a rising tide lifts the average level of the sea. The result is that many of my audience keep the Five Precepts. It is also not difficult to illustrate that kindness to your colleagues, family and to yourself, brings much more comfort into your life. So my disciples become less angry and more forgiving. There is so much medical evidence to prove that traditional Buddhist meditation practices case the stress of modern life and relieve so many other related problems. So the members of my temple are all keen meditators. These three central Buddhist trainings – morality, kindness and meditation – when framed in the context of personal growth in happiness, attract so many to Buddhism. They relate to what many people consider as important to them.

When we focus on what is relevant to ordinary people, then Buddhism becomes important to them. They might begin with interest in solving their worldly problems, but that soon leads to the Path that liberates one from all suffering.

Examples

All this means nothing to the modern generation without high quality leaders to provide the inspiration. The growth of Buddhism relies crucially on living examples of virtuous, compassionate, wise and peaceful monks. People of the 21st century are sceptical. They withhold their belief until they see some evidence that it will benefit them. Does Buddhism help? Does it really lead to virtue, compassion, contentment and freedom? They are looking at us monks for examples of where Buddhism leads, before they will follow. How can we expect to inspire the questioning modern generation when monks live in luxury, more wealthy that the common person, when we are slack in our precepts and know little of serenity? The Dhamma is spread mostly by example, much more powerfully than by any sermon. As one well-educated Australian wrote in her recent book, before becoming a Buddhist she observed the monks in Perth for many months. When she saw that they were very frugal, kept their precepts, worked hard and were very happy, only then did she go for refuge and start calling herself a Buddhist. Actions speak louder than words.

So, for example, in Western Australia we have established monasteries for training Sangha leaders of both genders, what I call a 'monk factory' and a 'nun factory' By putting many resources into training high quality Sangha leaders we will be ensuring the supply of high quality examples for the next generation.

These are some of the strategies that have worked in Australia to make Buddhism the fastest growing religion there. We do not need to change the message of the Lord Buddha, nor do we need to change the monastic rules. We may fulfil our duty to the Greatest Teacher, our Lord Buddha, and spread the delightful Dhamma throughout all parts of our modern world, by making Buddhism PURE. That is, Presented in ordinary language, User friendly, Relevant, and with us monks as the inspiring Examples.

BUDDHISM AS EDUCATION: SOUTH AND SOUTHEAST ASIAN THERAVADA BUDDHISM

Sri Lanka

At present Buddhism is flourishing in some countries and facing difficulties in others. Theravada, for example, is the strongest in Sri Lanka, Thailand and Burma (Myanmar), but seriously weakened in Laos, Cambodia (Kampuchea) and Vietnam. From the sixteenth to the nineteenth centuries Buddhism had declined in Sri Lanka due to persecution by first the Inquisition and then the missionaries of its Christian colonial rulers. It was revived in the late nineteenth century with the help of British scholars and theosophists. As a result, Sri Lankan Buddhism is sometimes characterized as "Protestant" Buddhism, with the emphasis on scholarly study, pastoral activities by monks for the lay community and direct meditation practice for laypeople, not just for those with robes. The lay householder community has great faith, but sometimes complain of the scarcity of monks with a balance of study and practice.

Indonesia and Malaysia

Sri Lankan monks have been helping revive Theravada Buddhism in Bali, other parts of Indonesia, and Malaysia, where it had slowly died out by the end of the fifteenth century. This is on an extremely limited scale. Those showing interest in Bali are the followers of the traditional Balinese mixture of Hinduism, Buddhism and the local spirit religion, while in other parts of Indonesia and Malaysia, the audience is the overseas ChineseMahayana Buddhist community. There are also some very small new Indonesian Buddhist sects that are hybrids of Theravada, Chinese and Tibetan aspects.

According to the Indonesian government's "panchashila" policy, all religions must assert belief in God. Although Buddhism does not assert God as an individual being and is therefore sometimes characterized as atheistic, it is officially recognized because of its assertion of Adibuddha. This is, literally, the "First Buddha," and is discussed in *The Kalachakra Tantra*, which had flourished in Indonesia a millennium ago. Adibuddha is the omniscient creator of all appearances, beyond time, words and other limitations. Although represented by a symbolic figure, he is not actually a being himself. Adibuddha is more abstract and is found in all beings as the clear light nature of the mind. On this basis Buddhism is accepted, along with Islam, Hinduism and the Catholic and Protestant forms of Christianity, as the five state religions of Indonesia.

India

Buddhism slowly faded in the sub-Himalayan regions of India by about the seventeenth century. At the end of the nineteenth century, however, the Sri Lankans with the help of British scholars founded the Maha Bodhi Society for the purpose of restoring the holy Buddhist pilgrimage sites in India. They have been very successful and now have temples with monks at each of these sites, as do several other Buddhist traditions.

In the 1950s, Ambedkar started a neo-Buddhist movement among untouchables in western India. Hundreds of thousands have joined, mostly to avoid the stigma of belonging to the lowest caste. The emphasis is on gaining political and social rights for themselves. Ambedkar died shortly after founding this revival. Since then it has been headed by Sangharakshita, an Englishman who founded the Friends of the Western Buddhist Order as a new form of Buddhism especially designed for Western practitioners.

Thailand

In Thailand, influenced by the model of the Thai monarchy, the Buddhist monastic community has a Supreme Patriarch and a Council of Elders with responsibility for keeping the purity of the tradition. There are two types of monastic communities, those who dwell in the forests and those who live in the villages. Both are objects of great veneration and support by the lay community. The strong forest tradition of mendicant monks lives in isolated jungles and engages in intense meditation. It follows strict adherence to the monastic rules of discipline, which forms the focus of its study program. Village monks perform numerous ceremonies for the welfare of the local people. Their study, however, consists primarily of memorizing texts. In keeping with the Thai cultural belief in spirits, these monks also provide amulets to the laypeople for protection. There is a Buddhist university for monks, primarily for training monastics to translate the Buddhist scriptures from classical Pali into modern Thai.

Myanmar (Burma)

In Myanmar (Burma), the military regime has taken strict control of Buddhism under its Ministry of Religion. It has brutally destroyed the monasteries where dissidents had been living, particularly in the north of the country. Now the government is giving great sums of money to the rest of the monks in an effort to win their support and silence any criticism.

Burma has a long tradition of a balanced, equal emphasis on meditation and study, particularly of the "abhidharma" system of Buddhist psychology, metaphysics and ethics. Many monasteries having this approach are still open, and the lay population maintains great faith. Since the late nineteenth century, perhaps influenced by the British colonial occupation, there are many meditation centers where monk and lay teachers instruct Burmese laymen and laywomen in basic meditational practices to develop mindfulness.

Bangladesh

In southern Bangladesh, in the hills along the Burmese border, there are many isolated villages traditionally following the Burmese Buddhist tradition. Cut off from Burma, however, their level of understanding and practice is quite low.

Laos

In Laos, Buddhism is still taught and practiced in a rural setting in the traditional manner, but the monasteries are in poorcondition due to the American-Vietnam War. The lay Laotians still offer food to the monks on their alms rounds and go to the temples on full moon days. The meditation tradition, however, is extremely weak. Previously, the monks had to learn and teach Marxism, but now do not. People today need only pay lip service to communism and it is easier to become a monk.

Kampuchea (Cambodia)

In Kampuchea (Cambodia), Buddhism is being revived after Pol Pot's destruction and persecution, and especially with Prince Sihanouk as king, the restrictions are being slowly relaxed. Still, however, one must be over 30 or 40 to ordain, since the country needs the manpower. The head Khmer monk, Maha Ghosananda, studied meditation in Thailand, since it was mostly lost in Cambodia, and is trying to revive its practice there. Whatever forest tradition was left in the country was more concerned with gaining special powers rather than meditation.

Vietnam

Although there never was an equivalent of the Cultural Revolution in Vietnam, Buddhism is still considered the enemy of the state there, with monks continuing to challenge state authority and control. It is very difficult to ordain and many monks are still put in jail. Only token monasteries are open, mostly for propaganda purposes. The regime is more relaxed with the monks in the north, where the monastic institutions had coexisted with the communists during the Vietnam War. The regime is much more suspicious and hard on the monks in the south.

EAST ASIAN MAHAYANA BUDDHISM

Taiwan, Hong Kong, and Overseas Chinese Areas

The East Asian Mahayana Buddhist traditions deriving from China are the strongest in Taiwan, Hong Kong and South Korea. Taiwan has a strong monastic community of monks and nuns very generously supported by the lay community. There are Buddhist universities and Buddhist programs for social welfare. Hong Kong also has a flourishing monastic community. The emphasis among the overseas Chinese Buddhist communities in Malaysia, Singapore, Indonesia, Thailand and the Philippines is on ceremonies for the welfare of ancestors, and for prosperity and wealth for the living. There are many mediums through whom Buddhist oracles speak in trance and whom the lay community consults for health and psychological problems. Chinese businessmen who are the main driving force behind these "Asian tiger" economies frequently make generous donations to the monks to perform rituals for their financial success.

Korea

Buddhism in South Korea is still strong, although facing a growing challenge from Evangelic Christian movements. There are many monastic communities of monks and nuns with much popular support. The meditational tradition is particularly flourishing, especially of Son, the Korean form of Zen. In North

Korea, on the other hand, except for a token monastery open for propaganda purposes, Buddhism is severely repressed.

Japan

Japan has many temples beautifully kept for tourists and visitors, but many are commercialized. Although there are some serious practitioners, for the most part the traditions are extremely formalized and weak. From the thirteenth century, the Japanese have had a tradition of married temple priests with no prohibition against drinking alcohol. Such priests gradually replaced the tradition of celibate monks. Most Japanese follow a combination of Buddhism and the traditional Japanese Shinto spirit religion. They have priests perform Shinto customs and ceremonies for births and marriages, and Buddhist ones for funerals, with little understanding of either. There are some moves to adopt Buddhist methods for relieving work pressure in large companies, and one large Japanese Buddhist sect has an extensive program building Peace Pagodas around the world. There are also a number of fanatic doomsday cults that call themselves Buddhist, but in fact have little to do with BuddhaShakyamuni's teachings. Historically, some of the Japanese Buddhist traditions have been extremely nationalistic, based on belief in Japan as a Buddhist paradise. This derives from the Shinto cult of the emperor and the importance of belonging to the Japanese nation. Such traditions have given rise to Buddhist political parties that are extremely nationalistic and fundamentalist in flavor.

People's Republic of China

In Inner China, namely the Han Chinese areas of the People's Republic, the majority of Buddhist monasteries were destroyed and most of the well-trained monks, nuns and teachers were executed or imprisoned during the Cultural Revolution in the 1960s and 1970s. This was not to the same huge extent, however, as in the non-Han regions, namely Tibet, Inner Mongolia and Xinjiang. Today, a large number of Han Chinese of all ages in Inner China are interested in Buddhism, but the main problem is the lack of teachers. Many young people are receiving monastic ordination, but their quality is low. Most college-educated youth prefer to work and make money, while those who join monasteries are mostly from poor and/or uneducated families, primarily from the countryside. There are only a few qualified elderly monks and nuns left who survived the communist persecution and can teach, and no one of middle age with any training. There are government Buddhist colleges with two to four-year programs in many major Inner Chinese cities and pilgrimage sites, with political education as part of their curriculum. Relatively few of the newly-ordained Han Chinese attend them.

In general, the level of Buddhist education is extremely low in the Han Chinese monasteries. People are focusing primarily on the physical reconstruction of Buddhism at the moment – temples, pagodas, statues and so forth – and this requires putting time and effort into raising money and building. In some cases, the Chinese government is helping to finance the reconstruction. As a result, many Buddhist temples are now open as museums or tourist attractions, with the monastics being the ticket collectors and temple attendants. This allows for a veneer of "religious freedom," an image much sought by the Beijing government. Most reconstruction, however, is being financed by the local people, sometimes with foreign benefactors, and often by the monastics themselves. Some traditional ancestor-worship practices done in temples before the communist persecution are now being revived. There are, however, a few Chinese monasteries in various parts of Inner China that are active and have some level of study and practice.

CENTRAL ASIAN MAHAYANA BUDDHISM

Tibetans in Exile

Among the Tibetan traditions of Central Asia, the strongest is with the Tibetan refugee community around His Holiness the Dalai Lama in exile in India since the 1959 popular uprising against the Chinese military occupation of Tibet. They have restarted most of the major monasteries and several of the nunneries of Tibet, and have the traditional full training program for monk scholars, master meditators and teachers. There are educational, research and publication facilities to preserve all aspects of each of the schools of the Tibetan Buddhist tradition.

The Tibetans in exile have helped revitalize Buddhism in the Himalayan regions of India, Nepal and Bhutan, including Ladakh and Sikkim by sending teachers and retransmitting the lineages. Many monks and nuns from these regions are receiving their education and training in the Tibetan refugee monasteries and nunneries.

Nepal

Although the Tibetan tradition of Buddhism is followed among the Sherpa people of eastern Nepal and among the Tibetan refugees in the central part of the country, the traditional form of Nepalese Buddhism still exists on a limited level among the Newari people of the Kathmandu Valley. Following a blend of the late Indian form of Mahayana and Hinduism, they are the only Buddhist society that keeps caste distinctions within the monasteries. Since the sixteenth century, the monks are allowed to marry and there is a hereditary caste among them of keepers of the temples and leaders of rituals. Those who perform these functions must come from these castes.

Tibet

The situation of Buddhism in Tibet itself, which the People's Republic of China has divided among the five provinces of Tibet, Qinghai, Gansu, Sichuan and Yunnan, is still very grim. Of 6500 monasteries and nunneries before 1959, all but 150 were destroyed, mostly before the Cultural Revolution. The vast majority of learned monastics were either executed or died in concentration camps, and most monastics in general were forced to disrobe. Starting in 1979, the Chinese have allowed the Tibetans to reconstruct their monasteries, and much has already been rebuilt. The Chinese government has helped with two or three of them, but the vast majority has been through the efforts and finance of the former monks, the local populace and Tibetans in exile abroad. Thousands of young people have become monks and nuns, but the Chinese government is now imposing severe limitations and restrictions once more. Many police and government spies are disguised as monks and keep a close check in the monasteries. Monks and nuns have often led protests against the Chinese policies of suppression of human rights, demanding true autonomy and freedom of religion.

The Chinese communist authorities effort to control Buddhism in Tibet has surfaced most prominently with respect to the finding of the reincarnation of the Panchen Lama. The first Panchen Lama, living in the seventeenth century, was the tutor of the Fifth Dalai Lama and is considered the second highest spiritual leader among the Tibetans after the Dalai Lama. Upon the death of a Dalai Lama or Panchen Lama, the successor is chosen as a small child recognized as the reincarnation of his predecessor. The child is found upon consultation with oracles and thoroughly tested for accurate memories of people and objects from his former life.

Although the Dalai Lamas, since the time of the Fifth, have been both the spiritual and temporal heads of Tibet, the Panchen Lamas have never held a political position. Since the early twentieth century, however, the Chinese have tried unsuccessfully to split the Tibetans by supporting the Panchen Lama as a political rival to the Dalai Lama.

The Manchus, a non-Han Chinese people of northeast Asia, ruled China from the mid-seventeenth to the early twentieth century. They tried to win the allegiance of the Mongolian and Tibetan people within the sphere of influence of their empire by outwardly supporting Tibetan Buddhism, while always trying to manipulate and control its institutions and change its center of gravity from Lhasa to Beijing. In the mid-eighteenth century they declared that only the Manchu emperor had the authority to choose and recognize the reincarnations of the Dalai Lamas and Panchen Lamas through a system of drawing lots from a golden urn. The Tibetans ignored their claim; the choice of Panchen Lamas was always confirmed by the Dalai Lamas.

The Chinese communist government is avowedly atheistic, supposedly does not interfere in religious matters and has totally denounced all policies of the previous imperial dynasties that have ruled China. Yet in 1995 it proclaimed itself the legitimate heir of the Manchu emperors in having the authority to find and recognize the reincarnation of the Tenth Panchen Lama who had passed away in 1989. This was shortly after the abbot of the Panchen Lama's monastery located the reincarnation and the Dalai Lama officially gave his recognition to the boy. Subsequently, the boy and his family have been taken to Beijing and not been heard from since, the abbot has been imprisoned, and the Panchen Lama's monastery put under strict communist control. The Chinese authorities then ordered all high Lama teachers to gather at a ceremony in which they chose their own Panchen Lama reincarnate. Subsequently, the President of China has met with the six-year old boy and instructed him to be loyal to the Chinese communist party.

In addition to Chinese government interference, the main problem facing Buddhists in Tibet is a lack of qualified teachers. Only a handful of the old masters have survived the communist persecution and the few teachers available have received only two or a maximum of four years of training in a very limited curriculum at government Buddhist colleges established through the efforts of the late Panchen Lama. Although in general there is more study than in Inner China, many of the monasteries in Tibet are open as tourist attractions and the monks must work as ticket collectors and temple attendants. The lay population in general has very strong faith, but a large portion of the youth are being demoralized by the lack of employment due to the huge population transfer of Han Chinese and the ever-increasingsupply from Inner China of cheap alcohol, heroin, pornography and pool tables for gambling.

East Turkistan (Xinjiang)

Most of the monasteries of the Kalmyk Mongols living in East Turkistan (Xinjiang) were destroyed during the Cultural Revolution. Several have now been rebuilt, but there is an even more severe shortage of teachers than in Tibet. New young monks have become very discouraged by the lack of study facilities and many have left.

Inner Mongolia

The worst situation for Tibetan Buddhists under the control of the People's Republic of China, however, is in Inner Mongolia. Most of the monasteries in the western half were destroyed during the Cultural Revolution. In the eastern half, which was formerly part of Manchuria, many had already been destroyed by Stalin's troops at the end of the Second World War when the Russians helped liberate North China from the Japanese. The Cultural Revolution merely finished the devastation. Of 700 monasteries formerly in Inner Mongolia, only 27 are left. Unlike in Tibet and Xinjiang, however, there has been almost no effort to reconstruct them. There has been such a huge influx of Han Chinese settlers and intermarriage that much of the local Mongolian population, particularly in the cities, has little interest in their language, traditional culture or Buddhist religion. A few monasteries are open as tourist attractions and there are a handful of young monks, but they receive almost no training. In extremely remote areas of the Gobi desert, one or two monasteries are left with monks still performing the traditional rituals. But none are younger than seventy years of age. Unlike in the Tibetan regions where the grasslands are rich and the nomads have the resources to support rebuilding the monasteries and feeding new monks, the Inner Mongolian nomads of the Gobi who still have faith are extremely poor.

Mongolia

In Mongolia itself (Outer Mongolia) there had been thousands of monasteries. All were either partially or totally destroyed in 1937 under the orders of Stalin. In 1946, one monastery was re-opened in the capital, Ulaan Baatar, as a token symbol, and in the early 1970s a five-year training college for monks was begun there. It had a very abbreviated curriculum with a heavy emphasis on Marxist study. The monks were allowed to perform a limited number of rituals for the public who were carefully questioned by the government authorities.

With the downfall of communism in 1990, there has been a strong revival of Buddhism with the help of the Tibetans in exile in India. Many new monks are sent to India for training and 150 monasteries have been either re-opened or rebuilt on a modest scale, with several teachers coming from the Tibetans in India. Unlike in Tibet where the old disrobed monks have not rejoined the monasteries, only worked to rebuild and support them, many old monks in Mongolia have rejoined. Since most have not abandoned living at home with their wives at night and drinking vodka, there is a major problem concerning the monks' rules of discipline.

The most serious problem facing Buddhism in Mongolia today, however, is the aggressive American Mormon and Baptist Christian missionaries. Coming initially to teach English, they offer money and aid for people's children to study in America if they convert. They pass out beautifully printed, free booklets on Jesus in the colloquial Mongol language and show films. The Buddhists cannot compete. There are no books on Buddhism yet in the colloquial language, only classical, hardly anyone who could make such translations, and no money to print such books even if they were made. So young people and intellectuals are being drawn away from Buddhism to Christianity.

Russia

There are three traditional Tibetan Buddhist regions in Russia: Buryatia in Siberia near Lake Baikal, Tuva also in Siberia north of western Mongolia and Kalmykia to the northwest of the Caspian Sea. The Buryats and Kalmyks are Mongols, while the Tuvinians are Turkic. All the monasteries in each of these areas, except for three only damaged in Buryatia, were totally destroyed by Stalin in the late 1930s. In the late 1940s Stalin re-opened two token monasteries in Buryatia under strict KGB surveillance. Disrobed monks put their robes back on as uniforms during the day and performed some rituals. Several went for studies to the training college in Mongolia. After the fall of communism in 1990, there has been a large revival of Buddhism in all three regions. The Tibetans in exile have sent teachers, and new young monks are training in the

Tibetan monasteries in India. There are now seventeen monasteries reestablished in Buryatia. As in Mongolia, there is a problem of alcohol and the monastics who were former monks having wives. But unlike Mongolia these monastics do not claim to be celibate monks. There are plans under way to open monasteries in Kalmykia and Tuva. Christian missionaries are active in the three regions, but not as strong as in Mongolia.

There is also a great deal of interest in Tibetan Buddhism among Asians of other Buddhist traditions. Many Tibetan masters are invited from the community in exile in India to teach in Southeast Asia, Taiwan, Hong Kong, Japan and Korea. People find the clear explanations of Buddha's teachings found in the Tibetan tradition a useful supplement for understanding their own traditions. People are also attracted to the elaborate Tibetan rituals for prosperity and health.

Non Traditionally Buddhist Countries

All forms of Buddhism are also found throughout the world in nontraditionally Buddhist countries. There are two major groups involved: Asian immigrants and non-Asian practitioners. Asian immigrants, particularly in the United States and Australia, have many ethnic temples. This is also the case on a smaller scale in Canada, Brazil, Peru and several Western European countries particularly France. The main emphasis is on devotional practice and providing a community center to help the immigrant communities maintain their individual cultural and national identities.

Buddhist "Dharma centers" of all traditions are now found in more than eighty countries around the world on every continent. These are mostly frequented by non-Asians and emphasize meditation, study and the practice of rituals. The vast proportions of these centers are from the Tibetan, Zen and Theravada traditions. The teachers at these centers include both Westerners as well as ethnic Buddhists from Asia. The largest number are found in the United States, France and Germany. Serious students often visit Asia for deeper training. Furthermore, there are Buddhist study programs in numerous universities throughout the world and an ever-growing dialogue and exchange of ideas between Buddhism and other religions, science, psychology and medicine. His Holiness the Dalai Lama has played a most significant role in this respect.

The Art of Living

An important rule for a happy life is the ability to live harmoniously with other people. To be able to do that, we must recognise that there are many paths that people can take to reach the same goal. Therefore, we must not get unduly upset if other people practise customs or have opinions which are different from ours.

Manners and Customs

The standards of good manners differ among societies. In some countries, guests at dinner are expected to eat as noisily as possible. It is also not considered impolite if the guests belch at the end of the meal, since this indicates that they really enjoyed the meal. Such table manners would be considered rude, ill-mannered or uncivilised in other societies.

While in one country, putting one's finger in one's mouth or nose for any reason is considered most insulting, it means nothing in some other countries. Some people think it is degrading to be struck by a shoe, yet among other people, a slipper can be used for spanking a child.

We discover the peculiarities of the manners and customs prevailing in other societies most acutely when travelling. We should not prejudge too quickly what is right or improper. In themselves, manners are neither good nor bad. But when they cause harm or hurt the feelings of others, then we judge an action as being good or bad manners.

We are living in an ever changing world. We should not cling blindly to the traditions, customs, manners and rituals practised by our forefathers or ancestors who adopted these practices according to their beliefs and understanding capacity. Some customs or traditions handed down by our ancestors may be good, while others are less useful. We should consider with an open mind whether these practices are congenial and significant to the modern world.

In the Kalama sutta, the Buddha has given this advice about customs, traditions, beliefs and practices: "When you know for yourself that certain things are unwholesome (akusala) and wrong and bad for you and others, then give them up... And when you know for yourself that certain things are wholesome (kusala) and good for you and others, then accept them and follow them."

Today, some elderly people cannot tolerate the modern ideas and ways of living of the younger generation. They expect their children to follow the same age-old traditions of their forefathers. Instead of adopting such an attitude, they should allow the children to move with the times when the activities are harmless. Elders should call to mind how their own parents objected to certain popular modes of behaviour prevalent at the time when they were young. These differences in perception between the conservative parents and the younger generation are common sources of conflict within families. It does not mean that parents should hesitate to counsel and guide their children if they have gone astray due to some erroneous values. But when correcting them, it is good to remember that prevention is better than punishment. Parents should also explain to their children why certain practices are wrong, because children are not mature enough to reason why certain things are bad and certain things are good.

Allowing others the Right to Differ

If a person lives all by himself, then he will not have any problem with differing opinions. But if he has chosen to live in society, he must learn to deal with views and opinions of others even though they do not conform with his.

We are also living in a world where, apparently, might is right. The strong take advantage of the weak and the rich exploit the poor. If we cannot agree, we have to learn at least to agree to disagree. We should express our views gently and politely without trying to impose views on others by force.

Those who use physical force to overcome their opponents clearly show their inability to convince the opponents that they are right.

We find comfort in those who agree with us, but discomfort in those who disagree. Sometimes, others' opinions on our attitudes or actions may not be something we would like to hear.

But if we listen to them carefully, we will realise that there may be some truth in their opinions. This can give us a chance to improve ourselves if we are prepared to change our ways. The world is like a garden with different kinds of flowers. Like a bee gathering honey in the garden, we should be selective in choosing what is good in an opinion and leave behind what is not.

Patience and Tolerance

Those who can remain cheerful during difficult times are admirable and a source of inspiration to others. They can avoid conflicts by seeing the lighter side of things.

A wise man can avoid a quarrel by answering jokes and remarks directed at him with another joke. When you play a game, you should not show your temper when you lose. By doing so, you not only spoil the fun of the game, you may lose the game completely.

Every person is responsible for making a better world by planting the seeds of patience, love and honesty deeply in the human heart.

Eventually, a new era will blossom not only during his lifetime but also for generations to come. He would be a cultured man who left the world better than when he came into it.

Some may say that this is impractical and too idealistic to follow. Some are cynical and wonder if man who is struggling to eke out a living in a hostile world can cultivate love and kindness. While this is by no means easy to accomplish, perseverance and determination can make this concept become a reality.

Diplomacy

You cannot hope to achieve peace by correcting each and every person in this world. In the same way, you cannot remove the world of stones and thorns to ensure the pathway is smooth. To feel comfortable walking on uneven ground, we should learn to guard our senses and to have peace of mind since we cannot succeed in removing disturbing objects from the world.

There are many ways to correct a person if he is wrong. By criticising, blaming and shouting at him publicly, you will not be able to correct him. You only make him more adamant in his views. Correct him without humiliating him. This is by far the most common way to avoid making more enemies. If you kindly point out his mistakes, he is more likely to listen to you, and some say he will thank you for your guidance and kindness.

Whenever you express your views regarding certain matters, avoid harsh words spoken with anger so as not to hurt the feeling of others. Always express your views gently and politely. On the other hand, you should not lose your temper or show your sulky face when your faults are pointed out. You may think that by raising your temper, showing an ugly face, and shouting at others, you can intimidate others into overlooking your shortcomings. This is a false and wrong attitude to adopt. Rudeness, yelling, anger and swearing are a weak man's imitation of strength.

The historical Buddha Shakyamuni was born around 560 B.C.E. to a royal family. From early childhood, he was surrounded by wealth and beauty, and enjoyed a sophisticated education. The texts describe him as tall, strong, and blue-eyed. When he was 29 years old, he left the palace for the first time and encountered an old person, a sick person, and a dead person, experiences he had never known before. He then realized that nothing was permanent and left his palace to meditate in the mountains and forests of Northern India. After a six-year search for lasting meaning, he recognized the nature of mind while in deep meditation and reached enlightenment in what is Bodh Gaya in Northern India today.

The Buddha's teachings, which make beings fearless, joyful, and kind, are the main religion in several East Asian countries. Since the early seventies, the profound Buddhist view with its vast number of methods has inspired and fascinated a growing number of people in Western cultures.

Buddha teaches about ultimate and conditioned existence in a way that makes Buddhism directly relevant to our daily lives. Understanding this makes the experience of lasting happiness possible. Buddhism does not proclaim dogmas; rather, it encourages critical questioning. Using the right meditations, the intellectual understanding of the teachings becomes a personal experience. Additional methods solidify what is reached in meditation. The goal of Buddha's teachings is the full development of the innate potential of body, speech, and mind. Through his teachings, Buddha is seen as a timeless mirror of mind's inherent potential.

Liberation and Enlightenment

In the process of becoming liberated, one first discovers that body, thoughts, and feelings are in a constant state of change. Therefore, there is no basis for a real existing ego or "self." Realizing this, one no longer feels like a target and stops taking suffering personally. Enlightenment is the second and ultimate step. Here, the clear light of mind radiates through every experience. In every moment, mind enjoys its self-arisen abilities and everything becomes spontaneous and effortless.

Cause and Effect – Karma

Karma means cause and effect. It does not mean fate. The understanding that each of us is responsible for our own lives makes it possible to generate positive impressions consciously. This brings happiness and helps us to avoid the causes of future suffering. Positive states of mind may be strengthened effectively through the methods of the Diamond Way, while negative impressions waiting to mature can be transformed into wisdom.

REFERENCES:

1. Agocs, T.: A Vision of Buddhist Education from Central Europe, A Paper presented at the 1st International Conference of Buddhist Universities in Bangkok, 27 May 2007.
2. Brady, R.: Realizing True Education With Mindfulness, pp.77-97 in: Prof. Le Mahn That and Ven. Thich Nhat Tu (editors): Buddhist Education: Continuity and Progress, Culture and Information Press, Hanoi, 2008.
3. Kassabian, A.: Mindfulness Meditation: Calming Classrooms One Breath at a Time, pp. 127-158 in: Prof. Le Mahn That and Ven. Thich Nhat Tu (editors): Buddhist Education: Continuity and Progress, Culture and Information Press, Hanoi, 2008.
4. Waldron, W.: Modern Education as Foundation of Buddhist Modernity, pp. 239-252 in: Prof. Le Mahn That and Ven. Thich Nhat Tu (editors): Buddhist Education: Continuity and Progress, Culture and Information Press, Hanoi, 2008.
5. Dr. B. R. Ambedkar - -"Buddha and His Dhamma" Siddhartha Publication Mumbai, 1957.
6. Dr. B.R. Ambedkar - - "Annihilation of Caste"
7. Dr.B.R. Ambedkar - - "Writing and Speeches" The Education Department, Government of Maharashtra, Mumbai 1987.
8. Mr.Bhagwan Das- "Buddhism in India" Dalit Liberation Today, June 1997, New Delhi.
9. H.H. Dalai Lama - - "A Human Approach to World Peace."
10. H.H. Dalai Lama — "Compassion and the Individual"
11. Dhananjay Keer - -"Dr. Ambedkar's Life and Mission" Popular Prakashan, Mumbai, 1971, "Revival of Buddhism"
12. Dr. Prof. Ananda W.P. Guruge - - "What In Brief Is Buddhism" Published by Mitram Books, A Subsidiary

of, Dhamma Healing Way. Inc. Monterey Park, CA. USA, 1999.

13. W.J. Basil Fernando - - " Demoralization and Hope" A Comparative study of the Ideas of N.E.S. Grungtvig of Denmark and B.R. Ambedkar of India, A Publication of Asian Human Rights Commission, Hong Kong, 2000.
14. Venerable Narada Mahathera - - "The Buddha and His Teachings" Buddhist Missionary society, Kuala Lumpur, 1988, "Is Buddhism A Religion"
15. Venerable Dr. K. Sri Dhammananda - - Ven. Narada Mahathera, Dr. G.P. Maklalasekera "Gems of Buddhist Wisdom" The Buddhist Missionary society, Kuala Lumpur.
16. S. Krishna (Anand) –"The Buddha the Essence of Dhamma and its Practice" Publication By, Samrudh Bharat Publication, Mumbai, August 2002
17. The Times of India — "100 Indians who made a difference this Century" Monday, December 6, 1999. Mumbai.
18. Venerable Bhikkhu Vinayarakkhita, Dharmayatana, Maharagama, Sri Lanka.
19. Dr. BabaSaheb Ambedkar... "The Man who made all the difference."

3

The Value of Buddhism

(The Faith of the Future)

"To set aside each sin of old,

To leave no noble deed undone,

To cleanse the heart:—in these behold

The teaching of the Awakened One!"

In order to accurately estimate the value to Humanity of any particular religious system, it is necessary at the outset to assume the critical attitude of mind, and to judge it, not by its own claims to be regarded as the only Truth, not by its promises or threats concerning the Hereafter, not even by selections from its Sacred Books—for herein much depends upon the selector's views—but by the effect it has had in the past on the lives of its adherents and by the extent to which its adoption would meet the needs of modern progress and of modern thought. The questions which must be considered in this relation are these:—to what extent has the Religion we are discussing served to promote human solidarity in the past; to what extent has it tended to overcome the evil passions, the blind prejudices and the innate savagery of mankind, and brought peace and happiness on earth; to what extent is it capable of rendering practical answer to the great problems of our latter age?

If these tests are applied to the Buddhist Religion we believe that it will be found that, alike in its civilising value in the past, as revealed by the history of two thousand five hundred years, and in its possibilities for promoting peace, progress and the general happiness of the modern world in the future; Buddhism stands unrivalled, nay, unapproached, amongst the great Religions of to-day. But before proceeding to the discussion of these questions, it will be necessary to first point out some few widespread misconceptions regarding the nature of Buddhism, for it is only after the removal of these misconceptions that a fair judgment concerning this much misunderstood Religion can be arrived at. These misconceptions may be summed up as follows:—Firstly, that Buddhism is a 'heathen' doctrine, whose adherents worship idols and pray to stone and wood; Secondly, that it is a mysterious sort of affair, connected with miracle-mongering and 'esotericism'; and, Thirdly, that it is a backboneless, apathetic, pessimistic manner of philosophy, with annihilation as its goal and aim, tending to the subversion of all useful activities, well enough for 'the dreamy peoples of the Orient,'—as those who know them least delight in calling them,—but totally unsuited to the more active and energetic nations of the West.

The reason of the first of these misconceptions is very simple. Travellers from Western Lands come to Eastern Countries, and visiting Buddhist Temples, they see there images of the Buddha, they see the shrine before the image thronged betimes with kneeling and adoring crowds, murmuring sentences in an unknown language, offering lights and flowers before the Master's shrine. And they at once jump at conclusions. These people, think they, are idolators, these images of the Buddha are their god, the murmured words their prayers to their divinity, these flowers and scents and lights, offerings they think acceptable to the thing of stone or wood before which they bow. The facts are true,—but nothing could be further from the truth than these deductions. For, in the first place, Buddhists do not believe in any God (in the Occidental acceptation of a Supreme Being who can hear and answer prayers) at all; the images before which they kneel are representations only of One whom, for His love for all mankind, and because He found the Way to Peace, they worship in gratitude:—a man, long since passed 'into that utter passing away which leaves nothing whatever behind'. They are not praying—seeing that in their conception there is no one to pray to, Buddhists do not pray at all;—and the offerings they make are but a symbol of their reverence for the Great Teacher, and a means of concentrating their minds on the meaning and the truth of the words they are saying. Just as we love to see the portrait of one dear to us when death or distance has deprived us of their presence, so do Buddhists love to have before them the representation of the Master; because, more than aught else in the world, this representation brings them to think upon the incomparable Life He lived, the love He had, the Law He taught—and that is all. The words they say are meditations, and not prayers:—Buddhists think that the more they contemplate the life of the Master, the Truth He taught, the Order of those who are striving to obey His precepts to the uttermost ; the better, the truer, the nobler will their own minds become—and that is their great ideal in life. And so they recite to themselves the Virtues of the Master, His Law, and His Order,—knowing that thinking of things holy always exalts and elevates the mind—hoping thus to bring a little of those virtues to manifest in their own lives. The things they offer as they kneel are object-lessons in the Truth that they are trying to realise, and, offering, they are murmuring, not prayer, but meditation on the lesson that those oblations teach. One of these meditations—that used in the Offering of Flowers—we will give, that our readers may gain an idea of the thoughts in the minds of these kneeling crowds:—

"These flowers I offer in memory of Him the Lord, the Holy One, the Supremely-enlightened Buddha, even as the Enlightened Ones in ages past, the Saints and Holy of all times have offered. Now are these flowers fair of form, glorious in colour, sweet of scent. Yet soon will all have passed away—withered this fair form, faded the bright hues, and foul the flowers' scent Thus even is it with all component things:—Impermanent, and full of Sorrow and Unreal :—Realising this may we attain unto that Peace which is beyond all life!"

Believing, as he does, in the universal dominance of the Law of Righteousness, it would indeed seem to the Buddhist to be not merely futile, but even wrong to 'pray' for this or that:—he realises that his circumstances are the outcome of certain Laws, and would no more think of praying to these than a physicist would pray to gravitation not to act upon a stone.

The second misapprehension—that Buddhism is a Religion of the mysterious and of the occult,—had its rise in the fact that the Western world Þrst came in contact with this Religion through translations from the voluminous Sanskrit works which sprang into existence during the period of the decadence of Buddhism in India—when the animistic superstitions of the people were recrudescing on every hand:—a period about eight hundred to a thousand or more years after the Great Decease of the Founder of Buddhism.

These works consist in part of translations from the original Pâli Scriptures and chiefly of original works foisted on the Buddha or His great Disciples, but shewing clearly, both by their style and matter, that they could not possibly have sprung from the same source as the Pâli Scriptures. Later on, these latter were discovered by Europeans in Burma, Ceylon and Siam; and as in many essential features the Pâli and Sanskrit works are widely different, it became a problem to ascertain which were the original and authentic Teachings of the Buddha. Historical criticism, in the hands of Dr. Rhys Davids and other eminent scholars, has now laid this problem at rest for ever:—it has been shewn that the Pâli Scriptures are the representatives of the earlier and original teachings, and that the later Sanskrit works bear about the same relation to these as the Latin monkish works of the Middle Ages might do to the Christianity of Christ.2 We shall hope in a future issue to be able to lay before our readers the collected evidence for this conclusion, from the pen of one most competent to deal with the matter; as this evidence has, so far as our knowledge goes, been nowhere collected together yet, but is scattered through many various works. One another thing has tended to enhance the conception of Buddhism as a mystic Religion, namely, the fact that the founders of a widely-spread mystical movement called Theosophy used—and some of their followers still use,—many Buddhist technical terms in their works;—one of the earlier of these, indeed, being termed 'Esoteric Buddhism'; and containing as one of its fundamental teachings that very doctrine of the existence of an immortal soul (Sansk. Âtman) in man which the Buddha so constantly denied.

In the early days of the Theosophical movement, when the real Buddhist Scriptures were accessible only to a few scholars of Pâli it was a very natural mistake; but it has had the unfortunate effect of widely spreading the belief that Buddhism is concerned with those very animistic conceptions which it alone, amongst the Religions of the world, had utterly rejected. To represent the Buddha as having taught the existence of the Âtman in man, as is done in many of these Theosophical works, in face of the fact that in almost every division of the voluminous Scriptures of Buddhism the opposite doctrine is inculcated with unwearying reiteration, is about on a par with an endeavour to represent the Founder of Christianity as maintaining the nonexistence of a Father in Heaven,—when in the Christian Scriptures scarcely an utterance of the Christ is recorded which does not contain the assertion of that Father's existence. And, just as devoted Christians would be inexpressibly shocked were anyone to write of their Master as having taught the non-existence of the Heavenly Father—in defiance of the Christian Scriptures themselves,—so are we Buddhists filled with grief when we find attributed to our Master that very doctrine which He again and again denounced as the chief stumbling-block to the Religious Life;—as the first of the Fetters of the Mind which must be cast off before a single step can be taken on the Path of spiritual progress.

We think that if our friends the Theosophists were to take the trouble to study our Scriptures, and if they understood how deeply Buddhists feel on this point, that they would surely cease from thus misrepresenting One for whom they also profess the profoundest veneration. lithe Buddha indeed preached the doctrine of the Existence of the Soul in man, then He, judged by His own Teaching, had not won the lowest of the Paths, the State of Sotâpanna, which can be attained alone by him who has cast off the first Three Fetters of the Mind:—Sakkâyadimmhi, the Theory of Individuality; Vicikicchâ, Perplexity or Doubtfulness; and Silabbatpârasâsa, or the Belief in the efficacy of Ritual and Rule.[1] But whilst we naturally resent the misuse by Theosophists of. Buddhist terminology, their assumption to know more of our Religion than we ourselves, and the attribution to our Lord of the very doctrine which was in His eyes the most profound delusion to which man is subject; we cannot but be too deeply grateful to them for the immense service they have done in enlarging the religious horizon of the Western world—a service without which our own efforts would fail of their effect.

We regard, indeed, the Theosophical movement as the necessary forerunner of true Buddhist ‘reaching, for had the doctrine of Anatta, (the non-existence of any immortal principle in man), been mooted generally in the West twenty-five years ago, it would have aroused a hostility so considerable as to make the spread of the Religion hopeless.[2] In conclusion we wish to state, with what authority long study of the Master's Teaching, and the Yellow Robe can give us, that there is nothing whatever of an esoteric nature about Buddhism—it is all open to the light of day, and we are too proud of it to deem some part of it necessary for concealment; that the Buddha forbade His followers to perform miracles in public; and that, when about to pass away He declared to His best-loved disciple:—"I have preached the Truth without making any distinction between exoteric and doctrine: for in respect of the Truths, Ânanda, the Tathâgata has no such thing as the closed fist of a teacher who keeps some things back."[3]. As to the last of these misconceptions, that the Goal of Buddhism is annihilation, that it is a Pessimism which has no further hope than death, and that its teaching undermines the energy of its adherents, rendering them undiligent and apathetic; we may say at once that nothing can be further from the truth. Buddhism indeed admits the existence, nay, the vast preponderance, of sorrow and of evil in the life we live; but it is the whole teaching of the Religion to shew how that sorrow and that evil can be eliminated, and a happiness beyond our dreaming gained; and the whole practice of Righteousness and Meditation that that teaching inculcates is but a means to this end. To *admit* the existence of sorrow and of evil is surely but to admit an undoubted fact:—whilst, as we understand it, Pessimism is not only the *admission* of the preponderance of III but the belief that Ill cannot be remedied:—which is precisely the very idea that Buddhism most strenuously denies.

In its assertion of the power of culture over evil, of nurture over nature, Buddhism is surely no Pessimism, but rather the proudest Optimism ever declared to man in the guise of a Philosophy or a Religion. To say, again, that Buddhism aims at final extinction is not true—the Goal of Buddhism is not in the hereafter, but here in the life we live—its Goal is a life made glorious by self-conquest and exalted by boundless love and wisdom, and that Perplexity to which we have referred as one of the first three of the ten Fetters of the Mind which must be broken before that ideal life can be attained includes all such speculations as "Shall I exist or not after my death?" As this question of the nature of the Goal of Buddhism is dealt with in a separate article in this issue, it is unnecessary to further refer to it here. Finally, as regards the charge of apathy, this again has been made by those who have not understood the meaning and the purpose of Buddhism, and the falsity of the belief that this Religion tends to subvert the will and to paralyse the useful activities of man, is well set forth in an essay by Mrs. C. A. F. Rhys Davids, a reprint of which will be found amongst our Publications.

The whole practise of Buddhism is one long training in strenuous effort, known to us as the Great Fourfold Struggle:—the struggle to suppress old evil states of mind, to prevent new evil states arising; to cultivate to their fruition good states already existent, and to induce new good to rise; and to do this necessitates an unceasing effort of will, a constant attitude of alertness and watchfulness of mind. 'Strenuousness' we are taught 'Strenuousness is the Immortal Path,—sloth is the way of death. The Strenuous live always,—the slothful are already as the dead;'[16] and this teaching is echoed throughout the whole of the Buddhist Scriptures. "Impermanent are the Tendencies—therefore do ye deliver yourselves by Strenuousness"[17]—this was the last charge of the Buddha to his followers,—a charge repeated by the Buddhist Monk each time he recites the Five Precepts to the people. A Religion which thus places the necessity for earnest effort, for 'non-procrastination' (Pâli, Apparnâda) so much in the foreground:—which regards it, indeed, as one of the essentials of all true progress, can hardly be justly held to conduce to atrophy of mind and will.

These misapprehensions laid at rest, we can now pass on to the discussion of those vital questions set forth at the beginning of this chapter, *viz.*, what service has Buddhism rendered to the cause of humanity and of civilisation in the past, and to what extent can it offer a solution to the problems of the modern world to-day?

As regards the first of these questions, Buddhism has, in our opinion, done more to promote the true civilisation of the world than any of the great Religions which we know. For the true value of a Religion surely lies in its power to overcome the passions, ignorances and above all the prejudices of mankind, in its power to promote the general happiness and to bring peace on earth. We may, I think, take it for granted that all the great Religions have in some measure tended to make better men of their adherents; but, unfortunately, with the sole exception of Buddhism, the good that they have done their own devotees by such ethical teaching as they inculcate, has been outbalanced by the terrible wrongs that those same adherents have inflicted on innocent outsiders;—fruits of the dark bigotry and cruelty innate in man, for which religious dogmas have proved only too convenient outlets. Whether we consider the brutal persecutions of the Buddhas under Sankarâcârya in the name of the three million Gods of the Hindu Pantheon; the oceans of blood shed by the followers of Muhammed in the name of Allah; or the long persecutions of every form of liberty of thought in the name of the Christ; we find that the annals of all have been stained indelibly with the blood of the innocent; and to the extent to which they have fostered bigotry and all manner of cruelty, they have been rather scourges than blessings in the world. Buddhism, on the other hand, albeit it now numbers five hundred millions of adherents, albeit that its dominion extends amongst races so far apart as the nomad dwellers of the steppes of Tartary and the inhabitants of tropical Ceylon, can, alone amongst the great Religions of the world, make the proud boast that its altars have been from the beginning unstained with human blood:—that not one life has ever been sacrificed in the name of Him, who taught love and pity as the chiefest Law of Life. What good Buddhism has done in the world,—and it has been the redemption of the savage tribes of Thibet and Tartary, it has augmented the immemorial civilisation of China, it has ennobled the national life and nature of the great people of Japan,—what good it has done has been good unalloyed; and we think that the fact that its dominion over its adherents has been so great for good that they have never fallen into the dark abyss of intolerance, have never dared employ the Master's Name as excuse for their own cruelty, is perhaps the best proof of all of the perfection of its ethical teaching, of its true value to humanity, its true power as a civilising agent.

Finally, as to the worth of Buddhism to the modern world, and its capacity for furthering the progress of the modern Civilisation. We maintain that in this respect the adoption of Buddhism would imply an advance in humanity comparable only in its magnitude to the advance in knowledge which the West has made in the past hundred years, and this for the simple reason that it unites in itself, and vivifies with a new meaning, all the great movements for the suppression of ancient barbarisms and the promotion of peace and true prosperity which are being mooted in the West to-day.

The first of the Five Precepts which are binding on every Buddhist is the abstention from the taking of life, and the general adoption of this Precept as a guide in life would mean an immeasurable advance in humanity and in civilisation. It would mean the substitution of rational arbitration for the horrors of warfare, and hence a vast reduction in those armaments that constitute so heavy a drain upon the resources of modern States; it would mean the abolition of capital punishment—a relic of barbarism out of keeping with modern progress; it would extend also to the animal creation the principles of humanity (and surely humane treatment should not be accorded only to those who, like human beings, are capable of self-defence), and abolish not alone the brutalities of the slaughterhouse, but also the necessity for maintaining a class of men in an inhuman profession, in order to pander to the appetites of more civilised classes who would themselves recoil in horror from that slaughtering of animals that they are so careless of delegating to less fortunate men. The adoption of the Fifth Precept,—the abstention from intoxicants—would mean at one stroke a vast reduction in insanity and crime, and the abolition of one of the greatest curses of the age a curse that the threatens to undermine, not only the stamina of those who indulge in it, but to plant in their offspring the seeds of an inevitable decadence, to undermine in future generations that central mental control which alone constitutes the difference between sanity and insanity.

Buddhism, again, is the only great Religion in which the injurious distinctions between the sexes are entirely absent; and where, as in Burma, that Religion is thoroughly practised and lived up to, women are in every respect as free as men:—free in the holding of property, free to claim divorce on the same grounds as men, having an equal claim with men upon their children;—freer by far in all essential points than are their sisters of the Western Nations.

In the direction of education, again, Buddhism—holding as it does that all crime and evil in the world spring but from Ignorance—would in its adoption imply a great and notable advance. For it is not only that instruction in the arts and sciences is set forth in the Buddhist Scriptures as an essential part of the duty of parents to their children;[18]but that the mental training which is an essential part of the practise of Buddhism, would supply one of the greatest needs of humanity to-day. It has always seemed strange to us that modern thought, which lays such stress upon the culture of the physical body, which has developed such perfect systems of cultivating every muscle of the human frame, should so far have evolved no analogous system for the exercise and development of the higher faculties of mind:—faculties not less amenable to proper treatment than are the muscles and sinews of the body they control. Of course, in a sense, all modern education *is* a cultivation of certain of these faculties by use; but it is only *some* amongst them that are reached by the present methods, whilst others, more important by far to the well-being of mankind, are totally neglected.

Buddhism maintains that, in exactly the same way as a muscle can be atrophied by disuse, or cultivated to its full growth and function by a careful systematic use, so can the mental powers be atrophied or enhanced. And for this reason, regarding as it does the principles of solidarity as being the essential of all true culture, it inculcates the exercise of these faculties by a definite system of mental practises. Thus, for example, one of the chief causes of sorrow in this world is anger or hatred,—which causes grief not only to the man who hates or is irritable, but also to all humanity, of which he forms an integral part. And how to overcome that cause of Ill? By cultivating, says Buddhism, the opposite faculty of Love. And the way to do this is very simple we *practise thinking*thoughts of love concerning all beings:—practise, at some definite time each day, until the strength of the faculty of Love thus gained has banished from our lives the possibility of hate. And so with sympathy, with compassion, with all the higher powers of mind:—there is in Buddhism a definite manner of training these, training them by a regular practise of thinking thoughts that conduce to their development. Is it less important to Humanity at large that we should be able to love, to have sympathy with others' joy; compassion with their suffering; than that we should be able to solve an algebraical equation? Surely not, if we are to gain in all that is greatest and noblest in our human nature, if we are to come nearer to the realization of Humanity, the fulfilment of the purpose of our race.

And so the introduction of Buddhism would see a new departure in educational methods; a new and higher rendering of the meaning and purport of education itself:—making of it, not alone a means of endowing men with the knowledge essential to progress in life, but also of elevating humanity as a whole, of cultivating those principles of solidarity upon the extension of which a true and lasting progress must always depend. And this, we Buddhists think, should also be the idea underlying the treatment of criminals. The criminal, according to our ideas, is a person who is lacking in that moral control which in the ordinary man inhibits criminal instincts, and to 'punish' such a person by the 'solitary system or by making him break stones or pick oakum, is from our point of view absurd:—more, such a system is itself criminal, when, after degrading the man utterly alike in his own esteem and that of others, after stultifying what little intelligence and higher aspirations he possessed originally by harsh treatment and the compulsory performance of useless tasks, he is turned loose upon the world to breed new offspring, to whom he must necessarily communicate both his inherited mental weakness, and that acquired during his years of treatment as an animal in a modern gaol. It is necessary, of course, to safeguard society from the depredations of such men, but it is folly, and worse than folly, to so treat what is really a disease of the mind as to make that disease doubly worse, and then allow the criminal thus manufactured to return to the world and perpetuate the mental degradation to which the prison system has reduced him in generations of his descendents, who by force of their heredity must tend to go the way he went. The true cure for crime—for that of the habitual criminal, at least—is surely to endeavour to cultivate the missing faculties, the higher mental control (which oakum-picking and the like is hardly likely to effect), and, failing this, to segregate the subject, to prevent him perpetuating his species—without making all his life a hell. The object of civilised punishment should surely be, not to torture the man that has done evil; not to cut off either his nose and ears, as used to be done; nor his remaining mental faculties, as is now the usage; not, most of all, to so ill-use him as to frighten others from committing the same crime, (for apart from its innate injustice, experience has long shewn the folly of 'deterrent' legislation);—but to protect society from the criminal, to make of his necessary punishment a means of reform, to convert him from a menace to a useful servant of the State. Nor should such a system of criminal treatment be denounced, as it too often is, as a mere 'sickly sentimentalism'; for it would strike at the true source—which is but a form of mental disease—of habitual criminality, and in a few generations enormously diminish the proportion of crime in the world; and to effect such diminution is surely the aim and object of all criminal legislation. That object, we know only too well, is not attained by the system at present in vogue:—is the adoption of a method more certain, more scientific, more humane, to be decried merely because of its humanity?

The dissemination of such views as these, forming as they do an integral portion of the teachings of the Buddhist Religion, will, together with the exposition of that Religion itself, constitute the platform of our present Review; and we cordially invite the co-operation of all who, whether calling themselves Buddhists or not, are interested in the propagation of these ideas. To aid in the promotion of a better understanding of the Laws of Life, in which knowledge the secret of true happiness lies hid; to help to bring love to dwell in the hearts of men in place of selfishness, pity where cruelty grew; to advance the spreading of such teachings as shall aid the backward and the fallen of our race, and uplift them to their human birthright through the sympathy of the strong; to teach that true humanity is not alone the love of man, but of every weakest and meanest living thing upon the earth; and, last and chiefest of all, to declare in the hearing of mankind that Treasure of the Truth our Master taught, whereof these things are but some solitary gems:—these are the objects of our new Review, the programme of our little portion in the symphony of universal life. We shall rejoice indeed if this our work shall serve to right one atom of the wrong on earth, to bring one gleam of light into one darkened mind, or one pure flower of love to bloom in the arid desert of desire:—it is for this that we have striven in the life we live, for this that we have followed in the Faith the Master taught, for this that we now send some little of His Message unto all the world.

'Truth'—it is written in our Sacred Books—'Truth verily is Immortal Speech'. Knowing this so, we send forth from the East these echoes of an ancient Faith:—a Faith so old that the great hills have wasted and the galaxies of heaven have changed, since first the Master of Compassion taught it beneath the Himâlayan snows, under the watching stars of the still Indian night. Have yet the ages dimmed either the love He taught, shrouded the Wisdom of His Words, or sealed the entrance to the Way of Peace He shewed? Nay, surely,—and whatsoever of that ancient Truth may linger in the tale we tell, whatever of His Teaching yet resounds in this, its faroff echo, *that* will find place within the hearts of these who wait for it;—*that* will endure, after our lips are dumb in death. The rest is naught, all other speech is vain:—Truth the Immortal will alone survive; will live on through the ages, shrined in the Temple of Humanity; until the fires of Passion, Hatred and Delusion shall be quenched for ever, and the Veil of Nescience be torn aside:—till all mankind, blent at the last in one fair Brotherhood of Peace, shall own one Law, one Hope, one Faith:—that Faith of Pity and of Wisdom and of Love which shall survive all lesser lights,—fair blossom on the Tree of Human Thought; the Faith of all Humanity, the Faith of the Future!

BUDDHIST EDUCATION AND PEDAGOGY: CHALLENGES AND OPPORTUNITIES

The emerging profit-driven global economy is guided by unbridled development and gigantism. Such an economy is also coming under ever increasing domination of science and technology. Such a development is not only cutting us off from nature and one another but also undermining natural and cultural diversity. One major consequence of this is that our very survival is threatened. Moreover, the global economy is overwhelmingly controlled and run by consumerism and salespersons in which things are bought not because people need them but because they want them. The modern economic notion that more production of goods would make people happy is misplaced.

As pointed out by Schumacher, "An attitude to life which seeks fulfillment in the single-minded pursuit of wealth- in short, materialism- does not fit into this world, because it contains within itself no limiting principle, while the environment in which it is placed is strictly limited... The modern economy is propelled by a frenzy of greed and indulges in an orgy of envy, and these are not accidental features but the very causes of its expansionist success... such causes... carry within themselves the seeds of destruction" (1973: 17-18). Thus, we need to seriously examine not only our attitudes and lifestyles but also our policies that govern the use of renewable and non-renewable resources, science and technology, and the scale and direction of industrialization.-

As compared to this, Buddhist economy is based on the motto of happiness and welfare of maximum number of people (bahujanahitâya bahujanasukhâya: Vinaya Pitaka.I.21). Buddhist Economics does not necessarily see unbridled modernism and westernization as a positive phenomenon as it is responsible for many of the major problems that we face today. A modern Buddhist scholar, for instance, has pointed out that "Modernity is rejected because it is seen as a form of life that has in a short period of time despoiled the landscape and done irreparable damage to the environment (Lancaster 2002: 1-2).

Not only the inherent value of life itself but also the interdependence and reciprocity of human and other forms of life are a fundamental Buddhist belief. Thus, nature and humanity on the one hand and humans amongst themselves on the other are seen as mutually obligated to each other. A living entity can neither isolate itself from this causal nexus nor have an essence of its own. In other words, as part of the Dependent Arising (paticcasamuppâda), humans are seen as affecting their environment not only through the purely physical aspects of their actions, but also through the moral and immoral qualities of such actions.

That is, karmic effects sometimes catch up with people via their environment. It is thus said that, if a king and his people act unrighteously, this has a bad effect on the environment and its gods, leading to little rain, poor crops and weak, short-lived people (Anguttara Nikâya.II.74-76). This message is also strongly implied by the Aggañña Suttanta of the Dîgha Nikâya (III.80-98), which shows how in the beginning nature was bountiful, but it became less so when humans began to take greedily from it. When they began to harvest more rice than they needed, it was not naturally able to grow quickly enough.

This necessitated cultivation which in turn caused division of land into private fields, so that property was invented. Origin of private property became the root cause of different social and economic ills. Here, then, is a vision of how sentient beings are affected by what they take from their environment.

Our current socioeconomic system promotes competition rather than cooperation. This is bound to generate conflict and resentment-.

A society founded upon the Buddhist Dharma recognizes that one should aim at promoting the good of the greater unit to which one belongs, and as a minimum one must not look for one's own satisfaction in ways that may cause harm to others. Thus, in Buddhist approach to social and economic develop-ment, the primary criterion governing policy formu-lation must be the well-being of members of the society as a whole. Production must serve the real needs of the people, not the demands of the economic system. In such a system, economic de-velopment would be guided not by maximum consumption but sane and rational consumption furthering human well-being.

Buddhism promotes a wide distribution of basic necessities so that no one has to suffer deprivation as deprivation is the root cause of social conflict. Thus, talking about the cause of social conflict, the Buddha pointed out that, "goods not being bestowed on the destitute poverty grew rife; from poverty growing rife stealing increased, from the spread of stealing violence grew apace, from the growth of violence, the destruction of life became common" (Dīgha Nikāya.III.67).

Hoarding wealth in any form is looked down upon in Buddhism (A.III.222) and if a wealthy person were to enjoy his wealth all by himself only, it would be a source of failure for him (Sn.v.102). In fact, pride of wealth or economic snobbery is given in Buddhism as a cause of one's downfall (Sn.v.104). As pointed out by Fromm, the present system generates greed and selfishness in which personal success is valued more highly than social responsibility. "It is no longer shocking when political leaders and business executives make decisions that seem to be to their personal advantage, but at the same time are harmful and dangerous to the community... At the same time, the general public is also so selfishly concerned with their private affairs that they pay little attention to all that transcends the personal realm" (Fromm 1976: 10-11). Our modern dinosaur society has become a greedy society and we do not know when enough is enough. A society driven by greed loses the power of seeing things in their wholesomeness.

"The hope... that by the single-minded pursuit of wealth, without bothering our heads about spiritual and moral questions, we could establish peace on earth, is an unrealistic, unscientific, and irrational hope... the foundations of peace cannot be laid by universal prosperity, in the modern sense, because such prosperity, if attainable at all, is attainable only by cultivating such drives of human nature as greed and envy... making inordinately large demands on limited world resources and... (putting rich people) on an unavoidable collision course- not primarily with the poor (who are weak and defenceless) but with other rich people" (Schumacher 1973: 18-19). Thus, "given unlimited desires, even the greatest production cannot keep pace with everybody's fantasy of having more than their neighbors. Necessarily, those who are stronger, more clever, or more favored by other circumstances will try to establish a favored position for themselves and try to take advantage of those who are less powerful, either by force and violence or by suggestion... (Conflict in the society) cannot disappear as long as greed dominates the human heart" (Fromm 1976: 114).

Buddhism, even though speaking in atheistic and secular terms, aims at the liberation of human beings from egoism and greed as they are the main cause of misery and harm. There is no doubt that environmental disaster is to a great extent due to the insatiable greed of humans. Buddhism on the whole, though does not mind wealth and prosperity, but they have to be acquired and used in full accord with the ethical norms. Human tendency to have- to possess- which the Buddha called craving (tanhâ), is the basis of present profit-driven global economy fostering greed. As compared to this, Buddhist economy would base itself on what Fromm called 'to be'- to share, to give, to sacrifice (Fromm 1976: 105-106).

In the present profit-driven global economic system anything that is 'uneconomic' is sought to be obliterated out of existence. "Call a thing immoral or ugly, soul-destroying or a degradation of man, a peril to the peace of the world or to the well-being of future generations; as long as you have not shown it to be "uneconomic" you have not really questioned its right to exist, grow, and prosper" (Schumacher 1973: 27).

However, in Buddhist view of things, profitability alone cannot be an adequate measure of whether something is "economic" or not. Buddhist economics would take into account not only the profitability of a given activity, but also its effect upon people and environment, including the resource base. The higher animals have an economic value because of their utility, but they are not a meta-economic value in themselves. "If I have a car, a man-made thing, I might quite legitimately argue that the best way to use it is never to bother about maintenance and simply run it to ruin. I may indeed have calculated that this is the most economical method of use. If the calculation is correct, nobody can criticise me for acting accordingly, for there is nothing sacred about a man-made thing like a car. But if I have an animal-be it only a calf-or a hen-a living, sensitive creature, am I allowed to treat it as nothing but a utility? Am I allowed to run it to ruin? It is no use trying to answer such questions scientifically. They are metaphysical, not scientific, questions. It is metaphysical error, likely to produce the gravest practical consequences, to equate "car" and "animal" on account of their utility, while failing to recognize the most fundamental difference between them, that of "level of being"(Schumacher 1973: 84-85).

By pointing out that the vulgar chase of luxury and abundance is the root-cause of suf-fering, Buddhism encourages restraint, voluntary simplicity, and con-tentment. "The cultivation and expansion of needs is the antithesis of wisdom. It is also the antithesis of freedom and peace. Every increase of needs tends to increase one's dependence on outside forces over which one cannot have control, and therefore increases existential fear. Only by a reduction of needs can one promote a genuine reduction in those tensions which are the ultimate causes of strife and war" (Schumacher 1973: 20). Thus, Buddhist economics based on ideals such as being content with little, avoiding wastefulness, voluntary simplicity i.e., fewness of desires (appicchatâ), and contentment (santutthi) aspires to pave the road to peace and happiness. Contentment is the mental condition of a person who is satisfied with what he has or the position in which he finds himself (santussamâno itarîtarena: Sutta-Nipāta.v.42).

The question arises as to how can a person remain content in the midst of so many economic difficulties. From the Buddhist point of view, economic and moral issues cannot be separated from each other. From the Buddhist point of view mere satisfaction of economic needs without spiritual development can never lead to contentedness among people. Just as poverty is the cause of much crime, wealth too is responsible for various human ills. In the consumer society wealth is merely seen from a materialistic point of view. The result of such an attitude is that its possessor is never satisfied and does not have the correct attitude towards it. However correct attitude towards wealth from the Buddhist point of view is very important because it views material wealth as only required to meet bare necessities. Moreover, wealth must be earned only through righteous and moral mean.

Generosity (dâna) and liberality (câga) are always linked in Buddhism with virtue. Moreover, by doing so one gets rid of selfishness and becomes more unacceptable to others because "one who gives makes many friends" (Sutta-Nipâta.187). It is not necessary to have much to practice generosity because giving from one's meager resources is also considered very valuable (Samyutta Nikâya.I.18; Dhammapada.224). Generosity is one of the important qualities that make one a gentleman (Anguttara Nikâya.IV.218). The Buddha compares the man who righteously earns his wealth and shares it with the needy to a man who has both eyes, whereas the one who only earns wealth but does no merit is like a one-eyed man (Anguttara Nikâya .I.129-130). To build up a healthy society, therefore, liberality and generosity have greatly to be encouraged.

As pointed out by Schumacher, "(f)rom the point of view of Buddhist economics... production from local resources for local needs is the most rational way of economic life... the modern economist... tends to take statistics showing an increase in the number of ton/miles per head of the population carried by a country's transport system as proof of economic progress, while to the latter- the Buddhist economist- the same statistics would indicate a highly undesirable deterioration in the pattern of consumption" (1973: 42).

The fig-tree glutton (udumbarakhâdika) method blamed by the Buddha (Samyutta Nikâya.IV.283), the method of shaking down an indiscriminate amount of fruit from a fig-tree in order to eat a few, is precisely the same as the one employed in drift-net fishing, where many more animals are killed than utilized. Today we understand natural capital as the sum total of renewable and non-renewable resources, including the ecological systems and services that support life. It is different from conventionally defined capital in that natural capital cannot be produced by human activity. What was unimaginable 50 years ago was the speed with which the loss of natural capital would affect humankind. Humanity cannot continue to consume the planet's limited resources at the rate to which it has become accustomed. Such an attitude is bound to have catastrophic consequences. The human economy does not operate in an infinite expanse capable of providing an inexhaustible supply of re-sources. When the economy expands, it does so by absorbing into itself more and more of the re-source base of the extremely fragile and finite ecosystem and by burdening the ecosystem in turn with its waste. But long before the human economy reaches that limit, it will cross a threshold point beyond which the delicate fabric of the ecosystem will be damaged so badly that it shall no longer be capable of sustaining higher forms of life.

We may already be very close to that threshold and as human population grows further, the stress on the environment is bound to rise to even more perilous level-s.

Since human beings are social creatures who naturally come together for common ends, this means that a social order guided by Buddhist principles would consist primarily of small-scale communities in which each member can make an effective contribution. Only small-scale social arrangements can rescue people from the portending future disaster. Considered from a Buddhist point of view, the huge polluted mega-cities and uncaring bureaucrats and politicians typical of our age are unsuitable for a proper welfare of sentient beings.

The most suitable and compatible economy would be small-scale and localized. Such an economy would use simple technology which would not drain natural resources and in it production would be aimed principally at local consumption, so that there would be direct face-to-face con-tact between producers and consumers. Large-scale technologies are dehumanizing and morally wrong. Schumacher called for human-scale, decentralized, and appropriate technologies. People can only feel at home in human-scale environments. If economic structures become too large they become impersonal and unresponsive to human needs and aspirations. Under these conditions individuals feel functionally futile, dispossessed, voiceless, powerless, excluded, and alienated. "Wisdom demands a new orientation of science and technology towards the organic, the gentle, the nonviolent, the elegant and beautiful" (Schumacher 1973: 20).

Thus, in the Buddhist concept of economic development, we should avoid gigantism, especially of machines, which tend to control rather than serve human beings. If bigness and greed can be avoided, the Middle Path of Buddhist development can be achieved, i.e., both the world of industry and agriculture can be converted into a meaningful habitat. "Some in the industrial countries have learned at first that material prosperity without spiritual development is ultimately unsatisfying" (Anonymous 1983: 18). "Strange to say, technology, although of course the product of man, tends to develop by its own laws and principles, and these are very different from those of human nature or of living nature in general. Nature always, so to speak, knows where and when to stop. Greater even than the mystery of natural growth is the mystery of the natural cessation of growth. There is measure in all natural things- in their size, speed, or violence. As a result, the system of nature, of which man is a part, tends to be self-balancing, self-adjusting, self-cleansing. Not so with technology... (which) recognises no self-limiting principle- in terms, for instance, of size, speed, or violence. It therefore does not possess the virtues of being self-balancing, self-adjusting, and self-cleansing" (Schumacher 1973: 120).

Our economy is already big enough and our technologies too smart and too powerful. What we need most of all is streamlining and downsizing: cutting down on weapons production, on industries dedicated to wasteful luxuries, on conspicuous con-sumption as the engine that drives the economy. Instead we need qualitative improvements to make our technologies more humble and humane, more benign towards the total bio-sphere.

Economic justice and social equity are essential so that no one is deprived of a fair standard of living. As Schumacher said the problem children of the world are the rich societies and not the poor (1973: 126). "To live peacefully, we must live with a reasonable degree of equity, or fairness, for it is unrealistic to think that, in a communications-rich world, a billion or more persons will accept living in absolute poverty while another billion live in conspicuous excess. Only with greater fairness in the consumption of the world's resources can we live peacefully, and thereby live sustainably, as a human family" (Elgin 1993: 42).

Well-documented scientific studies have now clearly established that each living creature has its place in the biosphere, whereby it plays its unique role is part of the collective balance. The egalitarianism of rights to life is therefore based on scientific realities such as the unity of the living world, its vast diversity (a key factor in evolution) and the complementary nature of its different components. The right to have humanizing work that is dignified and meaningful- right livelihood (Sammâ-âjîva) as it is known in Buddhism. "The study of Buddhist economics could be recommended even for those who believe that economic growth is more important than any spiritual or religious values... It is a question of finding the right path of development, the Middle Way between materialist heedlessness and traditionalist immobility, in short, of finding "Right Livelihood" (Schumacher 1973: 45). The righteous householder aims at harmonious living (dhammacariya, samacariya) (Majjhima Nikâya.I.289; Samyutta Nikâya.I.101) and compassion (karunâ) which is "the desire to remove what is detrimental to others and their unhappiness" (Sutta-Nipâta.v.73). This is the concept of the well-adjusted and balanced person, who while he seeks pleasure, exercises a degree of restraint and limits his needs and avoids greed (visamalobha) (Dîgha Nikâya.III.70).

The Buddhist values mean that environment should not be over exploited. As the Tibetans say very wisely that not too much of anything that is precious should be taken from the earth, as then its quality fades and the earth is destroyed (Morgan & Lawton 1996: 93). The Buddhist ideal, in fact, is co-operation with nature, not domination. As pointed out by

E.F. Schumacher, the world is ruled from towns where the feeling of belonging to an ecosystem is not realised. This results in a harsh and improvident treatment of things upon which we ultimately depend, such as water and trees. Moreover, modern economics does not distinguish between renewable and non-renewable materials, as its very method is to equalise and quantify everything by means of a money price. The cheapest is automatically the one to be preferred, as to do otherwise would be irrational and 'uneconomic.' From a Buddhist point of view "non-renewable goods must be used only if they are indispensable, and then only with the greatest care and the most meticulous concern for conservation. To use them heedlessly or extravagantly is an act of violence... The Buddhist economist would insist that a population basing its economic life on non-renewable fuels is living parasitically" (Schumacher 1973: 43-44).

Thus, a new relation must be established between people and nature, one of cooperation not of exploitation. Buddhism enjoins a respectful and non-violent attitude towards ecology. "Every follower of the Buddha ought to plant a tree every few years and look after it until it is safely established, and the Buddhist economist can demonstrate without difficulty that the universal observation of this rule would result in a high rate of genuine economic development independent of any foreign aid" (Schumacher 1973: 43).

Pollution and accumulation of large amounts of highly toxic substances is an important feature of the emerging global economy. However, as pointed out by Schumacher, this is an ethical, spiritual, and metaphysical monstrosity which "means conducting the economic affairs of man as if people really did not matter at all" (1973: 119). "An entirely new system of thought is needed, a system based on attention to people, and not primarily attention to goods- (the goods will look after themselves!). It could be summed up in the phrase, "production by the masses, rather than mass production." What was impossible, however, in the nineteenth century, is possible now. And what was in fact- if not necessarily at least understandably- neglected in the nineteenth century is unbelievably urgent now. That is, the conscious utilisation of enormous technological and scientific potential for the fight against misery and human degradation- a fight in intimate contact with actual people, with individuals, families, small groups, rather than states and other anonymous abstractions" (Schumacher 1973: 56).

The driving force of such an economy would be the pro-motion of well-being both material and social, not commer-cial profit and unrestrained expansion. As pointed out by Fromm, the development of profit-oriented "economic system was no longer determined by the question: What is good for Man? But by the question: What is good for the growth of the system? One tried to hide the sharpness of this conflict by making the assumption that what was good for the growth of the system (or even for a single big corporation) was also good for the people. This construction was bolstered by an auxiliary construction: that the very qualities that the system required of human beings- egotism, selfishness, and greed- were innate in human nature; hence, not only the system but human nature itself fostered them. Societies in which egotism, selfishness, and greed did not exist were supposed to be "primitive," their inhabitants "childlike." People refused to recognize that these traits were not natural drives that caused industrial society to exist, but that they were the products of social circumstances" (Fromm 1976: 7-8). "The technology of mass production is inherently violent, ecologically damaging, self-defeating in terms of non-renewable resources, and stultifying for the human person. The technology of production by the masses, making use of the best of modern knowledge and experience, is conducive to decentralisation, compatible with the laws of ecology, gentle in its use of scarce resources, and designed to serve the human person instead of making him the servant of machines" (Schumacher 1973: 126).

We are trying to satisfy nonmaterial needs with material goods. For Buddhism material satisfaction merely pro-vides a starting point for the pursuit of higher goals. The Buddha called upon people to wake up and liberate themselves from the illusion that craving for things leads to happiness. It is not cleverness but wisdom which can "enable us to see the hollowness and fundamental unsatisfactoriness of a life devoted primarily to the pursuit of material ends, to the neglect of the spiritual. Such a life necessarily sets man against man and nation against nation, because man's needs are infinite and infinitude can be achieved only in the spiritual realm, never in the material. Man assuredly needs to rise above this humdrum "world"; wisdom shows him the way to do it; without wisdom, he is driven to build up a monster economy, which destroys the world, and to seek fantastic satisfactions, like landing a man on the moon. Instead of overcoming the "world" by moving towards saintliness, he tries to overcome it by gaining preeminence in wealth, power, science, or indeed any imaginable "sport"" (Schumacher 1973: 24). Spiritual health and material well-being are not enemies: they are natural allies. A Buddhist approach to economics would distinguish between misery, sufficiency, and glut. Economic growth would be good only to the point of sufficiency. Limitless growth and consumption would be disastrous.

Further, whereas Buddhist economics would be based squarely on renewable resources, modern economics is based on the ruthless exploitation of nonrenewable resources and recognizes no limits to production and consumption- a non-sustainable system. "Economics without Buddhism, i.e., without spiritual, human, and ecological values, is like sex without love... While the materialist is mainly interested in goods, the Buddhist is mainly interested in liberation. But Buddhism is "the Middle Way" and therefore in no way antagonistic to physical well-being. It is not wealth that stands in the way of liberation but the attachment to wealth; not the enjoyment of pleasurable things but the craving for them... From an economist's point of view, the marvel of the Buddhist way of life is the utter rationality of its pattern- amazingly small means leading to extraordinarily satisfactory results... For the modern economist this is very difficult to understand. He is used to measuring the "standard of living" by the amount of annual consumption, assuming all the time that a man who consumes more is "better off" than a man who consumes less. A Buddhist economist would consider this approach excessively irrational: since consumption is merely a means to human well-being, the aim should be to obtain the maximum of well-being with the minimum of consumption... The ownership and the consumption of goods is a means to an end, and a Buddhist economics is the systematic study of how to attain given ends with the minimum means" (Schumacher 1973: 38-41).

Buddhist economics is very different from the economics of modern materialism, "since the Buddhist sees the essence of civilisation not in a multiplication of wants but in the purification of human character. Character, at the same time, is formed primarily by a man's work... properly conducted in conditions of human dignity and freedom" (Schumacher 1973: 39). It is unBuddhistic to consider goods as more important than people and consumption as more important than creative activity. Such an aim was made explicit in the Green Buddhist Declaration, prepared by members of the international Buddhist community for discussion at the World Fellowship of Buddhism in Colombo (1980): "We believe that since world resources and the ecosystem cannot support all peoples at the level of the consumption of the advantaged nations, efforts towards global equity must be coupled with efforts towards voluntary simplicity, in one's individual life-style and through democratically-determined policies. The economic structures which encourage consumeristic greed and alienation must be transformed." Unfortunately, in present-day globalizing world, moral sentiments are viewed as irrelevant to business and economics. Business principles are taken to be essentially restricted to profit maximization. Moreover, as pointed out by Amartya Sen, "a departure from profit maximization need not necessarily be benign, nor need moral sentiments be invariably noble. Some of the worst barbarities in the contemporary world have been committed by self-sacrificing racists- ready to do harm to some people even at great cost or risk to themselves. Indeed, this process continues today with relentless persistence... The rejection of a self-centered life can go with the attempted advancement- sometimes violent promotion- of the perceived interests only of a particular group or community (excluding others), and even with wilfully inflicting damages on another group or community" (Sen 1997: 6). This is where Buddhism and the value-system proposed by it become important.

Briefly, Buddhist Education is a practical, clear-cut, tried and tested holistic training programme to be followed in one's daily life. It encompasses a method and technique of living to help one to meet the problems and challenges in life as well as to make the best of the limitless opportunities that life has to offer. In this sense, Buddhist Education is a holistic education programme, based on the practice and practical application of the Dhamma. It is far from being an academic study to satisfy one's intellectual gratification. On the contrary, Buddhist Education calls for resolute self-effort and a firm self-commitment to not only learn but to also skilfully train oneself in the Teachings of the Buddha. As such, Buddhist Education engages all of one's faculties – the emotions as much as one's intellect and will.

The Buddha did not want anyone to blindly follow the Noble Path He unravelled for the benefit of all humankind without regard to a person's own life-experience. He wanted disciple monks and lay-adherents whose own experimentation provided them shraddha or confidence obtained through a right understanding of the Dhamma. It was for this reason that the Buddha consistently underlined this cardinal requirement of self-inquiry and self-development in one embracing the Dhamma. We must therefore not overlook this basic requirement of Buddhism which we are to first fulfil. So before everything else, one has to undergo oneself, the spiritual experimentation or orientation.

THREE DOMAINS OF LEARNING IN BUDDHIST EDUCATION

It is a matter of great significance, especially in the context of learning psychology, which the Buddha had over 2600 years ago, identified three distinct levels or domains of learning namely, pariyatti, patipatti and pativedha. According to Buddhist Education, pariyatti constitutes the theoretical foundation that is required in learning and understanding the Buddha Dhamma. However, we have to be mindful that a theoretical foundation would only enable a person to experience the Dhamma at a superficial level. On the other hand, a person could still experience the deeper meaning and relevance of the Dhamma without having to be erudite in the scriptures and to eloquently recite suttas. Buddhist scriptures are replete with examples of how disciple monks and lay followers of the Buddha, possessing relatively low intelligence, could attain great spiritual uplift. A classic example was Cula Pantaka who could not even commit a simple verse to memory. Yet, he was able to attain Arahanthood simply by practicing concentration and removing defilements from his mind. Simply put, in Buddhist Education possession of a high level of intelligence is not a qualifying pre-requisite or pre-condition for spiritual advancement.

A theoretical study of the sacred texts must not therefore be looked upon as the be-all-and end-all of Buddhist Education for this will limit one to only a superficial involvement with the profound Teachings of the Buddha. From possessing a theoretical foundation of the Dhamma, one should advance to patipattior the practice of the Dhamma through inquiry, investigation and self- experience. Skilful practice of the Dhamma in daily life is absolutely necessary for one to progress to the third domain of learning and self-training namely, pativedha — the realisation of Insight Wisdom. The Buddha had always stressed that in order for one to come to grips with the realities of life one has to come to terms with one's own spiritual development. To really understand and benefit fully from the Dhamma, one has to progress beyond the theoretical plane and immerse oneself in the method and technique of practicing and applying the Buddha's Teachings in daily life.

The Buddha had always stressed that in order to benefit from the Dhamma one has to practise his Noble Teachings with understanding and depth. This is because the Dhamma is a complete education and training programme which we are to infuse into our day-to-day living. The Buddha persistently admonished His disciples and lay followers that he was only a Teacher, Guide and Role Model of one who had understood, lived and experienced the Dhamma. Throughout His forty-five years in teaching the Dhamma, He laid stress on the Eternal Doctrine as a way of wholesome living rather than an esoteric philosophy for scholarship or for theorising. On many occasions he refused to be drawn into useless speculation and debate when he knew that the discussion would not lead the opponent to understand the nature of his existence and the realities of life.

It is significant to note that in modern teaching psychology too, three distinct levels of learning are recognised namely, the cognitive, affective and psychomotor domains. The cognitive domain of learning deals with bare knowledge such as facts, figures, data and theories. This essentially knowledge-based learning focuses on the acquisition and retention of facts or information such as Siddhartha was a Sakya prince; his father was King Suddhodana; he attained Supreme Enlightenment and so on. As these learning deals essentially with acquiring and regurgitating knowledge, the inner being, in terms of one's emotional feelings, thinking process and mind-set remains largely uninvolved or affected. It is because of this fact that the cognitive level or domain of learning is referred to as a 'passive' process.

On the other hand, the affective and psychomotor domains of learning involve, among other things, critical observation, self-reflection, self-analysis and the synthesis of different facts, ideas and viewpoints. The thrust of the affective domain of learning is for one to develop a deep, probing, inquiring mind. This is similar to the penetrating, analytical and objective, mental make-up and thinking that is typical of the Buddha's life since his childhood. Here the individual has to establish for him or herself what is significant in a subject, analyze and synthesize the facts, ideas and viewpoints that are involved and to independently form objective judgments and conclusions. In this way, the individual progresses from the domain of possessing knowledge or facts on a specific subject to developing his or her observational skills, ability to reflect, sieve, conceptualise and evaluate the different facts and details. In the process objectivity is sharpened objectivity which enables a person to think clearly and with a critical mind.

The development of the mind is central in Buddhist Education. In the context of daily living, this helps one to discriminate, for example, between wholesome and unwholesome thoughts and actions.

In terms of practising and internalising the Dhamma, the affective domain of learning and training is without question an essential ingredient and is linked to harnessing the pool of information and facts in the Dhamma that is to be relied upon for one to arrive at sound conclusions, decisions and actions in our daily life.

The psychomotor domain of learning advances an individual a step further in learning. As the term itself suggests, this level of learning deals with the total person, that is, the body and mind concurrently. In this domain, both the psychological (meaning the thinking, attitude, mental make-up, emotions, sentiments and feelings) and the behavioral (in reference to personal skills, talents, conduct and volition or actions) aspects of learning are involved in unison. It is in this domain that the practical application and practice of the Dhamma impacts forcefully on the development of the individual.

Viewed from the perspective of Buddhist Education, the psychomotor and the affective domains of learning, relates to the living or 'being' aspects of Buddhism. Here the individual becomes mindful of living the Dhamma. The focus of the learning and training is on developing. human values and virtuous qualities such as metta, karuna, muditha, upekkha. Thus it is in the psychomotor domain that the practical application of Buddhism in terms of actual day- to -day practice of the Dhamma is ingrained.

THE FUTURE OF WOMEN IN BUDDHISM

The future of humanity relies on the procreative power of women, since the future of the human species literally depends on women's special power to give birth to children. Yet women's procreative potential is not the only reason to believe that women hold the key to the future. In addition to our biological gifts, we women have many other skills and talents to offer humanity. And Buddhist women have unique strengths and potential to succor our crisis-ridden planet.

In recent decades, attention to the topic of women in Buddhism has expanded dramatically. Since the 1960s, interest in Buddhism has grown exponentially throughout the world, facilitated by great Buddhist teachers, new research and publications on Buddhism in modern languages, the Internet, the growth of outstanding Buddhist educational centers, and an abundance of vibrant Buddhist social service activities. Especially in Western countries, the Buddha's teachings on peace, compassion, ethics, and human psychology have had a significant impact. Buddhist thought and culture have permeated Western culture to a remarkable degree, from religion to politics, the arts, and the marketplace. This new wave of interest in Buddhism has coincided with new educational and professional opportunities for women and an increasing awareness of women's capabilities and potential. Yet, unfortunately, women do not always have access to Buddhist education, nor are they equally represented in Buddhist institutions. Although the Buddha taught a path to liberation for the benefit of all beings, full recognition and equal opportunity do not extend to women in many Buddhist traditions. If the Buddha's teachings are liberating, shouldn't they be equally liberating for both women and men?

The answer to this question is fairly obvious. The Buddhist teachings speak about the nature of the mind and how to purify the mind of the delusions that cloud it in order to achieve lasting peace and happiness. The nature of the mind, which is pure awareness, is identical for women and men. The human potential to dispel delusion and realize perfect happiness is also identical for women and men. This means that the Buddha's teachings are equally liberating for both women and men. So why is it that most of the stories of realized beings in Buddhist history speak about men? If all human beings can practice the Buddha's teachings and become free of greed, hatred, and ignorance, why don't we have more stories about realized women? If all living beings have the potential to become free from suffering, why don't we hear more about women achieving liberation?

In recent years, these questions have led to serious reflection and research among Buddhist scholars and practitioners about women's roles and potential in Buddhism. Many new books have appeared about women in Buddhist history and in contemporary Buddhist traditions. Many books have been written by women authors about their practice and insight into the teachings of the Buddha. The American Buddhist nun Pema Chödrön, one of the most popular Buddhist writers today, has been featured in a wide range of media, from Newsweek magazine to *The Oprah Winfrey Show* on television. Her books have become influential among people of all religious backgrounds and no religious background. Many studies document how women are taking new roles in Buddhist organizations and becoming highly respected as Buddhist teachers, especially in Western countries. The only remaining question is: What is holding Buddhist women back?

Before we tackle that question, perhaps we need to locate the question within present global realities. As the world becomes more advanced scientifically and technologically, it is painfully obvious that many areas of human development have not kept pace. We can now communicate to any precise point on the planet in a fraction of a second and disseminate information to millions of people with the click of a mouse, yet human beings are still enslaved to the same old negative emotions that have plagued humanity for millions of years. Wars and corruption continue to rage. Greed and hatred spin out brutish strategies to control others and their resources.

Sadly, we have become more skilled at killing and cheating greater numbers of people with far less effort than ever before. Today, more human beings live in slavery than ever in human history. Children as young as six years old are sold into the sex trade, including many Buddhist children. Shortages of basic necessities like food and water affect millions of people, while a tiny fraction amass obscene wealth. Even in the so-called developed countries, our food, air, and water have become contaminated to a frightening degree. Virtues like loving-kindness and compassion seem to be in short supply.

For thoughtful Buddhists, the answer is easy. As the Buddha taught, we need to recognize and eliminate the sources of human suffering: greed, hatred, and ignorance. If we can address the root causes of these problems, both as individuals and as a society, we have a good chance of transforming the world and changing the course of human history. But greed, hatred, and ignorance will not go away without effort. That means that we need to study and practice the Buddhist teachings sincerely and intensively in order to really change things. We need the teachings and we need teachers to explain them, but perhaps more important, we need living examples of people who model Buddhist values and can serve as sources of inspiration to others. We need qualified Buddhist teachers who have developed a heart of compassion, sufficient wisdom, and skillful teaching methods to motivate others on the path. Sad to say, there seems to be a shortage of inspiring teachers in the world today.

The Buddha set a great example and continues to inspire millions of people even today. By leaving his luxurious life in the palace and setting off to discover the meaning of human existence, he demonstrated the importance of making life meaningful. Making a living and taking care of our young are very important, but they are not the ultimate purpose of human existence. Other animals - even ants and honeybees - also make a living and take care of their young, and some seem to do a better job of it than human animals do. What sets human beings apart from other animals is our higher intelligence and our special capacity for spiritual practice. We have the capacity to unlock the secret and discover the meaning of life. By avoiding unwholesome actions and doing good deeds, we can achieve happiness in this life, higher rebirth in the next, or, if we really get to work, even perfect enlightenment. But we need teachers and we need role models to help us on the path.

This is where Buddhist women come in. If humanity is going to survive, we need all the help we can get. We can no longer afford to squander half of our precious human resources by ignoring or devaluing women's spiritual potential. Nowhere do the Buddhist texts say that teachers need to be male. Nowhere does the Buddha say that being a woman is the result of bad karma, though this rumor continues to circulate in Buddhist societies. In fact, when King Pasanadi bemoaned the birth of a daughter, the Buddha said that a girl child may turn out to be better than a son. When the Buddha's stepmother asked to join the Buddhist order, he confirmed that women have equal potential to achieve the fruits of the path, including liberation. Therefore, there should be nothing stopping women from practicing the Buddha's teachings, achieving realizations, and becoming the inspiring role models that humanity so badly needs. In fact, if a woman sets her mind to it, she may turn out to be a better practitioner than a man. By practicing the Six Perfections - generosity, ethical conduct, patience, joyful effort, concentration, and wisdom - women can proceed directly to buddhahood. By developing loving-kindness, compassion, and wisdom, women can awaken and help lead sentient beings out of suffering.

Since women make up half the world's population, we need to do our part to help address the serious problems that affect humanity today. Women already do more than our share in raising ethical, compassionate children, which is the key to humanity's future. Whatever gender we may happen to be in this lifetime, we need to set aside any misconceptions we may have about women's capabilities and encourage women to become the role models we wish to see in the world. We need to cut through any false thinking we may have about women's limitations and realize that all human beings have equal potential for awakening. Spiritually speaking, there are really no limitations. If we set our mind to it, we can purify the delusions that make us unhappy and, in their place, generate limitless love for all living beings. In a mind of pure love, no darkness can exist. If we cultivate patience, lovingkindness, contentment, and wisdom, then anger, hatred, greed, jealousy, attachment, pride, and negativity can no longer afflict us. A heart of pure compassion is happy, contented, and a source of happiness for others.

Of course, we cannot purify the mind all at once. We need to be constantly alert and mindful, moment to moment. With daily practice, conflicting emotions will have less and less power over us, freeing up tremendous energy that we can use to help alleviate the sufferings of living beings. A person with a pure and loving mind can bring limitless good to our suffering world. As half the population here on planet Earth, women share the responsibility for global transformation equally with men. With full access to the Buddha's liberating teachings, women can shoulder our responsibility and work to benefit the world by embodying the values of peace and love that he taught. There is no aspect of contemporary life that would not benefit from Buddhist values.

If Buddhist women understand the logic of this proposition, then we must take our responsibility seriously. To work toward liberation for the benefit of the world is the highest meaning we can give our lives. The bodhisattva commitment to work toward becoming a perfectly enlightened being in order to liberate all beings from suffering is called *bodhicitta.* Once we generate this pure and perfect aspiration, we begin working step-by-step toward the goal of buddhahood. According to the Mahayana teachings, all sentient beings have this excellent potential. Women and men alike have the seed of awakening within, waiting to take root. Not only *can* all sentient beings become perfectly enlightened, they definitely *will* realize their potential and become buddhas; it is just a matter of time. One of my Tibetan teachers said: "The only difference between us and Buddha Shakyamuni is that we are lazy." Isn't it time for us to get down to the hard work of purifying our minds and realizing that potential?

The first step toward freeing ourselves is to disengage from fruitless activities and eliminate the conflicting emotions that are causing us problems and sapping our energy. We can accomplish this by being vigilant in recognizing and dispelling negative emotions as soon as they arise. Destructive emotions are our worst enemies, more dangerous than any external enemy. For example, when anger arises, there is a danger that we may act on it, speak hurtful words, or do something to harm ourselves or others. If we allow anger to rage unchecked, we may lose control and strike out or even kill someone. We need to stay alert and catch anger as it arises. Even anger's subtler cousin, irritation, can be remedied with the application of patience.

To take another example, when desire arises, there is a danger that we may act on it. We may wish to buy consumer items that we do not need, contributing to the depletion of the earth's resources and cluttering up our homes and our minds. Attraction to physical beauty and the enchantment of desire may get us into some sticky situations. It can lead us into unsuitable partnerships, causing great confusion and suffering to ourselves and others. We need to be mindful and catch desire as it arises. By recognizing the mind's tricks, we can avoid getting ensnared in unwholesome, complicated situations. As the Buddha said, "Contentment is the greatest wealth."

The second step toward freeing ourselves is to put the Buddha's teachings into action in our everyday lives. Reciting the sutras and reflecting on loving-kindness are no longer enough. Isn't it time to actively engage in relieving the sufferings of the world? This begins in our own family, neighborhood, and workplace and gradually extends to benefiting needy beings wherever they may be. Buddhist social activism can take many forms, from family counseling to international relief work. We may volunteer in a hospice, a hospital ward, or a prison ward. We may make contributions to education projects or hurricane relief. Whatever forms our activism may take, it is clear that

Buddhists need to become more socially engaged in alleviating the daunting problems that beset the human family today. We can practice the virtue of generosity by giving our time and resources and also enhance our minds through the practice of compassion. This is a win-win situation.

Do women have greater potential for the inner work of purifying the mind and a greater responsibility for the outer work of compassionate social action? I believe that all human beings have equal potential and share equal responsibility. Yet women seem to work especially hard. The United Nations has documented that 60 percent of the world's work is done by women, though they are often not compensated. History has shown that women are exemplary caretakers for beings in need, yet their loving-kindness and generosity are often undervalued. Many women skillfully alleviate the day-to-day sufferings of those who are ill, weak, or unable to take care of themselves, yet their compassionate contributions may be overlooked or overshadowed by other people's wishes and expectations. Women often set aside their own spiritual development in order to care for others, leaving little time for formal Dharma practice. How do we resolve this dilemma?

One solution is to transform caregiving into a bodhisattva practice. If we are able to generate the bodhisattva attitude, every compassionate action can become a bodhisattva practice. But caring for others does not mean that we need to put our spiritual development on hold. We need to balance our time between spiritual practice and service. Understanding when, where, how, and how much to practice and how to serve requires wisdom, personal honesty, and sometimes courage. Developing wisdom requires educating ourselves to continually deepen our understanding of the Buddha's teachings.

The Buddha's teachings are a treasure trove. They are not simply to be chanted. We need to put them into action. Women are developing the confidence to learn and apply these teachings here and now. We have a special responsibility to awaken our wisdom and compassion and apply these priceless values. We can take inspiration from great practitioners, past and present, both women and men. Today a global movement, led by the Sakyadhita International Association of Buddhist Women, is inspiring and encouraging Buddhist women to work together and optimize our potential for enlightenment.

Human life is precious and fleeting. By making the most of every moment and working together, the future can be very bright. Women definitely have the power to transform the world.

THE APPEAL OF BUDDHISM IN MODERN WORLD

Buddhism is spreading rapidly around the world now. There are Buddhist centers in many European countries, North America, South America, South Africa, Australasia, and so on. We find Buddhists in Europe not only in the Western capitalist countries, but also in the socialist countries of the East. For example, Poland has about five thousand active Buddhists.

Buddhism appeals very much to the modern world because it is reasonable and scientifically based. Buddha said, "Do not believe in anything that I say just out of respect for me, but test it for yourself, analyze it, as if you were buying gold." Modern-day people like such a nondogmatic approach.

There are many dialogues between scientists and Buddhist leaders, such as His Holiness the Dalai Lama. Together they are discussing and investigating what is reality. Buddha said that all problems come from not understanding reality, from being confused in this regard. If we were aware of who we are and how the world and we exist, we would not create problems out of our confusion. Buddhism has an extremely open attitude in examining what is true. For example, His Holiness the Dalai Lama has said that if scientists can prove that something Buddha or his followers taught is incorrect or just superstition, he would be happy and willing to drop it from Buddhism. Such an approach is very attractive to Western people.

Since learned masters of the past have adapted Buddhism to the culture of each society to which it has spread, it is only natural that teachers today need to present Buddhism in different modern countries in slightly different ways. In general, Buddhism emphasizes a rational explanation. Within this context, however, different points and approaches need more emphasis depending on predominant cultural traits.

Buddha taught such a variety of methods, simply because people vary so much. Not everyone thinks in the same way. Consider the example of food. If there were only one type of food available in a city, it would not appeal to everyone. If, on the other hand, different foods could be had with varied flavors, everyone could find something appealing. Likewise, Buddha taught a large variety of methods for people with a wide spectrum of tastes to use to develop themselves and grow. After all, the objective of Buddhism is to overcome all our limitations and problems and to realize all our potentials so that we can develop ourselves to the point at which we can help everyone as much as is possible.

In some Western countries that emphasize psychology, such as Switzerland and the United States, teachers usually present Buddhism from the point of view of psychology. In other countries where people prefer a devotional approach, such as many Southern European lands and in Latin America, teachers tend to present Buddhism in a devotional manner. People there like to chant very much, and one can do that in Buddhist practice. People in Northern European countries, however, do not enjoy chanting as much. Teachers tend to emphasize an intellectual approach to Buddhism there.

Many people in Eastern Europe are in a very sad situation. The Buddhist teachings appeal to them greatly because many find their lives empty. Whether they work hard at their jobs or not seems to make no difference. They see no results. Buddhism, in contrast, teaches them methods for working on themselves, which do bring results that make a difference in the qualities of their lives. This makes people unbelievably appreciative and enthusiastic to throw themselves fully into practices such as making thousands of prostrations.

In this way, Buddhism adapts itself to the culture and the mentality of the people in each society, while preserving the major teachings of Buddha. The principal teachings are not changed – the aim is to overcome our problems and limitations and to realize our potentials. Whether practitioners do this with more emphasis on the psychological, intellectual, scientific, or devotional approach depends on the culture.

How is Buddhism Adapting to the Twentieth Century in General?

Buddhism is adapting by emphasizing a rational scientific approach to its teachings. Buddhism gives a clear explanation of how life's experiences come about and how to deal with them in the best manner possible. Then it says do not accept anything on blind faith; think for yourself, test it out and see if it actually does make sense. This resembles science asking us to verify the results of an experiment by repeating it ourselves, and only then to accept the results as fact. Modern people do not like buying something without examining it; they would not buy a car without testing it. Likewise, they will not turn to another religion or philosophy of life without checking it first to see if it really makes sense. That is what makes Buddhism so appealing to many people of the twentieth century. Buddhism is open to scientific investigation and invites people to examine it in that way.

Buddhism and thai Education

When we speak about Buddhism and education, we tend to invoke the past when temples were centers of learning and monks were the teachers in charge of education. Making reference to the historical role of the monk as teacher is a way of showing the educational value of Buddhism in society — which once really existed. But at the same time, this type of reference amounts to a self-accusation, because these values no longer exist. Furthermore, turning one's back on the confusion and void of the present and finding amusement and pride in the richness of the past might be viewed as a symptom of people who have run out of hope, people who are trying to escape the sorrow of the present by referring to the past and finding pleasure and fulfillment there. This nostalgia is not an auspicious phenomenon or a sign of progress that should delight us.

On the one hand, this chapter is like some other chapter in one respect: it turns back again to reclaim the past when temples were the center of education and learning in Thai society and when monks had the important role of trainer and teacher of the populace. On the other hand, this article will not revert to describing how the temple was the source of education and how the monks were its bestowers — I will only refer to these things to link them with present conditions. The important point is that I will make sufficient references to show that, even at the present time, Buddhism has not completely lost its importance in education; it still has a residual or latent role, and sometimes these residual things have great importance for Thai society.

There are two kinds of important Thai customs related to Buddhism and education that are fundamental to the current situation:

(1) There exist customs in which the temple is the center of education and learning for the people and monks are the teachers who carry out the duty of training others. This custom may be almost invisible to present-day city dwellers, but for villagers in the distant countryside it is still apparent. Even though the temple may not be the center it was in the past, it is still a path or a last refuge.

(2) There exists the custom of being ordained and studying (*buat-rian*). This can mean entering the monkhood along with studying, or being ordained and then being obligated to study, or ordaining for the express purpose of studying. This might even mean being a monk for as long as one wishes to study, and after studying, those who want to stay in the Order can stay, and those who do not can leave. This has become the custom of temporary ordination. One aspect of this custom still well known today is the "three-month ordination," which has tended

to shrink to one month, half-a-month, even one week. When a person has remained in the monkhood for a time, he is free to leave the Order whenever he wishes.

Actually, these two customs are one and the same thing; but here I have divided them into two because the effects of these two aspects — which have come down to us to the present day — are different, as we will see below.

There are two important events and conditions that have resulted in the present state of Buddhist education:

(1) The state established a system of education following the Western model and separated education for the masses away from the temples. At first, this was done with the cooperation of temples, giving them an important element of responsibility. But later, the two gradually became more and more distant to the point that the state and the temple might be considered completely separate in educational matters.

(2) The state has not been successful in establishing education for the general public and has not been able to give its people an equal opportunity to receive an education. Largely this is because some people have not had access to this important opportunity. Some people have lost access to education for geographical reasons, in that many places do not have access to a school; and some have lost out for economic reasons, because if a student studies well and has no money, schooling must cease.

Saying this amounts to criticizing the government as the primary cause of such degeneration, but actually it is not this way. The two points mentioned above are accepted facts, especially point number two. Educators themselves often raise this issue for discussion, and the government is trying to find a way to rectify this. The points that follow are intended as constructive criticisms. Because the conditions of the nation are this way, this still allows the temples and the Sangha a role and some importance in education; but if the government were to successfully perform the two activities mentioned above, the temples and the Sangha may completely lose their role, shrinking in importance in the area of education. We do not have to turn to the past to make suppositions about this; in the present we can see this more and more clearly. Wherever the government expands and spreads its educational services, the role and importance of the temples and the Sangha are reduced or change. It is understandable that the condition that will disappear most slowly, which will help the temples and the Sangha still maintain a role and importance in education for some time to come, is the lack of equal opportunity in education related to economic conditions. As soon as the government can successfully solve the two problems above, then the educational role of the temple and the Sangha will change, fade, or completely disappear. All of this depends upon working with knowledge that can keep pace with this situation and whether or not, or to what degree, people are willing to face the truth.

The current conditions resulting from the clash between the two customs and causes just mentioned can be summarized as follows:

1. When the state does not have enough power to offer education to the masses and is not able to provide equal opportunity to the people, the poor peasants and villagers in the countryside still depend upon the custom of being ordained and studying. For them, the temple continues to be a source of education, a channel, or path. We can even say that this alternative exists as a "path of mobility" (*thang phan*), which allows children to receive a certain amount of education. This also has many other effects, such as:

   (a) Most of the so-called permanent monks and novices in Thailand who reside at temples (numbering approximately 230,000) come from poor farming families in the distant countryside. These monks and novices flow into the temples in the major cities for further education. This makes the temples, even in the capital city, a community for upcountry people right in the middle of the city (more than 90% of the monks and novices residing at temples in Bangkok are from the countryside);

(b) Normally, even though these monks and novices have the duty to study coursework related to Buddhism, because of their background (and some other good reasons), they are inclined to desire worldly studies as well-and this inclination increases, especially when their contemporaries are seen studying in the government system. If the temples and the Sangha are willing to accept these monks and novices into the Order, then it becomes their duty to determine how they will motivate them or force them to study courses related to Buddhism and to decide how much they should yield to their needs for worldly education. It is also normal that the needs and attitudes of monks and novices of school age will not always coincide with Sangha Elders or the ecclesiastical administrators of the Sangha. The greater the gap between their perceived needs and the education offered by the Sangha, the stronger the conflict becomes. To put it in the terms used by some modern people: the situation has become sharply polarized. When the situation has reached this point, it ordinarily follows that the administrators of the Sangha only increase their concern; having become very concerned, they are likely to strictly (or even forcefully) make the monks and novices remain within the framework they stipulate. In modern terms, this is called working on the minus side (in a negative or destructive way). Whenever these administrators have sufficient power to control others successfully, they are overjoyed, but the overall conditions decline each time. The best method for attaining positive results is to follow an old Thai custom: employ a policy of tactful conciliation and allow both sides to reap benefits. To further illustrate this point, Thai custom is not averse to using a "path of mobility"; quite the opposite, it supports using it, but it insists that those who tread this path must help to maintain it. The more the path is walked, the more progressive it becomes — including all those who walk the path, the path itself, and the community that has formed around this path — and the more everyone thrives together. Aside from this, there will still be a certain number who will remain in the Sangha and work there.

(c) When monks and novices from the countryside flow into this path of mobility for education in the city and there is no flow back to the countryside, this makes for a further loss, a continuous loss of strength on the part of the countryside. In the cities, even though a monk may be well educated, this still is not enough for him to acquire the status of being a leader; whereas in the outlying areas, whatever knowledge the monks and novices may have (or do not have), the villagers regard them as leaders. But the truly qualified monks who might provide good leadership in the countryside jam into the cities, which make for a two-fold loss.

(d) When the role of the Sangha and the condition its education has to depend on the deficiencies of the state education system — especially for potential ordinands — then as soon as the state education system arrives (or the local economy develops), the ordination of young boys as novices decreases or disappears entirely-except for those novices ordained according to custom at cremation ceremonies (*kan buat na fai*) and those young students who agree to be ordained for a short period during their summer recess. There are always some novices around, but they have come to be novices from the distant countryside where the state education system has not yet reached. This is the cause for an ever-increasing lack of monk-leaders in the countryside; this lack goes hand in hand with a decline of the temple and the Buddhist religion.

2. Meanwhile, inside the structure of the state education system, the higher the students go, the more necessary it becomes to move into the urban areas. Some middle-class people upcountry may have the partial means to send their children to study within the state system, but this still is not sufficient to support them completely. Therefore, when their children progress to higher levels of study and are to enter the market towns and major cities, they are often put in the care of the urban temple as dependents of the monks. This makes the temple a kind of dormitory or boarding house for students from the countryside enrolled in the state system. This condition has even more obviously turned urban temples into communities for people from the countryside. While at the same time, the temples have, in yet another way, become places offering support to the state education system.

3. Part of the custom of being ordained and studying that still remains in principle, even if incompletely, is ordaining for the three-month rainy season (*khao phansa*). But this custom has been, to a large degree, disturbed by the state education system. Because most young people do not have the opportunity to be ordained when they reach the proper age, they must wait until they are graduated, or postpone this even further due to work, a career, or a government post, for example. At any rate, this custom still is of great benefit to Thai society in the following ways:

(a) Young men in the cities — given the surrounding conditions and the lifestyle there — are estranged from the customs of their own society. Ordination is a tool for pulling them back to be complete Thai people, not strangers to their own culture and customs.

(b) For the young men living in the countryside, it can be of especially great benefit. In the eyes of this writer, I see the training and daily life in the temple, even during this temporary ordination period of three months, as real education and of greater benefit than the schooling received during the early ages of primary school (*prathom*) grades 1-4. It is education that brings life to bear on studies, and it is studying based on real life within the surrounding conditions, culture, and customs, which involves a relationship with the local community. We say that ordination makes a person ripe or mature (*suk*). This rite of passage still holds true in the countryside, because it makes those monks enter into adulthood, preparing them to become a complete member of a community. In addition to learning the traditions and customs of the community, monks attain knowledge they can put to good use or use to serve the needs of society. Furthermore, many rural youngsters graduate from the fourth grade (*prathom* 4) and go off to live in the midst of the rice fields, almost completely forgetting their courses, even reading and writing Thai. When they enter the monkhood they can reconsider and apply that knowledge so that it can be revived again. This value of ordination according to custom is especially clear during these times in which Thai educators are charging that schooling in this country has been treading the wrong path for a long time and that modern education alienates students from their own culture, communities, and customs.

Nevertheless, it is most unfortunate that the three-month ordination continues to fade even in the countryside, which makes the stay in the monkhood become shorter: one month, half-a-month, or even seven days. Daily training deteriorates. Many places have monks residing idly for a matter of days. Some temples lack leadership and do not even have monks with enough seniority to become abbot; temples often house monks who have been in the monkhood only one to two years, and they continue to act as abbots for some of the previously mentioned reasons. The benefits of the custom of ordination are, therefore, in decline.

4. While monks and novices from the countryside currently use the "path of mobility" for attaining the benefits of education, studying some worldly courses and some Buddhist courses along the way, in the end, most of them end up leaving the Order — this is the ordinary state of affairs. At the same time, the Sangha, or the monks in administrative positions, are all caught up in trying to control or contain this situation, partially out of anxiety and confusion and partially due to confidence in their own power — this has engaged people in a fight to the finish. In the meantime, a new trend has arisen: Some young, modern people — many with a good education and a lot of worldly experience — have become bored with the world or have come to see the value of Buddhism. They have been willing to leave their homes and carry out their intention to ordain for life. While at the same time, it has become clear that the Sangha was not prepared to receive this group of people, especially in terms of providing for their proper education. Most of these people cannot find much meaning in the existing ecclesiastical education and have a wide circle of relations with groups of students in institutions of higher learning for laymen, which also have groups studying about Buddhism; and these groups exist beyond the confines of the Sangha system itself. It is true that the ordination of people of this calibre is something that should be viewed as a positive sign, but if the educational system cannot meet their needs, then this may lead to negative results. If the Sangha has not made arrangements to accommodate and assimilate this group, then it is foreseeable that this new trend could become a strong force that could challenge the whole educational system and administration of the Sangha-a matter could escalate within a short period of time.

5. Not long after the state education system had parted ways with the temple, other aspects of lay life gradually moved away as well. Yet in the rural communities, some people still depend on the temple for education, and life is still more closely tied to the temple in accordance with tradition and custom than it is in the cities. Furthermore, after older generations pass away, if the later generations who hold responsibility in the government and modern society are no longer familiar with the temple and monks and come to have any relationship with them, it will be like strangers meeting — they will not truly meet each other on common terms, nor will they understand each other's problems. In fact, these people are likely to misunderstand each other very easily. All of this is due to the distance between the temples, the state, and urban society, which breeds the following undesirable attitudes:

(a) Most city dwellers are not familiar with the temple and Sangha that constitutes a community right in the middle of their own society. Only seeing its outward form and its occasional superficial movements, they do not know what it is nor how it exists. They then paint a picture in their minds: seeing monks study and then disrobe, they criticize and complain saying that the monks exploit the temple for their own education and take advantage of the laypeople; after the monks disrobe, they take jobs away from laypeople; or seeing no social role on the part of monks, they say that monks are listless and useless in society. Actually, some of the criticisms leveled by these people are, to a certain extent, correct, but because the reasons for these attitudes are not based on understanding and knowledge, this brings about more bad results than good — at least it does not contribute to the solution of problems.

(b) Currently, it is as if many of the people in important positions of responsibility in the state education system do not understand the situation. Or, to put it even more broadly, it seems that the state itself does not know, does not understand the traditions and relationship between itself and the Sangha in the area of education-forgetting how, over time, the state had partial responsibility for the education of the Sangha — and so it does not take the correct stand on education for the monks, and sometimes it even ends up causing confusion and conflict. For example, on occasion, some people have been known to say that the education of the monks is the monks' business, and the education of the nation is the nation's business — it is everyone for himself, different people, different work. But occasionally, some people are given to saying that this education for the monks has been conducted by the monastic institutions themselves and there are no laws to recognize it — it is, therefore, a kind of "outlaw" education.

(c) The patronage and support of the religion, since earlier times, has had, among other things, the goal of promoting and encouraging religious education, both directly and indirectly. But when the educational activities of the temples continued to decrease, the meaning of this — in terms of the relationship between support of the religion and support of Buddhist education — also decreased until it has been almost completely lost. You can see that the supporters of Buddhism in this later period now focus on materialism, putting up more and more grand structures or monastic buildings — and even the Sangha guides the people in this direction.

(d) The Sangha has become accustomed to feeling that education for the masses is currently the responsibility of the government and the Sangha is only involved in teaching the monks and novices about Buddhism. This feeling is deep-rooted to the point that, generally, when someone mentions religious education, the Sangha sees this only in terms of monks and novices and what goes on in the temples. The monks do not look beyond the

> fence or the wall of the temple. It does not occur to them that, "I ought to have a modicum of responsibility for the religious and ethical education of the children and young adults at large." They, therefore, do not get involved in knowing how village children receive their ethical training. Even if they were to talk about or criticize these matters, they would do it with the attitude of someone who is outside the realm of responsibility.

Having said all of this, I have not wished to chastise or criticize any particular person or group. In fact, everyone and all groups are the product of all the causal factors mentioned above. The best path is one of cooperation, of helping each other to study and understand the facts, accept the truth, and come together to change and solve these problems. The most unfortunate thing is that many people, especially those in positions of responsibility — either civil or ecclesiastical — tend to dream up imaginary criteria, saying: "things must be like this" or "things must not be like that." When real life conditions do not fit their notions, they absolutely refuse to listen and are unwilling to investigate the truth further with a mind open to considering the related causes and effects. These people have good wishes for Buddhism and are concerned about its activities, but it is the concern and good wishes of these very same people that contribute to the escalating seriousness of different problems. And it is the opposing or negative actions of these very people that have led to a kind of cooperation with their "perverted" monks, creating a field of battle for a fight to the bitter end. This, in turn, has helped to eliminate any possibility of common benefits or mutual happiness — and in the end this often may even contribute to the final destruction of Buddhism. Aside from the people at the administrative levels and those in positions of responsibility, we must admit that there are some monks and novices who do intentionally use the temple as a path for further study, for actual personal career benefits in a way that can be called using the "path of mobility" without helping to care for the path. There are also monks and novices who tread this path of mobility mindful of the reason for doing so, thinking that they will look after the path; but some of these monks are like seeds that break away and disperse, coming to rest just beneath the surface of the earth, crumbling, deteriorating, and rotting in the middle of the field instead of withstanding being tread upon, rolled over, dumped upon, and waiting quietly to grow, without anyone noticing, until the time is ripe and flowers bloom, making people willing to appreciate — by their show of beauty — the real fruits to be admired.

THE PLACE OF WOMEN IN BUDDHISM

The position of women has been a subject of considerable interest in recent decades. In all societies, particularly in the West, there has been a rethinking of the position accorded to women in all spheres of activity. This has resulted in a significant change in the role played by women in social, economic and even political life. This reappraisal has also touched on the question of the position accorded to women in the main religious traditions of the world. In Christian countries the issue of the ordination of women has become a highly controversial topic, and some Churches are facing the prospect of dissension, and even schism, on this question. It is therefore opportune to consider the place accorded to women in Buddhism.

Sanghamittâ Day is particularly appropriate topic to reflect on concerning this question. This day, which falls on the full-moon day in the moth of Unduwap of the Sinhalese calendar (November-December in the Western one), is particularly important for Sri Lanka Buddhists. It marks the anniversary of the arrival of the Bhikkhuni Sanghamittâ, reputedly a daughter of the Emperor Asoka of ancient India, in Sri Lanka on a historic mission. Sanghamittâ brought with her two treasures. The first of these was the establishment of the Bhikkhuni Order in Sri Lanka, thus complementing the work of her brother Mahinda Thera who not only introduced the Order Bhikkhus into Sri Lanka but is also credited with the introduction of Buddhism itself to Sri Lanka. The second of the treasures brought by Sanghamittâ was a sapling from the

Bodhi tree under which the Buddha had attained enlightenment. It is ironic that whereas the Bhikkhuni Order (which because of its self- sustaining nature could have continued indefinitely) has disappeared in Sri Lanka, the Bodhi tree (a much more transient entity subject to the law of *anicca*) still flourishes in Sri Lanka. There is perhaps a lesson here on the difficulty of perpetuating a Buddhist institution which has to be based on human endeavor of a high quality, than in looking after and venerating a non-human object, which is unfortunately all too common with many Buddhists.

The role of women in Buddhism could be considered in several ways. We can, for instance, compare the position accorded to women in both the religious and the secular life in India before the Buddha's time with that after the establishment of Buddhism, and consider whether the Buddha's teaching resulted in a change radical or otherwise. We can see whether the Buddha's teaching accords to women a position different to that accorded to men, as is the case in many other religious. We may consider whether the accident of the sex of one's birth helps or retards progress on the Buddha's path, and indeed whether gender is itself a chance event or caused by pre-existing factors. The part played by women in the early history of Buddhism, notably during the Buddha's own time, could be considered as providing a clue to the place accorded to women in Buddhism. In this connection the events surrounding the establishment of the Bhikkhuni Order need to be re-examined, as there is a measure of misunderstanding on this question. The influence of Buddhism on the position of women in the countries where Buddhism became a living presence could be highlighted. In this connection the significant facts pertaining to the mission of Sanghamittâ to Sri Lanka deserves notice. Finally the position of women in Buddhism could be contrasted with that accorded to women in the other great religious traditions of the modern world.

While the attitude of the Buddha to the role of women was an enlightened one, even when judged by the standards of the modern age, it must not be thought that everything that is said on this subject in Buddhist writing, even in the Pali Canon itself, measures up to the high standard expected of a Buddha. There are many explanations for this, not least of which is the fact that most of these works were written down several centuries after the Parinibbâna of the Buddha, and that during this time the teachings were sustained by monks, some of whom might not have been entirely free from the prejudices of the age. It is interesting to note that such "backsliding" occurs most commonly in the later works, e.g. in the prose sections of the Jataka (which incidentally are non-Canonical). And popular Buddhism took liberties of its own with this aspect of Buddhist teaching as it did with several others.

It is not possible to consider all these issues in a talk of this length. Only a few comments can be made on each of these questions. In particular it is not possible to comb the Buddhist texts to collect all the relevant issues relating to the position of women ill Buddhism. Fortunately this is not necessary as a small literature on this subject has accumulated since the late Ms I. B. Horner wrote her book *Women under Primitive Buddhism* well over 50 years ago. This book presents a comprehensive account of this question, and is still in may ways the best source on this question.

But no apology is needed to revive this question at a time when the position of women in religious life is undergoing a critical re-examination in many places.

The Pre-Buddhist Position of Women

The social matrix in which Buddhism arose was one which accorded to women an inferior position. In this regard Indian society did not differ radically from that in other places, and in some respects its treatment of women may actually have been more liberal. Indian religion in the Buddha's time is usually designated as "Brahmanism" to distinguish it from Hinduism, which in its classic form was a post-Buddhist development.

The position of women under Hinduism is well-known. Some idea of this position could be gleaned from the classic

Hindu Dharmashâstras of which the Manu-smirthi, popularly knows as the "Laws of Manu", is the best known. This work describes the duties of women as follows"

"By a girl, by a young woman, or even by an aged one, nothing must be done independently, even in her own house. In childhood a female must be subject to her father, in youth to her husband, when her lord is dead to her sons; a woman must never be independent". (Laws of Manu, V, 147-8).

Women were prevented from performing religious rites, and even the knowledge of the Vedas was to be kept away from them (IX, 18). The question for historians is how far these laws were in force at the time of the Buddha. The Hindus claim a divine origin for the laws of Manu, but they were probably complied later when Hinduism had assumed its rigid form centuries after the Buddha's time. However the Brahmanical religion of the Buddha's day, though somewhat better in this respect, did not accord spiritual parity to women. The primordial principle in the Vedic-Upanishadic philosophy which was dominant in the Buddha's time, was the male-principle (purusha), and this provided justification for the exclusion of women generally from social and spiritual activity.

It was in contrast to this attitude which reserved spiritual achievement for males that the Buddha proclaimed a message that was to be universal, one designed for the good of humanity as a whole without exception as to race, caste or sex. One of the classic titles given to the Buddha is "sattâ devamanussanam" or "teacher of gods and humans". If the Buddha had been regarded as a teacher of men, as opposed to women the term "purisa" (which is the Pali counterpart of "itti", woman) would have been used in this classic description, rather than the generic term manussa. More generally the teaching of the Buddha is referred to as one that could lead all beings (sattâ) to liberation, in whatever realm they lived and whatever form they assumed. However another of the classic description of the Buddha describes him as "Purisadammasârathi", or "charioteer of men to be tamed". Some might see in this sexist language, but what it probably means is precisely what it says, viz that men are subject to more violent misdeeds and have to be "tamed" to a greater extent than women.(1)

While the change in attitude towards women brought about by the Buddha has to be appreciated it must be remembered that he was not alone in this regard. The Jains too took a more enlightened attitude towards women when compared to the dominant Brâmanical religion. But Jainism unlike Buddhism did not concede the possibility of ultimate spiritual liberation to a woman, although a woman could become a man. Some, but not all, Jain sects extended their religious orders to women.

Women and the Buddha's Path

There is very little, if any at all, in Buddhism that identifies it with a particular sex. The Buddha himself was historically a man, but the essence of Buddhism does not involve any extolling of the personality of the Buddha (unlike say the Christian extolling of the person of Jesus in his capacity as the Son of God). What the Buddha discovered was a universal law which existed independently of all the Buddhas, and which others, male or female, can discover by following the directions of the Buddha. The cult of the Buddha's person, the worship of relics, the conduct of the "Buddha pûjâs" and the like, were all later developments, both in the Theravada and the Mahayana, and have scant justification in the discourses of the Buddha.

Later academic speculation has raised the question whether a female could become a Buddha or a Bodhisattva. Mahayanists have taken an affirmative position (e.g. the cult of Kwan Yin as a Bodlihisattva who heeds the pleas of those in distress), but the Theravadan position is less clear. Some have claimed that the Buddhas have to be males, others have taken a more ambiguous position. The correct way to approach this question is to regard it as another of those profitless questions which the Buddha left unresolved (avyâkata), as it is irrelevant to the question of release from samsâra. There can be only one Buddha in a given Buddha-era (despite what some of the Jâtakas may imply), and the present era happened to have been inaugurated whether by necessity or coincidence, by a male, Siddhartha Gautam.

Another way to regard this question is that even though the male-female identity is set at birth, this is only true of a particular birth. The Buddhists doctrine of rebirth asserts that gender can change over successive transmigrations. Thus in the samsaric sense there is no male or female, but only a single karmic stream. This is hardly surprising given that the anattâ doctrine ensures that there is not even a persisting personal identity over the samsaric stream. This is another reason why the Dhamma for the most part ignores the sexual identity of persons.

Unfortunately a contrary view has gained some popularity in Buddhist countries, mainly due to the influence of the Jataka stories. In these stories men tend to be men and women tend to be women (e.g. Siddatta and Yasodarâ are said to have been consorts over countless births).(2) As mentioned earlier, these stories are later accretions to the Buddhist tradition meant for popular consumption, and as we have them the essence of the stories seem to run counter to the fundamental Buddhist principle of anattâ. Only the stanzas in the Jatakas, which are bereft of narrative material, are considered canonical in the Theravada tradition. Another popular misunderstanding in many Buddhist countries is that negative ("unskillful") karma results in a man being reborn as a woman, and positive ("skillful") karma has the opposite effect. There does not seem to be any authoritative basis for this belief. In fact, the workings of the law of kamma is one of the unknowable questions for those who have not reached enlightenment. What factors result in a person becoming a male or a female were not discussed by the Buddha. Thus popular beliefs with regard to this are without foundation in the Buddha-dhamma.

On his deathbed the Buddha exhorted his followers to abide by the teaching, the Dhamma, which was to be the supreme guide. The Dhamma, of course, has no gender; the question is whether gender has anything to do with making the pursuit of the Path easy or difficult. The answer to this again is clear - the Buddha's path could be practiced by anyone, male or female. The eight components of the Noble Eight Fold Path are usually collected into three groups-Sila or Morality, Bhâvanâ or spiritual growth, and Pa ñ ñ ā or Wisdom. The practice of morality may in some minor respects involve different kinds of conduct for the two sexes, but in the practice of the path gender has no relevance. The highest achievement of Buddhism, supreme enlightenment, is available to both men and women. This was stated categorically by the Buddha, well before there were any female Arahants, when he answered Ananda's question as to whether women could reach enlightenment in the affirmative. The point made here is so self-evident that it would not justify any more elaboration.

Buddhist practice, in its purest form, has no place for ritual. It is in the conducting of rituals in most religions that sex-typing becomes important and questions of precedence, ritual purity, and the like arise. Later developments in some Buddhist countries have seen the emergence of some rituals, but even this kind of simple rituals have not involved any typing by the sex of the devotee. Buddhist rituals usually involves simple forms of worship, chanting or symbolic offerings, and all of these are available for men and women on equal terms.

In this connection it must also be mentioned that Buddhism has no place for a priestly class. Buddhist monks are sometimes mistakenly referred to as "Buddhist priests", but this is wrong use of terminology and should be avoided by all Buddhists. The role of the priest in religious life is to officiate between the faithful and the God , and Buddhism being essentially atheistic, has no place for a God or priest. Thus Buddhism has been spared the problem now all too evident ill theistic religions of women protesting their exclusion from the priestly circle. The position of monks and nuns in Buddhism will be considered in a later section.

The disciples of the Buddha, especially the more perceptive of the female followers, appear to have grasped very well the principle that the Dhamma was neutral with respect to the gender of the person following its dictates. There are not many direct references to this question, but an incident reported twice in the Sutta Pitaka is very relevant to this and must be considered. This records the taunt of Mara to the Theri Soma that no woman could reach "the high ground of the wise" because she has only the "two-finger knowledge (dvangulapa ñ ñ ā)", an allusion to cooking where the consistency of the cooked rice is tested by pressing it between the fingers. The refutation of Māra, as given hi the Sanyutta Nikāya, is worth quoting in full:

ittibhâvo kim kiyirā
cittamhi susamāhite

ñ ānamhi vattamānamhì
sammādhamma.m vipassato

What matters being a woman
If with mind firmly set

One grows in the knowledge
Of the Right Law, with insight?

yassa nûna siyā eva
itthāham puriso ti a

kiñci va pana asamîti
tam Maro vattum arahatîti

Any one who has to question

Am I a woman or am I a man

And does not oneself really know

Over such a one will Mara triumph

The version given in the *Therigâthâ* preserves the essential first stanza which asserts the irrelevance of the "female condition" (*ittibhāvo*) to spiritual progress, but replaces the second with a more conventional stanza:

sabbattha vihatā nanadi

tamokkhadho padālito

evam janāhi pâpima

nihato tvam asi antaka

With pleasures overcome everywhere

And the mass of ignorance torn away

Know this, 0 Defiled One,

Driven out art thou at last!

Whether this involves some later reworking by monk compilers we shall never know. It is however a fact that the *udānas* recorded in the Therigâtha are somewhat disappointing if we were to look in them for evidence on the question that is considered here. In most respects what the Theris see as the travails of life from which they seek escape into the ineffable, are not different from those identified by the theras in the *Theragāthā*.

THE SECULAR POSITION OF WOMEN IN BUDDHISM

When we consider the position accorded to women in ordinary life we have to note that the Buddha's teaching was primarily concerned with individual spiritual emancipation. This emancipation would be manifested in the worldly conduct of individuals, but the Buddha was not interested in establishing and perpetuating a particular worldly order, for whatever actual regime that would be put in place would in a Buddhist sense be unsatisfactory. In this respect Buddhism differs from other religions where private and public affairs were brought within the gambit of religious regulation.

Thus Buddhism does not take such things as marriage (where the position of women is important) as a religious "sacrament".. as it is, for instance, in Christianity or Hinduism. The Buddhist position was that these matters have to be regulated by society thorough some kind of social, political or legal process. It is only required that such arrangements should not be in fundamental conflict with the Dhamma. It is possible to have many different kinds of social and family arrangements which are compatible with the broad framework of the Dhamma. Thus matters like divorce, inheritance of property, etc. are entirely regulated by social processes, and there is considerable freedom for individuals in these arrangements. In matters like marriage, divorce, ownership of property, personal political or religious beliefs, etc. wives were allowed considerable liberty, and this was something that was to astonish Christian missionaries to Buddhist countries.

Nonetheless in his discourses to the lay person the Buddha does express views, and recommend practices which he considered as compatible with the Dhamma. Sometimes the Buddha's views happened to coincide with commonly accepted social principles, sometimes they were contrary to these views.

Thus for instance, in a society which considered male children to be more desirable than female ones, the Buddha held a different view. When King Pasenadi of Kosala, while still an adherent of the Brahmanical religion and thus shared its values, was disappointed that his Queen Mallika bore him a daughter, the Buddha told him: "A woman-child, 0 Lord of men, may prove to be a better offspring thən a male" (San. Nik, iii, 2, 6). It is possible to see in this a kind of diplomatic response to prevent the King developing an aversion to his Queen who was a Buddhist, but the sentiment expressed is genuine, and in keeping with the rest of the Buddha's teaching.

A few discourses given to householders emphasize the more worldly aspects of living, and of these the Sigalovada Sutta is the best known. This Sutta has been dissected to get actual rules of conduct on a wide variety of secular matters. This is a wrong way to approach the question. In this Sutta the Buddha was not laying down a code of domestic jurisprudence but instructing the Brahmin Sigala on certain basic principles. Of these the ones that are relevant here are the duties of wife to husband and vice versa. The Buddha lays down rules in this regard that could be considered common sense and eminently sensible. They conform to the mores of the time. The actual details are not important, but what is important is that the Buddha emphasizes the principle of reciprocity. Thus just as the wife has duties prescribed vis-a-vis the husband, so has the husband towards the wife. The equal burden of responsibility and duty laid on both husband and wife is the hall-mark of the Buddha's attitude to the role of women in the family life. In this Sutta the Buddha identifies qualities in women (beauty, wealth, kin, sons, virtue) which would make them the superior partner in a marriage, but these qualities are those generally accepted in society in the Buddha's time. The Sigalovada Sutta presupposes a monogamous system, but some of the royal patrons of the Buddha practiced polygamy having large harems, but they were not admonished for this by the Buddha. This was a matter belonging to social convention, and the Buddha preferred not to pontificate on it.

At other places in the Pali Canon there are references to the position of females that might not satisfy a modern exponent of "women's liberation". Thus the Dhaniya Sutta of the Sutta Nipata extols obedience in wives (reminding us of the Christian marriage vow imposed on wives to "obey" their husbands). Then there are the various lists of kinds of wives that appear in the Vinaya and the Sutta Pitaka, with the occasional hint that the more docile the kind of wife the better. But it must be remembered that these opinions do not have any kind of binding force, and are not always consistent with statements elsewhere. In a compilation as large as the Pali Canon such inconsistency on relatively minor matter is to be expected.

If one were to get a general principle on the question of the relation between the sexes it is the principle of reciprocity and non-dominance that emerges in the Buddhist writing. Even in the later Jatakas it is sometimes stated that woman who live in fear of their husbands are not true wives (No.537).

The Order of Bhikkhunis

This is often regarded as crucial to the evaluation of the role of women in Buddhism. What can be concluded is that while Buddhism passes this test it does so with a few minor qualifications.

Every religion has jealously guarded entry into its innermost sanctum. In many religions the doors of this sanctum are barred to women. In Buddhism one could consider the Sangha as forming part of the core of the Buddha Sâsana (Dispensation of the Buddha). It is part of the Triple Gem to which all Buddhists go for refuge. There is some argument as to whether the Sangha consists of those who have formally undertaken to follow the rules of the Vinaya, or consists of those who have "entered the stream" be they monk or lay, but we shall not consider this questions here, and take the popular view that the Sangha consists of the former.

As is well-known that the Buddha established the Order for Bhikkhus a few months after his enlightenment, and established the Bhikkhuni Order only five years later. The facts relating to the establishment of the Bhikkhuni Order are well known and need not be recounted here in full. We have Maha Prajapati G6tami, the foster mother of the Buddha, expressing her wish to enter the Order; we hear of the Buddha's rejection of this request; we see Prajâpati Gotami persisting in her request, and even following the Buddha over long distances; we then hear of Ananda's pleas to the Buddha on her behalf; and we have the Buddha's final consent.

The establishment of thc Bhikkhu Order is considered as something revolutionary in religious history. It is the first time that we have a body of men coming under a strict discipline not discharging a priestly function, all earnestly engaged in seeking a way of release. Previously ascetics were individual wanderers (*samanas*), not belonging to a body corporate. The Jains are sometimes credited with first establishing a religious Order but the Jain orders were something intermediate between the isolated Hindu ascetic and the organized body of samanas that constituted the Bhikkliu Sangha.

The extension of the monastic principle to women was even more revolutionary. Involvement of women in the religious life has at most times been either non-existent or dubious (as for instance in the case of the Indian devadasis and their counterparts in other countries). In course of time Prajāpati Gotami's wish to become a Bhikkhuni became the common aspiration of many women. Perhaps they saw in the Bhikkhuni order a freedom that they could not find in the secular life, where they were bound down by the rules of a society which accorded little importance to women.

The Buddha's decision to sanction the establishment of an Order for women in the fifth year after his enlightenment was a landmark in Buddhist and Indian history. But by the standards of the modern age it was marred by the special rules which the Buddha imposed on the Bhikkhunis. Thus Prajāpati Gotami had to agree to 8 special rules (*garudhammā*) before she was ordained, and these rules were later incorporated in the Bhikkhuni Vinaya. These rules could be summarized as follows:

Bhikkhus were always to have precedence over Bhikkhunis in matters of salutation, etc. irrespective of any other consideration.

Bhikkhunis could not observe the annual retreat (*vassa*) in a district where there were no Bhikkhus.

Bhikkhus had to set the dates for Bhikkhuni Uposatha ceremonies.

Confessing transgressions by Bhikkhnis had to done before the assembly of both Bhikkhus and Bhikkhunis.

Certain judicial processes in case of Bhikkhunis had to be undertaken by both the Sanghas.

Upasampadā initiation of Bhikkhunis should be given by the Bhikkhu sangha as well.

A Bhikkhuni should never abuse a Bhikkhu.

Bhikkhus can officially admonish Bhikkhunis, but not vice versa

That these rules involve a subordination of Bhikkhunis to Bhikkhus cannot be denied. Some of the rules may be explained in terms of practical necessity. Thus Rule 2 recognized the dangers to which Bhikkhunis would be exposed to if they spent the long period of retreat in isolated areas. Rules 3 and 6 might have been set up to see that the procedures in the newly established Bhikkhuni Order would correspond to and benefit from similar procedures in the already established Bhikkhu Sangha.

Rule 7 seems to be a restatement of the precept regarding "wrong speech". But Rules 1 and 8 cannot be seen in any other light than a concession to male superiority. In practical terms Rule 1 must have been the most irksome, and even humiliating in a society where the protocol attaching to salutation was very strict. The usual Buddhist rule which guided seniority was the number of years a person had spent in the Order, and while this continued to apply to Bhikkhus and Bhikkhnis considered separately, any individual Bhikkhuni had always to pay respect to any Bhikkhu however junior the latter may have been. It is not surprising that it was from this rule that Prajâpati Gotami sought exemption (unsuccessfully despite the support of Ananda).

Yet whatever be the explanation the rules lack reciprocity between males and females, and would not suit the present age. Unfortunately the extinction of the Order of Bhikkhunis must mean that this question has to remain an academic one. On his deathbed the Buddha gave permission to revise the less important rules of the Vinaya, but the offer was never taken. Whether this contributed to the extinction of the Bhikkhuni Order we shall never know. A few more comments will be made in connection with Sanghamittâ and Sri Lankan Buddhism.

The special rules for Bhikkhunis have come for criticism from certain Western observers. In Christianity there were no female priests, and therefore no equivalent to Bhikkhunis. The closest that we have are the various orders of Christian nuns (whose equivalents in Buddhist countries are the women who take the ten precepts). The position of Christian nuns vis-a-vis monks and male laity is distinctly worse that the position of Bhikkhunis under the Vinaya rules. At least the Bhikkhunis did not have to acknowledge (after the death of the Buddha) a male person as the spiritual head (as for instance Christian nuns would have to acknowledge the Pope or the Bishop).

The subordination of Bhikkhunis to Bhikkhus could be seen as one relating to protocol rather than to spiritual progress. Even amongst monks it does not follow that a more senior monk is necessarily more spiritually advanced than another who is a junior in terms of years spent in the Order. Similarly while Bhikkhunis may rank lower than Bhikkhus in terms of formal position they can be more advanced in terms of spiritual attainment.

Women in Early Buddhism

Once the order of Bhikkhunis was founded a large number of distinguished women from various social backgrounds came to adorn this Order, attracted by the power of the Buddha's teaching and the freedom which the new Order offered them. Many of these Bhikkhunis attained to the supreme bliss of enlightenment. The stories, sayings and deeds of these distinguished Bhikkhunis are recorded in many places in the Pali Canon, most notably in the *Therigātha*, a compilation of verses uttered by these Theris when they saw the clear light of the Dhamma, and which constitutes a part of the Khuddaka Nikaya of the Sutta Pitaka.

Amongst those in the *Udāna* are recorded in the *Therigāthā* are some of the best known names in early Buddhism. The include Prajāpati Gotami, who was the first Bhikkhuni, Uppalavannâ and Khema, who are traditionally regarded as "foremost of the Bhikkhunis", Kisāgotami and Patacâra, who figure in the best known stories in early Buddhism. The members of the order belonged to all walks of life. Some were former courtesans like Ambapāli and Vimala, others were of royal lineage like Sumeda and Sela. There were distinguished exponents of he Dhamma like Dhammadinnâ, scions of noble or merchant families like Bhadda Kundalkesa, Sujāta, and Anopama, not to mention those of humbler origins like Punnika the slave girl, or Chanda the daughter of a poor Brahmin. The actual numbers of Theris involved is not known. Patacâra is credited with having 500 personal followers, and there are several unnamed Thens to whom sayings are attributed.

The accomplishment of these Theris of old is that they gave living proof of the Buddha's utterance (Sam.Nik., 1, 5, 6):

yassa etâdisa.m yāna.m

ittiyā purisassa va

sa ve etena yānena

nibbanasseva santike ti

This is the only vehicle

Be it a woman or be it a man

The one who takes this vehicle

Can reach the peace of Nibbāna

where the chariot referred to is the Buddhā-Dhamma. Apart from these Theris and Arahants there were many women from all walks of life who embraced the Buddha's teaching. They became upāsikās and sāvakas, students and servitors of the Buddha and the Sangha. Their names have gone down in Buddhist legend and their piety is well known. These stories do not need repetition here.

Concluding Remarks

By way of conclusion we may reflect on the heritage of Sanghamittâ and compare the Buddhist position on the role of women in religious life with that of the other dominant religions.

However strong was the role of women in the Buddha's day once the charismatic presence of the Buddha ended with his death, the Bhikkhuni sangha too appeared to have entered into decline. While the Bhikkhu Sangha has continued in unbroken succession in many parts of the world (though not in the land of its birth) the fate of the Bhikkhuni Sanglia is less well recorded.

The Buddha is credited with the prophecy that the lifespan of the Buddha Sâsana would be curtailed because of the creation of the Bhikkhuni order. Whatever value be added to such prophecies, it is a fact that after the period foreseen by the Buddha (500 years) Buddhism saw the great bifurcation between the Mahayana and the Theravada streams. Even the Theravada which is the closest of these two streams to the original views of the Buddha, developed numerous tendencies which were not seen in the Buddha's day. The rise of the Mahayana has had some implications for the role of women in Buddhism. It has been claimed that the Mahayana entertained a more positive attitude toward the role of women than the Theravada. However, the early Mahayana masters were all male. Indeed it is the claim of some Mahayana sects that the Buddha established a line of patriarchs with Maha Kassapa as the first. This line of patriarchs naturally all consisted of males. When Chinese orders of Bhikshunis were finally established this was done with the aid of Theravada bhikkhunis from Sri Lanka.

While the Mahayana bhikshuni orders still survive the fate of the bhikkhuni order in Theravada countries has been different. In India itself not only the bhikkhuni order but also the bhikkhu order came to an end. But before this happened both orders were established in Sri Lanka which henceforth became the source of Theravada Buddhism. There is no evidence that a Theravada bhikkhuni order has existed in any country other than India and Sri Lanka. Whereas the Bhikkhu order was exported to countries in South-East Asia this does not seem to have been the case with the Bhikkhuni Order.

Sanghamitta's role in bringing the Bhikkhuni Order to Sri Lanka has been noted earlier. She seems to have had a great initial success with many of the leading ladies of the country including those of royal blood taking to the monastic life. From Sri Lanka the Bhikkhuni Sangha was taken to China in the fifth century by enterprising Sri Lankan Bhikkhunis. Other than this very little is recorded of the activity of Bhikkhunis in Sri Lanka. We do not even have the exact date as to when the Order vanished in Sri Lanka. This also meant the extinction of the Theravada Bhikkhuni order in the current dispensation of Gautama.

The question for the modern age is whether the Bhikkhuni order should be revived, and if so how this could be done. In Sri Lanka and other Theravada countries women who want to play a more active role than that of lay followers of the Dhamma can only take the Ten Precepts.

The dominant opinion amongst the Sangha in Theravada countries is that there is no possibility of resuscitating the Bhikkhuni Order. This follows from the traditional requirement of an appropriate lineage for the perpetuation of a particular Order. Thus Bhikkhunis have to be ordained by other Senior Bhikkhunis although the Vinaya also requires the participation of Bhikkhus. Those who argue for the revival of the Bhikkhuni Order argue that technically the lineage of Sanghamitta Theri still continues to flourish in a few places where Chinese Buddhism still flourishes. True, the Mahayana practices differ from those in the Theravada. But if the technical requirement of an unbroken lineage is what is needed to revive the Bhikkhuni Order a way could be found by using this curious survival of the heritage of Sanghamitta Theri in a foreign land. But that Bhikkhus must also participate and the conjunction of Mahayana Bhikshunis with Theravada Bhikkhus to re-establish a Theravada Bhikkhuni Order will run into serious difficulty from both sides.

But even without a Bhikkhuni order there is ample scope for the participation of women in Dhamma work. The Buddha has not said that enlightenment can come only from formal adherence to a monastic order. Both laymen and laywomen have become arahants in the past. Thus the door to the highest goal of Buddhism is not barred to women simply because the Bhikkhuni order has become extinct.

A few comments of the Buddhist position of women with that of other religions may be made. We have had occasion to make a few remarks on the position of women under classic Hinduism. Modern Hinduism has not changed much, although there has been some elevation in the social position of women. Women cannot still officiate as priests ill the Hindu religion.

Christianity has traditiotially been a masculine religion mainly because its main dogma relates to a God considered as a male ("Father") and a prophet-teacher Jesus who is considered as his "Son". The centerpiece of the religion is the Father-Son relationship, and it is not surprising that women have been relegated to a secondary place and denied spiritual equality with men. Jesus considered himself to be a Jewish Messiah, and did not challenge Jewish views on this subject. His comments on the role of women are at best ambiguous. None of the 12 original disciples were women. The modern Christian Church was constituted out of the claims of Jesus by St Peter, who is well-known as a misogynist, and the subsequent record of Christian Churches has reflected this quite well. Now there are moves to ordain women priests in some Christian denominations but these moves have led to much dissension.

The position of women in Islam is well known. They too are denied full access to religious functions, and in some countries even access to the mosque. It is disturbing that the revival of Islamic fundamentalism is threatening to undo some progress that has been made in some Islamic countries.

Thus whatever comparison we may care to make with other religions the Buddhist view on this question is not only enlightening but unique.

THE ROLE OF RELIGIOUS BELIEFS IN EARLY CHILDHOOD EDUCATION: CHRISTIAN AND BUDDHIST PRESCHOOLS IN JAPAN

The views of teachers and directors in four Christian preschools and four Buddhist preschools are examined in this qualitative study of early childhood education in Japan. In Christian preschools, the guiding principle was that each child was a precious gift of God. This belief resulted in a play-oriented curriculum that maximized the choices available to children. Teachers also attempted to encourage children's creativity and their ability to formulate thoughts and express them to others. A particular focus was helping children appreciate each other as individuals and learn to form relationships based upon that appreciation. In Buddhist preschools, the curriculum was designed to strengthen children's virtue, intellect, and physical well-being. Activities were teacher structured, with an emphasis on attaining literacy and numeracy skills. Lessons were delivered in a whole group context, with an emphasis on absorbing content rather than encouraging personal exploration and expression. The clear implications of these different religious perspectives suggest that similar analyses be undertaken in the United States, where very little research has been conducted on church-based preschools.

Introduction

The United States is one of the most religious countries in the world, with a majority of the population claiming affiliation with a religious group. After a historical period of relatively strict separation between church and state, religious values are again beginning to receive explicit recognition in some public educational settings. For example, Congress recently voted to allow the Ten Commandments to be posted in public school classrooms. Additionally, many states are debating whether to allocate public funds to charter schools sponsored by religious organizations, another breach in the wall of separation (Fuller, in press).

In the research literature on K-12 schooling, there has been a growing scrutiny of religious schools. One focus has been on the manner in which the values inherent in the religious doctrine are embodied in the expectations for teachers, students, and parents, including such issues as student comportment in and out of school, teachers' discipline practices, and the nature of teachers' communication with parents. Research in Catholic schools suggests that children benefit when parents and staff communicate with each other and share such values as commitment to hard work and respectful behavior toward adults(e.g., Bauch, 1993; Coleman & Hoffer, 1987). The literature on home schooling has also begun to track the role of religious values in shaping curriculum and pedagogical practices (Huerta, in press).

In contrast to this burgeoning literature in the K-12 area, there has been little attention to the functioning of early childhood programs that operate under religious auspices. A few studies of child care quality have included religious affiliation as a variable, and so far the findings have been rather contradictory. In the National Child Care Staffing Study (Whitebook, Howes, & Phillips, 1989), for example, researchers found that church-sponsored centers paid higher wages than for-profit centers, but they lagged behind nonreligious, nonprofit centers in the provision of other employee benefits. On the other hand, analysis of a national survey of nearly 2,000 centers found that employee salaries were lower in church-related centers than in any other type, and the analysis also found less evidence of a planned curriculum and parent participation in church-related centers than in any other type (Fuller, Raudenbush, Wei, & Holloway, 1993).

Work to date has not closely investigated the goals and expectations of staff at church-based schools, nor have studies assessed aspects of children's learning and development that may be most relevant to the goals of the schools. More research, particularly in the form of qualitative investigations, is needed to better understand the ways in which the "rules for living" espoused within various religious organizations are instantiated in preschool organizations.

In the study reported here, a qualitative approach was utilized to understand the goals, values, and expectations of Japanese early childhood education programs affiliated with Christianity and Buddhism. By talking at length with teachers and directors of these programs, I sought to understand how their values were embodied in the practices and curricula of the schools. These data underscore the importance of understanding how collectively held belief systems inform educational practice.

The system of early childhood education in Japan is quite extensive. Over 90% of Japanese children attend at least 2 years of a licensed preschool (*youchien*) or child care center (*hoikuen*) (Boocock, 1989). Public preschools are funded by state and local government (with some tuition contributed by parents), but approximately 80% of children attend private preschools, some of which are affiliated with a religious organization (Ministry of Education, Science, and Culture, 1994). All preschools and child care centers are subject to oversight by the national government, which develops regulations pertaining to such issues as the dimensions and basic facilities available and the level of required teacher preparation. However, preschool directors have considerable latitude in formulating their own programs, resulting in more diversity in the areas of materials, activities, and curriculum than is seen at any other stage in the Japanese educational system (Peak, 1991; Tobin, Wu, & Davidson, 1989). Shinto, Buddhism, and Christianity, which have been intertwined with each other for over a century in Japan, create a rich tapestry of spiritual and philosophical thought that has had a profound impact on the nature of preschools (Wollons, 1993). (Note 1)

The theoretical basis of this study is located in the literature at the intersection of anthropology and psychology (Shweder et al., 1998). In this literature, individuals involved in the socialization and education of young children are presumed to hold cultural models that guide their actions (e.g., Harkness & Super, 1995). Cultural models are "presupposed, taken-for-granted models of the world that are widely shared (although not necessarily to the exclusion of other, alternative models) by members of a society and that play an enormous role in their understanding of that world and their behavior in it . . . [and which] frame experience, supplying interpretations of that experience and inferences about it, and [provide] goals for action" (Quinn & Holland, 1987, p. 10). Cultural models include beliefs or conceptual schemas (e.g., "children should be seen and not heard") as well as behavioral scripts (e.g., steps to take when a child acts in an aggressive manner toward a peer) (D'Andrade, 1992; Holland, Lachiotte, Skinner, & Cain, 1998). However, cultural models are not necessarily associated with broad social categories like nation or ethnicity (Kondo, 1990); they can be generated within smaller social units as well (e.g., working class families in the Shitamachi section of Tokyo).

Furthermore, for important topics like rearing and educating children, a number of cultural models are available in a given community. This cultural "pool" of beliefs and practices may contain elements that are in tension, or even in fundamental conflict, with each other (Kojima, 1986, 1988). Within Japanese preschools affiliated with religious organizations, there may therefore be sharply divergent models as to how human relations should be organized and socialized in young children (see also Shore, 1996; Holloway, Fuller, Rambaud, & Eggers-Piérola, 1997).

Sample and Methods

The data are drawn from interviews and observations conducted in 1994 and 1995 in 32 early childhood settings (27 preschools, 5 child care centers) in Tokyo and the Kansai area, which includes the major cities of Osaka and Kobe. Introductions to site directors were provided by officials in the regional association of private preschools and by colleagues in local universities.(Note 2) The sample was selected to ensure variation across type (preschool, child care center), location (urban, suburban), and auspice (private, public).

The visit to each setting included an observation of approximately 1 hour in a classroom serving 4-year-olds and an interview with the director and one or more teachers, conducted by the author and a Japanese bilingual associate. (Note 3) The open-ended interview, which lasted from 1 to 3 hours, was designed to probe cultural models regarding goals of the preschool experience, theories about the role of the teacher in facilitating learning, views about discipline and control, details of the curriculum and activities, and perceptions about the family and its relationship with early childhood education. The observations were used as a source of examples to deepen these extended conversations. All interviews were tape recorded; in addition, detailed notes were kept during the interview.

Subsequent to the first round of data collection, a deductive process of preliminary data analysis occurred. Field notes and interview notes were reviewed and analyzed using a preliminary coding framework. Initial data displays were developed—within-case displays were created to highlight the key cultural models in each preschool, and cross-case displays were used to highlight differences and similarities across preschools (Miles & Huberman, 1994). In the second round of data collection, 3 schools were selected from the pool of 27 preschools. The author and a Japanese associate spent at least 5 days in each setting, observing in a classroom of 4-year-olds and conducting further interviews with staff. A running record was kept during the observations, with the focus being a description of the teacher's activities and utterances. Field and interview notes were reviewed regularly to develop hypotheses that could be probed in subsequent interviews and observations (Strauss, 1987).

At the end of the data collection period, all interviews were translated and transcribed by a bilingual Japanese doctoral student in education. The original Japanese terms used for key childrearing and educational concepts were retained along with the translated equivalents. A coding system was developed that permitted sections of narrative to be tagged with global categories (e.g., goals, activities, teacher-child relations, discipline, role of the parent, and issues of individualism and group orientation). The transcriptions were then coded using a qualitative software package.

The final stage of analysis involved a number of activities. First, all passages associated with each of the key codes were examined to obtain a sense of the variation that existed within each code. Next, the entire corpus of transcripts and field notes was reviewed to learn how the categories fit together at each school. A matrix was generated listing the central findings pertaining to each category for each preschool. These steps resulted in the confirmation of earlier hypotheses about the clusters of cultural models that were shared by subgroups of the preschool staff. Brief case studies of particular schools were written to use as a point of discussion in focus groups and informal interviews with Japanese informants—including parents, parent educators, and faculty in departments of psychology and early childhood education. Reactions and commentary from these informants as well as field notes and written material provided by the preschools (i.e., curriculum guides, parent newsletters, and promotional materials) were used to understand and contextualize the interview data. This paper is built primarily upon the comments of directors and teachers from four Buddhist preschools and four Christian preschools (Catholic and Presbyterian).

FINDINGS

Christian Preschools

Directors in each type of school articulated cultural models that guided their school's curriculum and vision of appropriate practice. We begin this discussion with the Christian schools. Although these schools spanned a variety of denominations, both Catholic and Protestant, they shared a number of cultural models that informed their programs. The amount of time devoted specifically to learning about Christianity varied among the schools.

Most schools included a daily morning prayer and a prayer before and after meals. Attending a church service of some kind once a week was common. In the more actively religious schools, there was a designated time for listening to Bible stories. At Christmas, they engaged in a number of activities; for example, literature samples obtained from two Catholic preschools each feature a photograph of the Christmas performance, which was an enactment of the Nativity. Although the schools spanned a variety of denominations, including Catholic and Protestant organizations, the staff held a number of cultural models in common.

The Christian directors built their programs around the view that God's love is the primary message of Christianity. According to this central cultural model, children are gifts from God, and each one should therefore be highly appreciated (*hitori hitori o taisetsu ni*). For example, Ms. Watanabe, director of Hikari preschool, expressed the following sentiment:

Jesus Christ delivered God's message of love. The love of God means that God loves each individual child. Each individual child is precious because he or she is a gift sent by God. Through his or her parents, each individual child is delivered by God. We sincerely appreciate God's production of children

Children at a Christian Preschool Practice a song for An Upcoming Performance.

This cultural model had two direct implications for the daily routine at Christian preschools. One way of respecting the individual was to allow the children considerable freedom in deciding what they wanted to do. Accordingly, free play formed the basis of the curriculum in all the Christian schools. For instance, as he came to realize the fundamental importance of individual self-determination in Western religious thought, Mr. Kobayashi, director of Arima preschool, became more and more convinced that it was essential to avoid teacher-centered activities:

We respect children's spontaneous activity (jihatsuteki koudou). *In the past, the children went to the chapel once a week to pray. They had to walk with their hands folded. It was teacher centered, and the adults ordered the children around. The children tried to respond properly. I tried to destroy that atmosphere. I didn't like it because . . . the teacher's desire was different from the desires of the children. If the children aren't paying attention during a story, it means it is not interesting to them—and the teacher shouldn't just tell them to be quiet.*

A second implication was that the teachers placed a priority on encouraging children to articulate their own ideas and to integrate their views with those of their classmates. For example, the teachers at Arima held a class discussion after every art period to elicit children's opinions and ideas about the morning's activities. I observed Ms. Nagatomi, a teacher from Arima, handle such a class meeting for the purpose of discussing a "junk art" project in which children used tape and glue to create individual objects from household items like egg cartons and tissue paper boxes. The projects were imaginative and intricate: a peacock whose tail could stand up when pulled with an attached string; a cardboard jewelry box with tissue paper cut into small squares and pasted to resemble stained glass; a serving of assorted sushi, complete with rosette of ginger and a wedge of plastic grass. Ms. Nagatomi picked up each project and asked its creator to say something about it. She then built on the child's comment, sometimes soliciting suggestions from the class as to how the project could be extended or how problems the creator had experienced could be solved. This carefully conducted discussion is consistent with the Arima philosophy of combining individual attention with developing an awareness of others and skills in interacting with them. As this glimpse indicates, the teachers were careful to nurture the children's imagination and self-expression, both artistic and verbal. But Ms. Nagatomi was careful to balance this focus on the individual with attention to how the children interacted in the group context.

*Three-year-olds just tend to put a couple of boxes side by side and say, "That's it." . . . But only they themselves know what they are making. Then they realize that others may see their creations differently. They realize the importance of how the other party sees their productions. Through the creation of a work, they learn to develop a common understanding (*kyoutsuu rikai*). This is my goal. . . . Instead of one child learning a particular subject, we try to involve all the children in the shared learning.*

Children use Tape during a "Junk art" Activity at a Christian Preschool.

Teachers in Christian preschools were particularly welcoming of children with disabilities because they felt it was valuable for the nondisabled children to encounter someone who had characteristics that differed quite saliently from their own. Through daily interactions with children who were different from them in some ways, the students were thought to gain an appreciation for each individual but also to learn how to form relationships in spite of those differences. As the teacher at Arima said:

As you may have noticed, we have a handicapped child in the class. I pay particular attention to that child, but I also ask other children, "Please help him while I am working with these other children." At first, his learning or working speed was very different from the others. Because of that, he had difficulty in getting along with them. Gradually, however, he became involved with other children. In that process, the children came to understand each individual's differences and started to acknowledge each individual's characteristics. I think this process applies to children's mutual interactions in general.

Perhaps because of the connection that their religious beliefs provided to Western thoughts and values, the directors of Christian preschools that I visited were more interested in learning about and adapting Western theories of early childhood education than were directors in other preschools. For example, Ms. Ishida, the director at Aizawa preschool, had sought wide exposure to Western theories of early childhood education. She had attended classes in the Montessori method, although the major emphasis of her training at a local Christian college had been on the methods of Froebel. She was also exploring in workshops the ideas of constructivists like Constance Kamii and was cautiously implementing new strategies for fostering children's emergent literacy, even though they appeared to contradict the Ministry of Education's policy of leaving literacy to the elementary schools. Activities on the day I visited presented many opportunities to build literacy skills. The 4-year-old children were making vegetable soup with a recipe that featured written directions accompanied by pictures. The 5-year-old children were re-creating their experience at a summer fair. Using large cardboard boxes, they constructed food stalls and activity booths. Their writing skills came into play as they created signs, menus, price lists, and other artifacts.

A parent volunteer reads with two students at a Catholic preschool.

Montessori materials are available at this Catholic preschool.

Not surprisingly, the Christian preschools were the most similar to American schools of any that I visited. The cultural models inherent in Christian thought have obviously permeated the views of children in the United States to a profound extent. However, it should be noted that these models have been interpreted by Japanese early childhood educators and combined with Japanese cultural models; this appropriation process results in an orientation toward strengthening the individual's powers of self-expression, fostering self-knowledge, and cultivating personal interests—but the teachers expect children to use these skills to build relationships and form the ability to function well in group settings. This dual emphasis on individual development and social connection makes these schools likely to serve as models of good practice for American educators, who are apt to value these particular cultural models (see also Kotloff, 1993).

BUDDHIST PRESCHOOLS

From the front, the Tennoji Buddhist Preschool building looks more like an insurance company than a preschool. The imposing modern structure is three stories high, with many windows whose darkened glass prevents outsiders from seeing in. Yet, when one moves through the entryway and passes through the hall to the play yard, the peaked, tile roof of a traditional Buddhist temple looms into view. A close examination of the school philosophy at Tennoji and the other Buddhist schools reveals how three traditional elements of Buddhist thought have been artfully synthesized with modern preoccupations about preparation for elementary school.

*Virtue (*toku*) as a Goal of Preschooling.* The essence of virtue, according to the staff at Tennoji, was in developing a sense of consideration for others (*itawari no kokoro*). They felt that kindness and consideration should be extended to all living things, including animals and plant life as well as humans. They emphasized this message in the weekly prayer service at the temple, and they provided practical experiences, like caring for the preschool's plants and animals.

Children attend a service at the Buddhist temple associated with the preschool.

The emphasis on showing consideration for others is consistent with Buddhist teachings on compassion. For Buddhists, both wisdom and compassion are needed to help relieve the pain and suffering of the human condition. Buddhist ethics include "a deep sensitivity to the life of the cosmos, an ecological consciousness which combines esthetic refinement with a sense of responsibility" (Dumoulin, 1994, p. 65). Japanese Buddhism is particularly explicit in its strong emphasis on compassion. For example, one of the strongest and oldest schools of Japanese Buddhism, the Shingon sect, urges its followers to practice Four Embracing Acts: charity, kind speech, beneficial acts, and adapting oneself to others.

For the director at Suma Buddhist preschool, informal daily prayer was another important vehicle for teaching compassion:

*Through a variety of activities, we would like children to appreciate the spirit of Buddha. Putting one's hand together in prayer is the most important activity, particularly in today's society. . . . We teach the children Buddhist song and show them how to offer flowers to the altar celebrating Buddha's birth. . . . Obviously, young children do not understand a deep philosophy like this, but I want teachers to convey gentle feelings to the children. Through activities, we would like the children to appreciate gentle feelings. . . . Japanese put their hands together in prayer before eating a meal. They take doing so for granted. In Christianity, people say "Amen," which corresponds to the Buddhist chant of "*Namuamidaibutsu.*" A sense of gratitude is what we should consider most important. But it is today's Japanese people that tend to forget the importance of this activity, which is the foundation in life . . . children should extend their gratitude and then have a meal. Also they should extend their gratitude to their parents. They acquire this as a habit and this is most important.*

The Buddhist directors tried to be gentle in their exhortations about prayer as the means for developing a mind of appreciation. However, they were also quick to point out that

Buddhism called for strength and determination as well as kindness:

> *Raising cheerful, gentle, and healthy children (*akaruku sunao genki na kodomo*) is our overall philosophy. This is from the Buddhist belief in which being strong, happy, and gentle is emphasized. You might think that in Buddhism you are generous to everything. This is not necessarily true. Living in a strong way is important in Buddhism. By being strong, I mean that one should do anything with confidence and determination.*

The view among the Buddhist directors I spoke with was that children were like wild animals and needed to be tamed in preschool. At Tennoji, 3-year-old children were considered to be a particular challenge because they do not understand the school rules, resulting in a situation that is "chaotic" and leaves teachers feeling as if they are "fighting a war." As one teacher put it:

> *I try to tame one child after another every day. I first try to tame those children who seem to adapt easily. I may tame one child today but may not be able to do so tomorrow. . . . By July [4 months into the school year], all the children have become calm and quiet except for a couple of children who are still naughty. . . . By now [November], they are calm and quiet.*

One of the least desirable characteristics of the unsocialized person, according to the directors, was a tendency to act in a selfish, egocentric manner. Therefore, the staff members at the Buddhist preschools were careful to enforce desired behavior firmly. As the director of Suma explained:

> *I am afraid to say that Japanese people have not yet developed the notion of democracy. If children are left as they are, they tend to be selfish. Japanese people in general tend to equate democracy with being self-centered. Japanese tend to ignore discipline unless they are told to observe discipline. When it comes to developing children's individual character (*kosei*), I think it is important to allow them to play freely and at the same time to discipline them. But children tend to do only*

what they want. They tend to seek self-centered individualism. They tend to ignore the notion of love or empathy (omoiyari). *Thus we tend to feel that we need to control children. This is a very important aspect of Japanese education.*

In this passage, the director of Suma argues that Japanese people are by nature selfish and that they need structured socialization experiences to become "human" rather than animalistic. This view contrasts sharply with the opinions of the Christians, who emphasized the idea that children are "precious gifts" from God. It is interesting that Japanese Christian early childhood educators hold this benign view, while the Buddhistsarticulate a more negative view of human nature, one that is similar to that of conservative Christian educators in the United States. The view of many evangelical American Christians is that adults must be vigilant to prevent children from succumbing to the wickedness that is the legacy of the original sin (Cleverly & Phillips, 1986).

Another strategy for avoiding individualism was to feature large group activities as much as possible. In a pamphlet for parents, the director makes an argument for large class sizes: "I suspect that most of you [mothers] think that small class sizes, such as 5 or 10 children per teacher, are better for your children. I do not think so. Among 20 or 30 peers in a class, the children are more motivated to learn by competing with each other. Therefore, class sizes of 5 or 10 students are not good at all. Of course, parental overprotectiveness (*kahogo*) is not good. Children aged 4 to 5 need a group" [translation].

Another component of the group orientation is developing the child's weak points rather than allowing him or her to focus on strengths, again illustrated in the parent brochure: "Young children need balanced care that focuses on various aspects of development such as music, intelligence, creativity, and health (physical ability). In a*youchien* there are future artists and future scholars. There are also future athletes, and yet it is not a good idea to develop only their athletic abilities. If you improve only the musical ability of a child who is good at music, this child will have unbalanced overall ability" [translation].

Children at a Buddhist preschool learn to play the drums.

*Obtaining Knowledge (*chi*).* Buddhists have traditionally focused on wisdom and faith as the key to salvation, in contrast to the Christian doctrine of love. Buddhism holds that ignorance, in combination with desire, are the forces that prevent people from moving beyond the pain of life on earth. A primary strategy for attaining knowledge is to study sacred texts. The texts themselves are considered authoritative, so the believer is a "hearer of the word." Expression of Buddhist faith has traditionally focused on "pious copying out of scripture," a practice that is still considered meritorious (Dumoulin, 1994, p. 55). Schools established by Buddhist monks from the 18th to the 19th centuries featured intensive study of classical texts (Sato, 1998).

In the Buddhist preschools I visited, students were strongly encouraged to orient themselves toward external sources of knowledge, including both texts and the teacher. At Tennoji, this approach was partly illustrated by the children's memorization of sacred chants. In addition, they spend most of their day sitting at desks receiving instruction from the teacher. Literacy is a major focus of the curriculum, including instruction in reading *kanji*(Chinese characters) and writing *hiragana* (the simplified syllabary). Children engage in poetry reading and writing, and they learn the basics of grammar. They are involved in activities for the purpose of "developing their intelligence" (*chi no kaihatsu*), in which a wide range of materials are used to stimulate basic cognitive skills such as visual perception and memory, as well as such Piagetian principles as seriation and class inclusion. In addition, children attend classes in art, ballet, English, instrumental music, and choral singing.

Children pair up for a game at a Buddhist preschool.

Children use glue and markers during an art activity at a Buddhist preschool.

At Sannomiya preschool, a more radical curriculum emphasizes decontextualized cognitive stimulation. Children are exposed to complex visual and auditory patterns, which they memorize, with no exploration of the meaning of the stimuli.

For example, in one exercise, teachers clap out a complicated rhythm for children to repeat. Children are shown flash cards representing the flags of nations around the world and call out the name of the appropriate country. They memorize poetry in archaic Japanese. According to the director, a Buddhist monk, the purpose of these activities is not to learn facts, but rather to receive brain stimulation in a rhythmic, fast-paced tempo:

Cramming children's heads with knowledge is wrong. What children need is intellectual stimulation, as can be seen in what we do with children's language development. Visual stimuli represented by literacy are important so that children absorb many things from the environment. Children's brain functioning is strengthened by absorbing a lot of things from their environment.

This approach to learning is consistent with what Hori (1994) calls "ritual formalism," the method used for teaching in Japanese Zen monasteries: "By ritual formalism, I am stretching one term to cover several kinds of behavior: repetition, rote memorization, behaving according to traditional prescription. In ritual formalism, students imitate form without necessarily understanding content or rationale. They are instructed in 'what' to do but given very little instruction in 'why' and 'how' to do it" (p. 21).

What unites the Buddhist preschools, then, is an emphasis on the ultimate authority of text and teacher as the source of knowledge. This view contrasts with the Christian emphasis that knowledge results from children's individual exploration in combination with teacher-guided social interaction among peers.

The Significance of the Body (tai). In the Zen tradition, composing one's body for meditation—sitting and breathing correctly—is crucial practice for attaining higher consciousness. By emptying oneself of physical discomfort, emotions, and thoughts, one achieves unity of mind and body and detachment from the self. Analysis of the moral implications of the physical state is commonplace in Japan, in Buddhist as well as secular contexts.

In many of the preschools, not just those that were Buddhist, the children were constantly reminded to sit up straight and keep their feet together. In the Buddhist preschools, posture was just one of the concerns directors expressed about the physical development of the children. At Sannomiya preschool, for example, the children sat on benches rather than chairs in order to strengthen their back muscles and prevent them from lounging.

They received constant reminders about how to position and move their bodies. When the teacher called attendance, for example, each child was required to raise his hand upon hearing his name. The teacher watched to be sure the child's arm was pitched at the proper angle, with fingers together and straight. The Tennoji preschool's pamphlet explicitly links posture and spirituality: "Going to the shrine makes one's spine straighten. One feels renewed, formal, and serious. One grows in appreciation for Buddha who protects us all" [translation].

Because much of the day was occupied with academic classes and music instruction, the children at strict Buddhist preschools had little opportunity to engage in physical activity. When it did occur, physical exertion was routinized and teacher structured. For example, children at Sannomiya preschool received direct instruction in how to shinny up a pole. Six children at a time approached their respective poles and waited at the bottom. Upon a signal from the teacher, they shinnied up and held their position until she blew her whistle, at which time they slid down and yielded to the next group. Physical activities at Buddhist preschools were sometimes designed to provide a challenge that would help toughen the children. This was especially true at Sannomiya preschool, where the director purposely designed a field trip to include experiences that would be physically challenging for the children.

Children Line up for Morning Exercises at a Buddhist Preschool

The directors in the Buddhist preschools were also concerned about the spiritual and physical effects of receiving proper nutrition and exercise.

The director at Sannomiya was concerned that Japanese children were overweight, out of shape, and "mentally sloppy" due to inactivity and poor diet. He deplored mothers who wished their children to be excused from strenuous exercise because of being "too weak":

My response [to such mothers] is, "If you insist on [exempting your children from physical activity] you must be sure that you can take full responsibility for your child's entire life." I would say, "Your child is not intrinsically weak. Instead, you have made him weak because you did not give him opportunities or experiences."

A notation on the brochure for Tennoji preschool sums up the connection between nutrition, group orientation, and spiritual awareness. A list of five positive attributes of their preschool included the following: "The perfect lunch system!! Everyone eats the same thing, and everyone eats everything that is served because we are showing our appreciation to the living things whose lives we are taking."

The Buddhist schools I visited were among the largest of any schools that I saw; some had over 600 pupils. If the present economic uncertainties continue, these schools will likely continue to be a very appealing method for parents interested in giving their children a head start in school.

On the other hand, their espousal of conservative political philosophy and adherence to traditional values may drive away parents with no personal knowledge of or fondness for the pre-War days (Allison, 1996). The demands for obedience are at odds with a powerful cultural model that sees children under 7 as little treasures that should be treated indulgently (Boocock, 1989), a model that may have become even stronger in recent times (Vogel, 1996).

Conclusion

The Japanese are sometimes described in Western writing as a nonreligious people. But it is more accurate to say that Japanese people express religiosity in a way that differs from that of Americans. Japanese appear more willing to mix and match religions, often invoking Shinto at birth and marriage, and Buddhism when faced with death. Yet, in spite of factors that work to blur the distinct philosophical contribution of the various religions, we have seen concrete ways in which the ideologies of Christianity and Buddhism continue to influence Japanese preschools.

The clear effects of religious beliefs on the curricula and practices in these preschools suggest that similar analyses of American preschools are warranted. In the past decade, researchers and policy experts have been grappling with the feasibility of a global definition of child care quality that could be applied across all institutions in any community across the country.

The elements of "appropriate practice" have been articulated by the National Association for the Education of Young Children (NAEYC). These recommended practices were based primarily upon the child development research literature, as well as practitioner experiences (Bredekamp & Copple, 1997). This viewpoint tends to privilege the "scientific" approach to raising children, with little explicit recognition of the fact that collectively based ideologies—including religious beliefs—may proscribe values and practices that conflict with the approach favored by many researchers. At the current time, there is so little information available about the philosophical bases, and favored practices, of church-based schools that it is impossible to speculate on the nature of possible tensions. As early childhood educators increasingly advocate moving toward "partnerships" and "dialogues" between early childhood educators and parents (Holloway & Fuller, 1999)—with each contributing their perspectives and knowledge to the conversation—the exploration of the role of religious beliefs will be increasingly imperative.

REFERENCES:

1. Dhammapada v. 183.
2. Dr. Rhys Davids' 'Notes on the History of Buddhism,' in his American lectures; and the Introductions of the translations in 'Sacred Books of the East' and the 'Dialogues of Buddha.'
3. *Ibid*; p.211
4. In the Pali texts the term *puriso* is often used not in its strict meaning of "man" but to denote a human being in general, just as the term *putta* is used to denote "child" rather than "son" that it literally means. This is also true of many languages, and it is only now that language is coming to be used in a strict non-sexist manner.
5. Even though none of the Jâtaka tales in the Pall Canon represent the Bodhisattva as a woman some of the iconographic representations of Jâtaka scenes at the Sanchi stûpa represent the Bodhisattva in a female form. Thus the Buddha was not a male person in all his previous births.
6. Some Western ladies who have become Buddhists and wishing to play a deeper role than that possible by being lay disciples have donned the yellow robe and have called themselves "nuns". There does not appear to be a justification for this in the Theravada tradition. The terms "monk" and "nun" have usually been used to denote Bhikkhu and Bhikkhuni, and as the latter has become extinct the term "nun" must now refer to those who undertake the 10 precepts. Usually those who follow these rules wear a white robe rather than a yellow robe. To prevent confusion it is best to restrict the yellow robe to those who have been ordained into Sangha orders following the currently prevailing methods.
7. It is rather difficult to obtain a clear sense of the number of religious preschools in Japan. Many preschools that

are housed on the grounds of religious organizations are not particularly affected by the religious beliefs of the host organization (Tobin, Wu, & Davidson, 1989); in these cases, the motivation for running a preschool is primarily financial. In 1990, there were 1,636 Christian preschools in Japan, of which two-thirds were Protestant and one-third Catholic; these numbers represent approximately 10% of preschools, which numbered 14,988 in 1990 (Christianity Almanac, 1990). I was unable to find any report of the number of preschools affiliated with Buddhist temples, but 40% of Buddhist temples raise funds through nonreligious activities, and among these activities, running a preschool is one of the most common. The most committed Buddhist directors are members of the Buddhist Nursery and Kindergarten Association; this association reports membership of 598 child care centers and 763 preschools (Japan Buddhist Nursery and Kindergarten Association, 1998).

8. In Japan, it is essentially impossible to gain access to preschool staff without some assistance from an intermediary. The faculty and officials who assisted with introductions were asked to select randomly among institutions falling within the categories established by the researcher (e.g., public vs. private preschools).
9. I have conducted several studies of Japanese education and child rearing over the past 15 years and authored numerous publications on these subjects (Holloway, 1988, in press; Holloway, Fuller, Azuma, Kashiwagi, & Gorman, 1990; Holloway, Kashiwagi, Hess, & Azuma, 1986). The data reported in this article were collected during a 6-month stay in the Kansai area sponsored by Fulbright. I have moderate proficiency in Japanese. During all interviews and observations, I was accompanied by a native Japanese speaker who was either a professional in early childhood education or developmental psychology.

10. Allison, Anne. (1996). Producing mothers. In Anne E. Imamura (Ed.), *Re-imaging Japanese women* (pp. 135-155). Berkeley: University of California Press.

11. Bauch, Patricia A. (1993). Improving education for minority adolescents: Toward an ecological perspective on school choice and parent involvement. In Nancy Feyl Chavkin (Ed.), *Families and schools in a pluralistic society*(pp. 121-146). Albany: State University of New York Press. ED 367 449.

12. Boocock, Sarane Spence. (1989). Controlled diversity: An overview of the Japanese preschool system. *Journal of Japanese Studies*, *15*(1), 41-65.

13. Bredekamp, Sue, & Copple, Carol (Eds.). (1997). *Developmentally appropriate practice in early childhood programs* (Rev. ed.). Washington, DC: National Association for the Education of Young Children. ED 403 023.

14. *Christianity almanac* [Kirisutokyo Nenkan]. (1990). Tokyo: Kirisuto Shinbunsha [Christianity Newspaper Company].

15. Cleverly, John F., & Phillips, D. C. (1986). *Visions of childhood: Influential models from Locke to Spock*. New York: Teachers College Press.

16. Coleman, James S., & Hoffer, Thomas. (1987). *Public and private schools: The impact of communities*. New York: Basic Books.

17. D'Andrade, Roy G. (1992). Schemas and motivation. In Roy G. D'Andrade & Claudia Strauss (Eds.), *Human motives and cultural models* (pp. 23-44). New York: Cambridge University Press.

18. Dumoulin, Heinrich. (1994). *Understanding Buddhism: Key themes*. New York: Weatherhill.

19. Fuller, Bruce (Ed.). (in press). *Charter schools and the paradox of radical decentralization*. Cambridge MA: Harvard University Press.

20. Fuller, Bruce; Raudenbush, S. W.; Wei, L.; & Holloway, S. D. (1993). Can government raise child care quality? The influence of family demand, poverty, and policy. *Educational Evaluation and Policy Analysis*, *15*(3), 255-278.EJ 471 906.

21. Harkness, Sara, & Super, Charles. (1995). Culture and parenting. In Marc H. Bornstein (Ed.), *Handbook of parenting: Vol. 2. Biology and ecology of parenting* (pp. 211-234). Mahwah, NJ: Erlbaum. ED 389 417.

22. Holland, Dorothy; Lachiotte, W., Jr.; Skinner, D.; & Cain, C. (1998). *Identity and agency in cultural worlds*. Cambridge, MA: Harvard University Press.

23. Holloway, Susan D. (1988). Concepts of ability and effort in Japan and the United States. *Review of Educational Research, 58*(3), 327-345. EJ 393 061.

24. Holloway, Susan D. (in press). *Contested childhood: The changing world of Japanese preschools.* New York: Routledge.

25. Holloway, Susan D., & Fuller, Bruce. (1999). Families and child care institutions: Divergent research and policy viewpoints. In Suzanne W. Helburn (Ed.), *The silent crisis in U.S. child care. Annals of the American Academy of Political and Social Science* (Vol. 563, pp. 98-115). Thousand Oaks, CA: Sage Publications.

26. Holloway, Susan D.; Fuller, Bruce; Azuma, H.; Kashiwagi, K.; & Gorman, K. (1990). The family's influence on achievement in Japan and the United States. *Comparative Education Review, 34*(2), 196-208. EJ 412 238.

27. Holloway, Susan D.; Fuller, Bruce; Rambaud, Marylee F.; & Eggers-Piérola, Costanza. (1997). *Through my own eyes: Single mothers and the cultures of poverty*. Cambridge, MA: Harvard University Press.

28. Holloway, Susan D.; Kashiwagi, Keiko; Hess, Robert D.; & Azuma, Hiroshi. (1986). Causal attributions by Japanese and American mothers about performance in

mathematics. *International Journal of Psychology, 21*(3), 269-286.

29. Hori, G. V. S. (1994). Teaching and learning in the Rinzai Zen monastery. In T. P. Rohlen and G. K. LeTendre (Eds.), *Teaching and learning in Japan* (pp. 20-49). New York: Cambridge University Press.
30. Huerta, L. (in press). Losing public accountability: A home schooling charter. In Bruce Fuller (Ed.), *Charter schools and the paradox of radical decentralization.* Cambridge, MA: Harvard University Press.
31. Japan Buddhist Nursery and Kindergarten Association [Nihon Bukkyo Hoiku Kyoukai]. (1998). *Outline of the Japan Buddhist Nursery and Kindergarten Association.* Tokyo: Author.
32. Kojima, Hideo. (1986). Japanese concepts of child development from the mid-17th to mid-19th century.*International Journal of Behavioral Development*, *9*(3), 315-329. EJ 344 351.
33. Kojima, Hideo. (1988). The role of belief-value systems related to child-rearing and education: The case of early modern to modern Japan. In Durganand Sinha & Henry S. R. Kao (Eds.), *Social values and development: Asian perspectives* (pp. 227-253). Newbury Park, CA: Sage Publications.
34. Kondo, Dorinne K. (1990). *Crafting selves: Power, gender, and discourses of identity in a Japanese workplace.* Chicago: University of Chicago Press.
35. Kotloff, L. J. (1993). Fostering cooperative group spirit and individuality: Examples from a Japanese preschool.*Young Children*, *48*(3), 17-23. EJ 460 160.
36. Miles, Matthew B., & Huberman, A. Michael. (1994). *Qualitative data analysis* (2nd ed.). Thousand Oaks, CA: Sage Publications.
37. Ministry of Education, Science, and Culture. (1994). *Education in Japan: A graphic presentation.* Tokyo:

Gyosei Corporation, Research and Statistics Planning Division.

38. Peak, Lois. (1991). *Learning to go to school in Japan: The transition from home to preschool life*. Berkeley: University of California Press.
39. Quinn, Naomi, & Holland, Dorothy. (1987). Culture and cognition. In Dorothy Holland & Naomi Quinn (Eds.),*Cultural models in language and thought* (pp. 3-40). New York: Cambridge University Press.
40. Sato, Manabu. (1998). A social history of classroom life and management in Japan: The dilemma of teaching and learning. In Nobuo K. Shimahara (Ed.), *Politics of classroom life: Classroom management in international perspective* (pp. 189-214). New York: Garland Press.
41. Shore, Bradd. (1996). *Culture in mind: Cognition, culture, and the problem of meaning*. Oxford, England: Oxford University Press.
42. Shweder, R. A.; Goodnow, J. J.; Hatano, G.; LeVine, R. A.; Markus, H.; & Miller, P. (1998). The cultural psychology of development: One mind, many mentalities. In William Damon (Series Ed.) & Richard M. Lerner (Vol. Ed.), *Handbook of child psychology: Vol. 1. Theoretical models of human development* (5th ed., pp. 865-937). New York: Wiley.
43. Strauss, Anselm L. (1987). *Qualitative analysis for social scientists*. Cambridge, England: Cambridge University Press.
44. Tobin, Joseph J.; Wu, David Y. H.; & Davidson, Dana H. (1989). *Preschool in three cultures: Japan, China, and the United States*. New Haven, CT: Yale University Press.
45. Vogel, Suzanne Hall. (1996). Urban middle-class Japanese family life, 1958-1996: A personal and evolving perspective. In David W. Shwalb & Barbara J. Shwalb (Eds.), *Japanese child rearing: Two generations of scholarship*. New York: Guilford Press.

46. Whitebook, Marcy; Howes, C.; & Phillips, D. (1989). *Who cares? Child care teachers and the quality of care in America*. Oakland, CA: Child Care Employee Project. ED 323 032.

47. Wollons, Roberta. (1993). The black forest in a bamboo garden: Missionary kindergartens in Japan, 1868-1912.*History of Education Quarterly, 33*(1), 1-35. EJ 482 412.

4

The Fundamentals of Buddhist Education System

It is necessary for us to a have correct understanding before practicing Buddhism; otherwise, all the time spent in cultivation will be futile, as the most superior result will not be attained. Therefore, I would like to briefly explain the true nature of Buddhism.

Chinese history tells us that about three thousand years ago, Buddha Shakyamuni, the founder of Buddhism was born in Northern India. He lived seventy-nine years and dedicated forty-nine of them to teaching. In 67 AD, one thousand years after he entered Nirvana, these teachings were formally introduced into China.

Prior to acquiring a good knowledge of Buddhism, we need to understand the terms Buddha, Dharma, Buddhist Dharma and Buddhist teaching, as they are important to our cultivation. Buddha is a Sanskrit word, meaning "wisdom and enlightenment". Why was it transliterated as Buddha and not translated into wisdom and enlightenment? The meaning of "Buddha" is so profound and extensive that these two words were insufficient to cover the original meaning. Therefore, transliteration was used with further explanations.

In essence, Buddha means wisdom. In application or function, it means enlightenment. There are three levels of wisdom. First, "General and All Knowledge Wisdom" is the correct understanding of the noumena, or essence, of the universe. It is the wisdom of knowing the general aspect of all existences, the wisdom of Theravada sages. Second, "Differentiation Wisdom" is the wisdom that can correctly comprehend all the infinite phenomena of the universe, the wisdom of knowing the discriminative aspect of all existences, the wisdom of Bodhisattvas. How did these phenomena arise? From where? In what way? What were their results? Third, "Overall and Perfect Knowledge Wisdom" is the exhaustive and perfect perception and comprehension of the truth of life and the universe without the slightest doubt or error, the wisdom of Buddhas. Buddha Shakyamuni, possessing all three of these kinds of wisdom, completely understood the true reality of life and the universe.

The function of wisdom is enlightenment. There are three classifications of enlightenment. First is "self-enlightenment", a state in which one possesses no erroneous thoughts, views, speech or behavior. Arhats and Pratyekabuddhas in Theravada Buddhism have attained this level of self-enlightenment, but have not yet generated the Bodhi mind to help others achieve enlightenment. Second, is "enlightenment of self and others", a state in which one helps others to reach enlightenment after achieving his or her own. Bodhisattvas in Mahayana Buddhism have attained this level. Third is "Perfect Complete Enlightenment", a state in which one reaches perfection in both enlightenment for self as well as helping others to reach enlightenment. This is the state of Buddhas.

The Buddha told us that this perfect wisdom and virtue are innate to all beings. The sutras, recorded teachings of the Buddha, tell us that "all sentient beings can attain Buddhahood." and "every being possesses the wisdom and virtuous character of the Buddha". In other words, all beings are equal to Buddhas in nature. However, due to our discriminating and wandering thoughts and attachments, which are the root cause of all sufferings and disasters, we have temporarily lost our original Buddha nature. Thus, we continue being born into the endless cycle of birth and death.

The more we rid ourselves of these wandering thoughts and attachments, the more we will experience freedom from suffering, and the more wisdom and enlightenment we will uncover. Once we completely free ourselves from discriminating and wandering thoughts and attachments, our fixations to certain ideas or objects, we will regain our lost Buddhahood; our original perfect enlightened state, our self-nature Buddha.

Possessing great wisdom and enlightenment enables us to truly know all that exists and all that is infinite. This includes matters and objects as tiny as a speck of dust or the finest hair on the human body, to those as great as the infinite universe. All of these are the objects of our perception, or wisdom and enlightenment.

The Buddha used the word Dharma to symbolize all these infinite phenomena. Buddhist Dharma or Principle, is the infinite wisdom and enlightenment, the perception of all things and laws in life and the universe. Chinese people often say that Buddhist Dharma is as infinite as the object perceived is infinite and the wisdom perceivable is infinite. This wisdom is innate to our self-nature.

The Buddha said, "Our innate perception and the objects in the universe perceived are ONE not TWO." When we think about it logically, if the Buddha's words are complete and perfect, then we can believe that this wisdom and enlightenment are ultimate and perfect. However, if perceived and perceivable are opposites, then wisdom can hardly be complete and perfect, but rather it is limited.

The Buddha told us that knowable and known, perceivable and perceived are ONE not TWO. This is called the One True Dharma Realm, the most genuine, perfect and highest realm as explained to us in the "Flower Adornment Sutra." The Western Pure Land of the Pure Land School also belongs to and is not separate from the One True Dharma Realm. This Western Pure Land, was created by Buddha Amitabha as an ideal place of cultivation as those who are born there are no longer subject to reincarnation within the six realms.

In 1923, a well-known Buddhist scholar, Mr. Jing-Wu Ou-Yang gave a speech at Nanjing Normal University in China, entitled "Buddhism is Neither a Religion Nor a Philosophy, but the Essential for Our Modern Time." It caused considerable sensation. His well-documented speech gave much conclusive support to the proper definition and viewpoint of Buddhism.

WHAT IS BUDDHISM?

This question arises in all those who wish to better understand it. Buddhism is a most virtuous and perfect education directed by the Buddha towards all sentient beings in the universe. This education covers a boundless range of phenomena and principles that is much broader than what is currently studied in modern universities. In regards to time, it encompasses the past, present and future. In regards to space, it encompasses everything from our daily lives to the infinite universe. Buddhism is an education of the wisdom and understanding of life and the universe. It is not a religion. The teachings of Confucius concerns one lifetime. The teachings of the Buddha cover infinite lifetimes.

How can we tell that Buddhism is an education? Today, the terms teacher and student are only used in school. However, we call Buddha Shakyamuni, our Original Teacher. We call ourselves students, as did our predecessors in ancient China. This is unlike religions in which the god and his or her disciples do not have a teacher-student relationship, but rather a parent-child relationship. In Buddhism, however, it is clearly stated that the Buddha is the teacher and we are the students. Bodhisattvas and we are classmates; they were the Buddha's former students while we are his current ones.

Furthermore, a monk or nun is called He-shang, which is the transliteration of the Sanskrit word meaning a direct mentor who provides teachings and acts as our personal guide. We share a close teacher-student relationship with this individual. Temples, or Way Places, have only one He-shang. Teachers who teach on behalf of the He-shang are called Asheli. Their speech and behavior can be models for us to follow. Others who do not directly teach would be called Dharma masters or Fashi. They are like teachers whose lectures we do not attend or those who do not directly teach us. All these terms are characteristics of education and are not found in religion.

For further examples of how Buddhism is an education, we can examine Chinese way places where the activities are held. The way place is an educational institution combining Buddhist teaching and art, similar to the combination of a modern school and a museum. Nowadays, people pursue the arts in everything. Buddhism, however, practiced artistic teaching as early as three thousand years ago.

The staff organization of the way place further illustrates the similarity to modern schools. The He-shang is equivalent to the principal of the school, deciding policies, making plans for courses of study and employing the teachers. Reporting to the He-shang are three associates or program executives, who are in charge of everything directly related to teaching, advising and disciplining, and general services. In China, a traditional way place was regarded as a Buddhist University. From this administrative structure, we can further see that Buddhism truly is an education.

THE FIVE FORMS OF BUDDHISM TODAY

Currently, there are at least five forms of Buddhism. The first form is the traditional Buddhism I have just discussed. It is the education of the Buddha's teachings. This original form is rarely seen today. The other four forms are deviations of this one.

The second form is religious Buddhism. Although originally not a religion, it has become one in the past few hundred years. Today, it is difficult to deny this. Why? The external form of Buddhism today is indeed that of a religion. It is no longer the education found in a traditional way place where cultivators had up to sixteen hours a day for both lessons and cultivation. The lessons included listening to lectures and discussions. The cultivation session included either Buddha name chanting or sitting meditation. Study and cultivation were used hand in hand to strive for the right and proper understanding and practice, to purify practitioner's minds and to eventually attain the state of enlightenment.

Since the monks and nuns spent sixteen hours a day on study and cultivation, there was little time for discriminating or wandering thoughts, and so achievement could be attained relatively quickly. Unfortunately, this traditional form of Buddhism is seldom seen nowadays in way places for many of them have become a place to make offerings, to pray for blessings and to conduct memorial services. It is little wonder that people regard Buddhism as a religion.

The third form is philosophical or academic Buddhism often found as a course in college. This is inappropriate. Why? Buddhist education is a complete university in itself, including all branches of learning. But now it is reduced to merely a philosophical discipline. Regarding it as such, we miss the importance of the fact that the teachings are a necessity for all sentient beings. Why? Because these teachings can resolve all problems ranging from those in our current lives to those in the future, including even those of birth and death. Buddhism's scope is broad and profound and regarding it as merely an academic field of study is frankly, another deviation. These two forms cause no serious harm to society. Religions try to encourage people to be good. Philosophy strives to pursue truth and to gain knowledge.

The fourth and most recent deviation is Buddhism as a show. It consists of a few hours of music, singing and dancing with a short talk in between. However, the fifth form is a deviation that has gone too far, that of the distortion of Buddhism into a cult. This deviated form has appeared in the last thirty to forty years. The exploitation of Buddhism by evil cults has gone too far. In the name of Buddhism, they take advantage of the weaknesses of human nature, creating chaos by cheating, and misleading people, endangering the safety of the public. Some of their propaganda and deeds can sound extremely enticing and appealing. However, if we join their activities, which doom us to ruin, by the time we realize our mistake, the damage will have already been done. It will then be too late to regret. Therefore, we need to choose wisely which form to practice in order to receive the true benefits.

Holistic Education and Vipassana

Education, said Albert Einstein, is that which remains when everything that is learnt in school is forgotten. If we evaluate modem education by this definition, its chief outcomes can easily be identified as aggressive competition, pride and envy. At its best, the modem educational system imparts some professional knowledge and skills, but it lacks any cultivation of heart. The result is only to make the students conceited materialists. Consequently, at an age when children should be dreaming of beauty, greatness and perfection, they now dream about sensory titillation and wealth, and spend time worrying about how to cam money [1]. No wonder that our society today is being devoured by the twin devils of acquisitiveness and unabashed consumerism, with the resultant serious social problems of corruption, strife and violence; and ecological problems such as environmental pollution and the rapid depletion of resources which threaten the very survival of humankind on this planet. Thinkers and philosophers of all hues [2], whether in India or abroad, agree that a complete revamping of the educational system is a prerequisite for the solution to these serious maladies besieging mankind. For, unless human beings become harmonized within themselves, through a fundamental change in their animal instincts-which should be the most important purpose of education-all changes in their outer circumstances, will ultimately be overwhelmed by their instinctual, animal brutality.

A Vision of Holistic Education

Education should be concerned with the totality of life and not with immediate responses to immediate challenges [3]. Broadly speaking, four different but inter-related aspects of human life can generally be recognized: viz., the physical, emotional, intellectual and spiritual. Holistic education should cultivate all these aspects in full measure. For example, physical education should include not only the performance of physical exercises to keep the body fit, but also the training to use the senses and physical framework wisely.

Similarly, emotional education should emphasize the type of training of mind that develops the positive human emotions of universal love, compassion, forbearance, humility, equanimity, etc., and eradicates the baser instincts such as greed, envy, pride, aggressiveness, etc. In this way, one can establish a healthy relationship with society.

Intellectual education should require not only the development of the ability to think, but also the ability to act independently, rationally and logically on the basis of a deep understanding of the various phenomena of nature.

Finally, spiritual education should cultivate a refinement of the mind, to manifest that elusive "fourth dimension" of the human personality from which springs forth an intuitive understanding of the very purpose of our existence, and a clarity of what ought to be done to achieve it. It is quite clear that the modern educational system completely sidesteps the emotional and spiritual aspects of the human personality, and caters only to physical and intellectual growth-and this, too, only in a superficial manner[4]. It is not as if the educationists and education planners have not been aware of this deficiency, for as early as 1966, the Kothari Commission recognized the need for inculcating social, moral and spiritual values through education [5]. But the way to achieve this in a composite society like India, where the notions of caste, creed and religion are very strongly entrenched, has defied a universally acceptable solution. There have, of course, been many attempts to impart moral education indirectly through various means such as prayers, discussions and contemplation sessions, etc. Even direct attempts have been made through meditation methods, lectures and discourses in various institutions such as Christian missionary schools; Islamic schools; Anglo-vedic schools; schools associated with the Ramakrishna Mission; ISKCON; Maharishi Mahesh Yogi centres; the Krishnamurti Foundation; and the

Saibaba Trust, etc. However, these approaches have not been able to gain wide acceptance.

There exists in India and many other countries today, a scientific method of control and purification of mind which, if properly integrated with the educational process, has the potential of becoming a universally acceptable technique for nourishing the emotional and spiritual dimensions of human personality. This technique, an ancient science of mind and matter, is called *Vipassana* meditation. Following is a brief description of the technique and how it can be integrated into modern education.

VIPASSANA MEDITATION

Viewed from the perspective of holistic education, *Vipassana* meditation can be described as a technique of purifying the mind of its baser instincts so that one begins to manifest the truly human qualities of universal goodwill, kindness,- sympathy, tolerance, humility, equanimity, etc., and simultaneously gains an insight into the true nature and purpose of human existence. This is achieved in a very scientific manner through a systematic cultivation of Right Mindfulness coupled with non-reactivity; that is to say, development of the habit of paying penetrating attention to whatever is happening in our total organism-the body with its five senses and the mind which operates in and through it-without any admixture of subjective judgments or reactions. The quality which purifies the mind at the deepest level is the mental factor of objectivity, or equanimity, which develops from the constant, thorough understanding of the impermanence of all components of the mind-body phenomenon (ref. [8], p.258).

An important prerequisite for the systematic practice of *Vipassana* is scrupulous observance of five basic moral precepts- viz., abstention from killing, stealing, false speech, sexual misconduct, and intoxicants-since any willful violation of these precepts causes violent mental agitation which makes it impossible to observe the mind objectively. Of course, *Vipassana* practice also helps one to gain the mental strength needed to observe the moral precepts in day-to-day life. While the complete details of this systematic practice are best learnt in a meditation camp under the careful guidance of a teacher, some salient features of the technique and its theoretical basis are explained here.

The foundation stone in the cultivation of Right Mindfulness (or Awareness) consists of paying attention to the body (ref. 8, pp. 2542591. The practice of systematic self-observation begins by focusing attention on the respiration (ref. 9, p.5), the breath coming in and going out of the body. This practice-called *Anapana*-is an exercise in cultivation of, right awareness, not regulation or control of the breath (such as *praa.naayaama* or other breathing exercises). There is just a silent "bare observation" of the natural flow of respiration, with a firm and steady attention free from any strain. One observes the length of the breath, short or long. To aid the development of concentration, the student is advised to focus the attention on finer details, such as which nostril the breath is coming in and going out, or where the breath is touching in the area around the nostrils.

The whole exercise is one of observing the reality as it is, without any preferences or reactions. It is quite natural that in the beginning it will not be possible to focus the attention continuously on the breath, even for a minute or two. The habitual tendency of the mind to wander away from the assigned task comes to the fore very quickly, allowing the student to experience for him or herself the turbulent nature of the mind. The student learns to observe this fact itself dispassionately without feeling dejected about the repeated "running away" of the mind-and once again focuses one's attention on the breath.

With the systematic practice of *Anapana* for a few days, the concentration increases, and a natural calming and equalizing of the breath takes place. As the breath is very intimately related to the mind, this leads simultaneously to a tranquilizing of the mind-in fact, of the entire life-rhythm [61. The mind also becomes sharp enough to observe subtler realities of the body-mind complex, e.g., the sensations occurring in the area around the nostrils where attention is focused during the practice of mindfulness of breathing.

This leads us to the next step in the cultivation of Right Mindfulness, viz., awareness of the bodily sensations (ref. 9, p.21). The object of meditation now is body sensation. Sensations occur on the body, but they are felt by the mind. When one is investigating the internal experience of one's sensations, one is actually observing the interaction of mind and matter (*Vedanaa-samosara.naa sabbe dhamma:* Everything that arises in the mind is accompanied by sensation) (ref. 8, p. 253). Moreover, sensations *(vedana)* provide the crucial link between the impact *(phassa)* upon the six sense doors and the resultant reaction of craving and aversion *(ta"nhaa)* which is the root cause of all suffering [7; 8, p.2551. This profound discovery is, in fact, one of the most fundamental aspects of the teaching of the master scientist of mind and matter, Gautama Buddha.

The practice of *Vipassana* consists of "feeling" the sensations throughout the body without any reaction or evaluation whatsoever, thus developing equanimity at a very deep level. This is of course more easily said than done, because our subconscious mind, which is constantly "feeling" the body sensations, has the stubborn, recalcitrant habit of reacting to these sensations in a particular manner. It habitually reacts to pleasant sensations with craving and to unpleasant sensations with aversion, thus strengthening the mind's conditioned tendency to run after sensory pleasure and to run away from pain.

The exercise of awareness and equanimity in the face of the entire spectrum of sensations acts to gently break this habit pattern. One repeatedly observes the sensations as they actually are: constantly changing-arising, staying for some time, fading away, and giving rise to other sensations. Through this repeated practice, the habit of reaction is replaced by an experience of the truth of *anicca* or impermanence. The student is trained to focus one's attention on the changeful nature of the sensations, thereby gradually correcting the conditioned habit of evaluating them as pleasant or unpleasant. This scientific method of observing the sensations as they really are-without any evaluation based on past conditioning-is what is described by the word *vipassana. Vipassana,* a Pali word, literally means "to see things as they really are"-in their true nature, their true characteristic of impermanence *(anicca).*

One can thus gradually train the mind to observe the bodily sensations in an objective manner-without any notion of their being G4my sensations"-in the same way as one would dispassionately observe the waves arising and disappearing in the sea. With the practice of this objective observation, the attitude of "enjoyer ship"-one of the chief manifestations of ego-is thus enfeebled.

The attitude of remaining equanimous towards all internal phenomena arising from the interaction of mind and body is simultaneously strengthened, as the student repeatedly observes the fact of the evanescent nature *(anicca)* of the mind-body process.

The systematic practice of mindfulness of sensations integrates within itself other important aspects of the cultivation of Right Mindfulness, viz., the mindfulness of the state of mind and the contents of the thought at any given moment (ref. [91, p.25). As the alertness and objectiveness of the meditator increase (by the. continual practice of non-reactive observation of sensations), he or she can quickly become aware of the mental reactions which keep arising from time to time. As an adjunct to the main practice of mindfulness of body sensations, a student practices from time to time the bare registering of one's state of mind. One observes the various mental states without self-justification or self-condemnation. This practice reveals the changing nature of the mental states, and thereby strengthens the mediator's conviction about the *anicca* of all body-mind phenomena.

The most significant consequence of *Vipassana* practice is that it gives the mind a natural slant towards the goal of full enlightenment, the complete liberation from all bondages. Simultaneously, one develops the steadfast confidence that all hindrances on the Path can be overcome.

Role of *Vipassana* in Education

We can now understand how *Vipassana* can fill that vital gap in modern education-viz., the training of mind, leading to a balanced, harmonious and purposeful life. *Vipassana* meditation imparts a way to observe all the phenomena of this sensory world objectively and impersonally under the penetrating gaze of an equanimous mind. The multifold benefits which accrue from this practice are being discussed at length in this seminar and have formed the basis for research conducted by the *Vipassana* Research Institute (Igatpuri, India) in many areas of human activity. Here, only those aspects related to the field of education are being discussed.

The attitude of "bare attention" (bestowed by a mind at once aware and non-reactive) slows down the transition from thought to action, allowing the practitioner more time-those crucial few moments needed to come to a mature decision. The tendency of the base, animal instincts to overpower the faculty of human reason can thus be effectively checked, leading to a gradual reduction in negative traits such as rashness, intolerance, intemperance and aggressive behaviour which characterize modem youth. This emotional education should naturally lead to a marked improvement in the student-teacher relationship, which has been constantly deteriorating over the years due to the corroding influence of a materialistic world view coupled with the negative traits mentioned above.

On the positive side, this training of non-reactive observation of facts, coupled with the insight of *anicca* enhances one's ability to face the vicissitudes of life squarely and equanimously without taking recourse to such escapist alternatives as smoking, alcohol and drugs, which have become the bane of modern society. This attitude of equanimity also reduces the obsessive preoccupation with indulgence in unending materialistic desires, thereby allowing space for the manifestation of the so-called "higher needs"-the self-actualization needs of meaningfulness, justice, truthfulness, service, love, compassion, etc., which modem psychology recognizes as essential components of basic human needs [10]. Recent research has shown that people able to manifest these "higher needs" are generally much more creative and innovative, because self-actualization needs provide "a more durable fuel for creativity" than the drive for sensual gratification [11].

The observation of mental contents is also a powerful tool of self-education because it reveals to the mediator a very clear picture of his weak points and strong points without doing damage to his self-esteem. The habitual attitude of hurriedly glossing over one's weaknesses, or blowing one's strengths out of proportion, is thus checked. One gradually gains the inner strength needed to overcome one's weaknesses without a need to exercise a violent exertion of will or forceful repression, both of which are harmful in the long run. This candid self-examination promotes honesty towards oneself, increases one's tolerance of others' faults, assists in the development of humility and compassion, and reduces vanity.

The attitude of Right Awareness coupled with equanimity closely corresponds to the disposition of the true scientist and scholar, which is characterized by clear definition of the subject, unprejudiced receptivity for the facts, exclusion of the subjective factor in judgment, and deferring judgment until a careful examination of the facts has been made (ref. [6], p.39). This practice should therefore be of great help in augmenting the scientific temper.

Vipassana meditation reinforces the scientific outlook in another much more direct way. Every meditator, after some length of practice of mindfulness of sensations, reaches a state where he experiences the whole body as a mass of vibrations[12]. This experience is in line with the quantum-relativistic description of matter. This direct experience provides much more clarity about the nature of matter than the scores of mathematical formulae produced by classroom descriptions.

Another important benefit of the systematic practice-especially of mindfulness of breath, which is of crucial significance in education-is improvement in one's ability to concentrate on a task. As explained earlier, the essence of the practice is to train the mind to keep the attention continuously on an object (viz., the breath), and to minimize the drifting of the mind into futile daydreams, which are the chief obstacle to concentration. The training of observing the mental states also comes in handy. Once such daydreams have arisen (whether during meditation or during normal activity), if one briefly makes these daydreams themselves an object of close observation, their power of distraction is drastically curtailed and they get quickly dispersed. This results in a quick retrieval of concentration.

The attitude of impersonal non-reactive observation is of profound value in the ultimate deliverance of the mind from all bondages, which is the true purpose of spiritual education. To quote Venerable Nyanponika Thera (ref. [6], p.43): "The inner distance from things ... as obtained temporarily and partially by bare attention, shows us, by our own experience, the possibility of winning perfect detachment and the happiness resulting from it. It bestows upon us the confidence that such temporary setting aside may well become one day a complete stepping out of this world of suffering. It gives a kind of foretaste, or at least an idea, of the highest liberty, the 'holiness during lifetime' that has been alluded to by the words 'in the world but not of the world.' "

To achieve this objective, the principal requirement is to develop an insight into the basic characteristics of life. Impermanence (*anicca*) is the fundamental characteristic with which a*Vipassana* student is continually confronted. As this experience becomes ingrained, realization of the other characteristics-viz., of suffering *(dukkha) and* egolessness (*anattaa*)-automatically develops, leading one to a clear understanding of the purpose of life and the way to achieve it-the very acme of spiritual education.

Concluding Remarks

It should be evident from the preceding brief description that *Vipassana* meditation is a purely scientific technique, a universal culture of mind, which does not subscribe to any sectarian beliefs, dogmas or rituals. It should be universally acceptable, therefore, as an integral part of education. Its benefits have been corroborated by thousands of practitioners-both young and old belonging to diverse castes, creeds, countries and religious beliefs. Vivekananda dream of evolving a "man-making education" [2] could be fulfilled by the integration of *Vipassana* into modern education. It is high time that an action plan in the field of education be drawn, at least on an experimental scale, to scientifically validate the efficacy of *Vipassana* over an extended period. Some of the crucial issues which need to be addressed include:

1. How to motivate the students, teachers and management of schools and colleges to introduce *Anapana* and *Vipassana*, and reduce resistance from unwilling students and teachers?
2. The extent of training needed before authorizing educational staff members to teach meditation in schools and colleges.
3. The format and minimum duration of in-house camps organized to initiate young students to *Anapana* meditation, keeping in view the practical constraints (especially of overnight stay).
4. How to maintain continuity of practice within the tight schedule of schools and colleges?
5. Should there be a formal course on meditation in the curricula of schools and colleges?
6. How to assess the beneficial influence of *Vipassana* on teachers, students and the teaching-learning process?
7. How to integrate *Vipassana* with the student counseling services in the schools and colleges?

A properly thought out action plan if sincerely implemented should ultimately pave the way for the formation of institutions, which can impart truly holistic education. Such institutions would make a crucial contribution to developing wholesome individuals and a harmonious society.

REFERENCES

1. *Krishnamurti on Education*, Krishnamurti Foundation, 1992.
2. *Swami Vivekananda on Education*, compiled by T.S. Avinashilingam, Sri Ramakrishna Mission Vidyalaya, Coimbatore, 1993.
3. "A New Education," *All India Magazine*, Sri Aurobindo Society, Oct. 1990; and On Education, All India Magazine, Sri Aurobindo Society, Nov. 1990.
4. P.L. Dhar and R.R. Gaur: "Appropriate Engineering Education," paper presented at National Workshop on Technology Assessment, a Futuristic Viewpoint, 1IT, Delhi, 1988.
5. *Report of Education Commission* (1964-66): Education and National Development, Ministry of Education, Govt. of India, 1966.
6. Venerable Nyanaponika Thera., *The Heart of Buddhist Meditation*, Rider, London 1962.
7. Amadeo Sole-Leris., *Tranquillity and Insight*, Shambala, Boston 1986.
8. Sayagyi U Ba *Khin Journal,* Vipassana Research Institute, Igatpuri, India, 1991.
9. *Mahaavatipa.t.thaana Sutta"m,* Vipassana Research Publications, Igatpuri, India, 1993.
10. A. Maslow. *Motivation and Personality*, New York; Harper Press, 1954.
11. Pradeep N. Khandwala, "Fourth Eye: Excellence Through Creativity;" A.H. Wheeler an 0.1 Allahabad, 1984.
12. P.L. Dhar and R.R. Gaur., *Science and Humanism-Towards a Unified World View*, Common Wealth Publishers, New Delhi, 1992

5

The Fundamentls of Buddhist Education in Practice

What is the ultimate goal of the Buddha's teachings? It is to attain the Perfect, Complete Enlightenment. Transliterated from Sanskrit, it is called Anuttara-samyak-sambodhi. Out of respect, this phrase was maintained in its original form rather than translated. There are three stages within this enlightenment: "Proper Enlightenment", "Equal and Proper Enlightenment", and "Perfect, Complete Enlightenment".

The Buddha told us, that although scientists, philosophers and religious scholars may have reached a good understanding about life and the universe, this realization is neither complete nor proper. Why? Although they have obtained some understanding, they are far from having freedom from worries, from ending their afflictions. They still indulge themselves in the Five Poisons of greed, anger, ignorance, arrogance and doubt. They remain mired in all the troubles of human relationships and are swayed by personal feelings. In other words, they are human.

If a person has severed greed, anger, ignorance, arrogance, doubt and afflictions, it will be acknowledged that this person has attained the first level, that of Proper Enlightenment. He or she will be called an Arhat, similar to the initial academic degree in Buddhism. Arhats differ from Buddhas in the way that they use their mind. They use it in the same manner we do. The difference is that we still have afflictions while Arhats do not.

The next higher level of enlightenment is that of Equal and Proper Enlightenment, represented by Bodhisattvas. They resemble Buddhas in motivation but have not yet reached the same level of enlightenment. The minds of Bodhisattvas are genuine; they remain forever unchanged and are similar to those of Buddhas. Buddhas use the full and perfect true heart. Buddhas represent the highest level of enlightenment, which is the Perfect Complete Enlightenment.

In Buddhist classic literature, the perfect, true mind of a Buddha was symbolized by a full moon. The mind of a Bodhisattva was symbolized by a crescent moon, which was neither full nor perfect. And the mind of an arhat was symbolized by moonlight reflected from the surface of water it is not real.

These three levels of enlightenment can be compared to our college educational system. The level or degree of Arhat is similar to earning an undergraduate degree. The level of Bodhisattva is similar to earning a Master's degree and the level of Buddha is similar to earning a Doctorate's degree. The word Buddha is not exclusive to Buddha Shakyamuni, but is a common title for any being who has attained the perfect complete enlightenment. Thus, Buddha, Bodhisattva and Arhat are only names or titles to represent the levels of enlightenment or a degree we receive in Buddhism. And they are most certainly not deities to be worshiped.

So, a Buddha is one who has fully comprehended the truth of life and the universe and acquired the ultimate and perfect wisdom. This is also the goal of Buddhist education; to enable beings to attain this same level of wisdom. Therefore, Buddhism is an education of wisdom.

THE OBJECTIVES OF THE BUDDHA'S TEACHINGS

The principle of Buddhism is to break through all superstitions and delusions. It is to resolve delusion to attain happiness and enlightenment, to eliminate suffering to gain serenity and purity of mind. What is delusion? When we do not thoroughly and properly understand the phenomenon around us, we tend to be deluded, to have wrong ideas, which lead us to make mistakes. Then we suffer ill consequences as a result. However, if we have correct understanding about life and the universe, we will be free from mistakes in thought, judgment and behavior. Then our result, or effect, will be favorable. Thus, resolving delusion to attain enlightenment is the cause and eliminating suffering to attain happiness and purity is the effect.

Only through resolving superstition and delusion, can enlightenment be attained. This is the objective of the Buddha's teaching. This wisdom will enable all beings to differentiate true from false, proper from improper, right from wrong and good from bad. It can help us to establish a dynamic and caring attitude toward life and our surroundings. So, we can clearly see that Buddhism is neither passive nor obsolete, nor is it retreating from society. As said in the "Buddha Speaks of the Infinite Life Sutra of Adornment, Purity, Equality" and "Enlightenment of the Mahayana School" or the "Infinite Life Sutra," Buddhism can perfectly solve all afflictions and problems. It enables us to obtain true and ultimate benefits by creating fulfilling lives, happy families, harmonious societies, prosperous nations and a peaceful world. These are the objectives of the Buddha's teachings for our world now. The ultimate objectives of abandoning all worries thus transcending the six realms are even more incredibly wonderful. Therefore, we can see that it is an education that will enable us to attain truth, virtue, beauty, wisdom and genuine eternal happiness.

The Original Vow of Earth Treasure Bodhisattva Sutra the Great Perfection

After understanding the goals and principles of the Buddha's teachings, we need to deepen our understanding of the Dharma. What is the Dharma? It is the true reality of life and the universe, all the teachings of the Buddhas, which are included in sutras. These ancient textbooks documented all of the Buddha's teachings and were recorded by his students. The most basic one of Mahayana Buddhism is the "Original Vow of Earth Treasure Bodhisattva Sutra." It can be regarded as a textbook for first grade students, within which, the truth was clearly explained, not with spoken language but with emissions of light. The sutra, as told by Buddha Shakyamuni, begins with his emitting infinite bright lights called:

1. Great Perfection Brightness Cloud,
2. Great Compassion Brightness Cloud,
3. Great Wisdom Brightness Cloud,
4. Great Prajna Brightness Cloud,
5. Great Samádhi Brightness Cloud,
6. Great Auspicious Brightness Cloud,
7. Great Good Fortune Brightness Cloud,
8. Great Merit Brightness Cloud,
9. Great Refuge Brightness Cloud,
10. Great Praise Brightness Cloud.

Although ten kinds are given, it does not mean that there are only ten. The number ten is regarded as a symbol of perfection, a complete cycle symbolizing infinity.

What is called perfection in the "Earth Treasure Sutra" is infinity in the "Infinite Life Sutra." Not only can life be infinite, everything can be infinite! However, of all infinities, that of life is the most important. We may have boundless wealth and immeasurable good fortune, but how can we enjoy them if we do not have sufficient life spans? Therefore, the Pure Land School uses "infinite life" to symbolize all infinities. In the "Earth Treasure Sutra," the ten Brightness Clouds represent this concept. "One is all and all is one" clearly explains the infinite cosmos and life.

Upon what did the Buddha base his teachings of life and the universe? First is the Great Perfection Brightness Cloud. The great perfection of Tibetan Buddhism is the true self-nature in Chinese Buddhism. The true self-nature is great perfection. The following nine clouds of compassion, wisdom, etc. are perfect, everything is perfect. This great perfection is our own innate, true self-nature. It was from this initial point that the Buddha imparted the infinite teachings to us, thus revealing the true nature of all phenomena in the universe. Everything that the Buddha taught is innate to us. It is the original true self-nature within each of us. The purpose of his forty-nine years of teaching was to help us to learn how to live happy and fulfilling lives. This unique and complete education is for all sentient beings and is much more vast and extensive than our modern educational system.

People work hard everyday. What drives them to get up early in the morning and work long hours before coming home? It is the pursuit of prestige and wealth, especially wealth. Would people continue to work if they could not receive payment or some degree of prestige after having worked for a whole day? Of course not. Most would become listless and unwilling to work. Therefore, for most people, the driving force in our society is wealth, followed by prestige.

Buddhas and Bodhisattvas desire neither wealth nor fame yet they work harder than we do. What is the driving force behind this conscientious teaching while expecting nothing in return? It is the second Brightness Cloud, the Great Compassion Brightness Cloud. It is like a mother's love for her children, especially her newborn baby, but it is more profound in depth. A mother does so out of natural love and compassion, asking for nothing in return. This love is called a heart of compassion. The compassion of the Buddhas and Bodhisattvas towards all sentient beings is boundless, unconditional and universal. It is the eternal driving force that compels them to help all sentient beings. Therefore, the Great Compassion Brightness Cloud follows the Great Perfection Brightness Cloud.

In order to teach others, we practice cultivation as well as encouraging others to do likewise. We do so to sincerely introduce Buddhism to other people. What is our driving force?

Compassion. But if we do so for wealth or fame, then it is purely business and this is totally wrong for it violates the very spirit of Buddhism.

In fact, the circulation of the teachings, including sutras and reference works should be unconditional. Copyrighted materials do not accord with the true spirit of Buddhism. Every time I am presented with a Buddhist book, I first check for the copyright page. If it says "This book is protected by copyright; any unauthorized printing of this book shall lead to punishment", I will not read the book. If asked why I do not want to read it, my answer is that any true and good knowledge should benefit others unconditionally and that reprinting should be allowed. It would be a waste of time and energy to read copyrighted books. Only the writings of those who are broadminded and kind-hearted and who sincerely practice what they teach deserve to be read and studied. How can we expect a narrow-minded, profit-seeking person to write kind things and conclude them with the great perfection?

Compassion is built on rationale and is free of emotions. To be otherwise, it is delusion and therefore is wrong. There are two Buddhist sayings, "Compassion is the essence; convenient means is the way to accommodate people with different capacities". The other seemingly says the complete opposite, "Compassion often incurs misfortunes and convenience often leads to immorality". The reason behind this apparent contradiction is that if we ignore rationality and instead yield to emotion, compassion then often results in misfortune while doing favors for someone gives rise to immorality. Hence, this is followed by the Great Wisdom Brightness Cloud, the third of the ten great perfections. Perfect wisdom gives rise to perfect compassion. Wisdom is the method of convenience. Only by wisely utilizing various methods of wisdom and compassion, can we help sentient beings be enlightened and freed from sufferings.

The next brightness cloud is the Great Prajna (Intuitive Wisdom) Brightness Cloud. What is the difference between intuitive wisdom and wisdom? The "Great Wisdom Sutra" states, "Prajna innocence, knowing everything". It is intuitive wisdom without knowing and yet knowing everything. Without knowing is intuitive wisdom; knowing everything is wisdom. In other words, one is essence and the other is function. From a different perspective, wisdom is the knowledge of things and the realization of truth. Intuitive wisdom, our original wisdom, is that which can free people from worries and afflictions. Acquired wisdom is that which can interpret all phenomena in the universe. It arises from the original wisdom. If we cannot completely attain the great perfection of the universe, how can we teach about it to others?

When worries are completely eradicated and ignorance dispelled, we can attain our own great perfection and restore our original ability. From that point on, we are in a state of total awareness and capable of doing everything, we are all-knowing with infinite abilities. The brightness clouds of wisdom and intuitive wisdom contain profound meanings and are the perfect complete wisdom.

How do we attain wisdom? It is innate to our self-nature, but it is now hidden. Where is it? The Buddha told us that it is not permanently lost just temporarily lost. When we attain enlightenment, we can uncover this wisdom. Then how can we free ourselves from delusion and recover our original ability? One method taught by Buddha Shakyamuni is deep concentration, which is also called the Great Samádhi Brightness Cloud. Samádhi is another transliteration from Sanskrit meaning the proper enjoyment, which has the same meaning as deep concentration.

Buddhism emphasizes cultivation or correcting our thoughts and behavior. It is to correct everything that arises from our body, mouth and mind, the three karmas of erroneous behavior, speech and thoughts. To correct the three karmas, we start from the mind as the Zen School teaches, "cultivation should start from the root". What is the root? The mind. If our mind is proper then our thought, speech and behavior will likewise be proper.

In Buddhism, there are innumerable methods of practice. All of these methods are ways for concentration in cultivation. Not only the Zen School emphasizes concentration in cultivation. All the schools do, although they may not all use the term meditation.

Pure Land Buddhism calls it One Mind Undisturbed or purity of mind. Tibetan Buddhism explains it as Three mystic practices, the three karmas of body, mouth, mind corresponding to those of the Buddha. Used here corresponding means concentration. We can see that various schools emphasize the same principles. They simply use different terms to describe it. Therefore, since all lead to the same goal, all methods are equal and no one method is better than another.

We can choose whichever method best fits our manner of living and level of achievement and understanding. The most important point is to concentrate on just one method. The more methods we try to follow, the more confused we will become. The more confused we are, the more difficult it is to succeed. This is very important, as Samádhi or deep concentration, is the key to success in our learning and cultivation. We explain these as the Three Learning's of precepts or self-discipline, deep concentration and wisdom. Self-discipline leads to deep concentration. From deep concentration arises wisdom. Therefore, intuitive wisdom arises from deep concentration. This deep concentration in our self-nature is called the Great Samádhi Brightness Cloud.

Of the ten brightness clouds, the first five explain fundamental principles and the latter five explain the methods. The fundamental principles are the basis of Buddha Shakyamuni's teachings. The following are the five methods.

First is the Great Auspicious Brightness Cloud. What does auspicious mean? For most of us, auspicious means to get what we deserve. If we obtain what we do not deserve, then it is not auspicious. The meaning of auspicious in Buddhism is much more profound: throughout the universal existence, nothing is beyond our knowledge and experience. This is great auspiciousness. For example, when we are mindful of Buddha Amitabha and vow to be born into the Western Pure Land, we will attain birth into the Western Pure Land. If we vow to be born into the Flower Adornment World, we will attain the stage of awakening of Buddha Vairocana. This is the original meaning of auspicious.

In our world, Buddha Shakyamuni taught different methods for different levels of understanding and this is the utmost auspiciousness. First, the Buddha's teachings never contradict the true reality of life and the universe. Second, the Buddha always adapted his teachings to fit the audience's level of comprehension. His teachings would be a failure if they proved to be incomprehensible for the listeners or if they were too simple and boring. Neither of these would be auspicious. Therefore, the appropriate teaching is most auspicious. The Buddha conveys all that he wishes to: we hear all that we can understand and absorb. This is the utmost, the greatest and perfect auspiciousness.

Nowadays, people pursue wealth, knowledge, health and long life. This is called good fortune. If the Buddha asks us to learn and practice Buddhism but we do not receive what he said we would, then we will reject the teachings. Why? If we cannot get what we wish for now, how can we believe we will receive what is promised to us for the next life? It is all too distant and uncertain. When will we get to enjoy the promised great reward? However, if we can receive benefits now, we will be much more likely to believe in the promise of even greater rewards in the future. By truly practicing Buddhism, we will attain all that we wish for.

This is similar to a tree blossoming and bearing fruits. Only when we see the beautiful blossoms, will we believe there will be good fruits. If the flower does not bloom, how can we believe there will be fruit? Therefore, we have the Great Good Fortune Brightness Cloud following the Great Auspicious Brightness Cloud. We must cultivate the cause before we can attain the effect.

The next guiding principle is represented by the Great Merit Brightness Cloud. All Buddhas spent a long time, one hundred eons, cultivating good fortune after attaining Buddhahood. Why? A Buddha cannot help sentient beings if he himself does not have good fortune. People will not believe in a teacher who talks of it but obviously lacks it. However, when the teacher has good fortune and explains that it comes from cultivation, then people will listen and follow his or her teachings. Therefore, only if the teacher has good fortune and virtue in addition to wisdom can he or she help sentient beings. Thus, the Buddha taught us to cultivate both good fortune and wisdom. However, good fortune is different from merit in that merit is the one that helps us to transcend the cycle of birth and death. We accumulate merit by practicing the Three Learning's of precepts or self-discipline, deep concentration and wisdom.

In our practice, we need to rely on the next principle of the Great Refuge Brightness Cloud. This is not what is usually thought of as taking refuge in the Triple Jewels of the Buddha, the Dharma and the Sangha. Rather, it is to return to and rely upon the Triple Jewels, the great perfection of our self-nature.

The Great Praise Brightness Cloud symbolizes educating others about Buddhism, praising the perfect and infinite merits and virtue of the self-nature. What does Buddhism teach us? To attain our perfect self-nature. Zen Buddhism often says that we should search for the original state of our perfect self-nature.

In summary, Buddha Shakyamuni emitted light at the beginning of the "Earth Treasure Sutra." This light has many more infinite, boundless meanings than the ten brightness clouds discussed. The first five brightness clouds are the Great Perfection of self-nature and the last five are the function of the self-nature. These ten comprise the basis of the Buddha's teachings and are to be found in many sutras, often represented by emissions of light. Many people read of the brightness clouds without any real understanding of the profound meanings within. Not only this sutra, but also all sutras start and flow from the Great Perfection. We will benefit much more from reading sutras once we understand these representations.

THE GREAT PERFECTION OF MAHAYANA BUDDHISM

The sequence of practice in Mahayana Buddhism is represented in China by the four Great Bodhisattvas: Di Tzang (Earth Treasure) of Jiuhua Mountain; Guan Yin (Great Compassion) of Putuo Mountain; Wen Shu Shi Li (Manjushri) of Wutai Mountain; and Pu Xian (Universal Worthy) of Emei Mountain.

Earth Treasure means stored treasure of the great mother earth, which represents our mind. Without the earth, nothing could survive. So, the Buddha used the earth as a metaphor for our mind, which is the Great Perfection. It encompasses infinite compassion, wisdom, intuitive wisdom, auspiciousness, good fortune, merit and virtue. Therefore, all that the Buddha told us in the sutras is infinite, is the Great Perfection. Understanding this will enable us to find the boundless meanings within.

The "Earth Treasure Sutra" explains that we begin our learning and practice by being filial to our parents and respectful to our teachers and elders. Buddhism is an education of honoring teachers and revering their teachings, which is based on the foundation of filial piety. How can we expect a person who is not filial to his or her parents to respect his or her teachers? A teacher, regardless of learning and capabilities, cannot impart knowledge to a student who lacks respect and does not listen.

Therefore, only when we honor teachers and revere their teachings can we truly succeed in our learning of Buddhism. "The Original Vow of Earth Treasure Bodhisattva Sutra" is the sutra of the filial piety, which is the very heart of the Great Perfection. All other perfections arise from it. From here, we extend this loving and caring for parents to respecting teachers and elders. We keep expanding from here until we respect and care for all sentient beings without discrimination or attachment.

This is the enhancement and extension of Earth Treasure Bodhisattva and is the teaching of Guan Yin Bodhisattva. Therefore, without filial piety, there would be no great compassion. This is similar to building a house. The second floor must be built upon the first floor. In being filial to parents and showing compassion for all other beings, we should not use emotions. Rather we need to base this compassion on rationale and wisdom. Only in this way can we attain positive results.

Next is the third Bodhisattva, Manjushri, who symbolizes wisdom and Universal Worthy Bodhisattva who symbolizes the practice of filial piety, respect, compassion and wisdom in our daily lives. If we practice these principles when interacting with others, matters and objects, then we ourselves are Universal Worthy Bodhisattva.

The teachings of Universal Worthy Bodhisattva are perfect. As the "Flower Adornment Sutra" tells us, we cannot attain Buddhahood if we do not follow this teaching. Why? This Bodhisattva is perfect in every thought, every vow and every deed. Without true wisdom, the great vow of Universal Worthy Bodhisattva cannot be fulfilled.

These four great Bodhisattvas exemplify this understanding and represent the perfection of Mahayana Buddhism. Therefore, from Earth Treasure Bodhisattva, we learn filial piety and respect, from Guan Yin Bodhisattva, we learn great compassion, from Manjushri Bodhisattva we learn great wisdom and from Universal Worthy Bodhisattva we learn the great vows and conduct.

The Five Guidelines

Buddha Shakyamuni used innumerable methods to correspond with the level of attainment of his listeners. However, regardless of the particular method, he never deviated from the Great Perfection. In other words, all his teachings arose from the self-nature. Consequently, all methods are equal. It is like the harmony between the leading role and the supporting roles in the "Flower Adornment Sutra." If Buddha Shakyamuni is the leading role then all the other Buddhas are the supporting roles. When Buddha Amitabha is the leading role then Buddha Vairocana will be the supporting role. Any Buddha can take the leading role.

Harmonious cooperation between the roles is also found among the Bodhisattvas. If we regard Guan Yin Bodhisattva as the leading role in our learning of Buddhism, then the all Buddhas and other Bodhisattvas take the supporting roles. If Earth Treasure Bodhisattva takes the leading role then Guan Yin Bodhisattva and the others take the supporting roles.

This principle applies to sutras as well. When we choose the "Infinite Life Sutra" as our primary sutra then all the others become secondary. If we take the "Diamond Sutra" as the primary then the "Infinite Life Sutra" and the "Flower Adornment Sutra" become the secondary. All Bodhisattvas and all sutras are equal in nature. Whichever primary method is chosen it is praised as number one. However, saying that a certain method is number one does not mean that the others are less important or effective. If we forget this, then we commit a serious offense. What offense? Praising oneself and belittling others.

Consider the origin of the "Visualization Sutra." When Queen Vaidehi suffered from overwhelming family misfortune, she bitterly said to Buddha Shakyamuni: "Life is filled with of suffering. Is there not a place without suffering? I wish to live in such a world". By applying his supernatural abilities, Buddha Shakyamuni displayed for the queen all the worlds of all the Buddhas in the universe. She vowed to be born into Buddha Amitabha's Western Pure Land, the world of Ultimate Bliss and requested that Buddha Shakyamuni teach her how to accomplish this.

He taught her to practice the Three Conditions explaining that they were the fundamental causes of attaining Buddhahood for the Buddhas of the past, present and future. Therefore, they are a crucial part and foundation of our practice. The Three Conditions are the basis of Buddhism and crucial in our attainment of Buddhahood.

The Three Conditions

To be a virtuous person, it is necessary to first follow the Three Conditions. In sutras, we often see the phrase "good men and good women". What are the requirements for being good? Meeting each of the eleven principles contained in the three Conditions. Thus, we will see that the requirements are stringent. Good men and good women in the heaven and human realms need only meet the First Condition. Theravada sutras only require practitioners to fulfill the First and Second Conditions. But for Mahayana practitioners, good men and good women must meet all three. As we see in Mahayana sutras such as the "Earth Treasure Sutra" and the "Infinite Life Sutra," it is to live our lives in accordance with the eleven principles.

Failure to satisfy any one of the principles would prohibit a person from being considered good. Regardless of what the Buddha taught, the methods of learning and cultivation or the true reality of life and the universe, all accord with the Great Perfection. The eleven principles of the Three Conditions are likewise perfect in every word.

The First Condition: The Good Fortune Required to be a Human or Heavenly Being

The First Condition includes:

1. Being filial to our parents,
2. Being respectful to our teachers and elders,
3. Being compassionate and not killing any living beings and
4. Following the Ten Good Conducts.

Consider the first and second principles of being filial to our parents and respectful to our teachers and elders. The Chinese character for filial piety, "Xiao", is comprised of two parts. The top part "old" means the previous generations and the bottom part "children" means the future generations. This demonstrates that the previous generations and the future generations are actually one entity. They are ONE rather than

TWO. In our modern world, the existence of the generation gap has resulted in parents and children being TWO instead of ONE. This gap contradicts the principle of filial piety, which has no generation gap.

The past had its own past; the future will have its own future. The past had no beginning and the future will have no end. They are one. Filial Piety reaches beyond time and extends throughout the universe. In other words, it encompasses the entire universe. Who can practice the principle of filial piety to perfection? Only a Buddha can do so. Without having attained Buddhahood, we cannot achieve the Great Perfection in practicing filial piety.

Filial piety has profound meanings in Buddhism. It means to take care of parents physically, mentally and to fulfill their wishes. To further extend and enhance our respect and care for our parents, we have compassion for all beings in this world. As stated in a precept sutra, "All men are my father; all women are my mother". This is the broadening of our mind of filial piety so that it encompasses all beings in the universe, in the past, present and future.

Mahayana teachings are based on the principle of filial piety for without it there would be no principle of respecting teachers. It is illogical that we are not filial to our parents, yet respectful to our teachers. We could have ulterior intentions, for example, flattering the teacher to obtain a better grade. Filial piety and respect go together. At the same time that we are filial to our parents, we also elevate that filial piety to being respectful to our teachers. Only when we realize this truth will we truly appreciate the value of the principle of filial piety. The "Earth Treasure Sutra" is the Buddha's teaching of filial piety for only when we treat our parents with such respect can we uncover the infinite treasures within our own self-nature.

Being filial toward our parents is a virtue of our self-nature. Only virtuous acts can uncover our self-nature. It is the first and most fundamental principle of the Three Conditions. The Chinese respect ancestors even though they are distant from them by hundreds, thousands or even tens of thousands of years. They memorialize them on important festivals. Why? Their ancestors and they are all one entity. There is no gap between them. Sincerely memorializing our ancestors corresponds with our self-nature. If we remember and respect our ancestors, we will certainly be filial to our parents. When we are filial toward our parents, it naturally follows that we will respect our teachers.

When we disappoint our parents by not respecting teachers, not following their instructions and not studying hard, we violate the principle of filial piety. Also, siblings would do well to live in harmony. Not getting along with brothers and sisters will cause parents to worry thus also violating the principle of filial piety. By getting along with others at work, meeting responsibilities and abiding by laws, we will not cause our parents to worry, thus we accord with the principle of filial piety. These are a true perfection of virtue. Buddha Shakyamuni taught us to begin our learning from here. He is our original teacher from three thousand years ago. If we respect a teacher from this far in the past, how would we not respect our current teachers?

When we pay respect to an image of the Buddha, we are not worshipping him. We respect the image as a representation of our Original Teacher and therefore we pay our debt of gratitude to him. This is why the followers of the Buddha respect the Buddha's images as well as memorial tablets of ancestors. This practice has a far-reaching and widespread educational significance, for at the sight of them, we remember our obligation of caring for and respecting our parents, teachers and elders.

The "Earth Treasure Sutra" tells us about compassion after explaining the Great Perfection. Compassion is the third principle of the First Condition. Compassion is also a virtue of self-nature and crucial to our practice. When the virtue of filial piety and respect for parents and teachers is expanded, it becomes compassion. Compassion includes not killing any living being. This statement has profound meanings. Without a thorough comprehension of the "Earth Treasure Sutra," we cannot understand the true meaning behind not killing any living being.

Of all bad karmas, that resulting from killing is most serious. Why? All living beings have the natural instinct of fearing and evading death. Although killing is the direct retribution of the victim who killed the present killer in a previous lifetime, the current victim does not know this. He or she would not think, "I killed this person so now this person is killing me". If only the victim could understand this, there would be no anger at the retribution. Instead, the present victim will think, "You are killing me now. I will kill you next." This vengeance will be repeated in the endless cycle of birth and death and the mutual hatred will grow stronger and stronger.

This is the most terrible of all the bad offenses and is why we need so urgently to practice compassion for all beings. There are infinite ways to practice compassion, but in the Three Conditions, the Buddha particularly stressed not killing any living being. In other words, killing is an ultimate act of being un-filial towards our parents and disrespectful towards our teachers and elders.

The Buddha taught the basic Five Precepts and the first of these is also the first of the Ten Good Conducts, do not kill. Continuing to kill is to completely disregard his teachings and is an ultimate act of disrespect. This disrespect is tantamount to being un-filial to our parents. Consequently, if we ignore these instructions and kill, we are neither compassionate nor filial.

The fourth principle is "Following the Ten Good Conducts" which are criteria for good behavior and are to be found in many cultures and religions throughout the world. Buddha Shakyamuni told us that if we practice these good conducts, we would not fall into the three bad realms. Instead, we would likely to be born into the heaven realms if we practice these good conducts diligently. If we achieve the deep concentration along with the four immeasurable minds of loving-kindness, compassion, joy and letting go, we will rise to an even higher level of the heavens, the Heaven of Form and the Heaven of Formless.

The Buddha groups the Ten Good Conducts into three major categories: physical, verbal and mental. Physically, we are prohibited from killing, stealing and committing sexual misconduct. The last prohibition is for laypeople. For monks and nuns, the prohibition is to eradicate all sexual inclinations. Regardless of their good deeds or their ability in deep concentration, those who have sexual desires can only rise as far as the Heaven of Desire. This Heaven has six levels; the higher we rise, the lighter these desires.

A person who sincerely cultivates and has thus attained even the lowest level of deep concentration would be able to suppress sexual desires. At this level the Five Desires of wealth, lust, fame, food or drink and sleep would not arise. Although the desires are not completely eradicated, they can be suppressed by deep concentration. Only the one, who can resist temptations of desire, can attain this state and thus be born into the heavens above the First Level Meditation Heaven. Understanding this explains why attainment throughout this process is so difficult. When we are attempting to practice, we can first ask ourselves, "Can I resist the Five Desires of wealth, lust, fame, food or drink and sleep"? If we yield to temptation, we will not be able to rise to this level of heaven.

The second good conduct is to not steal. For instance, some people like to evade paying their income taxes. This is equivalent to stealing money from the country and the retribution from this is much serious than that from stealing private property. When we steal one person's property, we only have a debt to that one person. But if we steal property of the country, we will have a hopelessly insurmountable debt because then we will have stolen from and thus owe every taxpayer. For example, the United States has a population of well over two hundred million. Two hundred million creditors! Just imagine the consequences! Therefore, a sincere practitioner must be a law-abiding person devoted to meeting public responsibilities. One who does not violate the good deeds of no killing, stealing or sexual misconduct is said to be proper in physical conduct.

There are four verbal good conducts; no lying, abusive language, bearing tales and seductive words. First, do not lie. To lie is to cheat deliberately, it is dishonesty. Second, do not make rude or abusive remarks. Those who have this bad habit speak with no sense of propriety; their words can be irritating or very harmful.

Third, do not talk about others behind their back for this sows discord among people. A person says to Sam, "Tom has said something bad about you." And then this person says to Tom, "Sam has said something bad about you." Whether this person does so deliberately or unintentionally, he is bearing tales and gossiping. In our society, many people do this unintentionally. At times, so many people participate in this that the subject becomes distorted beyond recognition. A well-meant message or remark may become just the opposite after everyone who passes it adds or omits something. This can cause serious consequences ranging from discord among individuals to war among nations.

Fourth, do not use seductive words. These can sound very sweet and enticing but often conceal bad intentions. Just look at many of today's movies, singers and performers. They sound beautiful and look good but what are they teaching people to do? To lie, steal, or kill. Fifth, do not commit sexual misconduct. Practice chastity before as well as after marriage.

Finally, there are three mental good conducts; no greed, anger or ignorance. Greed includes being stingy, reluctant to give of our belongings, our knowledge to help others. This can become the greatest obstacle to overcome in our practice. The Buddha taught giving as a way to eradicate our greed. Some practitioners are able to resist any worldly temptations; however, they cannot resist the desire to learn many methods of practice. So, they have not truly rid themselves of their greed.

The Buddha has taught us to let go of all desires and greed. He did not ask us to turn to new objects for our greed. In the past, we sought worldly joys, now we seek and attach to Buddhist knowledge. The mind of greed is still there. Therefore, whether for worldly life or for Buddhist knowledge, we would do well not to be greedy. Greed is the source of all misdeeds and wrongdoing.

Greed leads to resentment and anger. Why? We become resentful and angry when our greed is not satisfied and this brings about immense worries and afflictions. Greed is the cause of the karma that results in us being born into the hungry ghost realm. By failing to rid ourselves of the resentment and anger caused by greed, we can be born into the hell realm. Ignorance, having no wisdom, results in us being born into the animal realm. In both worldly teachings and in Buddhism there is truth and falsehood, justice and injustice, right and wrong, good and bad. An ignorant person cannot tell the difference between them. He or she often confuses false and truth, bad and good. Whether this is done intentionally or unintentionally, this person is ignorant.

The Three Poisons are the biggest obstacles to our attainment of enlightenment. Buddhism, especially the Zen School, advocates starting our practice from the root, the mind. To start from this root, we need to sever our greed, anger and ignorance.

These three physical, four verbal and three mental deeds comprise the Ten Good Conducts. If we are filial to and care for our parents, respect and serve our teachers and elders, and are compassionate without any killing and practice the Ten Good Conducts, we will be regarded as good people by society. However, we still cannot be called "good men and good women" in the Buddhist sense because the criterion for this are higher than just these four principles. Thus, it is not easy for us to achieve even the basic standards.

The Second Condition: The Good Fortune Required to be a Theravada Sage

The second of the Three Conditions is:

5. Taking the Three Refuges,

6. Abiding by precepts laws and customs and
7. Behaving in a proper and dignified manner.

Mahayana Buddhism is based on the foundation of Theravada Buddhism, which was introduced into China during the Sui and Tang Dynasties, thirteen hundred years ago, but soon gave way to Mahayana Buddhism. Why did the Theravada teachings decline in China? In ancient times, people who learned Buddhism had already been nurtured in the Taoist and Confucian teachings, which were enough to replace the Theravada teachings. Since the Taoist and Confucian teachings were also similar to those of the Mahayana teachings, it was natural for the Chinese to accept them. Thus, the Theravada teachings were not practiced as Taoism and Confucianism served as the foundation of Mahayana teachings.

Consequently, Theravada teachings never really developed in China. Today, people learn and practice Mahayana but ignore Theravada Buddhism, Taoism and Confucianism. This is similar to ignoring the foundation and first floor when building a house. Such an attempt would not work because the house would be "a cabin in the sky". This is why we see so few Buddhist successors today.

Theravada Buddhism is established on the human-heavenly basis, which includes being filial to our parents, respectful to our teachers and elders, compassionate to others and diligent in practicing the Ten Good Conducts. With this base, we can meet the criteria to begin learning and practicing Buddhism. To be a Buddhist practitioner, after we have acquired basic understanding, we pay respect to the teacher and take the Three Refuges of the Buddha, the Dharma and the Sangha, the fifth principle of the Three Conditions. We pay respect to Buddha Shakyamuni and express the wish to follow his teachings for the rest of our lives. From this point on we will have the standards for changing our thought, speech and behavior.

Taking Refuge in the Triple Jewels is to take refuge in the Buddha, the Dharma and the Sangha. In ancient times, everyone understood the meaning of the Triple Jewels. Today however, many people misunderstand the meaning. When they hear the word "Buddha", they think of an image. When they hear the word "Dharma", they think of a sutra. When they hear the word "Sangha", they think of monks and nuns.

The Sixth Patriarch of Zen, Master Hui-Neng, foresaw the possibility that people in the future would misinterpret the meaning of the Triple Jewels. Therefore, whenever he taught he would not use the words Buddha, Dharma or Sangha. Instead, he used enlightenment, proper understanding and purity. These terms are more easily understood and less subject to misunderstanding. They are called the Triple Jewels of Self-nature, which are the true principles for us to follow. If we become misled here and follow an individual master, we will remain misled from now on. If that happens, how can we achieve any real attainment?

When we take refuge in the Triple Jewels, we first return to and rely upon the Buddha. For uncountable aeons, we have been wandering helplessly and miserably in the six realms. Now we have met a good teacher who shows us that we need to return from our confusion, delusion and erroneous thinking and to rely upon the awakening of our self-nature. Our self-nature was originally awakened. So, the Buddha that we rely upon is not to be found outside of ourselves but is innate to our self-nature. The Pure Land School teaches "Buddha Amitabha and the Pure Land are already within our self-nature". Buddha Amitabha, Buddha Shakyamuni and all Buddhas manifest from our self-nature. Therefore, what we rely upon is the Buddha or awakening of our self-nature. From now on we should be awakened and never again be deluded or filled with attachments, for if we do so then we have not turned back.

Next we return to and rely upon the Dharma, of which our thoughts and viewpoints of life and the universe completely accord with true reality. This treasure is only found within our self-nature. Buddha Shakyamuni taught us to return from erroneous thoughts and viewpoints and to rely only upon those that are proper. This is to return and rely upon the Dharma.

The Buddha did not tell us to blindly follow him but rather to be a dauntless independent individual and to find the truth by ourselves.

Next we return to and rely upon the Sangha, which represents purity of the Six Senses of sight, sound, smell, taste, touch and idea. Most of us will find that our six senses become polluted when they encounter external surroundings. When these are pleasing, we develop a heart of greed, which is pollution. When these are displeasing, we develop a heart of resentment and anger, which is pollution as well. We need to remember that the Five Desires of wealth, lust, fame, food or drink and sleep and the Seven Human Emotions of joy, anger, sorrow, fear, love, hate and desire are impurities of the heart. The Buddha told us that originally our self-nature was pure without impurities. We need to eradicate all impurities and rely upon our pure heart. This is to return and rely upon the Sangha.

In summary, taking refuge in the Buddha means being awakened and not deluded. Taking refuge in the Dharma means having proper viewpoints. Taking refuge in the Sangha means being pure and not polluted. These are the Triple Jewels of Self-nature that the Buddha taught us for our practice: awakening, proper viewpoints and purity. From now on, we need to forget our past and return to and rely upon these Triple Jewels and use them to correct our thoughts, speech and behavior.

When we attain one of the Three Refuges, we achieve the other two as well. Think about it. Will an awakened person have erroneous viewpoints? Will this person have an impure heart? Can a person with an impure heart and erroneous viewpoints attain awakening? The Buddha has shown us three guidelines to uncover our original self-nature and to attain Buddhahood. This is similar to a way place with three entrances, we only need to step through one and we are in!

Zen Buddhism uses the sudden enlightenment method to uncover our self-nature. However, only cultivators with superior capability and purity of mind can achieve attainment in this way. For example, the Sixth Patriarch of Zen, Master Hui-Neng only taught students with superior capabilities.

Other schools such as the Tiantai, Flower Adornment and Three Sastras (Discourse) Schools use the proper thoughts and viewpoints method by correcting thoughts and behavior following the guidelines in the sutras. However, this requires endurance and much practice because achievement takes a long time and we have to study many sutras.

The Pure Land and Tibetan Schools, however, emphasize practice through purity of mind through cultivation. It is logical that these two schools are popular today in the Dharma Ending Age. However, the Pure Land School does not require unusually superior abilities or a long period of time for practice. As it stresses the Buddha Name Recitation Method to attain purity of mind, it is much easier to practice and to reach attainment in than the Tibetan School. Again, although the doors to the way place are different, each of them will give us entry. Therefore, all methods are equal and the three methods of enlightenment, proper thoughts and viewpoints, and purity are in essence the same.

Thus, we need to acquire a clear understanding of the Triple Jewels of Self-nature and to know which method to choose as the basis for our practice. Only in this way will we find genuine refuge. Otherwise, we will remain ignorant of where to take refuge and upon what to rely.

Although we may now have more understanding of the Triple Jewels, we may still be confused as to how to practice them in our daily lives. Each school has its own representations of the Triple Jewels. For example, in the Flower Adornment School they are Vairocana Buddha, the "Flower Adornment Sutra," Manjushri Bodhisattva and Universal Worthy Bodhisattva and the forty-one Great Bodhisattvas, respectively. They are our role models to emulate.

The Triple Jewels of the Tiantai School are Buddha Shakyamuni, the "Lotus Sutra" and the Bodhisattvas named in the sutra, respectively. In the Pure Land School they are Buddha Amitabha, The "Infinite Life Sutra," the other four sutras and one sastra or commentary; Guan Yin Bodhisattva, Great Strength Bodhisattva, Manjushri Bodhisattva and Universal Worthy Bodhisattva, respectively.

We learn compassion from Guan Yin Bodhisattva and single-minded concentration from Great Strength Bodhisattva. "The Chapter on the Perfect and Complete Realization of Great Strength Bodhisattva" in the "Surangama Sutra" tells us how Great Strength Bodhisattva concentrated on the Buddha Name Chanting Method from the time he took refuge until the time he attained enlightenment. He taught us that the proper way to chant is the complementary practice of concentrating the six sense organs and continuous pure mindfulness of Buddha Amitabha. Pure mindfulness is to chant without "doubt, intermingling with other thoughts and methods", to chant with a pure mind. Continuous means uninterrupted with one sentence after another. This is the key to success in the practice of Buddha Name chanting, which was taught by Great Strength Bodhisattva.

Mr. Lian-Ju Xia wrote in his book entitled "Essentials for Practice of the Pure Land School" that Great Strength Bodhisattva was the founding patriarch of the Dharma realm. Initially, his comment greatly surprised me because I had never heard this before. Later, I understood what he meant and greatly admired him for his perception. Throughout the universe, Great Strength Bodhisattva was the first Bodhisattva to concentrate solely on the Buddha Name Chanting Method.

When Buddha Shakyamuni manifested in our Saha world, the first sutra he taught was the "Flower Adornment Sutra." In this assembly, the Ten Great Vows of Universal Worthy Bodhisattva concluded the sutra and guide us to the Western Pure Land. Thus, Universal Worthy Bodhisattva is the founding patriarch of our Saha world. Then, after the "Infinite Life Sutra" was introduced into China, Master Hui-Yuan of the Eastern Jin Dynasty, which was sixteen hundred years ago, built a cultivation hall and gathered together one hundred twenty-three fellow practitioners. They exclusively studied the "Infinite Life Sutra" and practiced the Buddha Name Chanting Method. Therefore, the three founding patriarchs of the Pure Land School are Great Strength Bodhisattva of the Dharma realms, Universal Worthy Bodhisattva of the Saha world and Master Hui-Yuan of China.

Years ago, my late teacher, Mr. Bing-Nan Lee, of Taizhong in Taiwan, suggested that I should introduce Pure Land Buddhism to the west. I established a Way Place in Dallas, Texas and called it the "Flower Adornment Society", the same name I used in Taiwan. When I brought statues of Buddha Amitabha, Guan Yin Bodhisattva and Great Strength Bodhisattva from China, they were too small for the twenty-one foot hall. I thought that it would be better to have larger paintings with western features to symbolize the introduction of the Pure Land Buddhism to the west.

Just one day before my departure for the United States, I received some paintings with the request that they be taken to Dallas. I still do not know who the donor was. The paintings were of Buddha Amitabha, Guan Yin Bodhisattva and Great Strength Bodhisattva. What a surprise! Buddha Amitabha had Indian features, Guan Yin Bodhisattva had Chinese features and Great Strength Bodhisattva had western features! The donor had the same idea that I had. The western features of the founding patriarch of the Dharma Realm symbolized the arrival of Pure Land Buddhism in the United States. Thus, the Pure Land Society was set up in the west. Mr. Lian-Ju Xia had been the first to suggest that a Pure Land Society be formed. But it was not to be in China, but rather in Dallas, Texas.

The Triple Jewels are also represented by images of Buddhas, sutras and monks and nuns. They are to remind us of the need to return and rely on the Triple Jewels of our self-nature. When we see images of the Buddha, they remind us to be awakened and not deluded when interacting with people, matters and objects. Without this daily reminder we will remain confused and wrapped up in worldly affairs.

The sutras are to be recited daily but not for the benefit of the Buddha. We recite them as another reminder of how to cultivate our mind and how to properly interact with people, matters and objects. For example, our daily conduct is an expression of the "Infinite Life Sutra" when we emulate the qualities found within it.

The image of a monk or nun, whether or not he or she has abided by the precepts, reminds us to keep our six senses from becoming polluted. We need to understand that we do not take refuge in individuals who pass on to us the meaning and the cultivation guidelines of the Triple Jewels of awakening, proper thoughts and viewpoints, and purity.

Although there is an uncountable number of methods, their objectives are the same. As is often said, "all roads lead to Rome" and "all methods are the same". Pure Land practitioners should never criticize or slander Zen, Tibetan or any other schools. Why? Because their objectives are the same as ours, they simply follow different methods. This is similar to our taking a bus while others chose to walk. We cannot say that they are wrong when all roads lead to the same destination. They have the freedom to choose their way. When I was in Huntsville, Alabama, a student asked me, "I am confused by so many methods. Which one do you think I should choose?" At the time, there happened to be a ball on the ground. I pointed to the ball and said, "Look at this ball. The surface has points countless as the number of methods. The teachings require you to find the center of the ball. You can reach the center from any point on the surface as long as you follow a straight line. You need not find a second or a third point. As an old saying goes, "Follow the road and you will get home. There is no need to circle around". He then understood that Buddhism pursues the true mind. Once we attain enlightenment, we attain everything. Therefore, no matter which method we choose, the key to success is concentration on one method. So long as we adhere to our chosen method, we will achieve deep concentration, attain wisdom and uncover the self-nature of Great Perfection.

From all of this, we can see how important the Triple Jewels are to us. Monks and nuns are the treasure of the Sangha. We need to respect all of them. We can learn from the good ones, as well as from those who do not follow the rules and guidelines. We emulate the former and use the latter to serve as negative examples.

If we fail to understand that taking refuge in the Triple Jewels does not mean following a certain person, then there will be the most serious of consequences, as we will fall into Avici Hell. Why? Throughout the universe, there is only one Sangha, an integral body. The Sangha in our present world is just a part of this whole. If we take refuge in and follow only one individual monk or nun, and regard that person as our only teacher and refuse to respect others, we will be committing "Splitting and sowing discord among the group". This is the fifth of the Five Deadly Offenses of murdering our father, murdering our mother, causing a Buddha to bleed, killing a Bodhisattva or an Arhat and disrupting the unity among the Sangha. Therefore, it would be even worse to choose only a certain monk or nun for refuge than not to take refuge at all.

Furthermore, we only need to take refuge once. It does not accomplish anything to take refuge from one person this time and then from another the next time. We may think that we can get much more protection if we follow many monks and nuns. However, as the saying goes, "A clay idol crossing a river cannot even protect himself". Nobody can protect us. Only when we take Refuge in the Triple Jewels of our self-nature, can we protect ourselves. Some of those here today, may have gone through a Taking Refuge Ceremony. If now, those who have done so, have a clearer understanding then they can properly take refuge in the Triple Jewels by following the principles of awakening, proper thoughts and viewpoints, and purity.

The sixth principle of the Three Conditions is abiding by the precepts, laws and customs. Of all the precepts the most important are the basic Five Precepts. My late teacher, Living Buddha Master Zhang-Jia once said, "The Three Refuges and the Five Precepts are so essential that all Buddhist cultivators need to abide by them every moment". Then he explained further, "It is like a train ticket for you to get from northern Taiwan to southern Taiwan. From the moment you board the train until you reach your destination, you must hold on to that ticket. You must not lose it, because you have to show it when you depart. Taking Refuge in the Triple Jewels and the first Five Precepts are as important to you as that train ticket". He further explained that if we part from the Triple Jewels and the precepts, we will lose the teachings and will no longer be a student of the Buddha.

The Five Precepts are no killing, stealing, committing sexual misconduct, lying and taking intoxicants. The first four offenses are physical transgressions of the self-nature. Whether or not we have taken the precepts, it is wrong to commit these acts. But for one, who has formally taken the Five Precepts, this will be considered as committing a double violation.

However, drinking alcohol and taking intoxicants is different. A person who has not taken the precepts is not guilty when drinking, however, a person who has taken the precepts and then drinks will have broken this precept. The purpose of refraining from intoxicants is to prevent us from committing the first four transgressions while under the influence. Therefore, intoxicants in themselves are not wrong. This is an example of why we need to understand the purpose of the Buddha's precept setting, its function and benefit.

When deciding whether to formally take the Five Precepts, the essence of all the precepts, we need to ask the Dharma Master to explain to us exactly what they mean. Only then we will know if and how to abide by them. Merely reading a book of the precepts does not necessarily ensure our commitment to keeping them.

Some people have complained that there are too many precepts and that it is too easy to violate them. Thus, they abandon abiding by the precepts. This is why most people prefer reading or listening to talks about the sutras while avoiding those on precepts. We need to remember that precepts guide us in our behavior and are the proper conduct of all Buddhas. If there were no precepts, there would be no Buddhism. If there were no courtesies, there would be no Confucianism. Merely reciting the sutras without practicing the teachings within them will result in our not receiving any of their benefits. True learning lies in practice and the precepts represent the practice of Buddhism. Thus, abiding by the Five Precepts becomes the standard for our daily lives and the guidelines for us to attain proper enlightenment.

When the Buddha was in our world, he was joyful and open-minded, whether taking part in daily life or teaching. And it was this joy and energy that attracted people and helped them to accept Buddhism. It is not meant to bind us, but to benefit all beings by bringing them joy and happiness. The formation of the precepts was to show us the right path to attain a happy and fulfilling life.

A good illustration is my late teacher, Mr. Bing-Nan Lee, who lived a simple and frugal yet happy life. For decades, he only ate one meal a day. But, whenever he was invited out for dinner, he accepted. On several occasions, he invited me to accompany him. Since I had been practicing the precept of not eating dinner for years, I felt very uncomfortable when being invited. Mr. Lee simply said to me, "Come with me! Come with me!" Later he spoke to me, "With this attachment, you will not be able to help people. Why? Because if you intend to help them, you must make them happy. Eating this dinner is not violating the precepts but rather it is lifting them. They invited you with good intentions. If you reject their invitations, they will look upon you as being closed to reason. Then they will not only reject Buddhism, but also will also tell others that we practitioners are arrogant and look down upon others. They may also urge them to avoid Buddhists. So, you could ruin the opportunity of an untold number of people to learn of Buddhism. Furthermore, this will result in the creation of negative karma for you". Therefore, he was not violating the precepts but was instead simply lifting them for this meant making others happy, helping them to learn of Buddhism as well as according with conditions.

When we arrived at one dinner, the host apologized, "I am very sorry that I did not know that my Mr. Lee does not eat after noon". The host was obviously deeply moved that Mr. Lee had accepted his invitation. We can see from this that Buddhism is flexible. However, it would have been entirely different if Mr. Lee, or one who practices this precept, wanted to eat something in the evening.

Many years ago when I was young, a friend told me a story about himself. It occurred during the Chinese War of Resistance against the Japanese invasion. After the fall of Nanjing, some Japanese soldiers chased the individual and two of his friends. The three fled to a temple and were saved by an old monk who shaved their heads, gave them monks clothing to put on and told them to blend into the large assembly of monks. When the Japanese soldiers arrived at the temple, they were unable to find the three and soon left. Thus, they were saved.

When the war was over, the friends returned to Nanjing wishing to repay their debt of gratitude. They invited the old monk to a lavish banquet. He arrived to find the table laden with chicken, duck, pork and fish. All of a sudden, they remembered that the monk was a vegetarian! They were extremely upset over their mistake and did not know what to do. But the monk acted like there was nothing unusual and picking up his chopsticks invited everyone to sit down. The three friends were greatly moved.

Did the old monk break the precepts? No! His behavior followed what is said in the sutras, "Compassion and kindness are the basis of Buddhism and skillful means are the method". He had used the first of the Four Beneficial Methods, making others happy. The old monk was moved by their gesture and did not blame them for their honest mistake. He had used the same method that the Bodhisattvas use to help people through the dharma doors. If the monk had been angry, he could have easily ruined their interest in Buddhism. But he was wise enough to use the opportunity to help guide three people. Therefore, we again see that Mahayana Buddhism is highly flexible, as it accords with the existing circumstances.

Let's look at strictly abiding by the precepts. The Five Precepts are the heart, the essence of all the precepts. Expanding further, we follow all the precepts as set forth by Buddha Shakyamuni, as well as the social norms, customs, rules and laws in every country. When in China we follow Chinese customs, rules and laws. When in the United States we do the same. In other words, precepts are rules we need to follow in our daily lives. The modern conveniences of transportation and communication have greatly increased opportunities for travel to different countries and regions of the world. We need to follow the advice of "When in Rome do as the Romans do". This is called strictly abiding by the precepts.

Many of the precepts taught by Buddha Shakyamuni were appropriate for that time but are no longer suitable today. Why? Our manner of living, dressing and eating is totally different from that of India several thousand years ago. For example, of the two hundred fifty precepts for monks, ten rules on the etiquette of dressing are totally unsuitable for today as ancient Indians dressed differently than we do. Eating is another area that has changed considerably. Therefore, when we recite and study the texts on the precepts today, we are learning "the spirit of the law and not just the letter".

Likewise, when we practice adhering to the precepts, the most important point is to follow their fundamental spirit, "Do nothing that is bad: do everything that is good". "To do nothing that is bad" is directed toward us. This is a Theravada precept to develop self-discipline and is to be followed conscientiously. It is what the Chinese call "Attending to one's own moral well being even while alone". When we practice self-discipline, we need to remain true to the precepts, even when we are alone. "To do all that is virtuous" is for the benefit of all beings. This is a Bodhisattva precept in teaching us how to interact with others. Precepts are the criteria for distinguishing between good and bad.

Because of the differences in the political system, philosophy and culture, the precepts needed to be modified when Buddhism was introduced into China. The rules established by Master Bai-Zhang, in the Tang Dynasty, were the modified versions adapted for China at that time, however, the essence remained unchanged. This is similar to a state revising the law from time to time. As new situations arise, it becomes necessary to amend some articles, but the principle remains the same. In China, way places in every province and regions have their own version of the precepts They need to mesh with the local conditions for people to follow them. This is simply a modification. If this is not done, then Buddhism will not survive. Only through this updating and modification will it be vital and constantly renewed, allowing it to be accepted and practiced around the world. The Buddha told us that if we can abide by the precepts and laws, we will have a tranquil body and mind, which will allow us to be free from worries and fear. Deep concentration arises from tranquility. Therefore, the precepts are essential to self-cultivation. If we break the law or the precepts, then our conscience will be plagued by guilt even if no punishment is meted out. Moreover, even if we avoid worldly retributions, there is no way to avoid our karmic retribution. When our body and mind are disturbed, we cannot concentrate on our practice. To practice successfully, we need to be tranquil. It is said, "Precepts or self-discipline lead to deep concentration, from which wisdom arises". In summary, the Second Condition, including abiding by the precepts, is a Theravada act of merit and the basis for practice.

The seventh principle of behaving in a dignified and proper manner means we act appropriately for the circumstances we are in. We act from the heart of sincerity and respect for all beings, animate and inanimate, to accord with social etiquette.

The Third Condition: The Good Fortune Required to be a Bodhisattva

The Third Condition is built upon the basis of the Second Condition and includes:

8. Generating the Bodhi mind,
9. Deeply believing in the Law of Cause and Effect,
10. Reciting and upholding the Mahayana sutras and
11. Encouraging others on the path to Enlightenment.

The eighth principle is generating the Bodhi mind. Chinese Buddhists primarily practice Mahayana Buddhism and wish to develop the Bodhi mind, the awakened mind that is genuinely free from delusions. It is the awakened mind that realizes this world is filled with misery and suffering. It is the compassionate and sincere mind, with every thought to attain realization for self and others. The Buddha told us that suffering exists throughout the six realms. Not only is the human life one of suffering, but heavenly life as well. The sufferings of the human realm are so numerous that it would take hours to describe them. Simply said, they are the Eight Sufferings of birth, old age, sickness, death, hardships, the inability to have what we want, being separated from our loved ones and being in the presence of those we dislike or even hate,

A person who has been born into the Form Heaven is one who has accomplished deep concentration as well as having severed the five desires for wealth, lust, fame, food or drink and sleep. In this realm there is no suffering arising from external circumstances such as famine, storm, sickness, etc., but the beings here still suffer the inevitable consequences of time, deterioration or decay of the body and finally the realization that they will not remain in this heaven permanently. With a physical body, we are mortal; we are born, we become old, we fall ill, we die. With material form, there is impermanence; there is creation, existence, annihilation and void.

A higher level is the Formless Heaven. Here, there is no sensuality, no form of male or female and no material form. The inhabitants have no sufferings arising from external circumstances or deterioration. However, here exists the suffering of the realization that nothing is eternal, nothing lasts forever, that the beings here are not in Nirvana. For example, one is not eternal, or able to remain in the Formless Heaven forever. Therefore, the only way to be free and happy is to transcend the three realms of the Desire Heaven, the Form Heaven and the Formless Heaven of pure spirit. How? By practicing according to the Buddha's teachings, for in this way we will truly generate the Bodhi Mind and be enlightened.

The Bodhi mind is fulfilled by the Four Great Vows of Buddhas and Bodhisattvas:

Sentient beings are innumerable,

I vow to help them all,

Afflictions are inexhaustible,

I vow to end them all,

Ways to practice are boundless,

I vow to master them all

Enlightenment is unsurpassable,

I vow to attain it.

Mahayana Bodhisattvas cherish the heart to help all sentient beings. They not only know their own suffering and try to help themselves, but they also want to help their families, relatives, friends; all sentient beings. To equally wish to help all beings, this is the great Bodhi mind. The "Infinite Life Sutra" tells us that Bodhisattvas are the "Un-requested friends of all beings". Even if you do not seek help from them, they come to help. They voluntarily introduce Buddhism to all and this is the pure cause of a Bodhisattva.

To help all beings, we need to first know how to help ourselves. To do this we first free ourselves from worries and afflictions. It is important for us to follow the Four Great Vows in the order listed. However, some practitioners practice the third vow of various methods before they practice the second vow, to be free from afflictions. Of the Four Great Vows, they want to achieve the latter two of learning all methods and attaining enlightenment, but not the first two of helping all beings and abandoning afflictions. Their attempts are like trying to build the third and fourth floors of a house without first building the first and second floors. Today, there are many practitioners, but few of them have succeeded. Why? They did not understand that first they needed to vow to help all sentient beings, for this great compassion is a critical driving force for us to truly study and practice. This is the heart of great kindness and compassion. Nor did they begin with the prerequisites such as eliminating delusions, greed, attachments and ignorance, which disturb and distress the mind. There are so many beings waiting for us to help them break away from their suffering. If we have no virtue, no knowledge, no ability, how can we help others? We do not attain Buddhahood for ourselves. This is the power of great kindness and compassion.

Years ago, when I first started to study with my late teacher, Mr. Lee, he placed three restrictions on me:

1. I was to follow only his lecturing or teaching,
2. I was to read no books or reference materials without his permission and
3. As everything I had previously learned was not recognized, I was to restart as a beginner.

The first blocked my ears, the second covered my eyes and the third cleared my mind. The requirements seemed so imperious and unreasonable. "What an arrogant and autocratic man he is", I thought. Yet I still accepted his restrictions and learned from him. I did not realize that these restrictions were precepts to help me to cut off my afflictions. My mind became purer with much less wandering thoughts after following his restrictions for just six months. His method helped me to practice the second great vow to end all afflictions.

I became very grateful to him. Although he had only asked me to follow his restrictions for five years, I volunteered to extend my study with him for another five. After ten years as his student and abiding by his rules, I had established a solid foundation in Buddhism. Thus, he lifted the ban and encouraged me to broaden my field of study. In other words, I could listen to any teacher, even ones with deviated thoughts. I could read any books. Why? He told me that all knowledge would be beneficial rather than harmful to me because I could distinguish between good and bad, right and wrong. I would not be misled by anyone. He likened it to a child who was innocent and young, needing to have the guidance and protection of parents before having the ability to judge and to make decisions.

Good teachers are truly compassionate and kind. They are patient in teaching and dedicated to their duty. They try to protect their students from contamination of the mind. It is crucial for us to be close to a good teacher; however, being close does not mean being next to the teacher but rather to listen to and follow their teachings. It is usually very hard to find one. We only meet the right teacher after many lifetimes. Some people have said to me that I was most fortunate to have met good teachers, but where could they find one? This teacher is to be encountered rather than sought and the chances for this are rare indeed. It is a matter of affinity and the right conditions maturing. We need to nurture the good root and opportunities. If we are unable to meet these rare teachers, then we can learn from ancient sages.

Mr. Lee modestly told me that he only had the ability to teach me for five years. He encouraged me to continue my studies by learning from his teacher, the late Venerable Master Yin-Guang. He advised me not to emulate people who were famous Buddhist scholars, who were knowledgeable in Buddhist studies, but who had not attained achievement in cultivation. Master Yin-Guang was currently the best teacher. When we cannot find the true knowledge of goodness in current teachers, we can turn to ancient sages. There have been many people who have succeeded with this method.

The first person in China to take an ancient master as his teacher was Mencius. He learned from Confucius, who had left his writings for later generations to learn from. Mencius only read Confucius' books and followed his teachings exclusively. He is acknowledged as a great sage, second only to Confucius. After Mencius, there were many others who succeeded in their academic pursuits using the same method. Another example is Master Ou-Yi of the Ming Dynasty, who was a patriarch of the Pure Land School.

As for finding a good teacher today, do not follow me, I am not eligible to be a teacher. Mr. Lee once advised me to learn from Master Yin-Guang. I recommend that you should select the best teacher, Buddha Amitabha and the "Infinite Life Sutra" for your practice. When we succeed in our practice, we will attain Buddhahood. The most important thing in Buddhism is to concentrate on and delve deeply into one method. Then we will surely reach deep concentration and attain wisdom.

In times past, people devoted to practice normally spent five years for this stage of learning and cultivation. During these five years, they would specialize in a certain method. Afterwards, they were allowed to study various sutras. At that point, I believe their understanding would be greatly improved and they will naturally understand the meanings in sutras. If we still have wandering and discriminatory thoughts, and have not yet awakened our wisdom, then even if we were to study for three hundred years, we would still not understand the meanings of the sutras and their commentaries.

Mr. Lee had set three restrictions for me, which I thought were his alone. In 1989, when I was lecturing in Singapore, Master Yan Pei invited me to give a lecture to a group of practitioners. Seeing that there were many young people, I told them of my past experiences and advised them to solely follow Master Yan Pei. I recommended that "If you follow one teacher and one method, you will surely succeed". After the lecture, Master Yan Pei invited me to have tea with him. He told me that when he was a young monk, his teacher had set the same three restrictions on him. Then I realized that the three restrictions were not the invention of one individual, rather they were the prerequisites that past masters set for their students.

Only then did I understand what "Inheritance of the tradition from the master" meant. When the teacher thinks that we are good students, he will require us to follow the three restrictions. He will first cover our eyes and block our ears so that no worries will intrude. When we truly have abandoned all attachments and gained wisdom, we will be allowed to study other methods. Therefore, extensive learning is conducted in the second stage rather than at the beginning.

Difficulties can arise if we engage in extensive learning at the very beginning. It is similar to hearing instructions from one master and beginning to follow him. Then we hear instructions from a second master and feel as if we were facing two paths leading in different directions. With three masters, we would be caught at a three-way junction and with four, we are stuck at a crossroads not knowing which way to go. Therefore, it is important to follow only one master at one time. Reading of ancient sages, monks, nuns and laypeople, we see that some followed their teacher for twenty to thirty years until they achieved some awakening. Only then did they begin to study extensively with other teachers.

Buddhist education is different from modern education in terms of concepts and methods. For instance, in a university, we must be very careful and take our time choosing our major. Buddhism however, is different. Here we are expected to awaken to perfect, complete wisdom first and then in the future we will become knowledgeable in all other departments of the university. Where do we start? From the intensive study of a certain method, just as is said in "Awakening in one sutra means awakening in all sutras". What does awakening mean? Awakened means to have attained wisdom.

Modern education is similar to building a pyramid. We read extensively and then narrow the scope of learning to specialize in one subject. This is a way of progressing from extensive to intensive learning. But, no matter how tall the pyramid or how large its base, the pyramid has its zenith. Buddhism is different. It is like a tree with roots, trunk, branches, leaves and finally fruits. It is an infinite process, starting from one point, the root, and then developing into the Great Perfection of the Self-nature. The result is that we understand everything. Worldly knowledge has its limitations after which there is no more to learn. Buddhism, however, is boundless. The wisdom of Buddhism is beyond the comprehension of average people. Buddhism may seem ordinary at the beginning, but the achievements we make later are inconceivable. On the contrary, worldly studies initially appear extensive and comprehensive but in the end, they provide no lasting accomplishment.

By following the Four Great Vows, we will eventually uncover our original self-nature. In the "Flower Adornment Sutra," Sudhana served as a role model for our cultivation. He not only taught us the principles and methods but also how to apply them in our daily lives. Manjushri Bodhisattva, Sudhana's first teacher, instructed him to follow the aforementioned three restrictions and to sever all afflictions, to accomplish self-discipline, deep concentration and wisdom. After Sudhana had attained original wisdom, Manjushri Bodhisattva then allowed him to travel extensively and to learn other methods by visiting fifty-three spiritual guides who represented different occupations and levels in society.

His last visit was with Universal Worthy Bodhisattva who taught him the Ten Great Vows, as well as how to chant "Amituofo" and to be born into the Western Pure Land, where upon meeting Buddha Amitabha, he attained perfect complete enlightenment. Without being born into the Pure Land and meeting Buddha Amitabha, we will only fulfill the second and third vows of severing all afflictions and mastering all methods but will find it difficult to attain Buddhahood.

In the "Flower Adornment Sutra," both Manjushri and Universal Worthy Bodhisattvas had reached the level of equal enlightenment and vowed to be born into the Pure Land. I was surprisingly pleased to discover this when I gave talks on the "Flower Adornment Sutra." I wondered why enlightened Bodhisattvas in the Flower Adornment World would want to be born into the Western Pure Land, considering how wonderful their own world was, it seemed unnecessary for them to do so. After thinking about it, I realized that they had vowed to go there to be able to attain Buddhahood in a short time. If not for this, there would be no reason to go to the Pure Land of

Buddha Amitabha. Suddenly, I realized that if we want to attain the perfect complete enlightenment, we need to go to the Western Pure Land. Only by understanding the "Chapter of Universal Worthy Bodhisattva's Conduct and Vows" will we know the proper way to study and practice Mahayana Buddhism. And when we truly understand, have awakened and generated the Bodhi mind, we will finally be free from delusions and attachments.

The ninth principle of the Three Conditions is to deeply believe in the Law of Cause and Effect. Earlier in my practice, I was puzzled by this phrase in the "Visualization Sutra." Why? It seemed to imply that a Bodhisattva had no understanding of the Law of Cause and Effect. If we know that good causes will result in good effects and that bad causes will result in bad effects, how could it be that a Bodhisattva was not aware of this? But the sutra urges Bodhisattvas to believe in cause and effect. I could not understand it.

Then I read the "Flower Adornment Sutra" and upon carefully reading the chapter about the Ten Grounds, I suddenly saw the light. It said that, "from the beginning to the end, the Ten Ground Bodhisattvas have always practiced the mindfulness of the Buddha". I then realized that the Bodhisattvas, from the first to the tenth ground and the level of equal enlightenment, all practiced the Buddha Name Chanting method. And I also came to understand that "Chanting the Buddha's name is the cause and attaining Buddhahood is the effect". Many Bodhisattvas were not aware of this, which is why Buddha Shakyamuni explained it in this sutra.

It was their firm belief in the above statement that led Manjushri Bodhisattva, Universal Worthy Bodhisattva and Sudhana to vow to be born into the Pure Land. It was after I had studied and lectured on the "Flower Adornment Sutra" that I came to understand this statement. Thus, it really is difficult to acquire this understanding.

The tenth principle of the Three Conditions is reciting and upholding Mahayana sutras, which help us to understand the true reality of life and the universe. With this understanding, we will know the proper way to think and behave as well as the appropriate method to use. Only when we truly accord with the teachings of the sutra, will we benefit. As practitioners, the least we need to do is to participate in the daily morning and evening sessions. The purpose of the morning session is to start a new day by reminding ourselves to base our thought and behavior on the Buddha's teachings. The purpose of the evening session is to reflect on whether we have followed the instructions. If not, then we need to earnestly regret and vow to correct our mistakes.

For the sessions, Pure Land Practitioners used to recite the "Amitabha Sutra," chant the Rebirth Mantra three times and then follow by chanting "Amituofo". The more times they recited "Amituofo", the better the result. This practice of single-mindedness was the same for morning and evening. The "Amitabha Sutra" appears simple but is actually extremely profound. To recite and benefit from it, we need a pure and quiet heart. The second time I lectured on the commentary of the "Amitabha Sutra," it took over three hundred sessions, which is an indication of its level of complexity.

I now recommend the "Infinite Life Sutra," which is easier to understand both in language and meaning. Since many people lead such busy lives, I suggest reciting Chapter Six for the morning session, which is comprised of the Forty-eight vows of Buddha Amitabha. It is the core of Pure Land Buddhism because true cultivators need to have the same compassion and vows as those of Buddha Amitabha. For the evening session, I recommend reading chapters thirty-two to thirty-seven, in which the Buddha teaches us how to end all wrongdoings, practice good conduct and how to interact with objects, matters and people in our daily living. If we can follow at least these chapters then we abide by the precepts.

If we can follow the above practices, be mindful of Buddha Amitabha and abide by the teachings in these six chapters, we would have the same mind, vows, understanding and practice of Buddha Amitabha and then we are Buddha Amitabha. But if we chant or read indifferently without applying the principles, then all the efforts we put forth will be pointless. The combination of morning and evening sessions was designed in ancient times and proved to be useful, for the people of that time had better understanding of what they were reciting. These sessions reminded people to behave in a proper manner and thus helped them to detect their faults. Today, however, people simply recite absentmindedly, like small children who sing a song with the right words to the right tune, but without understanding the meaning. Only when we become aware of the purpose and method of chanting the sutra can we actually achieve any results.

My late teacher, Mr. Lee, always told his students that when they listened to lectures, they needed to concentrate on understanding the principles in the sutra and not the words themselves. These principles are the laws governing the Buddha's teachings as well as worldly teachings. One, who thoroughly understands the principles of one sutra, can then use them to master all sutras. In other words, the student must conscientiously follow the methods taught by the teacher and do so wholeheartedly without being distracted by anything new and different.

To develop the Paramita of Patience, we need to persevere in our cultivation. People may recommend other methods or sutras as a better choice. Do not listen to them; do not pay attention to them until we have attained wisdom. Delve deeply into just one method. This is the key to success in our study and cultivation.

The eleventh principle of the Three Conditions is encouraging others to advance on the path to enlightenment. To do this, we extensively introduce Buddhism to those who are willing to learn. While the first ten principles of the Three Conditions are for self-benefit and cultivation, the eleventh is to encourage and help others to understand and practice Buddhism. To help others is the act of a Bodhisattva.

By fulfilling all the principles in the Three Conditions, from practicing filial piety for parents to encouraging others on the path to enlightenment, we will become the "good man and woman" of the Mahayana sutras. The "Earth Treasure Sutra" tells us that if we chant the name, make offerings to Earth Treasure Bodhisattva and accord with the teachings, then we can be born into the thirty-third Heaven one hundred times, without falling into the three bad realms.

In our world, we are considered a good man or woman after fulfilling the First Condition. The criteria in the Theravada teachings require us to meet the First and Second Conditions. However, in the Mahayana teachings, we are required to meet all three conditions. Therefore, when reading sutras, we need to ask ourselves whether or not we are qualified to be "good men or women". How much have I achieved? And does my conduct conform to the standards set forth in the Mahayana teachings?

THE SIX PRINCIPLES OF HARMONY

The Three Conditions are the basis for individual cultivation whereas the Six Principles of Harmony are the basis for group cultivation. The Sangha is a group of four or more people who properly practice the Buddha's teachings together, especially the Six Principles of Harmony. They are:

1. Sharing the same viewpoints or goals,
2. Abiding by the same precepts,
3. Living and practicing together harmoniously,
4. Not quarrelling,
5. Experiencing the inner peace and happiness from practicing together harmoniously and
6. Sharing benefits harmoniously.

Sharing the Same Viewpoints or Goals

This means mutual understanding or agreement. A group needs to share the same viewpoints of the principles and methods for study and practice. This is the basis for harmonious group cultivation.

If a society is to remain stable, its members need to live in harmony. Only harmony can draw us together in terms of opinions, ideas and our way of life. In other words, being harmonious can minimize the differences in human relations and improve equality. After that, peace and then finally, happiness can be achieved. To obtain happiness we must have a peaceful heart and body. Both Buddhist and worldly teachings emphasize the importance of harmony and respect.

A few years ago I went to Beijing and visited the Forbidden City, where there are three main palaces, the names of which all contain the word harmony. This shows that the early emperors of the Ching Dynasty, the last dynasty, tried to rule the country with harmony. However, the disharmony, which plagued the imperial family at the beginning of this century, ended the dynasty. Therefore, harmony is crucial for lasting peace and happiness.

Buddha Shakyamuni provided innumerable methods to practice but he did not intend that we try them all. We need to find the one most appropriate for us and then remember that the key lies in exclusive pursuit. In ancient times, the Pure Land School adopted three sutras and one sastra, now we emphasize five sutras and one sastra. As stated in an ancient Chinese textbook, "Of all the teaching principles, exclusive pursuit is the most important". Suppose some people like the "Infinite Life Sutra" while others prefer the "Amitabha Sutra." Can these two groups of people merge into one? They may merge, but they cannot practice harmoniously together, for when one half begins to recite the "Infinite Life Sutra," the other half will want to recite the "Amitabha Sutra." In order to create group unity, it will be necessary to set up two separate way places.

This explains why there are so many different way places even though we are all Pure Land practitioners. The same principle applies to choosing sutras with multiple commentaries. Which one will we use? This will result in a further setting up of way places. The same process can even occur when deciding which form of chanting to follow. Some prefer to chant slowly

"Namo Amituofo" while others prefer a very fast "Amituofo, Amituofo, Amituofo". It would be very difficult for the two groups to practice harmoniously together.

The people in ancient way places were able to achieve because everyone shared the same viewpoints and goals and practiced the same method without intermingling. Their very atmosphere was conducive to magnificence and peace. Thus, all those who entered naturally gave rise to respect.

Unfortunately, a common situation in modern way places is that the teachings of various schools are intermingled. Contradictions and conflicts are unavoidable, and it will be difficult for practitioners to focus, much less to succeed. So, it becomes evident that "Sharing the same viewpoints or goals" is crucial in a way place.

If the people in a group share similar ideas and viewpoints as well as the same interests and objectives, they can remain in harmony and thus form a Sangha. However, they may as well form a separate Sangha if differences arise. Otherwise, there would be conflicts and no one would succeed. By providing an infinite number of methods for cultivation, the Buddha meant to ensure that people of different viewpoints and interests would all be able to succeed in their cultivation. Thus, it is said that all paths lead to the same goal, as all methods are equal. This demonstrates the Buddha's great, compassionate heart, as he never forces anyone to practice one particular method.

As we have seen from the example in the "Visualization Sutra." Madame Vaidehi, being overwhelmed by the suffering in this world, asked Buddha Shakyamuni to tell her of a place where suffering did not exist. Instead of directing her to the Western Pure Land, he displayed all the Buddha lands for her so that she could choose one for herself. This is unlike most of us who want others to accept our opinion; "I have been practicing this method. It's great. Come and try it." When others have different ideas and viewpoints, this will often disrupt the harmony of the group and is the very thing we should guard against. The best way to introduce Buddhism is to provide a general introduction to the Mahayana teachings and practices and let others chose whichever method they prefer.

Those who prefer Buddha Name Chanting can practice together; those who prefer meditation can practice together. In this way, everybody has a place to go for cultivation and there is no need to pressure anyone into using one particular method. All methods are equal and were taught to meet our different needs, abilities and levels of understanding. Thus, each school should respect and praise the other. This is the true practice of the first harmony.

Abiding by the Same Precepts

When we live and practice together, we need to have rules and regulations for without them there will be disorder. Needless to say, the rules need to include the five fundamental precepts set by the Buddha. Rules vary for lay Sanghas and those at way places. The former conforms to the five fundamental precepts, the latter to the monk or nun precepts. In addition, common rules, regulations and local laws and customs are also to be observed. These all comprise the Permanent Resident Agreement of a way place. One or two members can be designated to draft the rules, which are then presented to the group for discussion and voting. Each individual living in the way place must abide by the agreement once it is set up. If every member respects and abides by the agreement, there will be no discord within the group, because all are have equal status and no special privileges are granted to anyone. Thus, the Sangha is truly democratic and law abiding.

Living and Practicing Together Harmoniously

The purpose of establishing a way place is to help everyone achieve in group practice. It is definitely not to help individuals escape their worldly responsibilities. It is a serious mistake to think this way, especially in the light of all the offerings way places receive from followers and the reality that every offering will have to be repaid, if not in this lifetime then in a future lifetime. The manner of living together does not mean that each person has his or her own room. If luxurious and comfortable facilities are available, it will be very difficult to achieve. Why? The "Earth Treasure Sutra" tells us that, "Every single movement or stirring of thoughts on the part of the living beings is karma and an offense". For uncountable eons we have been deluded and confused and have thus committed infinite wrongdoings. Consequently, we have developed and accumulated infinite bad habits. When with others, we usually try to be civilized and behave ourselves. But, when alone, we tend to indulge ourselves in doing whatever we feel comfortable with and easily forget proper conduct.

To counter this, members of the group share sleeping quarters. These quarters in a traditional way place were comprised of one large platform bed with a space for each person. Quilts were neatly folded as in an army barracks. Life in a way place was even more rigorous than that of the army and the monks and nuns were even more disciplined than the soldiers were. Only by living in such a disciplined way place, are we able to mold our temperament and reform ourselves through the Three Learning's of self-discipline, deep concentration and wisdom. This is true cultivation.

However, there are exceptions in way places. For example, the managing monk and the executive deputy chief, due to their responsibilities, have their own rooms, which are usually very small, in order for them to plan and take care of daily tasks without disturbing others. Monks and nuns, who are aged or ill, also have their own rooms. To accomplish our cultivation, this shared living is necessary, even in today's affluent society.

Not Quarrelling

All the members who live together need to do so without quarrelling. In this way, they can best concentrate their efforts on cultivation. When people are together, the most frequent act is that of speech, so speech karma is the easiest to commit. We have a proverb, "Illness enters by the mouth. Trouble exits from the mouth". Another is "More speech, more trouble". One, who eats too much, easily becomes sick. One, who talks too much, easily gets into trouble. Sometimes misunderstandings arise because the listener is sensitive while the speaker is careless. Both parties develop resentment and hatred, which gives rise to endless retaliation in the future. This is why ancient sages advised us to "Talk less and chant the Buddha's name more". The less we speak, the better it is for the less trouble we will be in. Ideally, we would only speak when it was necessary.

When I was in Los Angeles, a friend told me about the three-day Zen retreat his high-school son had attended. Once inside, no one was allowed to talk. The daily practice was sitting meditation, from 8 a.m. to 5:30 p.m. and from 7:30 p.m. to 9:30 p.m. Nothing else was done. Keeping silent for three days in a way place like this will help us to calm down and relax. The boy was so impressed that he wanted to go back for the longer winter session. The distinctive feature of such a way place is the harmony of silence and no quarrelling.

So, at a strict way place where chatting or other irrelevant talk is forbidden, there is virtually no opportunity for quarrelling. Almost exclusively, all we will find is the silent or voiced continuous chanting of "Amituofo" in the chanting hall. In a Tibetan way place, the chanting of mantras is ceaseless. For instance, during my early stage of Buddhist study, I was under the guidance of Living Buddha Master Zhang-Jia for three years. Through my observation, he never stopped silently chanting a mantra while moving his lips even when he was with visitors. He only paused to talk and as soon as he was finished, would resume his silent chanting.

This silent chanting while moving our lips is a form of practice called, "Diamond Holding". Master Zhang-Jia was one of the sincerest practitioners I have ever met. His mind was pure without any attachments or wandering thoughts. His teaching method was unique. He never spoke a word until he found the listener attentive and concentrated. He then spoke only a few words while looking directly into your eyes. Each of his words bore heavy weight, which his listener would never forget and would adhere to for the rest of his or her life. The goal of our practice is to eradicate all afflictions and attain the Buddha Name Chanting Samádhi. If we do not practice this method, it will be very difficult for us to achieve this goal.

EXPERIENCING THE INNER PEACE AND HAPPINESS FROM PRACTICING TOGETHER HARMONIOUSLY

This is to savor the Dharma joy. Whichever practice method we choose, the basic achievement we have in our practice is happiness. If we feel unhappy after beginning our practice, we have definitely encountered a serious problem. But the problem does not lie with the Buddha's teachings. We may have done something that goes against the principles of these teachings or we may have chosen the wrong method. Otherwise, the results would be evident; awakening from confusion and obsession, leaving sufferings behind and obtaining happiness.

With each passing year, we would have fewer worries while enjoying greater happiness and freedom. This is the evidence of success in our practice. If we are not achieving this, then we need to examine ourselves for the cause of our lack of success. If we can correct our mistakes, find the root of our afflictions and sever them, we can then attain the benefits of our practice. Practicing Buddhism is to experience life and to train our minds. Buddhist cultivation arises from our heart as we participate in daily life. What kind of heart do we cultivate? One of purity. When we have proper viewpoints and understanding and truly dedicate ourselves to Buddhism, regardless of who we are or what our circumstances are, whether good or bad, favorable or unfavorable, we will be able to reduce karmic debts and to plant the seeds of good fortune, wisdom and happiness. How then can we be unhappy? A feeling of joy naturally arises from our heart, as we savor the Dharma Joy. If we practice together harmoniously, everybody will attain this Dharma joy, everybody will attain achievement.

Sharing Benefits Equally

In ancient times, ordained people led a simple life with one meal a day. They received food donated by people in the village, rested under the trees at night and cultivated constantly. So, the way place was more like a school to educate the local community on Buddhism. Learned and far-sighted people built them with the financial support from those who were wealthy and held high status in the community. Then well-known and respected monks were invited to cultivate and conduct the teachings.

Way places were Buddhist educational institutions where everyone shared equally. If this principle were to be applied to society there would be no psychological imbalance and hence no social disturbances. At way places, none of the Six Harmonies can be neglected or else there will not be a true Sangha. As the Chinese say, "harmony in the family is the basis for any undertaking". Similarly, if a country is united, it will not be easy for another power to dominate it, because the power of unity is inconceivable. Consequently, if a family, company, social group or a country can practice three of the six harmonies of sharing the same viewpoints or goals, observing the same precepts, and sharing benefits equally, they will become prosperous.

We find an example in the business world. Since the Second World War, Japanese business has developed dramatically. After only half a century, these businesses were among the most successful in the world. Why? They have practiced these three harmonies. By sharing the same viewpoints and goals, the Sangha can reach common understanding. By abiding by the same precepts, all abide by the laws. By sharing all benefits equally, everyone is assured that there will be fairness in all things.

The importance of harmony also holds for the family. As the Chinese say, "Harmony in the family is the basis for any undertaking". One day, a student of mine asked for my opinion about the kind of person he should marry. I told him, "You should try to find someone who has the same viewpoints and goals that you do. Then you will help each other and enjoy a happy family life. You cannot just emphasize love for love is volatile and unreliable. It may fade after the two of you get married at which point everything can change". Therefore, a happy family life is built upon the basis of the Six Harmonies. If we do not understand this, it will be difficult for us to have a happy and enjoyable family.

The Three Learning's

We know that the very nature of Buddhism is education. It encompasses a large number of subjects, which cover the perfect knowledge of life and the universe. The textbooks for these subjects are sutras. However, not all of the sutras in India were brought to China. Because of the difficulties in the long journey between China and India in ancient times, both the Indian monks who visited China and the Chinese monks who returned after visiting India, had to limit the number of books they carried. They selected the most important ones and had to leave the others behind. So, all the books that were introduced into China were considered the essence of Buddhism.

However, after their introduction, not all of the books could be translated. Further screening had to be done and only the best and the most essential were selected for the difficult translation process. The project was financed by the central government. Experts, who were monks and laypeople from all over China as well as from foreign countries, were invited to participate in the mammoth translation effort. According to historical records, Master Kumarajiva's translation institute had over four hundred people while Master Xuan-Zhuang's institute had more then six hundred people.

The name of the translator that we see today at the beginning of the sutra is the chief of the institute and represents all the translators in the group. The Chinese sutras that we have today are fairly complete. However, the Indian Sanskrit versions have been largely lost with few remaining. After the Chinese sutras, the second largest collection is that of Tibet. Part of this collection was translated directly from the Sanskrit and the rest came from the Chinese versions.

Princess Wen-Cheng of the Tang Dynasty brought Buddhist sutras to Tibet when she was married to the Tibetan king. This is why the introduction of Buddhism to Tibet was some six hundred years later than the introduction of the teachings to China. As the Tibetan king built up belief in Buddhism, a new school from India found its way into Tibet.

An important part of the teachings are the Three Learning's of abiding by the precepts or self-discipline, deep concentration and wisdom. Accomplishment of these can relieve the suffering of this world. Buddha Shakyamuni told us how long the teachings would remain on this earth. The Dharma Perfect Age would last five hundred years. The Dharma Semblance Age would last one thousand years. The Dharma Ending Age, that we are now, in will last ten thousand years.

What are the sufferings of the sentient beings in our current age? The first is committing the wrongdoings of the Ten Bad Conducts. The Buddha taught us the First Learning of self-discipline to overcome these. The second suffering is the inability to remain serene and at peace. The Buddha taught us the Second Learning of deep concentration to achieve purity of mind and tranquility. The third suffering is ignorance. The Buddha taught us the Third Learning of wisdom to overcome our current state of ignorance.

Committing wrongdoings, being confused and remaining in ignorance are three of the major problems of sentient beings in our contemporary world. The Buddha will teach when these problems afflict the sentient beings in our world. However, if the beings are not ill, there will be no need for the Buddha to teach. The Diamond Sutra says, "in the end we even have to lay aside the Buddha's teachings, let alone worldly teachings". When beings are well, the teachings are unnecessary and introducing them might even lead to more problems. This is similar to a healthy person taking medicine every day and eventually falling ill.

Self-discipline cures our body, deep concentration cures our mind and wisdom cures our behavior. Therefore, a person who practices Buddhism is wise in thought, speech and behavior. So how could such a person be unhappy?

THE SIX PARAMITAS

Now that we understand the Three Conditions, the Three Learning's and the Six Principles of Harmony, how do we use them in our daily lives when interacting with people, matters and objects? To answer this Buddha Shakyamuni gave us the Six Paramitas of giving, abiding by the precepts, patience, diligence, deep concentration and wisdom. If we follow these in everything we do, from brushing our teeth in the morning until going to bed at night, we will be genuinely practicing.

The Paramita of Giving

The Giving of Wealth. Generally speaking, the majority of people seek wealth as their foremost pursuit for without it, life can be very hard. After this, people pursue intelligence and wisdom, health and long life. Regardless of whether they are in the east or in the west: whether they had lived in the past or are living now, these are major pursuits of humankind. If Buddhism is supposed to fulfill our wishes, can it provide these things for us? We have heard that "In Buddhism, every sincere plea will receive a response." Then why have most people not received what they wished for? They are not aware of the true reality of life and universe or the right method to fulfill their wishes. If we understand these principles and truths, all our wishes can be fulfilled.

The Buddha taught us that wealth; wisdom and long life are all karmic results. If we want to obtain the result, we must first nurture and establish the cause. Good causes result in good results: bad causes result in bad results or retribution. Where there is a cause, there will be a result and where there is a result, there was a cause. This is a law that never changes and the law around which all other laws in the universe revolve.

Consider someone who is very wealthy. How did this happen? It is not because the person is unusually clever or has better ideas to make money. Many other people are cleverer or have better ideas. Why are they not successful? The Buddha taught us that having wealth is the karmic result of a cause planted in former lifetimes. What was this cause? It was the giving of wealth.

The giving of wealth results in obtaining wealth, the giving of teaching results in obtaining wisdom, the giving of fearlessness results in obtaining health and long life. Therefore, if we wish to have wealth, wisdom and long and healthy lives in our future, we need to nurture and establish these causes in this lifetime. Only a small number of people obtain the results from causes they developed in their early years. Regardless of the time frame, we must develop the cause to receive the result. This is the Law of Cause and Effect. And this law never changes.

Giving is the most important requirement for practicing the Bodhisattva way. If we could sum up all the methods in Buddhism, we would find that all methods accord with the Six Paramitas. When we condense the Six Paramitas, we find that their essence is giving. One of the types of giving is that of wealth. When most people hear this, they often think of donating money to a group, church, temple or way place. This is wrong because such thinking is too narrow in meaning and is far from the true Bodhisattva way.

Selflessly remembering the welfare of others is the giving of wealth. Thus, everybody is practicing the giving paramita daily and in this way, we are emulating Bodhisattvas. We are just not aware of it. For example, when we get up in the morning and prepare breakfast for the family, we are practicing giving and kindness as did Universal Worthy Bodhisattva. By doing so we will be happy. In this way we will have no thought of "Poor me, my family regards me as a servant. I have to wait on them every day." If we complain like this, all the good fortune we have achieved will vanish. But once we change our complaints and problems into the Paramita of Giving, we will immediately enjoy the benefits of the joy and wisdom of the teachings.

An employee who works very hard every day to make as much money as possible or to receive a promotion is not practicing giving. However, if this employee works hard just to benefit the company and society, and not for the sake of money or a promotion, he or she is cultivating giving and will never be tired. I, myself, enjoy traveling around the world to help people to understand the Buddha's teachings, and in this way, am practicing the giving of teaching. I help others to better understand how to change their lives in the hope that they will be able to reduce their troubles, obtain joy and wisdom and thus be able to lead a better life.

In 1984, I made my third trip to Los Angeles. I went straight from the airport to the site where the speech was being held and began a talk that lasted nine hours. I delivered the talk while standing but at the end, it was the listeners who were tired, not I. The longer I spoke, the more energized I felt and the stronger my voice became. Why? Because I was so enthused about introducing the profound and subtle Buddhism to the listeners. This is the joy of teaching Buddhism and frankly, the best nutrition. Nowadays, people talk a great deal about health food. But it is false nutrition. Buddhists talk of keeping a pure, quiet and happy heart. Having this heart and obtaining this joy will enable us to remain healthy and young. Worry will only make us old and sick.

In the US, some social practices are actually giving. Most people pay for medical insurance for protection against catastrophic medical bills in the event they become ill. However, we are preparing for a possible illness when we make our monthly premium payments. In this way, we are bound to become ill. If we do not, then we will have wasted our money. But if we change our way of viewing this to the thought that our money has been used to help those that are sick, then we will have practiced giving and will never become ill. Why? Because we have developed the cause of no illness. If we give to and look after aged people, we will receive good karmic results in the future. When we ourselves become aged, then others will come to take care of us.

Today, most people have car insurance. If we think that we are making payments just to help those who may encounter accidents, then we will never encounter misfortune, because we have given of wealth and compassion. So, our way of thinking makes the difference in whether we are a Bodhisattva or an ordinary person. What is this difference? A Bodhisattva is awakened and always does things to benefit others, whereas ordinary people are always doing things to benefit themselves. When we do everything for others, we can get wonderful benefits, too wonderful to imagine. The kinds of giving are boundless and can be practiced any time, any day, any way.

In Buddhism, the giving of wealth consists of external and internal wealth. External wealth is comprised of worldly possessions whereas internal wealth concerns our body. For example, organ donation is an example of the internal giving of wealth as is helping others physically. If we volunteer to help others without expectation of benefit, we are again practicing the giving of internal wealth. We can practice this giving of internal wealth all the time.

We see that in the Buddhist criteria for good and bad, all deeds arising from the wish to help others are good and all deeds arising from selfishness are bad. This may all be difficult for a beginner to follow. Why should we not benefit ourselves? The reason why ordinary people cannot attain Buddhahood is due to the two attachments of self and all knowledge. By ridding ourselves of self-attachment, we attain the level of Arhat. By ridding ourselves of the knowledge-attachment, we attain Buddhahood. If our every thought is to benefit ourselves, our self-attachment will grow daily. Even as we plant some good causes, we will only increase our attachment. The Buddha told us that if we wished to transcend the cycle of birth and death, we must rid ourselves of both self and the knowledge-attachment. Self-attachments are afflictions that hinder us from attaining purity of mind. Knowledge-attachment hinders us from uncovering our all-knowing wisdom, our true wisdom.

The Giving of Teachings. The second form of giving brings us wisdom, intelligence and skill. Generally, it falls into two categories: Buddha's teachings and worldly teachings. To enthusiastically impart all of our knowledge to others, who are interested in learning, is the giving of teachings. It is not limited to the teachings of Buddhism. It could be teaching others cooking, engineering, etc. It is the unconditional and free imparting of knowledge or skills in any field.

A schoolteacher who instructs out of the sincere desire to help others is also practicing the giving of teaching. A teacher who does so just to earn a living or prestige is not. A genuine practitioner of the giving of Dharma is very enthusiastic and is never weary of giving. When we give for self-benefit, we will become disappointed upon failing to obtain prestige or other benefits and will thus loose our enthusiasm. On the other hand, a Bodhisattva is always compassionately working for the benefit of all sentient beings and never attaches any conditions to what is given.

In the "Infinite Life Sutra," the Buddha told us that of all the kinds of giving, that of the teachings is foremost. Worldly teachings do not get to the heart of the matter. Buddhism is a perfect education, which can help us to attain the boundless wisdom, virtue and skill to enable us to be free of all worries, leave the cycle of birth and death, put an end to reincarnation and ultimately to attain Buddhahood. This giving is perfect and remarkable, and is only found in Mahayana Buddhism. All Buddhas praise this giving. In Buddhism, the most important form of giving is that of books, audio and videotapes, CDs, as well as that of accepting other's invitations to lecture and thus, to create opportunities for them to learn the Buddha's teachings.

However, many currently circulated Buddhist materials are printed with copyright warnings. These are not the giving of Dharma but are commercial endeavors. Some Dharma masters, when requested to speak, ask how much they will be paid. These are not the true giving of the teachings. The act of a Bodhisattva is to benefit others, not self. If a person truly wanted to learn of Buddhism, a Bodhisattva would simply go to them to fulfill their wish. They would never do anything that would make it difficult for any person willing to learn, as long as the person could receive the true benefits from Buddhism

The Giving of Fearlessness. This form of giving has broad implications as it helps to remove the fears and insecurities of others. For example, if foreign forces were invading our country, we could join the army to help protect the citizens. If someone was afraid to go home alone at night, we could offer to go with him or her. Being a vegetarian is another example, because if we all followed this practice, then all living creatures would no longer regard us as a threat. Any act that helps sentient beings feel safe and secure is the giving of fearlessness. In doing so perfectly, we will definitely gain health and long life.

Emperor Qian Long of the Qing Dynasty, attained wealth, intellect, wisdom, health and long life. "Honorable as a great emperor and wealthy as one who possesses the entire world". He was truthful, clever, wise and lived a long life. He was emperor for sixty years and Supreme Emperor, Father of an Emperor, for four years. He was endowed with these great virtues because in his previous lifetimes he had practiced the cultivation of the Giving of Wealth, Dharma and Fearlessness.

The Buddha teaches that Bodhisattvas must practice the Paramita of Giving. Paramita means perfection. The question is how can we practice giving to the state of perfection? We do so simply by turning our thoughts around, by no longer thinking of ourselves but solely of others. In this way, we will be practicing "giving" anytime, anywhere. But, we will not yet have achieved perfect giving. Perfect giving is to let go, to be willing to give all that we possess and to help all others. Giving and gaining are one. If we have not practiced giving, we will not gain. When we give less, we gain less. When we give more, we gain more. Do you have fears, worries? Do you have birth and death, reincarnation? Why are you not willing to discard them? Giving is to part with all of these to attain great perfection and great freedom. This is the ultimate perfect giving, the Paramita of Giving. We start by parting with our material possessions and gradually part with everything. If we are able to let go of our afflictions, birth and death, then we will uncover the purity, wisdom and abilities within our self-nature.

The Paramita of Abiding by the Precepts

The second Paramita is Precept Observation, which means abiding by customs, rules, regulations and laws. Everything, big or small, worldly or beyond, has their own natural laws. We need to follow these for only by doing so, can we accomplish an undertaking quickly and perfectly. For example, within the family, we need domestic etiquette or seniority in human relationships to guide the behavior between parents and children, husband and wife, brothers and sisters. The manner of how things are accomplished needs to be followed. This is similar to cooking rice; we wash it, put it into the pot and then cook it. Without following the proper sequence, the rice will not be properly cooked.

This is even truer in learning and practicing Buddhism. If we want to achieve, we must follow the guidelines told to us by the Buddha: the Four Great Vows of Buddhas and Bodhisattvas. First, we vow to help all living beings. After that, we discard all worries, habits and attachments, to end all afflictions. Only then do we master all methods. Finally, we attain Buddhahood. Only when we become Buddhas, will we have the ability to help all beings and thus perfectly achieve the First Great Vow, "Sentient beings are innumerable, I vow to help them all".

Some may ask, "Is it really necessary to attain Buddhahood? Won't it be enough to become a Bodhisattva?" Although a Bodhisattva can help beings, he is unable to help a Bodhisattva who is equal or higher in attainment. For example, an Equal-enlightenment Bodhisattva cannot help another Equal-enlightenment Bodhisattva. However, a Buddha can help them as well as all others. Therefore, only when we attain Buddhahood, can we perfectly help all beings in the universe. With such a vow, we can generate the great compassion to help others, to be diligent in severing our afflictions and mastering all methods.

Today, many practitioners have not yet sincerely generated their vows although they recite them daily. Why do I say this?

Because they still have the mind of discrimination: ideas of favoring and disfavoring, self and other, love and hate. Consequently, they practice discrimination. They help people they like and ignore those they dislike. Theirs is not a genuine vow, is not a perfect vow. A perfect vow is that of a Bodhisattva and arises from the non-discriminatory mind. The Bodhi mind. It is wonderful, inconceivable and far beyond the minds of ordinary people.

The Paramita of Patience

In whatever we do, we need to exercise patience. As stated in the "Diamond Sutra," "All natural laws of the universe attribute their success to patience". Without it, we cannot succeed in anything. For example, to complete our college education, we have to be patient for four years. This audience needs to be patient to sit here for two hours listening to my lecture before you achieve perfection in this lesson. Without patience, we can never achieve anything, no matter how good our conditions are. Of the Six Paramitas, Buddha Shakyamuni in the "Diamond Sutra" stressed giving and patience in particular. They are the keys to success in cultivation.

It has been said that "It is difficult to handle matters, but it is even more difficult to interact with people". It was not so difficult to interact with people in the past, but now, it is. Why? Education in the past taught people the proper manner and behavior in which to conduct themselves. Today it teaches people how to make a living. It is no wonder that we do not know how to conduct ourselves. We are unable to understand the changing of our own emotions, much less those of others. Therefore, it has become increasingly difficult to get along with other people.

There are three categories of patience. First, tolerate the injuries of physical and verbal abuse. Patience is a virtue. With patience, we will have a quiet and pure mind; thus, it will be easier to attain deep concentration and achievement. When we successfully practice patience, we will gain the greatest good fortune. Second, we would do well to be patient with variations of the natural elements, hot and cold, summer and winter, hunger and thirst, as well as natural disasters. Third, be patient in the arduous course of our practice. Before attaining the joy of cultivation and before of our cultivation becomes strong, we will encounter many obstacles. However, once we get through this phase, we attain happiness. Why? Because we are on the right path. This is like traveling on an expressway. Before we can get on it, we keep circling and driving around trying to find the entrance. This is very frustrating because there are many cars in our way and we cannot drive fast. We have to remain patient. Once we get on the expressway, it is much more pleasant because traffic moves smoother and faster with no hindrances. Our practice of Buddhism is like this.

In the beginning, we move around, trying different methods and schools. Which one shall I choose? What shall I learn? Some people are fortunate because they only spend a few years to find the right method. Others are not so fortunate, and may take ten to twenty years or even a lifetime in the attempt to find the right method. Good fortune is the result of our good roots, merits and virtues, causes and conditions. With these, the Buddhas and Bodhisattvas will surely help us, as they never abandon anyone. And once we have the mind to accept their teachings, we will be helped by the Buddha to find awakening. Then our future will be bright.

Why, does the Buddha not simply tell us what we need to know? He did. But we did not listen. We were told the method, but instead thought to ourselves, "Well this may not be a good method. I heard that another one is better". We have thus argued with the Buddhas and Bodhisattvas. So, they have chosen not to come to us. Please carefully consider this. We need to be very patient before we can attain achievement. Without patience, we cannot advance to a higher stage, for patience is the prerequisite for deep concentration and diligence.

The Paramita of Diligence

The Chinese word for diligence is comprised of two characters meaning perseverance in a specialized field and progress. The two need to work together. Buddhism is neither conservative nor backward, but seeks daily improvement. Some say that Buddhism is no longer relevant. These remarks are erroneous because the people who said them did not know the Paramita of Diligence. Progress is good, but more important is progress with diligence. Currently, many great scientists in the west have made many discoveries. They persevered. They did research everyday and never stopped. The same applies to our learning Buddhism. We are practicing diligence when we choose one school or method and stay focused on our selection, studying until we excel in it, before advancing to another method. It is not effective to concentrate on different methods at the same time. Once we understand one method, we will understand all of them. This is known as "Once we achieve in one, we achieve in all". If we try to practice many methods before we are enlightened, they will become obstacles. Let me tell you what happened to one monk who specialized in the Buddha Name Recitation Method.

In the beginning of this century, Master Di-Xian had a student who became a monk at the age of forty so the student was almost the same age as the Master. The two had been childhood friends. Master Di-Xian, who was from a well to do family, had received a good education. However, his childhood friend was from a poor family and had received little education. When the friend grew up, he could only do manual labor and thus had a very difficult life.

One time, he went to visit Master Di-Xian. After staying at the temple for a few days, he told the Master that he too wanted to become a monk. "Why?" asked the Master. "Because life is too hard and I want to be a monk" replied his friend. The Master initially denied this request because he felt the rigorous training and sutra memorization would prove too much for someone who was illiterate and much older than novice monks usually are. The other monks would look down upon his friend. Feeling everything would prove too much for his friend, the Master denied the request. But the friend persisted and so the master gave in. Master Di-Xian said to him, "I will accept you as a monk. But I do not think you need take the vows of abiding by the precepts because you may not stand the rigor of the fifty-three day training. There are many deserted temples in the countryside, I will find you one to stay in." The Master arranged for some practitioners to provide meals for the new monk. He then taught his friend to chant "Namo Amituofo". "Just recite this phrase over and over. When you are tired, take a rest, when rested, resume your chanting. I am sure that you will greatly benefit from this".

And so the new monk isolated himself in the small temple and concentrated solely on his chanting. Three years later, he went to visit friends and relatives. He came back and told the woman, who had been doing the cooking for him, "There is no need to prepare food for me tomorrow". The woman thought the monk, who had not left the temple for three years had decided to re-visit his friends again the following day.

The next day, she went by the temple to see if he had returned. She went to the temple and called. Receiving no reply she went into the temple and found him standing, with his recitation beads in his hand. She greeted him but received no response. When she moved closer to him, she realized that he was dead but still standing! Never having seen anything like this before in her life, she rushed off to ask the others who were looking after the monk, what to do. They sent a message to the Master's temple informing him of the strange occurrence and asking what to do.

Due to difficulties in traveling, it took Master Di-Xian three days to arrive at his friend's temple. He understood that his old friend had been born into the Western Pure Land. He looked at the still standing dead friend and said admiringly to him, "You have proved that your decision three years ago to become a monk was a fruitful one. Not one of the Dharma masters or abbots at all the famous way places can match your achievement." For three years, the uneducated monk had done nothing but recite "Namo Amituofo". His single-minded, ceaseless recitation had resulted in his achievement of being freed from the cycle of birth and death and of being born into the Western Pure Land. The practice of diligence is important regardless of what we are doing. Whether chanting "Amituofo", sitting in meditation, chanting mantras, or studying sutras, we need to practice diligence.

In studying sutras, if we want to help ourselves as well as others, it would be best to specialize in just one sutra for study and lecturing. In this way, each time we study and lecture, we will reach a new state of mind, we will improve each time. A person who lectures on The "Amitabha Sutra" for ten years will become Buddha Amitabha. A person, who lectures on the "Universal Door Chapter" for ten years, will become Guan Yin Bodhisattva. A person, who tries to learn ten sutras in ten years, will become a jack-of-all-trades and a master of none. Now we can see how important diligence is!

Years ago, when I was a professor at the Buddha Light Temple, a Buddhist university in Taiwan, I recommended to the principal that each student specialize in only one single sutra, "This way in ten to twenty years, your Buddha Light will shine over the entire world". However, my idea was not accepted. If it had been, we would now have many experts giving Dharma talks. What a wonderful accomplishment that would have been! In this way people who wanted a talk on the "Amitabha Sutra," would have Buddha Amitabha to speak. People, who wanted a talk on the "Earth Treasure Sutra," would have Earth Treasure Bodhisattva to speak. Every graduate from the university would have become an expert! Only in this way can Buddhism become widely accepted.

So, I hope that all those who give Dharma talks will become experts instead of general scholars. For while such students appear to be knowledgeable in many areas, actually they are incapable of mastering anything. On the contrary, students who specialize exclusively in one subject will turn out to be versatile experts. All the Buddhas and Bodhisattvas are versatile, but they all concentrate on their respective teaching. To be diligent is to delve deeply into one method. The virtue and benefits of practicing the Paramita of Diligence in this way are infinite.

The Paramita of Deep Concentration

The fifth Paramita is deep concentration, which includes the concentration levels practiced within the heavenly realms and beyond. The concentration of the heavenly realms is comprised of eight levels. If we succeed in our cultivation of them, we will be born into the higher heavens. Beyond the heavenly realms, deep concentration is found in the realms of Arhats and Mahayana Bodhisattvas. Finally, the highest level of concentration is that practiced by all Buddhas. The key to all methods of practice lies in deep concentration.

It is a mistake to think that only Zen Buddhism practices deep concentration. Pure Land Buddhism uses Buddha Name Chanting to concentrate the mind. Tiantai Buddhism practices tranquility and contemplation, which is another form of deep concentration. Tibetan Buddhism uses the Three Mystic Practices, the three karmas of body, mouth, mind corresponding to those of the Buddha. So, although different schools use different terms, they all practice deep concentration. Therefore, in the Six Paramitas, concentration encompasses the above forms as well as all the phenomena in our daily lives.

What is this concentration? Being the master of our mind. We have goals, which will never be changed or influenced by the environment. Scientists succeed in their research because they do not allow themselves to be distracted by other concerns. So, they attain a scientific concentration. When we successfully practice the Buddha Name Chanting Method, we will attain the Buddha Name Chanting Samadhi, as did Master Di-Xian's student. If we are able to endure, we will become patient and thus be able to persevere and progress and thus attain deep concentration, which is the essence of our practice.

In the "Platform Sutra," the Sixth Patriarch, Master Hui-Neng explained that deep concentration was more than just sitting in meditation. He himself reached awakening upon listening to the "Diamond Sutra." Therefore, all of his lectures were based on the principles in this sutra. He said that meditation is not being attached to any phenomena.

Concentration is sustaining the mind of tranquility. In the "Diamond Sutra," Buddha Shakyamuni taught the proper attitude to have when encouraging others to practice Buddhism, "Do not attach to changing form, maintain the mind of stillness, do not be moved".

The "Flower Adornment Sutra" tells us of the fifty-three visits of Sudhana. When Sudhana went to visit Yuxiang, a venerable sage who practiced deep concentration, the boy could not find the old man. Where was he? The sage was not found to be sitting in meditation at home or in the way place. He was found roaming around a market. What was he doing there? Maintaining the mind of tranquility by practicing deep concentration and the principle of not attaching to phenomena. He was not sitting cross-legged facing a wall for hours, a position we often admire and expect of a master. We often find ourselves looking down on the Master of deep concentration whom we see bustling around in excitement. We do not yet realize that such a Master has reached a much higher level of attainment than many practitioners we see in the lotus position. A higher level of deep concentration or Samádhi can exist in all acts.

Why is deep concentration so important? Why did the Buddha caution us to stay away from form and to remain unmoved in our heart? Because all phenomena are illusory, like dreams, bubbles and shadows. They are unattainable. The Buddha sees through everything and urges us not to give rise to any discriminatory thoughts and attachments. If we can do so, then we will uncover our true self-nature and attain the Buddha's understanding of all things in the universe. This is the Paramita of Wisdom.

THE PARAMITA OF WISDOM

The Sixth Paramita is intuitive wisdom. We apply it in our daily lives, as we learn the Bodhisattva way. We know everything around us but we do not cling to it as we do our best to help others. Why? This act of helping others originates from the thought and practice of Buddhas and Bodhisattvas,

"Unconditional compassion for all others as we are all one entity". This is like a person naturally using the left hand to brush away a mosquito that is biting the right hand. Would the left hand ask why it should help the right hand? Of course not. They are part of the same body.

Today, we have temporarily lost our self-nature, not knowing that all beings and we are one entity. So we discriminate between others and ourselves becoming perplexed and obsessed, spreading confusion, committing wrongdoings and thus bringing sufferings to others and ourselves. The Buddha taught us how to break through delusion so that we would awaken to the truth that helping others is helping ourselves. Such a heart of compassion is unconditional because it originates from understanding of "Unconditional compassion for all others as we are all one entity".

In conclusion, everything has its own methods and continuity. This is abiding by the precepts. With endurance and perseverance, we will have patience. To specialize without slacking is diligence. To be master of our mind and not to be swayed by external condition is concentration. To thoroughly understand all phenomena is wisdom. Therefore, the Buddha taught us to adopt the Six Paramitas of giving, abiding by the precepts, patience, diligence, deep concentration and wisdom into our daily lives. In this way, we will be practicing the Bodhisattva way. It is a mistake to think that once we have accepted the Bodhisattva precepts, we will automatically become a Bodhisattva. If we are ignorant of the Six Paramitas and thus cannot apply them, then even if we have accepted the Bodhisattva precepts, we will be no more than clay idols unable to even help ourselves.

The Ten Great Vows of Universal Worthy Bodhisattva

Only when we have applied the first four of the Five Guidelines, the Three Conditions, the Six Principles of Harmony, the Three Learning's and the Six Paramitas will we truly be a student of the Buddha and thus be close to Bodhisattvas. Based on the foundation of the Six Paramitas, we can progress to the next level of our practice, which is comprised of the Ten Great Vows of Universal Worthy Bodhisattva. These vows were taught to us by the Buddha in the "Flower Adornment Sutra." This is the last stage of our cultivation leading to Buddhahood. We cannot practice the Six Paramitas and advance to the Ten Great Vows until we fulfil the first four guidelines. The main characteristic of Universal Worthy Bodhisattva is an immeasurably broad and compassionate heart. Every one of his vows is complete and perfect.

The First Vow: To Pay Respect to all Buddhas

Who are Buddhas? We read in the "Flower Adornment Sutra" that "Sentient or insentient, all attain wisdom". So all beings that have self-awareness and all things such as plants and minerals are Buddhas-to-Be. With respect for all beings and things, not just the present Buddhas, we will foster the heart of Universal Worthy Bodhisattva. His heart is different from that of most Bodhisattvas.

Buddhist practitioners are respectful to the Buddha, but this respect may not be completely sincere. Why not? If we are listening to a lecture, but suddenly think of an important appointment or have a call on our telephone or pager, what will we do? We will leave the hall immediately go to attend to business or the telephone call! So, our respect and belief are not genuine. If we were truly sincere and respectful, we would regard attendance at the lecture as our prime concern. But in fact, if we are listening to a talk on the sutra and someone tells us that there is a business opportunity that will make us one million US dollars, we will immediately leave the lecture hall. Our respect and belief are not genuine enough.

The profound respect of Universal Worthy Bodhisattva is perfectly genuine, regardless of whether it is for Buddhas, sentient beings or insentient objects. Why? He understands that they all have a Buddha nature. Therefore, offending a sentient being is offending a Buddha. Thus, we too should respect all beings. Then how do we act towards tables and chairs? They are also to be respected as beings, for everything is the result of the joint force of all causes. What is the right way to show respect for all things? Prostrate to them three times a day? No, that is the way of a Buddhist idiot. To show respect to material objects, we just keep them orderly and clean. For example, books go neatly into a bookcase. When doing something, we are earnest and responsible, trying to do it the best we can. We treat people, matters and objects with equal respect. This is the virtuous way of Universal Worthy Bodhisattva. This is the expanded and perfected way of the Six Paramitas, and therefore the most perfect and effective way for Buddhist cultivation..

The Second Vow: To Praise the "Thus Come One"

The second vow is to "Praise the 'Thus Come One'". Since, the first vow is "To respect all Buddhas" why do we not rephrase them as one, "Praise and respect all Buddhas"? There is a profound meaning within these two vows. "Respect all Buddhas" applies to behavior. When considering the form, we are to show respect for everybody, regardless of whether they are good or bad. Also, we are to respect all laws whether they are accepted or heretical. "Praise the 'Thus Come One'" applies to nature. So, there is a difference. We admire the good but not the bad, although we respect the latter as well. And therein lies the difference.

In the "Flower Adornment Sutra," Sudhana understood this very well. He respected and praised nearly every one of the fifty-three spiritual guides he visited. However, three of them he respected but did not praise; Fasumiduo, Shengrepoluomen and Ganluhuowang. The first was a prostitute and symbolized lust or greed. The second was a heretic and symbolized ignorance. The third was hot-tempered and symbolized anger, punishing those who caused him the slightest offense by plunging them into boiling oil or driving them into a hill of daggers. These three symbolized the Three Poisons of greed, anger and ignorance. To Sudhana, the three were to be respected but not praised. So, we see that praise is linked to virtue.

Only good characteristics and accepted laws deserve praise. But we still respect all beings and things because respect reflects purity of mind and the virtue of respecting others equally. We respect heretical beliefs while we praise accepted ones such as Christianity, which helps raise people to the heaven realms. This is not achieving the perfect, complete enlightenment, but it is infinitely better than heretical beliefs that will lead people to fall into the three lower realms. So, we praise Christianity. However, we never praise cults for they encourage people to commit wrongdoings.

We can see that there is a big difference between the first and second vows although both come from a pure and perfect intention.

The Third Vow: To Make Offerings Extensively

The primary characteristic of Universal Worthy Bodhisattva is an immeasurably broad and compassionate mind, which in Mahayana Buddhism is considered as the perfect function of the self-nature. Ordinary Bodhisattvas have seen to their self-nature, but it is partial, not perfect. Only the virtuous character of Universal Worthy Bodhisattva is perfect. All his vows are directed to all beings in the universe. Herein lies the difference between Universal Worthy Bodhisattva and ordinary Bodhisattvas who practice just the Six Paramitas. An offering to one Buddha is an offering to all Buddhas. His offerings are not only made to Buddhas but also to sentient and non-sentient beings. Therefore, "One is all and all is one". With this great broad-mindedness, we can attain the non-discriminatory and boundless perfection.

Universal Worthy Bodhisattva told us that of all the many kinds of offerings, that of the teachings is supreme. However, only the Buddha's teachings can help sentient beings break through confusion and delusion, to uncover the perfect self-nature, to become enlightened. No other kind of offering can do this. As Buddhism is an education, we are to honor the teacher and revere his or her teachings. Only in this way, can we attain perfect, complete enlightenment.

In the teachings of Buddha Shakyamuni, which sutra is the most important? In the Sui and Tang dynasties, over a thousand years ago, great Buddhist scholars studied and compared all of the sutras from Buddha Shakyamuni's forty-nine years of teaching. They agreed that the "Flower Adornment Sutra" was the most important. So, the "Flower Adornment Sutra" was commonly acknowledged as the perfect teaching. The scholars then made comparisons between the "Infinite Life Sutra" and the "Flower Adornment Sutra" and concluded that the "Infinite Life Sutra" was higher than the "Flower Adornment Sutra." They explained that the "Flower Adornment Sutra" and the "Lotus Sutra" are the two most important. In Chinese Buddhism, they are called the "First Vehicle Perfect Teachings". Both function as the guide to the "Infinite Life Sutra." Therefore, the "Infinite Life Sutra" is really the number one teaching.

When I first read this, I was very pleased because it agreed with my personal experience. It was the "Flower Adornment Sutra" that guided me to Pure Land Buddhism. I lectured on this sutra for seventeen years. Later, I only lectured on the "Chapter of Universal Worthy's Conduct and Vows" from the "Flower Adornment Sutra." During these seventeen years, I deeply comprehended the meaning of the Ten Great Vows of Universal Worthy Bodhisattva in guiding beings to the Western Pure Land. This Pure Land is the essence and the final destination of the Flower Adornment. From this experience, I realized that the ancient masters were right.

So we know what is the best and most important among all of Buddha Shakyamuni's teachings. However, it was only after Mr. Lian-Ju Xia, a Buddhist layman, edited a compilation of the five versions of the original translations of the "Infinite Life Sutra" that we could enjoy a perfect benefit. The great project of editing such an extensive literary collection demonstrated that Mr. Xia was not an ordinary person, but rather the manifestation of a Great Bodhisattva. This great being felt compassion for the sentient beings in our world, which revealed that the opportunity for many beings to attain Buddhahood, had matured. Thus, he manifested in our world to compile the sutra versions and propagate the Pure Land method during our Dharma Ending Age.

When I visited Beijing, a student of Mr. Xia presented me with a photo of his teacher. Upon returning to Taiwan, I printed an enlarged copy of the photo. Although it is not very clear due to repeated duplications, an amazing phenomenon is apparent. Behind Mr. Xia's head the image of a Buddha appears. Light is emitting from this image as well as from below his shoes. Although the photo has been reduplicated many times, we can still clearly see that the image over Mr. Xia's head is that of a Buddha sitting on his lotus seat. We placed the photo in a prominent position to express our gratitude to this great Bodhisattva for having given us such a gift and for guiding us in our cultivation and propagation of Buddhism.

The "Infinite Life Sutra" is the most important sutra for helping all beings to attain Buddhahood. It contains forty-eight chapters. Which chapter is number one? Of all the chapters, chapter six is the most important. It tells us of Buddha Amitabha's Forty-eight Vows. When we read the "Infinite Life Sutra," we see that Buddha Shakyamuni accorded with these vows when he introduced the history and background of the Pure Land.

Which of these vows is number one? The great scholars and monks in ancient China agreed that the eighteenth vow is number one. It tells us that ten recitations of Buddha Amitabha's name will result in birth into the Pure Land. In my early years of study, I questioned whether the Buddha had the ability to help a person to immediately become a Buddha, even if he or she was doomed to birth in the Avici Hell, the lowest of the hell realms. If the Buddha was unable to accomplish this, then his wisdom and ability were limited. To say that he had all virtues, perfect abilities was complimentary rather than factual. But, if the Buddha were capable of helping such a person become a Buddha, then I would believe that he was perfect in wisdom and capabilities, and was thus worthy of our admiration. This question remained unanswered until after I read the forty-eight vows of Buddha Amitabha in the sutra. Then, I realized that the Buddha's wisdom and virtuous character are indeed, perfect and universal.

The Buddha is indeed capable of helping a person who has committed serious offenses to become a Buddha. The question lies in whether or not the person believes and accepts. If not, then the fault lies with the individual, not the Buddha. So, after reading the "Infinite Life Sutra" we know that anyone who sincerely practices the recitation method will surely succeed.

In the earlier example of Master Di-Xian and the student who so successfully chanted "Namo Amituofo" for three years, the student knew in advance when he would be born into the Pure Land. He told the woman who brought his food daily, that she need not bring it the following day. After he passed away from this world, he remained in a standing position for three days waiting for his master to come to make final arrangements. His birth into the Pure Land was into the highest level. His accomplishment is proof of the eighteenth vow, which explains to us that this birth can be accomplished with just ten recitations of "Amituofo".

Anyone who firmly believes in this method surely has good roots, great merits and virtues. The "Infinite Life Sutra" explains that the monk's rebirth after such a short time of practice was due to his having made offerings to innumerable Buddhas in previous lifetimes. As a result, he was able to believe and practice. Without his good roots from previous lifetimes, he would not have been able to believe regardless of what his teacher had said.

The name of Buddha Amitabha contains infinite meanings. It is the name of the universe, so it includes everything. If we want to know the meaning of the name, we can read the "Infinite Life Sutra," the explanation of the name. If we want to understand the "Infinite Life Sutra" we can read the "Flower Adornment Sutra," for it is a detailed explanation of the "Infinite Life Sutra." If we want to understand the "Flower Adornment Sutra" we can read the entire Great Canon for it is the detailed explanation of the "Flower Adornment Sutra." By using this method to understand the sutras, we will know that the merit and virtue of the name of Buddha Amitabha are truly extraordinary.

This name alone contains all of Buddhism as well as all laws throughout the universe. Therefore, to chant this name is to chant all sutras. During the reign of Emperor Qianlong, there was a famous monk Ciyun Guan-ding. Among his many works is the "Directory to the Visualization Sutra," which tells us that when we seek escape from disasters we can resort to reciting sutras, chanting mantras or drawing divination slips. However, if a person has committed grave wrongdoings then the only thing that will work is to recite "Namo Amituofo". From this, we understand that this is the best method to follow when facing disaster. Many people do not know this so they resort to other methods. Therefore, a person who is ill may recite the "Medicine Master Sutra" and when faced with disaster may recite the "Universal Door Chapter". This person does not know that the merits and virtues of Buddha Name Recitation make it the number one method.

Then why did Buddha Shakyamuni not tell us so directly? Why did he teach us so many sutras and methods? Because many people do not believe in the Buddha Name Recitation Method. So, he kept the finest method for last. This is similar to what we see in the Taiwan Palace Museum. Most people consider the beautiful jade collection of the Qing Dynasty, to be more valuable than the bronze ware, which resembles pieces of metal, not realizing the bronze ware is the most valuable part of the collection in the museum. Similarly, most people do not realize the true value of Buddha Name Recitation. So, the Buddha had to teach all the sutras to guide sentient beings to the Pure Land.

Master Shan Dao told us that the only purpose for all Buddhas to manifest in the world is to tell us of the original vows of Buddha Amitabha. Today, we can truly understand, cultivate and propagate the Pure Land method. Truthfully, this is due to the support of the Triple Jewels. Also, the opportunities today for sentient beings to achieve attainment are very good. In the past five to six years, millions of copies of the "Infinite LifeSutra" have been printed and spread throughout the world. I have traveled around the world introducing and recommending this sutra. Many people have liked and accepted it. Seeing you here working and practicing so earnestly, I am very pleased and feel that my hard work has been rewarded. Therefore, if we can practice and widely propagate this method, than I can say that we have perfectly fulfilled the vow to "Make Offerings Extensively".

The methods used by Buddhas and Bodhisattvas are infinite in number. They are the display of great compassion and lead to birth into the Pure Land. For example, Universal Worthy Bodhisattva is the founder of Tibetan Buddhism. Also, Zhun Ti Bodhisattva, one of the great patriarchs of Tibetan Buddhism, is a manifestation of Guan Yin Bodhisattva. Both Universal Worthy Bodhisattva and Guan Yin Bodhisattva urge us to seek birth into the Western Pure Land. We ordinary people discriminate between Chinese and Tibetan Buddhism, but Buddhas and Bodhisattvas with their perfect freedom and non-discriminatory minds do not discriminate among the different schools. All eighty-four thousand methods lead to the same goal. With this understanding, we will naturally respect all methods and schools.

The Fourth Vow: To Regret Karmic Obstacles

Everybody has karmic obstacles. Every thought in a person's mind causes a karmic act, which in turn will certainly results in an obstacle. What is obstructed? Our true nature, within which there is infinite wisdom and virtue. There are two types of obstacles: those caused by afflictions and those caused by knowledge-attachment. We create these constantly. The Buddha told us in the "Flower Adornment Sutra," "All beings have the Buddha's wisdom and virtue but cannot attain them due to their wandering thoughts and attachments". Like a doctor, the Buddha pointed out the root cause of our illness. Attachments are the root cause of afflictions and wandering thoughts are the root cause of knowledge-attachment. For all methods, learning and cultivation is simply a matter of doing away with our wandering thoughts and attachments. Once we do this, we will uncover our Buddha nature. All the methods in Buddhism teach us to regret our karmic obstacles. Thus, to regret karmic obstacles is the key to our cultivation.

However, it is very difficult to remove these obstacles. Of all the methods, that of the Pure Land is unique. For even if we have committed an extremely grave crime such as one of the Five Deadly Offenses and are thus destined to fall into the Avici Hell, we can still remove our obstacles and attain Buddhahood. We need to feel remorse, vow to change and practice Buddha Name Recitation and accord with the Buddha's teachings to attain birth into the Pure Land. This is why Master Ciyun said that this recitation method alone is able to dispel obstacles, for they cannot be dispelled reciting sutras or mantras.

In the past few years there was a theory being circulated that said a person with remaining karma could not attain birth into the Pure Land. This greatly shocked and panicked Pure Land practitioner. When I went to Los Angeles in1984, I was asked if this was really true. On hearing the question, I smiled and said, "If it were true that no person with remaining karma could be born into the Pure Land, then the only person there would be Buddha Amitabha. What then is the use of going there?" The person questioned "Why?" I replied, "Have you ever heard of the four lands, three kinds and nine grades in the Pure Land?" He replied that he had read of them in the sutras. I told him "If no one with remaining karma had been born into the Pure Land, why are there four lands, three kinds and nine levels?" With this, he understood.

The division of lands, kinds and levels is based on the amount of remaining karma. With heavier karma, we are born into a lower grade: with light karma, a higher grade. I then explained, "Guan Yin Bodhisattva, Manjushri Bodhisattva and Universal Worthy Bodhisattva are all Equal Enlightenment Bodhisattvas. The sutras tell us that even Bodhisattvas of this high level still possess one degree of remaining ignorance. Isn't this a karmic act?" My questioner was relieved at my words. So even an Equal Enlightenment Bodhisattva goes to the Pure Land with remaining karma. Buddha Amitabha is the only one there without any karma. I then concluded, "Who says that a person with remaining karma cannot be born into the Pure Land"! My words seemed to help as the individual laughed merrily for he began to see that all beings in the Pure Land had gone there with their remaining karma.

Buddhism teaches us not to be angry or hold grudges against others. So, I added "It is not wrong to advocate extinguishing karma for it is good to carry as little karma to the Pure Land as possible. In this way the person can attain birth into a higher level".

Later, I went to New York. As soon as I got off the plane, I was asked the same question. People did not know the truth. As soon as I explained, they understood that it was not wrong to have karma. Extinguishing karma is good for it is feeling remorse for the obstacle.

Buddha Name Recitation is a sincere act of feeling remorse and vowing to change. However, when feeling remorse we must be sure that our heart is the same as Buddha Amitabha's, our vow is the same as Buddha Amitabha's and our behavior corresponds with that of Buddha Amitabha. How do we do this? With sincerity by not merely reciting with our mouth but with our heart. In this way, we will perfectly fulfill the teachings in the sutras. Only by doing so can it be said that we are true cultivators of the recitation method. Be sure that with every thought of "Amituofo" we have the same thought and vow as the Buddha. We need to turn his forty-eight vows into our own. Only in this way can we be rid of karmic transgressions.

The Fifth Vow: To be Joyful over Others Meritorious Deeds

This requires us to go against what seems so natural to us, jealousy. It is natural for humans to have this emotion. For example, small children appear unhappy when others receive more candy than they do. This is jealousy and it is a major obstacle to our self-cultivation. Universal Worthy Bodhisattva largely attributed this vow to jealousy. He taught us not to feel envy but rather to regard others meritorious deeds as our own and to further assist them in their endeavors.

This vow tell us to not only feel joyful over others meritorious deeds but to help them accomplish even more. If we are unable to offer assistance, we can at least express our joy and admiration. However, if we are able to offer assistance then it will be a true fulfillment of this vow. Remember that helping others is helping ourselves. We would do well to love and tolerate those who exceed us for in this way we will accomplish the virtue of this vow.

In ancient times, education in China was such that each succeeding generation was expected to exceed the current generation in accomplishment. If not, the education was considered a failure. People today however, are afraid that others will exceed them. When they teach others, they may hold back important information. This is called grudging teaching, which will incur the retribution of ignorance. Grudging money incurs poverty. These people are not aware how serious the retribution will be. We should strive to continuously progress in our cultivation of virtue, acquisition of knowledge, development of ability and improvement of the standard of life. Only in this way will education be successful with the entire society progressing.

It will be our responsibility in the next era to educate others. If we fail to attain virtue, knowledge and ability, we will not be able to help the next generation of sentient beings. Why? Look at today's children. The education they receive is leaning more and more towards science and technology while society is becoming increasingly complicated. Therefore, those who have vowed to help others will need to have a purer heart, greater wisdom and higher virtue to cope with the new era and opportunities. Jealousy and hatred are extremely harmful to our self-nature and hence should be extinguished. So, the virtue of being joyful over other's meritorious deeds will be even more important.

The Sixth Vow: To Appeal to the Buddha to Turn the Dharma Wheel

Since we benefit from the education we receive from the Buddha, what can we do to repay his kindness? Nowadays, most people enshrine and worship him, making daily offerings to his image on an altar. Is this the right way to repay him? No. These are only rituals to remind us not to forget the Buddha's kindness. The Buddha's wish is for all sentient beings to hear the truth, practice accordingly and receive the benefits to attain Buddhahood. The only way we can repay him is to take his heart as our own. Only in this way can we repay our respected teacher. Therefore, we can request the turning of the Dharma-wheel, in other words, we invite knowledgeable masters to teach us about the sutras. This is also the greatest good deed and virtue. Why? Because it brings the teachings to the world. But if no one invites Dharma masters to lecture, they will not have the opportunity to do so. So, people who invite them to give Dharma talks will obtain great merits.

Many people are willing to invite masters to chant or recite believing that they will receive inconceivable good fortune. But actually, they may not understand the meaning of what they are reciting. Therefore, if they invite the Dharma master to give a talk, then the good fortune, merits and virtues are even greater. The listeners will acquire a better understanding of the text and will be more inclined to recite the sutra and follow its teachings.

Unfortunately, if we want to invite a master to give a talk on the sutra today, we will find it hard to find an eligible one since there are so few. Many times, as I have traveled to give talks, I have been told that it was very difficult to find masters to speak. I have smiled and said, " Having a master to teach is a result. We need to plant the cause before we can attain this result. You are wishing for it without having planted the cause! Where on earth can we find such a deal!" What does "planting the cause" mean in this instance? To help train Dharma masters.

People like to listen to talks by senior, famous masters. Younger, unknown masters are normally inexperienced so fewer people attend their talks. Thus they become discouraged and thinking that giving talks is too difficult, they return to conducting ceremonial services. What should we do to help these less experienced masters? The younger and more inexperienced they are the more we need to attend their talks. This will encourage them to continue to practice and to improve.

However, even if we attend every one of the master's talks, we should not praise them. Unfounded praise is more harmful than slander. People may become very angry when slandered but for a person with integrity and enthusiasm the slander will only serve as a stimulant. The more embarrassed he or she becomes, the more determined he or she becomes. This person will do their utmost to achieve. However, if people praise and eulogize the master, he or she will think that they are so good that further improvement is unnecessary. This thinking leads to arrogance. Therefore, we should neither praise inexperienced masters nor make offerings to them. With too much money and fame, they will soon become tainted.

A person gives rise to the Bodhisattva heart and becomes a monk or nun but later becomes corrupt due to receiving excessive praise and offerings from followers. So, these followers are to blame for ruining this monk or nun. When the monk or nun receives the retribution, the followers will share the responsibility. Then whom should we make offerings to? The person with a firm mind for he or she will neither feel excited when praised, nor troubled when slandered. Only they deserve to receive the praise and admiration for only they will not be harmed by it. We would do well to strongly recommend this master to others, so that the master can help more beings.

To accept praise and offerings is very difficult. Buddhists say that, "A single grain from the donor is heavier than Mt. Sumeru. I will serve the donor like a bull in my next life if I do not transcend the six realms of reincarnation at the end of this one". So it is not easy to properly accept offerings. Even Buddhas and Bodhisattvas do not enjoy the offerings made to them, let alone we ordinary beings. However, when the donor wishes to foster good deeds and virtues, the master should accept the offerings and then pass them on to others.

Earlier in this century, Master Yin-Guang set a good example for us. His innumerable followers gave many offerings. He used all the money to print sutras. Following his example, I have also used all the money donated to print sutras. I then freely distribute the books to everybody. I had the thought that if I did not attain achievement in this life and transcend the six realms, I would at least not become a bull in my next life because everyone who had received my books would help to pay the debt for me! This is the transference of giving. In this way, everybody would share in the good fortune. This is the proper way of accepting offerings from followers.

Using the offerings for personal use is absolutely wrong and immoral. Even if the money is used to build a way place, the way place has to be used to promote Buddhism. Only in this way can the donor receive the merits and virtues. Otherwise, without propagation and cultivation, the way place will become a place of competition and conflict. Therefore, we must be very careful if we want to build a way place. My late teacher, Mr. Lee, once said, "When building the way place, everybody is a Bodhisattva doing their best to complete the work. But after the way place is built, everybody becomes a demon." Why? Because they are all trying to grab power and profit. They have forgotten their initial genuine intention in building the way place.

We have to be very careful when making offerings to a Dharma Master. The Buddha told us that there were four kinds of offerings that could be made to monks and nuns. The first is food and drink, without which they cannot survive. The second is clothing. If it becomes worn, provide new ones if there is not another one available. The third is medicine to be provided upon illness. The fourth is bedding.

Nowadays, followers offer monks and nuns houses and whatever good things they can afford. Then they live such a comfortable life that they no longer want to go to the Pure Land! The present life becomes so satisfactory that the goal to transcend the cycle of birth and death to attain Buddhahood fades. This is very harmful to their cultivation. They have left their secular home behind. To present them with a house is to urge them to return home. Isn't this harmful to them? Having received ownership of a house, they have again acquired property. This is regression of their cultivation.

The follower is then actually a criminal who will ruin the master. These people do not understand that this is harming Buddhism and damaging the spirit of the Triple Jewels. They think they are doing a good deed and accumulating much merit. When they see the King of the hell realms after they die, they will feel bewilderment at their punishment. We must have true wisdom to cultivate good fortune, merits and virtue in Buddhism. Followers need to be told of this but many masters are reluctant to tell them so because then they may not receive offerings.

What about me? I am determined to go to the Pure Land. I will not remain in this world to continue to bear the suffering. Thus, to tell the truth, I do not care whether you make offerings to me or not. It would be even better for me if you did not for it would save me a lot of trouble. Because of this, I started the Corporate Body of the Buddha's Educational Foundation, which is devoted to the printing and distribution of Buddhist books. I told the manager "Print more if there are more offerings. Print fewer if there are fewer offerings. There is no need to print any if there are no offerings, which is best".

When too many offerings are received, we have to take the trouble to select among all the Buddhist books to determine which ones are most suitable to print and then decide how best to print them. With no offerings, there would be no worries, no troubles. So we should not seek offerings, seek a way place or ask for anything. Then we will have a pure mind and a quiet heart on our path to enlightenment. Cultivating a pure mind and a quiet heart, helping others to cultivate the same and staying away from fame and profit is true cultivation.

We need to foster novice monks and nuns by placing them in hardships. If we cannot bear to see them experiencing hardship, we are harming them. When Buddha Shakyamuni was in this world, all of his students had only one meal a day and spent the night sitting under trees. Is this not a life of hardship? If we had been there, felt sorry for them and helped them out of their hardships, how could they have attained enlightenment?

The Buddha taught us to regard hardship as our teacher. Only by living most simply and frugally can we acquire a true Dharma heart and be firmly determined to transcend this world. So, hardships are good for us. If we are not willing to undergo hardship ourselves then we can at least respect those who are and not try to extricate them from their difficulties. Only when we sincerely help inexperienced monks and nuns to improve will we have good masters promoting Buddhism.

The Seventh Vow: To Request the Buddha to Reside in this World

The main purpose of the sixth vow is to introduce Buddhism to all people. If we hope to have accomplishment in our cultivation, the vow to request the turning of the Dharma wheel is not enough. Have you seen anyone attain enlightenment simply by listening to a talk on the sutra only once or twice in his or her lifetime? If this could happen, then enlightenment would be obtainable only when the Buddha was in the world and unobtainable when he was not. However, with our limited abilities we cannot do this, so we need to request the Buddha to reside in this world. In other words, we need a teacher who is with us every day so that we can be under their constant guidance and thus be able to reach enlightenment.

Years ago, I was asked by Professor Lee about my aspirations. I told him that I wished to travel around the world encouraging others to practice Buddhism. He nodded and told me that this was good, that I could achieve but I could not help others to do so. I asked why. He replied that I could only propagandize. He said that he had lived in Taizhong for more than thirty years and therefore many people had attained achievement. He went on to explain that if he had not lived in Taizhong but had simply visited to lecture once or twice a year than nobody would have had any achievement. To be able to help another, there needs to be an existing affinity. Without this affinity, even a Buddha cannot help us. By traveling around the world propagating Buddhism, we meet many people but the affinities with them are lighter. Staying in one place to conduct regular teachings needs stronger affinities.

I have benefited greatly from my travels as I have been freed from the concept of home. Every day I was either on the road or in a hotel. Where is my home? No home at all. Although I have places to give talks, I usually do not stay there for longer than a few weeks. The shattering of the idea of home has proven to be an escape for me.

If we want to reach any achievement, we need to request the Buddha to remain in this world. The Buddha himself is no longer here but his followers are, be they monks and nuns or laypeople. Those who are knowledgeable and virtuous can be invited to reside in our town or city to give teachings. In this way, we will be constantly under their guidance. It is easy to provide for masters of virtue and character because they lead simple lives. However, the Lecture Hall should look magnificent so that the listeners will like it and will thus develop respect for the way place. However, if the appearance of the hall is mediocre they might look down on the way place. People often set store by appearance and pay less attention to content. Although a person who knows the true value of things does not attach much importance to appearance, a splendid and imposing looking Lecture Hall is necessary for people to see initially.

Although the Lecture and Cultivation Halls are very impressive, the living quarters of the monks and nuns are very simple. If we look at the temples in China, we will understand. Even the head monk lives in a small room. The luxurious exterior rooms are only for laypeople and visitors. By carefully observing this we will know the right manner we need to have and the right methods we need to adopt. Doing so properly will enable Buddhism to take root, grow, blossom and bear fruit wherever we live.

From the above, we can see that among the Ten Great Vows of Universal Worthy Bodhisattva, the first seven are for a Bodhisattvas vows and conduct and the last three are the ways to dedicate all merits.

The Eighth Vow: To Constantly be a Diligent Follower of the Buddha's Teachings

Although the Buddha no longer resides in this world, we still have his sutras to follow and study. Following the sutras is the highest standard in our learning and practicing Buddhism.

The Ninth Vow: To Accord with all Sentient Beings

We need to accord with the wishes of all sentient beings in the universe. This is extremely difficult to do and is why the Chinese say that filial piety and according with others go together. Learning Buddhism is to honor filial piety and to accord with the being's wishes. While according, we need to look for the right opportunities to try to encourage people to stop committing wrongdoings. This will help them to break through delusion and attain enlightenment. However, to do this perfectly, we need to recognize the right way and time and for this, we need wisdom, expediency and flexibility.

The Tenth Vow: To Dedicate all Merits

This means dedicating all of our good deeds and merits to all the sentient beings in the universe. It means broadening our hearts so that the entire universe becomes one entity. Only when we have reached this state can we be said to have attained the Great Perfection.

In our learning and cultivation of the Pure Land, we use the five sutras and one sastra:

1. "The Buddha Speaks of the Infinite Life Sutra of Adornment, Purity, Equality and Enlightenment of the Mahayana School,"

2. "The Amitabha Sutra,"
3. "The Visualization Sutra,"
4. "The Chapter of Universal Worthy Bodhisattva's Conduct and Vows" from the "Flower Adornment Sutra",
5. "The Chapter on the Perfect Complete Realization of Great Strength Bodhisattva through Buddha Name Recitation" from the "Surangama Sutra" and
6. "Vasubandhu Bodhisattva's Report on the Way to Reaching the Pure Land."

We practice the Five Guidelines:

1. The Three Conditions,
2. The Six Harmonies,
3. The Three Learning's,
4. The Six Paramitas and
5. The Ten Great Vows of Universal Worthy Bodhisattva.

Very simple, very clear, not at all complicated. If we consistently follow these in our learning and cultivation, we are sure to succeed. In doing so, as an ancient sage said, "If ten thousand practice, ten thousand will succeed." Now we have the principles and methods of learning and cultivation. How do we interact with people, matters and objects in our daily lives? If we follow the above five guidelines, single-mindedly chant the name of Buddha Amitabha and seek birth into the Pure Land, we will definitely succeed.

THE RIGHT ORDER OF LEARNING BUDDHISM

Belief, Understanding, Practice and Attainment: We have looked at the basis for learning and cultivation and have had a brief introduction to the main practice guidelines. Now, let's look at the creative teaching methods of Buddhism. As Master Qingliang explained, in the "Flower Adornment Sutra" learning and cultivation can be divided into the four stages of belief, understanding, practice and realization.

The first stage is belief. When we are able to believe, then our conditions have matured. There is a saying "The Buddha is unable to help those who have no affinity with him". What is affinity? It is being able to believe. Even a Buddha cannot help someone whose conditions have not yet matured. However, when they have matured, the person will have belief. Then the Buddha can help. Religions are different from Buddhism in that once the believers have faith, they are saved, whereas, the belief in Buddhism, means that we believe in the benefits of Buddhism and accept one of the many methods.

Once we have the belief, we have to have understanding. Buddhism explains the truth of life and the universe. Only after we have acquired a true understanding of it can we begin our practice. Therefore, practice is based on understanding. If we do not understand the principles and methods, how can we practice? True practice is based on the foundation of principles and correct methods. The ultimate goal of practice is to achieve attainment, to attain the real benefit. What is attainment? It is the application of what we believe, understand and practice in our daily lives, to attain the ultimate enjoyment in life. For example, what we find in the "Infinite Life Sutra" is just what we think and practice. What we think and practice in our daily lives conforms to the sutra. This is attainment and true reality and this is what makes Buddhism so valuable.

Thus, we need to know the proper sequence of cultivation, which is belief, understanding, practice and attainment. When we speak of belief, first we believe in ourselves. This is where Buddhism differs from religion. In religion, the most important criterion is to believe in God. In Buddhism, the most important criterion is to believe in ourselves, not something outside of ourselves. We need to believe that we have the same Buddha nature. Believe that originally we were Buddhas. Believe that we are no different from the Buddhas. Believe that our true nature has become polluted and that once we remove this pollution we will uncover our true self-nature.

However, if we are always dwelling on thoughts that we have heavy karmic obstacles and fear that this will keep us from achieving attainment, then we definitely will not achieve. Why? If we do not believe that we can achieve, then even the Buddhas and Bodhisattvas cannot help us. Buddhas and Bodhisattvas can only help those who help themselves. Therefore, it is crucial that we have this confidence and belief in ourselves.

In addition, we also need to believe in the teachings of the Buddhas. We have been told infinite principles and methods. We will surely succeed as long as we follow them. After we have belief in ourselves, we need to have belief in the Buddha's teachings. Master Ou-Yi described this as believing in principles and in matter. Where does matter come from? From the principle, that is the pure mind of the true nature. All phenomena in the universe arise from the principle. They are related by the endless cycle of cause and effect. A cause gives rise to an effect, which in turn becomes the cause of the next effect. This process continues ceaselessly. Developing understanding and belief in true reality builds our confidence enabling us to seek thorough understanding of everything. Only in this way can we be free from confusion and doubt, which are obstacles in our cultivation and thus obtain enjoyment and smooth advancement.

In practicing Buddhism, it is most important to accept the teacher's instructions and practice according to the recommended methods. This has been the right way to learn since ancient times. The first requirement was to follow the five-year learning restriction, which was set by the teacher. In so doing, the teacher took full responsibility for whether the student succeeded or failed. This is the principle of honoring teachers and revering their teachings. This principle, however, no longer holds today for teachers are not responsible and students are not earnest. The principles of teaching are declining and this is the tragedy of our times. Students no longer respect teachers and teachers no longer sincerely help students to achieve.

The five-year learning restriction resulted in the student following just one teacher. It laid the foundation for the Three

Learning's of self-discipline, deep concentration and wisdom. It was the responsibility of the teacher to see that the student learned this. Consider Zen Buddhism. What did the teacher ask of the student for the first five years? They were assigned simple manual labor and asked to perform it earnestly, without change, every day. They were also to memorize the sutra. They were to read after completing their work and not to be concerned with anything else. The purpose of this labor was not to treat them as servants.

After a while the student felt bored and would think that he or she had worked very hard for five years without accomplishing anything. In actuality, he or she had acquired much without realizing it. What was acquired? Afflictions were greatly reduced and concentration was increased because of a ban against seeing and listening to many things. If the ban was properly followed, the students attained both good fortune and wisdom. What is good fortune? Working every day in the way place was cultivating the practice of giving. Since monks and nuns had no money to give away, they could work to cultivate the Paramita of Giving. Through the restrictions on listening and reading thereby concentrating the six sense organs, the students also acquired a pure mind and attained deep concentration. This is wisdom. So, the teacher taught the students to cultivate good fortune and establish the foundation of self-discipline, deep concentration and wisdom. The teaching was designed to be subtle yet effective. With the five-year learning restriction as a base, upon listening to one or two years of Dharma lectures, the students could become enlightened.

In the biographies of well accomplished monks and nuns we see that through this method many of them become enlightened in three to five years. Today, however, practitioners can live in a way place for thirty or fifty years, even a lifetime without awakening. They may have read numerous sutras but were still not enlightened. At most, they have memorized some general knowledge about Buddhism, but have done nothing to sever their afflictions or attain wisdom. So, we must try to find a good teacher for guidance. This advice may seem boring at first. But after the initial stage, we will be truly delighted and joyful in our attainment.

Many of us have made the big mistake at the beginning of our cultivation, of wanting to learn all different methods. Ancient learned monks and nuns started with the second of the Great Vows of Buddhas and Bodhisattva, "Afflictions are inexhaustible, I vow to end them all". In ending all afflictions, we will achieve deep concentration and attain wisdom. Then, the "Ways to practice are boundless, I vow to master them all". This is the correct order for cultivation. The mistake many people make is to attempt to study extensively without having severed afflictions. Master Qingliang called this "Understanding with no practice". These people concentrate only on understanding while neglecting the practice. They do not try to end their afflictions to cultivate a pure mind. As a result, they develop deviated viewpoints rather than proper views and knowledge.

PRACTICING THE THREE LEARNING'S CONCURRENTLY

What is the first step in learning Buddhism? Start by reciting one sutra. Do we need to understand it? No. For when we have not ended afflictions, our understanding will be erroneous. Then why do we recite only this sutra? By reciting the sutra, the Three Learning's of self-discipline, deep concentration and wisdom are accomplished together.

Self-discipline requires that we "Do nothing that is bad. Do all that is good". Reciting a sutra can prevent us from generating wandering thoughts so we will be prevented from doing anything that is bad. Sutras are words that flow from the Buddha's true nature. Nothing can surpass these words in virtue. Therefore, reciting a sutra is doing all that is good and results in the perfection of self-discipline so there is no need to practice the precepts one-by-one.

When reciting a sutra we must focus. By focusing, we cultivate concentration. Clearly enunciating every word correctly without any omission is the practice of wisdom. Therefore reciting the sutra properly is to practice the Three Learning's at the same time. Any attempt to analyze the sutra while reciting is in fact treating the sutra as a worldly book. This will result in none of the Three Learning's being accomplished and is not true cultivation. Never belittle the practice of sutra recitation, as it is the base of cultivation. Reciting for one hour accomplishes one hour of cultivation, reciting for two hours accomplishes two hours of cultivation, etc. Needless to say, the longer the better.

Many of my fellow practitioners in Taiwan and Dallas are reciting the "Infinite Life Sutra" ten times a day. So far, some may have chanted the sutra over two thousand times, thus they are very familiar with the text and only need thirty to forty-five minutes to finish one sutra. Reciting ten times thus means five or six hours of practicing self-discipline, deep concentration and wisdom. With so many hours devoted to cultivation, we will naturally develop a serene mind in just a few year's time.

Sutras flow from the pure and quiet mind of the Buddha. When we have developed a mind as pure and quiet, we will understand all we read in the sutra. The reason why the sutra is so hard to understand now is that our minds are filled with wandering thoughts. How can this mind be in harmony with one that is pure and quiet? This is why we do not understand the Buddha's words. So, if we want to learn from a good teacher, we need to trust and believe that their methods are proper and correct.

Just chose one sutra without being distracted by any others. If we chose to follow the Pure Land School, we recite and study the "Infinite Life Sutra." If we choose to follow the Tiantai School, we recite and study the "Lotus Sutra." If we choose to follow the Flower Adornment School, we recite and study the "Flower Adornment Sutra." When choosing a school, follow its principles and delve deeply into the sutra for five years. In other words sever all afflictions and try to develop a pure and quiet heart. This is the first step in learning Buddhism.

Frankly speaking, five years of learning and cultivating were enough for a practitioner to attain a pure mind in the past, because their minds were not as polluted as ours now are. In the past, children would remain innocent until around ten years of age. Then they would begin to be aware of differences between right and wrong, self and others. They would begin to develop such characteristics as greed, anger, ignorance and arrogance. Look at today's children. They start showing greed, anger, ignorance and arrogance when they are only a few years old! Where do they learn these things? From television. They are exposed to television every day. They naturally become polluted. They do not have the happy innocent childhood their parents had. How unfortunate they are!

I was born and grew up in the countryside and was neither sensible nor knowing of the world until I was thirteen. True Happiness is to remain innocent as long as possible in childhood and to not be aware of any of the suffering in the world. All I knew was how to play. Once we loose our childhood innocence, we are no longer happy. For then, we have to be constantly aware of others. So, I say that modern people are less fortunate than their predecessors were.

Once we have developed a pure and quiet mind and have attained wisdom, then we can begin to broaden our knowledge. We can see, hear and learn of anything that we are interested in, for now we have attained wisdom and will not be affected by our surroundings. Since we have self-control, the more we see and hear the wiser we will become and the greater our strength from deep concentration will be. How are deep concentration and wisdom increased? Remaining unmoved by surroundings will enhance deep concentration. Developing a clear and understanding mind will enhance wisdom. Then we can learn from other schools to further enhance our deep concentration and wisdom. First, we practice self-discipline, deep concentration and wisdom to attain our original wisdom. Then we can learn extensively to perfect our acquired wisdom. This is the way of learning from ancient times.

The Buddha told us in the "Great Prajna Sutra," "Innocent intuitive wisdom knows all". So, we must cultivate "innocence" first. The five-year method of practicing self-discipline results in our remaining innocent of the happenings in the world. When we are again in contact with the world, we will be aware of "Knowing all". This is the proper sequence and method to learn and practice Buddhism.

Ancient patriarchs not only abided by the rules set by Buddha Shakyamuni but also took Confucianism as the basis for their learning and practice. Chinese Buddhism has abandoned Theravada Buddhism in place of Confucius teachings. Chinese Buddhists as the basis for learning Buddhism adopted the Confucian five virtues of gentleness, kindness, respectfulness, thriftiness and humility. From this foundation, they developed the Three Conditions, the Six Principles of Harmony, the Three Learning's, the Six Paramitas and the Ten Great Vows. All the schools of Mahayana Buddhism adopted this framework of learning and teaching. In other words, we can accomplish our learning and cultivation in any school as long as we follow these principles and methods. So, we can say that the Five Virtues and Six Harmonies are the basis and a unique characteristic of Chinese Buddhism.

There was another advanced method of teaching and learning in Buddhism; continuing education for teachers. It was not until recently that this method again came into use. When he was in this world, the Buddha had many students. Some stayed with him because they had not finished their study and thus had not yet become independent. But others had reached some achievement. The latter were Bodhisattvas, who were responsible for spreading Buddhism. They went to different locations, set up way places and taught on behalf of the Buddha. Then they would return to where the Buddha currently was for a three months summer retreat for continuing education. This is similar to today's summer vacation when the students are out of school but the teachers cannot rest for they need to receive further training. So, the Bodhisattvas went back to be with the Buddha for a summer retreat. They listened to his teaching and thus were able to increase their concentration, wisdom and virtues. They also discussed difficulties they had encountered in their teaching and tried to find solutions. They learned from each other in seeking self-improvement. This system of continuing education has been infrequently seen in Chinese history.

It is advisable that way places and Buddhist societies conduct summer and winter retreats of Buddha name recitation and Zen meditation, seminars, etc. for short-term training. This is very effective and people are able to accept this idea of short-term continuing education. If we directly tell them that it is for severing afflictions; cultivating self-discipline, deep concentration and wisdom; and transcending the cycle of birth and death, only a few people will be interested and able to accept this concept.

Today, people differ in their concept of Buddhist education from those in the past. They want to learn more at the beginning of their study, not knowing that their method will limit their accomplishment whereas following the traditional method in practicing Buddhism can result in infinite benefits. In the past, many people have benefited from this traditional method, achieved in their cultivation and attained Buddhahood. However, at best, the present methods can only help us to get a doctorate of Buddhism, fame and wealth. But frankly speaking, it will not be easy for us to sever afflictions or transcend the cycle of birth and death. We should consider this very carefully.

The Artistic Aspects Of Buddhist Education

The Earliest System of Continuing Education: Buddha Shakyamuni gave lectures in many places, as did Confucius. In India, the Buddha and his students were invited by different groups to give talks. They would lecture in those areas for a while but did not remain permanently. As most of the Buddha's one thousand, two hundred and fifty students would follow him, it would have been very difficult for one place to support all of them. Only after Buddhism was introduced into China did Buddhist monks and nuns take up permanent residence in what was similar to a Buddhist educational institution. This came about because the introduction of Buddhism into China was supported and financed by the emperor. In India, people respected ascetics who traveled holding an alms bowl and therefore supplied them with offerings.

In China, however, people would have regarded this tradition as begging. Since the emperor, who respected them as teachers, had invited the monks to China, it would have been unacceptable to have them roaming the streets begging for food. Therefore, houses were built for them to live in and people were sent by the imperial court to assist the monks so they would not have to worry about their livelihood. By the Tang Dynasty, the system of Buddhist universities had developed. Masters Baizhang and Mazu were the initiators of these institutions. Master Mazu was the Eighth Patriarch of the Zen School and the third generation student of Master Hui-Neng, the sixth Patriarch of the Zen School. There is a Chinese saying that "Master Mazu built the university and Master Baizhang set up the rules".

What is this Buddhist University? It was the systemization of Buddhist teaching; the next step after what had been the verbal passing of teachings from a teacher to private students. After Master Mazu, the idea of the university continued to grow. This educational system was the special feature of Chinese Buddhism. The textbooks, lectures and teaching methods all attained the highest level of artistry as can be seen in the writing, music, images, architecture, offering implements, etc. Today, however, many of these perfect teachings are lost to us.

The Art of Buddhism

Today, the quality of Buddhist music has deteriorated. We are short of talented people, not only Buddhist artists with creative talents. Therefore, a Buddhist artist has to be profoundly learned for only then can he or she truly teach others and convey truth, goodness, beauty and wisdom. Ancient masters with high spiritual achievements composed Buddhist musical lyrics, but because the minds of today's people who chant them are not pure, their expression of them is also not pure. Spiritually, they have yet to achieve a state of awakening and are thus unable to move us. The artistic decline is caused by the lack of talented practitioners; it does not mean that Buddhism lacks artistic substance.

Anyone who has been to China and visited the Dunhuang murals or the Yungang grottoes, or the stone sutra texts found in Fangshan County, Beijing, knows how magnificent Chinese Buddhist artworks can be. The stone sutras were found in the years after the Cultural Revolution and are more extensive than the Great Buddhist Canon. Some of the sutras were translated at a later time than those in the Great Buddhist Canon. Fortunately, they survived in the Fangshan site. The stone slabs are carved on both sides with each beautiful character the size of a thumb. The entire project took four hundred years to complete, equal in scale to the building of the Great Wall. This recently discovered collection includes tens of thousands of stone slabs stored in seven caves. At present, only two of the caves are open to the public. We were filled with awe and admiration when we saw these stone sutras and could not help but admire our ancestors for having preserved such a legacy for us.

Today, schools and museums are separated. However, the system of Buddhist universities is similar to a combination of school and museum, for the art forms are educational, not just artistic. They exhibit inspiration and wisdom not discernable by average people. For example, when people see the many images of Buddhas and Bodhisattvas, they conclude that Buddhists worship many deities and therefore Buddhism is a religion and one of low standards at that.

Many people believe that an advanced religion worships only one god. They do not understand that Buddhism is not a religion, that we do not worship the images of Buddhas and Bodhisattvas but rather we regard them as teaching aids, which help us to understand the different methods of cultivation. One single image or method is insufficient to represent all phenomena in our world, so Buddhism uses many kinds of artistic works to represent them. Once we have understood the educational significance of Buddhist artistry, we will naturally give rise to admiration and appreciation.

All Buddhas symbolize our virtuous nature. All Bodhisattvas and Arhats symbolize the virtue of practice. Without the virtue of practice, the innate virtuous nature cannot be revealed. This complementary relationship is why the Buddha Table includes both Buddha and Bodhisattva images. The Buddha represents original nature and the Bodhisattvas represent the application of this nature. This original nature is empty, as it has no set form. All creations or form arise from this original nature and once there is form, there is application. The Buddha represents the original nature and the Bodhisattvas represent form and application. This is why in the "Flower Adornment Sutra," the Buddha does not comment on the teachings, for the original nature that is empty has nothing to say. But the Bodhisattvas do have something to say since they apply the principles. Not only is the original nature unexplained but also no thoughts arise from it. The saying that "Whenever I open my mouth I blunder; whenever I have an idea I am wrong" is said in terms of original nature represented by one Buddha. Why are there two Bodhisattvas to represent application? The infinite and innumerable form and application are divided into two categories; wisdom and practice or understanding and behavior. Practice corresponds with understanding. Understanding is the principle and practice is the application.

When we see the image of Buddha Shakyamuni, usually Ánanda and Kasyapa, two great Arhats are on either side of him. Buddha Shakyamuni represents our original nature. Ánanda, who is foremost in hearing, represents understanding and wisdom. Kasyapa, who is foremost in asceticism, represents practice. We may also see Buddha Vairocana, the wisdom body of Buddha Shakyamuni, with Manjushri Bodhisattva and Universal Worthy Bodhisattva on either side of him. Manjushri Bodhisattva represents understanding. Universal Worthy Bodhisattva represents practice.

Pure Land Buddhism regards Buddha Amitabha as the original nature with Guan Yin Bodhisattva representing compassion and practice, and Great Strength Bodhisattva representing wisdom and understanding. Due to these profound meanings, there cannot be two or more Buddhas and three or more Bodhisattvas.

Each Buddha represents a part of the virtuous nature. Every part of it is perfect so "One is all, all is one". Each name illustrates the virtues. For example, "Shakya" means kindness, teaching us that we need to treat others with kindness and compassion. "Muni" means stillness and purity. The whole meaning of Shakyamuni teaches us to behave toward others with kindness and compassion, to strive for purity of mind for ourselves. This is the meaning of Shakyamuni and is innate to our original nature. Amituofo is a Sanskrit transliteration. "Amituo" means infinite. "Fo" means Buddha. What is infinite? Everything, infinite wisdom, ability, long life, etc. But of all infinities, infinite life is the most important for without it all other infinities are useless. With it, we can enjoy all other infinities.

How can we gain these infinities? Infinity is none other than our self-nature, our original true nature. The Sixth Patriarch of Zen, Master Hui-Neng said, "Self-nature is innate; from self-nature arises all phenomena in the universe". In other words, it means infinity. What method do we use to obtain this infinity? We practice the teachings of Guan Yin Bodhisattva and Great Strength Bodhisattva. The former teaches us to be compassionate; the latter teaches us the single-minded concentration of Buddha Amitabha. Great Strength Bodhisattva taught us "Concentrate solely on Buddha Amitabha, without ceasing, without intermingling with other methods, and in this way we will surely attain wisdom and enlightenment".

Adding to this is the compassionate way of Guan Yin Bodhisattva. Behaving towards others with compassion and chanting only "Namo Amituofo" will enable us to enjoy infinite life. In this way we will develop our virtuous nature and uncover our infinite merits and virtues. Thus, when we pay respect to the images of Buddhas and Bodhisattvas, we need to understand that each is representative of a way of cultivation and of the truth of the universe.

The Hall of Heavenly Guardians

Buddhist architecture is also an artistic expression. From the exterior, the main cultivation hall appears to have two stories, but there is only one story inside. The external two stories represent "absolute truth" or the true reality of life and the universe, and "relative truth" or worldly views still clouded with delusion. The interior single story illustrates that both are the same truth. To the deluded, the two appear distinct and different; however, to the enlightened, they are one and the same.

Upon entering a way place, we first see the Hall of Heavenly Guardians. In the center of the hall is Maitreya Bodhisattva. To his left and right are the four Heavenly Guardians or Dharma Protectors. Maitreya Bodhisattva, known as the "Happy Buddha" in the west, is represented by the image of the historical monk Bu-Dai, a manifestation of Maitreya Bodhisattva. Maitreya Bodhisattva has a big smile that conveys "Want to learn Buddhism? Be happy and greet everyone with a smile. Do not constantly lose your temper or else you cannot learn Buddhism". This Bodhisattva also has a huge belly representing great broad-mindedness and equality of mind, teaching us to treat everything and everyone with generosity, patience and serenity. Only by emulating such qualities can we learn and practice Buddhism. Therefore, Maitreya Bodhisattva sits facing the door to tell all who enter, "only those who can accomplish this are eligible to learn Buddhism".

Standing beside Maitreya Bodhisattva are the four Heavenly Guardians or Dharma Protectors. They are symbolic guardians of the practitioners of the Buddhist way. Whom do they protect? They protect us by reminding us to educate ourselves and to safeguard the proper knowledge, which we should learn. Each guardian portrays a different aspect of thought or action.

The Eastern Dharma Protector symbolizes responsibility and safeguards the territory, which means that all of us are responsible for ourselves, our family, society and the country as a whole. How do we fulfill this responsibility? If each of us performs our duties well, fulfilling our obligations, we support each other and ourselves as well. In this way, society will be harmonious and the country will be prosperous and powerful.

The Southern Dharma Protector symbolizes progress and teaches us diligence. It is not enough to just meet our responsibilities. We need to make progress with each passing day for no progress means we regress. He emphasizes the importance of constantly cultivating and advancing our virtue, conduct, wisdom and ability, and to improve performance in our duties and our standard of living. From this, we can see that Buddhism is progressive, always leading the times.

The Western Dharma Protector symbolizes comprehensive vision and knowledge gained through exposure to the world. He represents the need to open our eyes to observe nature and humanity, to refine what we see and learn, and to distinguish good from ill.

The Northern Dharma Protector symbolizes comprehensive study and learning. Both teach ways of practice and how to achieve the goals in responsibility fulfillment and self-improvement. As the ancient Chinese said, "To read ten thousand books and to travel ten-thousand miles". Reading is the means for accomplishing the fundamental knowledge. Traveling ten thousand miles is to learn from observation. Through travel we see advantages of others and learn from them.

We also see their shortcomings, which can in turn serve as a warning to us so that we constantly improve ourselves. In this way, we can build a prosperous society and a safe country. In so doing, we safeguard the Dharma. So, the images of the Bodhisattvas and Dharma Protectors remind us to be diligent in the pursuit of our goals and responsibilities. So, we can see that Buddhism is neither a religion nor superstition.

The Four Dharma Protectors hold various objects to symbolize different aspects of the Dharma. The Eastern Dharma Protector of Managing the Nation holds a lute, which symbolizes the principle that we need to refrain from acting with undue haste but should keep to the middle path. It is like playing a lute, if the strings are too loose, it will not play. If they are too tight, they will break. We need to be responsible in our duties and do things in a proper, balanced way.

The Southern Dharma Protector of Growth holds the sword of wisdom that cuts away all troubles and worries. The Western Dharma Protector holds a dragon or snake that is twining around him.

The dragon or snake symbolizes change. Today, everything is constantly changing; only when we can see the truth will we be able to interact with ease and serenity. The Northern Dharma Protector holds an umbrella symbolizing protection from all the pollution that is around us. While learning, we need to safeguard our pure mind and quiet heart from becoming polluted. Furthermore, we need to understand the true reality of life and the universe, to have the wisdom and ability to properly interact with all people, matters and objects.

All of this can be learned from visiting the Hall of Heavenly Guardians. If we regard the Protectors as deities with magical powers who will protect us if we burn incense, prostrate and offer flowers and fruit praying for protection and safety we will be sadly mistaken. This is superstition. All the facilities, images of Buddha and Bodhisattvas and any offerings made are teaching tools designed to inspire our mind and wisdom. They also serve to remind us of the importance of being enlightened instead of deluded, virtuous instead of deviated, pure instead of polluted. These are the three principles of Buddhist teaching and practice.

Therefore, everything in a way place serves as a teaching aid. Even the offerings are educational. A container of water symbolizes the Dharma. The water is clean symbolizing that our minds need to be as pure as the water. It is calm without a single ripple, symbolizing the tranquility in our hearts. It is to have purity and equality of mind. Flowers symbolize the "cause" as the blossoming of flowers results in the bearing of fruit. Flowers symbolize the Six Paramitas. Fruits are not offered to the Buddha or Bodhisattvas to eat. They remind us that if we want the sweet fruit or the good result, we must cultivate and accumulate good deeds, the cause. Thus, everything we see in the way place is a teaching aid. The Buddhas and Bodhisattvas neither smell nor eat, they want for nothing.

We also see lamps, which symbolize wisdom and brightness; incense sticks, which symbolize self-discipline and deep concentration.

You will not see anything in the cultivation and lecture halls that do not symbolize some teaching. However, it is a sad loss that many Buddhists are totally ignorant of the educational significance of these objects.

They do not know why they burn the incense or why they make offerings to the images of Buddhas and Bodhisattvas. Their belief is actually superstition. Some people criticize Buddhists as being superstitious. These critics are right. Too many Buddhists are confused about Buddhism.

We need to be clear on what we are learning and explain this to the skeptics and critics, then I believe they will also want to learn. I have introduced Buddhism to people in China in this manner. After hearing my explanation, they said they had been ignorant of such a good thing and wished to learn more.

In conclusion, it is the genuine wisdom and infinite enlightenment in Buddhism that helps all sentient beings obtain true benefits and happiness. The Buddha teaches all beings with his boundless, compassionate heart. Throughout history Buddhist practitioners, whether they be of the Esoteric, Zen or any other School, have made great achievements following these principles and methods. Today, however, people know very little of the genuine principles and methods, so few have any real achievements.

In our Dharma-Ending Age, people have overwhelming obstacles from their accumulated karma. Under these circumstances, the Buddha Name Recitation Method is most effective due to its simplicity and expediency. It neither takes a long time nor requires special rituals. Anyone can practice it any time, any place. This is why so many people have achieved attainment. Taiwan is neither large in population nor in size, but in the last forty years, by my most conservative estimate, at least five hundred people have attained birth into the Pure Land to become a Buddha in one lifetime.

To succeed, we accord with the teachings in the five Pure Land sutras and one commentary, generate the Bodhi-mind and concentrate on mindfulness of Buddha Amitabha. The "Awakening of Faith Sastra" stated that, "Enlightenment is innate, delusion is not". Therefore, we definitely can uncover our innate Buddha nature and proper viewpoints. We definitely can discard what is not innate, our delusion, deviated viewpoints and impurities. Thus, we recite sincerely "Amituofo" to rid ourselves of our negative karmas and habits, to live simply and to practice diligently to attain the Buddha Name Chanting Samádhi. Then, finally we will attain freedom in body and mind, and understand the true reality.

We are free to go whenever we wish. If we choose to remain here for a longer time, that's all right. Since so many have achieved, why can't we? We have not sincerely chanted long enough. How long is long enough? According to ancient records, many have achieved after three years. After that, we no longer have any fears. We will feel perfectly safe and our minds will be at ease. If the Third World War were to start today and a nuclear bomb was to explode, we would simply say that it was time to go to the Pure Land. No pain, no fear, true freedom. This is what the "Infinite Life Sutra" said is "the true benefit given to all sentient beings". Adopt whatever teachings and practices are beneficial and effective. There is only one ultimate goal for us; benefiting all sentient beings, helping them free themselves from delusions and sufferings, and enabling them to attain happiness and enlightenment. If badgering or sternness works, use it. If gentleness works use it. But be aware that falsehoods, attachments, emotions and delusions have nothing to do with Buddhism or achieving our goal. I hope everyone will attain the goal of freedom from delusion, attachment and suffering, to attain happiness, tranquility and the perfect complete enlightenment.

Conclusion

Buddhism is adapting by emphasizing a rational scientific approach to its teachings. Buddhism gives a clear explanation of how life's experiences come about and how to deal with them in the best manner possible. Then it says do not accept anything on blind faith; think for yourself, test it out and see if it actually does make sense. This resembles science asking us to verify the results of an experiment by repeating it ourselves, and only then to accept the results as fact. Modern people do not like buying something without examining it; they would not buy a car without testing it. Likewise, they will not turn to another religion or philosophy of life without checking it first to see if it really makes sense. That is what makes Buddhism so appealing to many people of the twentieth century. Buddhism is open to scientific investigation and invites people to examine it in that way.

The Buddha's Methodological Approaches for Teaching and Learning

In Propagating his *religion*, the Buddha adopted various methodological approaches for teaching and learning, which may be summarized as follows:

1. Gradual Approach.

For imparting instruction to beginners, the Buddha, utilizing a psychological principle, was very careful to take into consideration their particular background and not to peach to profound, detailed principles of the subject all at once as that would scare them away. It were the more elementary doctrine that were imparted to them at first. Those who intended to follow his teachings were urged to accept at first the tenets and practices that were suitable to their aptitudes, tendencies and interests, and then the more profound doctrines were placed before them by stages. In this way too, the Buddha did not kernel of his teaching, but he began by urging his listeners to the practice of virtues such as generosity and rectitude to behaviour in their worldly vocation. He spoke of heaven with its rewards awaiting those lead a life of earnest purpose here below; and as soon as he knew that his hearers were fit to learn something deeper and higher, he proceeded to instruct them in the higher doctrines of the Four Noble Truths, and so forth.[2]

Even in teaching the Four Noble Truths, he proceeded n stages, from the concrete to the abstract principle, from effect to cause, i.e. from the phenomenal element of suffering as the obvious, to its causes, its cessation and the ways leading to its cessation. This approach shows the Buddha's attitude: " I do not maintain that the attainment of profound knowledge comes straightway; on the contrary , it comes by gradual learning, practice and progressive operation."[3]

2. *Approach of Adaptation.*

The present situation and circumstance where also used by the Buddha to impart his ideals to people. In order to gain over the hearers or the opponents to his view, the Buddha made use of a style which T.W.Rhys Davids characterized as 'pouring new wine into the old bottles.'[4]

This consists in the Buddha's giving a new meaning to words that were already current. He adapted traditional ideas and practices and adjusted his sermons to suit the temperaments of his hearers, a method that came to be known as '*upaaya-kosalla"m,*' i.e. the skilful policy (*expedient means)* of converting people[5] by which is meant that the Buddha possessed as one of his intellectual faculties the ability to comprehend the dispositions or tendencies of his fellow men (*naanaadhimuttikataa*).[6] Here, he claimed to know 'Brahma-God' and also preached 'the path leading to companionship with Brahma-God', by cultivating '*Brahmavihaaradhamma,*' i.e. the Four virtues for Excellent Abiding.[7] To mention another example, he also gave a brahmin an instruction in the 'ritualistic tenet' of washing away the sin. Instead of going into the river and washing it away by bathing, the latter was advised to take a bath in spiritual culture by harming no living beings, etc.[8]

3. Illustrative Approach.

By the expression 'illustrative approach' is meant the use of analogy, simile, parable *(upamaa)*, the use of fable and story drawn from ordinary life, in the Buddha's speeches along with beautiful verses in order to make them sweet, effective and attractive. It is often said in the texts: 'I will give you an analogy, for by means of an analogy some people of intelligence *(vi~n~nuupurisaa)*understand the meaning of what is said"[9] and 'a simile is employed in order to make the sense of a teaching clear.[10]

Thus, to teach the meaning of the 'Middle Way' *(Majjhimaapa.tipadaa)* to the Venerable Sona Kolivisa who was an expert in playing the lute in his earlier life, the Buddha made use of the analogy of playing the lute and observed that 'only when the lute' strings were neither overstrung nor overlaxed, it was tuneful and playable.' Similarly, the analogy of 'lust, hatred and delusion *(raaga, dosa, moha)* with fiery flames *(aggi)* was used to instruct the three brothers Jatilas, who, as the Buddha knew beforehand, believed in the 'the Fire worship.' He started: "Everything is in fiery flames: the eye, etc...are all in fiery flames.. By the fiery flames of lust, of hatred and of delusion by which all are kindled, produce and kindle the further fires of birth, etc.[11] Here and there in the *Pali* canon, especially in the *Jaatakas*, the Buddha is reported to teach his disciples by the use of fables and stories, and he added at the end of every instruction the moral the fable illustrated.

4. Analytical Approach.

The analytical approach of teaching is one of the most important characteristics found in the earlier texts. This is especially the case when the doctrine was meant for the more intelligent hearers or followers. The entire teaching of the Buddha is described as one which is of a critical outlook, to be verified and realized by the intelligent *(vi~n~nuu, prudent, wise),* who represent for the Buddha the impartial critic at the level of intellectual common sense.[12] As a matter of fact, almost the whole dialogue of the Buddha could possibly be included in this style of teaching. The Buddha himself claimed to be 'an analyst' *(vibhajjavaada);* when he was asked for his explanation of the truth of the proposition: 'The householder is accomplishing the right path....; the monk is not accomplishing the right path; he answered that one could not make an absolute assertion as to the truth or falsity of some propositions, but one should first analytically examine the nature of the subject of the subject of the discussions; the proposition in question means that, if both the householder and the monk were guilty of wrong conduct, them they are to be blamed, but if both of them conducted themselves rightly, they are to be praised.[13] The Buddha analytically reasoned with those who, being dialectically minded, came to discuss and debate with him.[14] And this shows his approach of teaching in what Oldenberg called 'Socratic fashion.'[15]

According to the Buddha, a teacher who is possessed of the four analytical powers will be not at a loss as regards both the meaning and the letter or theory of what he teaches.[16] The refers to the teacher's capacity for the analysis of meanings *(attha)* of reason or conditions *(dhamma)*, of educational medium *(nirutti)*, and of intellectual mastership *(or, rather, presence of mind, self-confidence- pa.tibhaana):* that is, he is capable of grasping the 'analysis of meaning', specifically and according to the letter, to explain the lesson in various ways, to teach it, expound it, lay it down, open it up, classify it and make it clear, and the same with the rest.[17]

5. Experimental Approach.

The Buddha did not want anybody to accept his teachings without one's critical spirit of experimentation. Since it is generally regarded as 'pragmatism' and 'rationalism' in the sense of 'utilitarian pragmatism,[18] canonical Buddhism is a verifiable system of philosophy experimentally discovered by the Buddha in the light of both failure and success in his experimental quest for the truth,[19] which is synthesized on scientific principles regardless of past traditions: observation of actual life, experiments asceticism, final deduction of a way to end ills, seeking the knowledge of nature-the knowledge which may be characterized as scientific on account of its basis of verification, etc.[20] The Buddha showed the disciples the example, by having tried the various methods practised by various systems prevalent in his time.[21] Therefore, his success in achieving enlightenment is not considered to be a mysterious single act, but an achievement through the development of natural faculties. Even knowledge of salvation is achieved only as the final phase of a gradual process of practice. He also identified himself as one of the Experimentalists (*di.t.thadhammaa-bhi~n~naavosaanapaaramippatta*) [22] i.e. those who have a personal knowledge of the truth through their own experience. He closed his discourses tot he Kalamas,[23] and to Bhaddiya, the Licchave,[24] with the remark that one should accept a doctrine as true only when one had experimentally realized by oneself its practical validity. "Let an intelligent person come to me, sincere, honest and straightforward; I shall instruct him in the doctrine so that on my instruction he could practise by himself in such a way that before long he would himself know and himself realize....[25]

The Buddha did not want his own statements easily accepted on his authority nor easily rejected but he rather demanded that they should be tested and worked out in the light of one's own experience, otherwise such statements would be fruitless. "Like a beautiful flower that possesses colour, but lacks perfume, so well-spoken words are fruitless to him who does not work them out:, the Buddha suggested: "on the other hand, well-spoken words are fruitful to him who sincerely practises them, like a beautiful flower that possesses both colour and perfume.[26] When asked to what extent one attained truth, he replied; "There is an attainment of the truth only by gradually following, developing, practising and experiencing the doctrines themselves"[27]practising, trying and experimenting with it, they may come to realize through their experience here and now the truth.[28]

Monks, what should be done by the Teacher for his disciples, seeking their good, out of compassion, that has been done by me for you.... concentrate on it and be not careless; do not reproach yourself afterwards. This is our command to you.[29]

When Ganaka-Maggallaana put a question to him: "Sir, what is the cause and reason why, though *Nibbaana* does exist, and even though you exist as adviser, some of your disciples on being exhorted and instructed thus by you, attain the goal, *Nibbaana*, but some do not,"[30] the Buddha replied: "...What can I do, brahmin, in this matter? (*It must be always remembered that)* a Tathaagata (*only)* shows the way."[31]

The importance of meditation: In contrast with modern education, Buddhism values first-hand experience higher than theory. Buddhist education should be concerned with more than just handing over factual knowledge. The Buddha taught a path of personal inquiry to put an end to suffering, and that path depends on direct experience. Therefore, the traditional methods of Buddhist mind-training – contemplation, meditation – could be taught at schools. The Buddhist view on the integral nature of human experience, where the intellectual and emotional sides of mind are equally appreciated, is highly relevant in the modern world, which is overly fragmented. Buddhism presents a path of mind-training, and education is nothing but that path. Since the full meaning of the Buddhist texts and teachings is not fully understood before one has direct experience in meditation, meditation is an indispensable part of Buddhist education. In fact, Buddhist educational institutions, if they have not been tainted by the values of the West, could well define themselves as schools of mental training. The usefulness of mindfulness methods in developing the "seven factors of enlightenment" (such as peace, joy, concentration etc.) has been demonstrated even outside the context of Buddhist education. It has been found indispensable for realizing true education in general. (Brady, Kassabian)

Finally, to encourage active Buddhist engagement in everyday affairs, we must open up new vistas of learning.

Hearkening back to spirit of the great Indian Buddhist universities such as Nalanda, we should try to apply the Buddhist principles in all walks of life, testing their truth in different disciplines. Just as Buddhist philosophy in India developed in constant dialogue with other schools of philosophy, we should also try to be at constant dialogue with science and the other religions.

NOTES AND REFERENCES

1. This method comes in close relation to the 'gradual course of training.'
2. Cp. M. I. 379f. D. I. 148; *Commentary of the Dhammapada*, p. 4f.
3. M. I. 479f; S. II, p 28f. A. I, p. 50f.; see also above not
4. Cp. Rhys Davids, *DB.*I, p. 142
5. D. III. 220.
6. M. I. 70f.
7. For more details, see M. II, p. 206ff.
8. M. I, p. 39f.
9. S.II. 114; M. I. 148.
10. M. I. 155; III, p. 275; *It.,* p. 114.
11. Vin. I. 34f.
12. Cp. D. I. 161ff.; II. 290ff.,; M. I. 400ff., 515f. A. II. 56.
13. M. II. 197ff. cp. The similar approach with the same context, S. I. 80f.
14. Cp. M. I. 376ff., 396ff.; D. I. 120ff; A. II. 190ff.
15. Cp. Oldenberg, *Buddha,* p. 189
16. A. II. 139.
17. A. II. 160f.; cp. GS. II. 167
18. See also A.C. Ewing, *The Fundamental Questions of Philosophy*, p. 56; De la Vallee Poussin, *Bouddhisme*, p. 129; S. Radhakrishanan, *India Philosophy*, I, p. 359; K.N. Jayatilleke: *Early Buddhist Theory of Knowledge*, p. 357

19. Cp. Jayatilleke, *op.cit.*, p. 464
20. A.K. Warder, *Early Buddhism and other contemporary System*, Vol. 18, p. 57
21. Cp. M. I. 77f., 81, 163f., 241f.
22. M. II. 211f. This term is employed by Jayatilleke, *op. cit.*, p. 172, 416
23. A. I. 189ff.
24. A. II. 190ff.
25. M. II. 44; cp. MLS. II. 238
26. *Commentary of the Dhammapada*. I. 383.
27. M. II. 174; cp. MLS. II. 363
28. M. II.22; III. 8f
29. A. III. 87, 89; cp. GS. III. 72
30. M. III. 4; cp. MLS. III. 53
31. M. III. 6.
32. Siddhi Butr-Indr, The Social Philosophy of Buddhism, Mahamakut Buddhist University, 1 st ed, 1973, PP.199-205

Bibliography

1. A,C. Taylor (Ed) *Patisambhimagga* , Pali Text Society, Vol. 1905, Vol. II, 1907

2. Alex Wayman, *Buddhist Insight*, Motilal Banarsi Das, Delhi

3. Amulya Chandra Sen, *Asoka's Edicts*, Calcutta, 1956

4. B.C. Law, *A Designation of Human Types* (Translation of Puggalapammatti), Pali Text Society, 1922

5. Bahadur Mal, *Religion of Buddha,* Vishveshvaranda Publication, Hoshirpur.

6. Bhikshu Jagadish Kashyap, (Ed) *Digha Nikaya,* Pali Publication Board, Nalanda, 1960

7. — (Ed) *Vindya Pitaka (Maha Vagga)* Pali Publication Board, Nalanda, 1960

8. ——(Ed) *Anguttara Nikaya,* Pali Publication Board, Nalanda, 1960

9. ——(Ed) *Patisambhiddamagga,* Pali Publication Board, Nalanda, 1960

10. ——(Ed) *Patthdnapakarna,* Pali Publication Board, Nalanda, 1960

11. ——(Ed) *Khuddaka Nikaya,* Pali Publication Board, Nalanda, 1960

12. —(Ed) *Samyutta Nikaya,* Pali Publication Board, Nalanda, 1960

13. –(Ed) *Dhammasangani,* Pali Publication Board, Nalanda, 1960

14. —-(Ed) *Vibhanga,* Pali Publication Board, Nalanda, 1960

15. B.M. Barua, *Asoka and his Inscriptions,* New Age publications, Calcutta, 1968, (Edition)

16. C.A.F.Rhys Davids (trs) *Psalms of the Early Buddhism: Pslms of the Sisters* (Translation of Therigatha) Pali Text Society, 1980 (First Published in 1909)

17. ——(trs) *Buddhist Psychological Ethics* (Translations of Dhammasangani) Pali Text Society, 1974 (3rd Edition)

18. D.D. Kosambi (Ed) *Visuddhimagga,* Bhartya Bhavan, Bombay, 1940

19. Edward Conze, *Buddhist Meditation,* Harper Torch Books, New York, 1956

20. F.L. Woodward (trs) *The Kindered Sayings* (Translation of Samyutta Nikaya) Pali Text Society, 1979

21. H.G. Wells, *Outline History of the World Arhant,* Jaipur, (2 Vols) 1989.

22. J.L. Shastry(Ed) *Ancient Indian Tradition and Mythology: Siva-pourna (Satarudra Samhita)* Moti Lal Benarsi Das, Delhi, Vol.II, Part.II

23. John Walters, *Mind Unshaken,* Ridder and Co, London.

24. Lord Chalmers, (trs) *Further Dialogues of the Buddha* (Translation of Majjhima Nikaya) Humphery Milford London, Vol.II, 111927

25. Mahesh Tiwary (Ed) *Puggala Pannantti Atthakatha,* Nav Nalanda Mahavihar, Nalanda, 1968

26. Narada Mahathera, (trs) *Dhammapada* (Text and Translation) Mahabodhi Society of India, Calcutta, 1943

27. Nina Gorkan, *Buddhism in Daily Life,* Dhamma Study Group, Bangkok.

28. N.N.Vasu, *Modern Buddhism-its Followers in Orissa*, Giyan Publishers, Delhi, 1986.

29. Nyantikoka, *Buddhist Dictionary- Manual of Buddhist Terms and Discussions,* Buddhist Publication Society, Kandy, Srilanka, 1980 (4th Edition)

30. P.V. Bapat and R.D. Vadekar (Edits) *Atthasalinini Poems,* 1942.

31. —(Ed) *Dhammasangani Pooma*, 1940

32. R.D. Vadekar (Ed) *Milinda-Panha,* Bombay University Publication, Bombay, 1943

33. Revatadhamma (Ed) *Visuddhimagga Vaaaranaseya* , Sanskrit Vishwavidalaya, Varanasi, 1967.

34. R. Mooris (Ed) *Anguttara Nikaya Pali*, Text Society, Vol.II, 1888, Revised Reprint 1976.

35. Romilla Thapar, Asoka *and the Decline of Mauryas,* Oxford University Press, Delhi, 1985.

36. Siddhi Butr-Indr, *The Social Philosophy of Buddhism.* (Bangkok: Mahamakut Buddhist University, 1st ed. 1973), pp. 199-205]

37. T.A. Gopinath Rao, *Elements of Hindu Iconography*, Paragan Book Reprint Corporation, New York, Vol.II, Part.I (Reprint of of 1914 edition)

38. T.W. Rhys Davids (Ed) *Yogavacara Manual*, Pali Text Society, 1896 (Reprint 1981)

39. T.W.Rhys Davids and Hermann Oldenberg (trs) Vinay Texts Sacred Books of the East series, Motilal Benarsi Das, Delhi, Part.III, 1965.

40. T.W.Rhys Davids and J.E.Carpenter (Edts) samrgala *Vilasini Digha Nikaya Atthakatha,* Pali Text Society, Vol.I, 1886

41. T.W. Rhys Davids and J.E, Carpenter (Edtts) *Digha Nikaya,* Pali Text Society, Vol.I, 1989 (Reprint

1975), Vol.II 1909 (Reprint 1982) Vol.III 1990 (Reprint 1976)

42. ——— and William Stede, *Pali English Dictionary,* Pali Text Society, 1959

43. Trenckent (Ed) *Majjhima Nikaya,* Pali Text Society, Vol.I, 1888.

Abbreviations

A – Anguttārā Nikāyā

M- Majjhimā Nikāyā

S- Sāmyuttā Nikāyā

Index

C

D

□□□